SPORTS ETHICS
IN AMERICA

Recent Titles in
Bibliographies and Indexes in American History

The Urban South: A Bibliography
Catherine L. Brown, compiler

Cities and Towns in American History: A Bibliography of Doctoral
Dissertations
Arthur P. Young, compiler

Judaica Americana: A Bibliography of Publications to 1900
Robert Singerman, compiler

Shield of Republic/Sword of Empire: A Bibliography of United States
Military Affairs, 1783-1846
John C. Fredriksen, compiler

Biographical Index to American Science: The Seventeenth Century
to 1920
Clark A. Elliott, compiler

The Natural Sciences and American Scientists in the Revolutionary Era:
A Bibliography
Katalin Harkányi, compiler

Changing Wilderness Values, 1930-1990: An Annotated Bibliography
Joan S. Elbers, compiler

The American Indian Ghost Dance, 1870 and 1890: An Annotated
Bibliography
Shelley Anne Osterreich, compiler

The Immigration History Research Center: A Guide to Collections
Suzanna Moody and Joel Wurl, compilers and editors

SPORTS ETHICS IN AMERICA

A Bibliography, 1970–1990

DONALD G. JONES
with Elaine L. Daly

FOREWORD BY THOMAS H. KEAN

Bibliographies and Indexes in American History,
Number 21

GREENWOOD PRESS
New York • Westport, Connecticut • London

Library of Congress Cataloging-in-Publication Data

Jones, Donald G.
  Sports ethics in America : a bibliography, 1970-1990 / Donald G.
Jones with Elaine L. Daly ; foreword by Thomas H. Kean.
  p. cm.—(Bibliographies and indexes in American history,
ISSN 0742-6828 ; no. 21)
  Includes indexes.
  ISBN 0-313-27767-2 (alk. paper)
  1. Sports—United States—Moral and ethical aspects—Bibliography.
I. Daly, Elaine L. II. Title.   III. Series.
Z7514.M66J66 1992
[GV706.3]
016.175—dc20   91-47538

British Library Cataloguing in Publication Data is available.

Library of Congress Catalog Card Number: 91-47538
ISBN: 0-313-27767-2
ISSN: 0742-6828

First published in 1992

Greenwood Press, 88 Post Road West, Westport, CT 06881
An imprint of Greenwood Publishing Group, Inc.

Printed in the United States of America

The paper used in this book complies with the
Permanent Paper Standard issued by the National
Information Standards Organization (Z39.48-1984).

10 9 8 7 6 5 4 3 2 1

Contents

Foreword

In 1990, the national college basketball champion was defeated in its bid for a repeat amid a cloud of pending NCAA sanctions against the school for discretions dating back more than a decade; a baseball pitcher who had been ejected from a 1990 playoff game for cursing at an umpire appealed his subsequent five-game suspension; that same player was joined by one other as the first professional athletes to sign guaranteed contracts for more than $5 million per year; fans booed a foreign-born college basketball player who resisted wearing an American flag patch on his uniform to support the Gulf War troops; an NBA All-Star spat at a fan during a heated argument and hit a young girl seated in front of his adversary; a boxing legend admitted to cocaine use; another boxer, a 41-year-old former heavyweight champ, attacked a rival boxer in a parking lot outside of a bar, after winning a comeback fight against a third boxer.

Meanwhile, a commission sponsored by the Knight Foundation issued a report recommending a series of reforms in intercollegiate athletics. The commission report noted that "fully one-half of all Division I-A institutions (the 106 colleges and universities with the most competitive and expensive football programs) were the object of sanctions of varying severity from the NCAA during the 1980's."

The sports world is in crisis. Even as professional leagues continue to set attendance records, even as the NCAA basketball tournament kitty fattens with each mad March, the X's and O's of athletic competition must themselves compete with scandals, rumors, and revelations for space on the news pages and programs that expose and exploit sports controversies. At times it is difficult to know whether these incidents set or follow the mood of society.

So many of our children idolize sports figures. What is a young fan's reaction to seeing a legend like Pete Rose sent to prison for tax cheating? Or to hear Rickey Henderson whine loudly that $3 million is insufficient payment for his own thievery? Or to the hockey player who promises--not threatens, but promises--to avenge an injury to his teammate? Or the baseball telecaster who openly advocates throwing message pitches with the deceitfully amusing appellation, "chin music"? Or to the Little League parent who attacked a rival coach during a game with a baseball bat?

Sometimes the parallels between sport and society are striking. How far different was the videotape of Los Angeles cops battering suspect Rodney King in March of 1991 from the film clip of the minor league hockey brawl in the 1990 season when a player held a fan down as his teammate beat the man with the man's shoe? How far different was the New England Patriots' harassment of reporter Lisa Olson from the sexual harassment that goes unreported in executive suites and on shop floors every day? Is the exclusion of Blacks from the links of so many private country clubs across America an anomaly in an otherwise integrated society?

Sports can be viewed as a microcosm of American culture, both good and bad. Along with the greed and the scandals, it gives us the artistry of a Michael Jordan, the heroics of a Kirk Gibson, and the teamwork of Duke's NCAA basketball championship run. Sports also mirrors society in its ethics, and as Drew University Professor of Social Ethics Donald G. Jones claims, we have much to learn from a careful study of the emerging field of sports ethics.

Don Jones, who has already published three bibliographies of business ethics literature, has done a first-rate job of compiling and introducing this first sports ethics bibliography. I am certain this will not be the last such compilation. It will prove invaluable to scholars, students, and journalists for years to come.

Thomas H. Kean
President, Drew University

Acknowledgments

Our debt of gratitude to Thomas Limoncelli, a Drew University undergraduate student and computer whiz, is great. He did the complicated and time-consuming work of printing out a camera-ready copy of this bibliography. We are also grateful to the library staff of Drew University, Lewis & Clark College, and the University of Washington. Finally, special thanks go to Ruth Friedman and Regina Diverio for excellent editorial contributions, and to Paula Massa for her winsome and professional clerical assistance.

Introduction

BACKGROUND AND GENESIS

Sports ethics is both a significant and hot topic in American society at the close of the twentieth century. The academic study of sport has always existed, but there has been an exponential growth in scholarly work on sport in the United States during the last two decades. In part, this is because sport plays such a major role in our society and has such a powerful impact from the standpoint of economics, morality, life-style, and values. Hence, philosophical, ethical, sociological, psychological, anthropological, historical, and to some extent, theological reflection on sport is a burgeoning enterprise.

The ethical analysis of sport has not been confined to the academy. There has been significant work in the popular media. Consequently, this bibliography includes not only books and articles from scholars, but also works from journalists, current and ex-athletes, ex-coaches, and other writers who have addressed the social and ethical issues of sports in contemporary society.

Problems of drug use, violence, payoffs, cheating, college sports, sexism, racism, sports medicine, gambling, exaggerated importance of winning, fan behavior, recruiting, labor relations in professional sports, children's sports, and other such issues have been subject to rigorous scrutiny by academics, journalists, current and ex-athletes, and culture critics of various sorts. This bibliography is a strong testimony to the serious attention sports ethics has been receiving in the recent past.

There are increasing numbers of courses on sports being taught in colleges and universities--sports ethics, history of sports, sociology of sports, sports and society, psychology of sports, and philosophy of sports. Because sports ethics is basically interdisciplinary, touching all of the above, this bibliography was created in order to provide a valuable reference tool for teaching and research in a variety of sports-related disciplines. One of the motivating aims for developing this volume was to provide a resource tool for students, coaches, athletic directors, recreation leaders, and school and university administrators having an interest and stake in sports. The genesis of this bibliography was also based on the expectation that it would be a valuable tool for journalists doing investigative reporting of sports and society issues.

METHODOLOGY

The methodology used to gather the citations included reviews of books, perusal of footnotes and bibliographies in books and articles, inspection of journals and magazines, and a review of standard indexes in both hard copy and through computer data retrieval services. The major journals used were: Journal of the Philosophy of Sport, Journal of Sport and Social Issues, Journal of Sport History, Quest, Review of Sport and Leisure, International Review of Sport Sociology, Phi Delta Kappa, Women's Sports and Fitness, Coach and Athlete, Olympic Review, Arete: The Journal of Sport Literature, Sociology of Sport Journal, Scholastic Coach, The Journal of Health, Physical Education and Recreation, The Journal of Physical Education, The Chronicle of Higher Education, and Journal of Sport Behavior. The index and reference resources consulted were: Social Sciences Index, Philosopher's Index, Books in Print, Humanities Index, Reader's Guide to Periodical Literature, Religion Index I and II, Public Affairs Information Service, New York Times Index, Education Index, Library of Congress Subject Index, Business Periodicals Index, Cumulative Book Index, Physical Education Index, and Sports Bibliography Index. In addition to these standard indexes, specific reference materials cited in the last section of this book, "Reference Materials," were invaluable in the development of this bibliography. The most helpful of those specific reference materials were the bibliographies of Sport Philosophy by Joy Theresa DeSensi for The Philosophic Society for the Study of Sport Proceedings and The Journal of the Philosophy of Sport.

Citations for books were verified on a cross reference quality check using the OCLC bibliographic data base, Books in Print, Library of Congress Subject Index, National Union Catalog of Books and the Library of Congress Subject Catalog, including numerous direct examinations of books. Journal, magazine, and newspaper articles were verified directly in numerous libraries including The New York Public Library, The Harvard University Library, The University of Washington Library, The University of Oregon Library, Oregon State University Library, and the Drew University Library. Approximately ninety-five percent of the articles have been directly verified in every way. This multiple methodology of citation gathering and verification has assured thoroughgoing quality control, resulting in a very reliable bibliography.

ORGANIZATION AND SCOPE

Five major categories structure this bibliography:

General Works and Philosophy
The Team, Players, and Coaches
The Game, Competition, and Contestants
Sports and Society
Reference Works

The main body of this bibliography is structured according to issues arising out of the three main environments of sports. The primary environment is the team and the various relationships entailed in that context. If the ethical issue arises out of an individual or dual sport, the primary environment is simply the player's modus operandi and/or the player's relationship with coaches, trainers, and doctors. The secondary environment is the game or contest involving the various relationships between and among players, opponents, fans, referees, officials, and the ethical issues engendered by competition. The third and macro environment is society. This section of the bibliography includes the wider social and ethical issues involving women and minorities in sports, the big business of college sport, the role of sport in society, children and sports, sport and media, academics and athletics, sport and politics, and other large societal issues.

The three main categories that organize this bibliography, representing the basic environments of sports, are placed between the first category, "General Works and Philosophy," and the last category, "Reference Works."

"General Works and Philosophy" contains books that involve sports ethics either directly or indirectly. In this category are a number of classics in the philosophic study of sport such as Man, Play, and Games by Roger Caillois, Competition and Playful Activities by James W. Keating, Sport, Culture and Society: A Reader on the Sociology of Sport edited by John W. Loy Jr. and Gerald S. Kenyon, Sport: A Philosophical Inquiry by Paul Weiss, Toward a Philosophy of Sport, by Harold J. VanderZwaag, and the classic phenomenology of play, games, and sport, Homo Ludens, by Johan Huizinga. This section also includes such recent philosophic inquiries into sport as Philosophy of Sport and The Question of Play by Drew Hyland, The Rules of the Game: Ethics in College Sport by Richard E. Lapchick and John B. Slaughter, and Sport in a Philosophic Context by Carolyn E. Thomas. Also in this section are such popular but erudite cultural criticism studies as Take Time for Paradise: Americans and Their Games by A. Bartlett Giametti, From Ritual to Record: The Nature of Modern Sports, by Allen Guttmann, and Sports in America by James Michener. All of these books treat specific issues of ethics and larger issues concerning the role of sport in society.

In the last section of the bibliography are reference works in fields interrelated with the discipline of ethics such as sports medicine, sociology, sports history, sports and literature, philosophy of sport, and works concerning sports in general.

The scope of this bibliography is not only indicated by the five major categories listed on the Contents page, but by the numerous entries in the cross referenced subject index, as well. For instance, if one is researching Little League baseball, not only is the relevant category "Children, Youth, and Sport" in the Contents, but the term "Little League baseball" is in the subject index. Or, if the subject matter is college basketball recruiting violations, one would go to the Contents and look under "Recruiting," "Cheating and Corruption," "Fans and Supporters," and "Big Time NCAA College Sport." In the subject index are some of the same terms and additional listings under "College Basketball," "North Carolina State," "NCAA Violation," "Boosters," and "Sports Mania."

The scope of this volume is also indicated by the subject headings that follow the citations. These subject headings were included because they provide more information in a shorter space than would prose annotations. The subject index does not duplicate subject headings for the citations. In many cases, the subject headings in the body of the text are longer and different from the subject index terms.

In addition to the Contents page, the subject index, and the subject headings, the scope of this volume is indicated by an alphabetically listed author index. Moreover, the interdisciplinary nature of this bibliography is indicated by the wide-ranging fields of study represented by these authors and the kinds of citations contained herein. While the pure discipline of sports ethics is primarily the province of philosophers, many of the contributions to the literature of sports ethics are from historians, theologians, sociologists, physical educators, feminists, psychologists, sports writers, players, and fans of all sorts. The philosophical purist might be critical of how wide the scope of this bibliography is and of the seemingly marginal and journalistic entries. Nevertheless, we intentionally decided to err on the side of comprehensiveness both in quantity and types of ethical perspectives. This effort yielded a total of 642 book entries and 2,232 article and monograph entries.

This volume covers mainly the two decades between 1970 and 1990, providing coverage of English language materials published primarily in North America with a focus on ethics and sports in the United States. There are exceptions to the time parameters and to the subject matter. In the interest of making this as valuable as possible, certain materials written prior to 1970 have been included if they were deemed especially relevant and significant. In addition, there are some entries that go beyond a strictly American focus to one of international sports ethics if there is a connection with the United States scene.

WHAT IS SPORTS ETHICS?

The term sports ethics combines two ordinary terms and point to two activities: sports, as a refined activity of play; and ethics, as a refined activity of intellectual reflection. Ethics has been connected to other terms. There can be medical ethics, business ethics, political ethics, engineering ethics, military ethics, criminal justice ethics, or professional ethics. In like fashion, the word sports has been linked to other terms such as sports medicine, sports journalism, sports law, sports history, sports psychology, or sports philosophy. Since understanding the meaning of any one of these concepts requires an understanding of each term, it follows that a definition of sports ethics logically flows from a definition of the two linked words sports and ethics.

DEFINITION OF SPORT

What is meant by the word sport? While there is an ongoing debate and discussion as to just what that term means, there is emerging consensus that whatever else sport might mean, the following four elements must be present in an activity for it to count as a sport:

1. The element of play.
2. The element of physical exertion.
3. The element of competition.
4. The element of order.

Play is the essence of sport, according to such theorists as Johan Huizinga, Roger Caillois, Eleanor Metheny, and Paul Weiss. The essence of play is fun. Hence, the starting place for conceptualizing the meaning of sport is with the meaning of play and the simple point of play--fun.

The word sport is derived from the Latin des-porto, meaning "carry away," and the Old French word desporter, meaning "to carry away from work." Being carried away from the ordinary world by exuberance, mirth, joy, amusement, and sheer fun is what characterizes play and constitutes the central element of sport.

As play, sport is an activity bracketed out of the mundane world where the players create a pretend world that is non-serious but utterly intense and absorbing. Huizinga likens this experience to aesthetics and religion where one finds a "sacred space" transcending the ordinary. As a "make-believe" activity situated outside of everyday life, sport has no serious function. It is non-instrumental. In its authentic expressions sport's value is intrinsic. Of course, sport may be used and valued for certain utilitarian purposes such as producing physical fitness, revenue, school spirit, entertainment, virtue, and fame, but these extrinsic gains are by-products of an intrinsic human experience when playing has its own reward.   Sport is valued in-and-of-itself as is the case with dancing, writing, poetry, meditating, or thinking.   As such, there is a link between sport and aesthetics, religion, pure science, and philosophy, all of which represent activities devoted to humanizing experience and not to utilitarian ends.

Concluding the discussion of this first element, we may say that sport is a refined and structured form of play.

The second element of sport--physical exertion--differentiates sport from other games.   Most sports are games.   There are the Olympic games, basketball games, baseball games, flag football games, volleyball games, and the game of tennis.   Not all games are sport, however.   Checkers, chess, monopoly, and gin rummy are games and they share all the elements of sport, except for one--physical exertion.

The philosopher Paul Weiss insists that chess is not a sport because it does not test what we have as a body.   All of the theorists of sport agree that physical activity and skill are at the apex of the structure of what constitutes sport.   All games involve the mind, but only sport games involve mind and body.   The best example of this is United States football, because it involves both mind and body in equal proportion.   Clearly, it is the most intellectual sport and is one of the most physical sports.   Some sports, such as track and field, do not require a lot of intellectual effort.   A sprinter of 100 to 200 meters or of a 400-meter intermediate hurdles race represents pure physical exertion.   Croquet, shuffle board, and golf call for moderate physical exertion, but still count as sport.

James Michener thinks that physical exertion and the concomitant health and fitness it brings "takes precedence over everything else."   Underscoring this point, Michener insists that, "specifically, a sport, to be effective, should place a demand upon big muscles, lung capacity, sweat glands, and particularly the heart."   If it does not, he says, "much of the potential value of that sport is lost."   While Paul Weiss and many other sport theorists emphasize the achievement of bodily excellence, Michener stresses the importance of sheer physical exertion.   "For myself," he writes, "I no longer have much interest in any sport that does not generate a vigorous sweat."   Wherever the emphasis might be put, it is clear that an essential element in sport is skillful physical exertion seeking to achieve excellence.

Competition, the third element of sport, is what differentiates sport from other forms of recreation such as mountain hiking, cross country skiing, jogging, or aerobic dancing.   These forms of recreation could only be sport if two or more hikers, skiers, joggers, or dancers were in a contest to see who could get some place first or who could endure the physical activity the longest.   If winning and losing are at stake, the physical activity then becomes a contest, and the actors become contestants.   A contest by definition has a specified goal requiring that the contestant complete a task in an effort to be victorious.   A sport contest involves strife and competition with and against others. Eleanor Metheny stresses the "with" aspect when she writes: "The concept of 'the good strife' is implicit in the word 'competition,' as derived from cum and pedere--literally, to strive with rather than against.   The word contest has similar implications being derived from con and testare--to testify with another rather than against him."

Of course, there is an implicit "against" included within this definition, as when two handball players join with each other in a struggle against each other to see who will win.

From an ethical point of view, competition has been viewed as bad and good. There is a vast literature condemning United States sports for overcompetitiveness and an exaggerated importance of winning.   Then there are those who emphasize the ethical value of testing a competitor's skill and prowess insofar as that requires discipline, courage, tenacity of purpose, temperance, and a capacity for fairness.   One justification of competitive sport is the opportunity it provides to find out who one is in relation to others, and that includes the physical, mental, ethical, and spiritual dimensions of life. This opportunity for self examination and inculcation of ethical values exists because, despite the ardent desire to win, a contestant must stick to the rules.

Sport, which is a refined form of play involving skilled physical exertion for the purpose of achieving victory over a competitor, requires order. Unlike such pure play as in playing dolls, tag, or hide-and-go-seek, where there is minimal attention to rules, sport is rooted in order and held together by rules. This fourth element in a definition of sport--order--is structured and achieved by two kinds of rules. The first kind defines and gives structure to the game with reference to the duration of the contest, the physical boundaries and spatial constrictions, the scoring system, the rest periods, time-outs, sanctions for rule violations, the role of officials, proper uniforms, the size and nature of balls and equipment, and how games begin and end. The creation of a game requires this kind of order because it is actually the creation of a pretend world. By creating its own time and space, sport becomes only loosely related to the real world of convention and laws, and hence, it needs to create its own structural and behavioral norms.

The second kind of rules has to do with the process of playing the game and what behaviors are permitted or proscribed during the contest. These rules function primarily to limit players and place obstacles in their path on their way to achieving their goals. Rules structure sheer finitude into games. Imagine the constrictions on a soccer player whose purpose it is to advance the ball down the field, but is not allowed to touch the ball with his or her hands, or the basketball player who has to either pass or dribble a ball to advance it and must play according to refined definitions of "traveling" and "double-dribbling" violations. Or consider the plight of six runners lined up to run 110 meters facing ten obstacles called hurdles. Most rules of sport are designed to prohibit the most efficient ways of achieving goals. As the philosopher Bernard Suits notes, "The simplest, easiest, and most direct approach to achieving a goal is always ruled out in favor of a more complex, more difficult, and more indirect approach." The general ordering of a game and the specific rules of the game have functional utility. They are sometimes designed to enhance excellence of performance, sometimes to create heightened interest and excitement on the part of players and spectators, and sometimes to achieve greater fairness and to mitigate harm.

Summing up the four elements--play, physical exertion, competition, and order-- that are its sine qua non, sport could be defined as a refined form of play removed from ordinary life, involving skilled physical exertion, in competition to see who wins, and with rules designed to enhance its purposes.

DEFINITION OF ETHICS

Ethics is the theoretical study of morality. As such, ethics is to morality what botany is to the structure and growth of plants, or what market research is to marketing. It is an academic discipline providing theories, concepts, norms, meanings, and guidelines for understanding, judging, and guiding a certain kind of activity or experience. In the case of ethics, it is the study of moral experience.

Two words from the above definition--study and morality--need further illumination. First, the word study means that ethics is a rational enterprise that proceeds in an orderly and systematic fashion. Clear thinking and objectivity are just as important in the field of ethics as in sociology, psychology, and anthropology. And as is the case with behavioral science and all other disciplines where there are different branches of a particular field, so in ethics there are different types of ethical study. There are descriptive ethics, normative ethics, and metaethics.

Descriptive ethics is similar to behavioral science. Its task is to describe the actual moral systems, conventions, norms, and behaviors of particular persons or groups. It could study gender difference in sports morality, contrast and compare the ethics of lawyers and investment bankers, or investigate the place of honor and cheating on college campuses. It consists in describing different theories and approaches of ethics. It may analyze codes of conduct or policies of large organizations, or it may assess character traits of certain persons.   One important task of descriptive ethics is to investigate empirically the various contextual variables that may surround a concrete moral problem or simply to identify value and duty conflicts and make reasoned predictions about what might happen if this or that choice is made.   This descriptive task is frequently prolegomenon to the normative task of ethics.

Normative ethics is the practical task of applying ethical theory to the actual world of human experience and making judgments and offering guidance as to what is good and bad about human conduct. Descriptive ethics and behavioral sciences are in the business of describing human behavior. Normative ethics prescribes and proscribes saying what is or is not permissible from an ethical point of view. Normative ethics functions to settle moral disputes when values or duties are in conflict. As a practical enterprise it may recommend policies, actions, procedures, and strategies and may offer practical justification for actions done or proposed.   Finally, normative ethics looks critically at the prevailing moral ethos of a group of society and evaluates the adequacy of the operative behavioral norms, ethical values, written and unwritten codes of conduct, and the moral system in general. For instance, if someone were to look critically at the ethos of Division I NCAA sports by applying ethical standards that transcend what actually is the prevailing moral climate, they would be doing normative ethics. Normative ethics could then offer guidance in systematically proposing, formulating, and justifying a new or modified system for the greater enhancement of big-time college sports.

Metaethics, the third approach to ethics, is concerned with establishing conceptual clarity regarding moral language used in doing normative ethics. When someone makes a normative judgment condemning an act of dishonesty, metaethics offers help in clarifying the meaning of such terms as lying, deception, or dishonesty. Likewise, if someone were to charge that a certain rule was unfair to smaller players in a sport, metaethics could seek clarity on the meaning of fairness and justice so that the normative task is done with more linguistic and analytic precision.   Unlike normative ethics, metaethics does not drive toward practical application of ethical theory and discourse, but it does help to analyze the theories, logic, and language used in doing the practical work of normative ethics.

In summary, ethics as a study and discipline includes these three interrelated, but discrete approaches--descriptive, normative, and metaethical.

If ethics is the theoretical study of morality, what is "morality"? What is moral experience or moral behavior? We know what a financial, culinary, sports, or aesthetic experience or behavior is, but what are the special features of morality? At its most basic level, morality has to do with harm. In the first instance, there is no moral issue unless there is some actual or potential harm involved. Hence, an immoral act always involves some injury to humans or to the human environment. In the second instance, morality is concerned with human benefit. On the positive side, moral experience and behavior involve human flourishing.   Ethics, then, as the study of morality, is fundamentally concerned with minimizing harm and maximizing benefit.   When metaethics attempts to provide and justify moral systems, the practical end of this theoretical task is to prevent or mitigate harm and to promote human welfare. When normative ethics applies such moral principles as justice, truthfulness, and sanctity of life to human experience in judgment or for guidance, the purpose is to reduce injury and to improve the human condition.

To put an emphasis on harm and benefit is not to suggest that morality and normative ethics involve only a calculation of what maims and enhances life. It does mean, however, that even if the emphasis is placed on the role of such prima facie duties as being honest, or on such universal moral principles as truth-telling, the heart of the matter has to do with harm and benefit. Lying is wrong not because a duty or principle is violated. Lying is wrong because in violating the duty or principle someone gets hurt. Sisela Bok, in her book, Lying: Moral Choice in Public and Private Life, makes this point compellingly when she declares: "Even Othello, whom few would have dared to try to subdue by force, could be brought to destroy himself and Desdemona through falsehood."

Flowing out of this concern in ethics for what harms and benefits have come two time-honored ethical principles--nonmaleficence and beneficence. The principle of nonmaleficence mandates two things--do no harm and risk no harm. This is the starting point for ethics and represents a general overarching imperative. The principle of beneficence says three things--promote human welfare, prevent harm, remove harm. In its simplest and most basic sense the task of ethics, as the study of morality, is to do the intellectual work of aiding those who would be guided by these principles.

Finally, in clarifying the meaning of ethics as a discipline and a mode of intellectual reflection, two large questions must be considered. The first and central question of ethics is "What is the good?" (Parenthetically, this is one of three large philosophical questions, the other two being "What is the true?" and "What is the beautiful?" The query about the "true" engendered theories of knowledge and epistemology. Concern for how to determine what is the beautiful produced the field of aesthetics just as concern for discerning the good generated the field of ethics.)

Ethics is concerned about some very concrete questions such as What is a good society? What is a good economic system? What is a good political system? What is a good educational system? What is a good marriage? What is a good doctor-patient relationship? What is a good sports contest? What is a good relationship between coach and player?

A second question follows, "By what standards do we judge the good?" In answering that question, philosophers and theologians over the course of western history have developed certain universal principles by which the good or bad, or the right or wrong, can be judged. The following list of principles represents some of the core norms for determining what is the good:

TWO OVERARCHING PRINCIPLES

Nonmaleficence
Do no harm
Risk no harm

Beneficence
Promote human welfare
Prevent harm
Remove harm

SPECIFIC PRINCIPLES
Sanctity of life
Dignity of life
Justice
Freedom
Equality
Truth-telling
Promise-keeping
Privacy
Confidentiality
Ownership rights
Loyalty
Functional Excellence
Public good

These are standards by which we may begin to judge the good or the bad of a situation. They are also standards that should shape and govern our behavior. Indeed, they are moral requisites of community. Truth-telling, for instance, is not just an abstract principle. It is a functional moral requisite of friendship, family, or any form of human community because honest communication is the basis of community. The same holds true for promise-keeping, which is a constitutive moral ingredient in nearly every interpersonal or group transaction. When someone says "I will meet you after the game," the central element of that transaction is a promise. These ethical principles can be regarded as abstract formal principles hovering over human experience to judge and guide. However, they should also be seen as constitutive elements of human experience that may actually be observed as a scientist observes elements that make up physical or life phenomena. Of course, when these rather general principles are pushed down into human experience they may become refined in rules, codes, habitual behavioral norms, or systems of adjudicating moral problems or differences. Just as a rule of law is rooted in some higher legal principle, so concrete rules of moral behavior are rooted in one of these higher moral principles.

In most any ethical dilemma one of these principles is at stake and two or more may be in conflict. To say these are universal principles is not to say that they are absolute because frequently they do compete. For example, in the case of what to do in the face of unjust aggression, the principle of beneficence--remove or prevent harm--competes with nonmaleficence--do no harm. The value of identifying the principles at stake in a given issue is that one is forced to establish priorities when justifying an action.

A final point needs to be made concerning these principles, and that is to say there is a very strong presumption that persons ought to conform to and be guided by these standards and that to violate any of them intentionally requires some moral justification.

This cursory explanation of what it means to say that "ethics is the theoretical study of morality" is drawn from philosophical studies, theological and religious studies, and, to some extent, the behavioral sciences. The field of ethics draws from all three disciplines but it is a discipline in-and-of-itself. Religious ethics and philosophical ethics are subspecies of ethics.

WHAT IS SPORTS ETHICS?

Sports ethics is a subspecies of ethics. The discipline of sports ethics is simply the discipline of ethics looking at one sphere of life--just as ethics looks at medicine, business, politics, war, family, and higher education. To be sure, sports ethics, like medical ethics, business ethics, and the ethics of other institutions and professions constitutes a distinctive field of thought encompassing unique practices, purposes, and values. However, sports ethics pursues its discipline by asking "What is the good and by what standards should we judge the good?" It pursues its discipline by raising other questions and approaching its special issues according to the methodologies developed in the larger field of ethics.

Albert Camus, the French existentialist writer, once said that it was from sports that "I learned all I know about ethics." While this may well be an exaggeration, as the philosopher Drew Hyland speculates, nevertheless those of us who have experienced sports know that ethics is a central and crucial dimension of that experience. Sports is a sphere of life where one's integrity, moral sensitivity, and ethical values are constantly tested. The opportunities to develop character, learn sportsmanship and fair play, and cultivate discipline and teamwork are many. On the down side, because of the importance of winning, there are manifold opportunities to cheat, take "cheap shots," engage in corrupt practices, and exhibit ill will toward others. Sport brings out the best and the worst in people. As such sport involves many ethical issues.

What are the salient ethical issues represented in this bibliography? They are highlighted in four distinct categories: "General Works and Philosophy," "The Team, Players, and Coaches," "The Game, Competition, and Contestants," and "Sport and Society."

In the first section, "General Works and Philosophy," there are numerous entries treating the metaethical questions of what is the meaning of play, recreation, leisure time activities, games, and sport. There are many entries devoted to the problem of defining these terms. The question as to how one critiques sport from a moral point of view is also a major theme in this section. There are also many articles and chapters treating such normative ethical issues as: Is competition a good or bad thing? Is the focus on winning and losing in sport good or bad? Should having fun be the raison d'être of sport? Is it licit to accept the notion of a "role-differentiated ethic" that legitimates certain behaviors in sport, such as football players hitting each other as hard as they can, which in other spheres of life would be considered a moral outrage? In this section there are also works that could be considered descriptive ethics. There are books and articles that describe the decline and corruption of sport in the late twentieth century. Interrelated with that issue are materials that employ sociological theories in analyzing the bureaucratization of sport and the overemphasis on statistics in sport.

Following the first and more general section of the bibliography are three categories representing the three environments or sport--the team, the game, and the larger society.

The section on the team deals with the relationships between coaches and players. Issues such as demeaning language, authoritarianism, physical abuse, lack of off-time control of players, playing with injuries, and fairness in the treatment of players are represented here. The style and actions of such well-known coaches as Woody Hayes, Vince Lombardi, Bobby Knight, Joe Paterno, Lou Holz, and John Thompson are scrutinized. What are acceptable training rules and policies governing player behaviors in practice, in games, and outside of sport? Who should set those policies? What are the players' obligations to the coach and team in terms of excellence? How should players balance the obligations to the team with obligations to the classroom? What about internal policies concerning drug use and testing? These are some of the ethical issues and questions involved in the primary environment of sport.

The issues flowing out of the second environment of sport--the contest or game--center around the conduct of players, coaches, officials, and fans. Abusive and excessive fan behavior is a major problem in United States sports. Numerous articles and chapters point out that fan behavior, starting with Little League and children's sport, going up through the high school and college years to professional sports, has sullied sport and contributed to its decline. Also in this section are many entries covering the good and bad of changes and reforms in sports in the recent past. Most of the changes in rules and policies, such as the new rules protecting National Football League quarterbacks, have served to make the games more difficult to play and presumably more interesting to fans. Sportsmanship, honorable behavior, and fair play are terms defined and discussed in many materials represented by the citations here. Some lament the loss of fairness and honesty in big-time sport. For instance, there was a time when professional tennis players would intentionally give back a point to an opponent after a bad call by an official. There are also anecdotes and illustrations of honorable behavior, as when track and field competitors help each other with techniques and evaluation of performance. Other issues represented in this section of the bibliography are recruiting practices, the role of agents, violence, point shaving, gambling, and the fairness and quality of officiating.

In the section covering the macro environment of sport--society at large--are many issues reflecting the problems of United States society and having an impact on that society. The deleterious and/or beneficial impact of the increasing bureaucratization and growth of children's sport has commanded much attention in the current literature on sports ethics. Clearly the liveliest topics covered are big-time college sport, the big business of sport, academics and college athletics, minorities and sport, women and sport, and the role of media and sport. All of these topics involve questions of honesty, justice, excellence, dignity, and integrity, including the larger issues of public good and harm. There is also literature discussing in more general and philosophical terms the benefit and harm of sport for individuals and the human community. To what extent does sport enhance human flourishing or to what extent does sport produce fierce competition in the business world? Related to this more general and philosophical topic is the attention given to the role of sport in society. The items represented under this rubric are concerned with the sociological impact of sports in both a micro and macro sense. For instance, there are entries that focus on the role of basketball in the inner cities, the role of high school football in Texas, the meaning of the Pittsburgh Steelers and the Pirates to their city, and the social function of high school and college basketball in Indiana. There are also citations that treat the more general questions of the impact of sports on the economy: sport as a shaper of societal values, the role of sport in influencing behavior, and the meaning of sport rituals to a culture. This section of the bibliography is the largest section, attesting to the overwhelming significance of sport in United States society.

In concluding this introductory essay, three general observations can be made. First, the immense quantity of works cited in this volume indicates an intense concern with sports ethics in the United States. Second, the high intellectual quality of a large number of book and article entries indicates that sports ethics is in the nascent stage of becoming a solid academic discipline. Finally, it is clear that many, if not most, of the major issues facing our society are reflected in the world of sport: money, race, education, gender, drugs, alcohol, labor relations, class, media influence, sexism, health, fitness, cheating, gambling, justice, and now AIDS and sexual lifestyles. As this book goes to press our society is still reeling from the recent announcement by Magic Johnson of the Los Angeles Lakers that he had tested positive for the HIV virus. This episode dramatically illustrates the point that sports mirrors society.

It is my hope that this bibliography will be a useful tool serving the needs of many who are involved in the serious and careful study of sport. More importantly, I would hope that in some way this reference work contributes to improving the ethics of sport behavior and ultimately plays some role in enhancing human flourishing through sport.

SPORTS ETHICS
IN AMERICA

General Works and Philosophy

Books

1. Avedon, Elliott M. and Brian Sutton-Smith. The Study of Games. New York: John Wiley and Sons, Inc., 1971. HISTORY, ANTHROPOLOGY, PURPOSE OF SPORTS, MILITARY, BUSINESS, EDUCATION, FUNCTION OF GAMES.

2. Baker, William J. Sports in the Western World. Totowa, NJ: Rowman and Littlefield Publishers, Inc., 1982. HISTORY, PLAYERS, FANS, HOW SPORTS BEGAN, EVOLUTION OF SPORTS, URBANIZATION, INDUSTRIALIZATION, INTERNATIONAL RELATIONSHIPS, MINORITIES, WOMEN, TELEVISION, BUSINESS.

3. Baker, William J. and James A. Rog (eds.). Sports and the Humanities: A Symposium. Orono, ME: The University of Maine at Orono Press, 1983. AMERICAN VALUES, MEDIA AND SPORT, ACADEMICS, BIG TIME COLLEGE SPORT, CRITIQUE OF SPORTS JOURNALISTS.

4. Barrow, Harold. Man and His Movement: Principles of His Physical Education. Philadelphia: Lea and Febiger, 1971. IDEAL AND MEANING, HISTORY, LEADERSHIP, VALUES.

5. Beisser, Arnold R. The Madness in Sports: Psychosocial Observations on Sports. Bowie, MD: The Charles Press Publishers, 1977. PSYCHOLOGY, CASE STUDIES, CONFLICT, FAILURE, RELATIONSHIP BETWEEN COACHES AND PLAYERS, ROLE OF SPECTATORS, ROLE OF SPORTS IN SOCIETY.

6. Butler, Alfred Joshua. Sport in Classic Times. Los Altos, CA: William Kaufmann Inc., 1975 (1930 reprint). GREEK AND ROMAN SPORTS, COMPARISON WITH MODERN SPORTS.

7. Caillois, Roger. Man, Play, and Games. New York: The Free Press of Glencoe, Inc., 1961. CORRUPTION, COMPETITION, FUNCTION OF SPORTS.

8.   Chu, Donald B. Dimensions of Sport Studies. New York: John Wiley and
     Sons, Inc., 1982. DEFINITION OF SPORT, PSYCHOLOGY, SOCIOLOGY, HISTORY,
     PHILOSOPHY, WOMEN, RACISM, EDUCATION, OLYMPICS.

9.   Csikszentmihalyi, Mihaly. Beyond Boredom and Anxiety: The Experience of
     Play in Work and Games. San Francisco: Jossey-Bass Publishers, 1975.
     ENJOYMENT, CHESS, ROCK CLIMBING, ROCK DANCING, POLITICS.

10. De Grazia, Sebastian. Of Time, Work, and Leisure. New York: Twentieth
     Century Fund, 1962. IDEAL AND MEANING OF SPORT, PLAY, PHILOSOPHY.

11. Dizikes, John. Sportsmen and Gamesmen. Boston: Houghton Mifflin, Co.,
     1981. DEMOCRACY, AMERICAN CHARACTER, HISTORY, RULES, WINNING AT ALL
     COSTS, CAPITALISM.

12. Dunning, Eric and Kenneth G. Sheard. Barbarians, Gentlemen and Players: A
     Sociological Study of the Development of Rugby Football. New York: New
     York University Press, 1979. RUGBY, ENGLAND, SOCIOLOGY, HISTORY, RULES,
     PROFESSIONALISM, SOCIAL CLASSES.

13. Ehrmann, Jacques (ed.). Game, Play, Literature. Boston: Beacon Press, Inc.,
     1971. NATURE OF PLAY, SPORT AND GAMES.

14. Ellis, Michael J. Why People Play. Englewood Cliffs, NJ: Prentice-Hall, Inc.,
     1973. DEFINITION OF PLAY, THEORIES OF PLAY, COMPETITION.

15. Galasso, Pasquale J. Philosophy of Sport and Physical Activity: Issues and
     Concepts. Toronto: Canadian Scholars' Press, 1988. MEANING OF SPORT,
     ETHICAL CODES, AESTHETICS, OFFICIALS, MORAL DIMENSION, PENALTIES IN
     GAMES.

16. Gerber, Ellen W. (ed.). Sport and the Body: A Philosophical Symposium.
     Philadelphia: Lea and Febiger, 1972. NATURE OF SPORTS, IDEAL AND MEANING,
     VALUES, AESTHETICS.

17. Giamatti, A. Bartlett. Take Time for Paradise: Americans and Their Games.
     New York: Summit Books, 1990. IDEAL AND MEANING OF SPORT, RITUAL,
     MYTHOLOGY, WORK AND PLAY, NECESSITY AND FREEDOM, PRO BASEBALL, ROLE
     OF SPORT IN SOCIETY.

18. Goldstein, Jeffrey H. (ed.). Sports, Games and Play: Social and Psychological
     Viewpoints. Hillsdale, NJ: Lawrence Erlbaum Associates, 1979. PLAY
     BEHAVIOR, GAME STRATEGY, SPECTATORS, SOCIOLOGY.

19. Grupe, Ommo, Dietrich Kurz, and Johannes Marcus Teipel (eds.). Sport in the
     Modern World: Chances and Problems. New York: Springer-Verlag, Inc.,
     1973. SOCIAL ASPECTS, IDEAL AND MEANING.

20. Gulick, Luther Halsey. A Philosophy of Play. New York: Charles Scribner's
     Sons, 1920. NATURE OF PLAY, GAMES, AND SPORT, DEFINITION.

21.   Guttmann, Allen. From Ritual to Record: The Nature of Modern Sports. New York: Columbia University Press, 1978. RELATIONSHIP BETWEEN PLAY AND CONTESTS, SOCIAL CONDITIONS, FOOTBALL, BASEBALL, INDIVIDUALISM, SOCIOLOGY, BUREAUCRACY.

22.   Harris, Dorothy V. Involvement in Sport: A Somatopsychic Rationale for Physical Activity. Philadelphia: Lea and Febiger, 1973. IDEAL AND MEANING, MOTIVATION, AGGRESSION, FEMININITY.

23.   Harris, Janet C. and Roberta J. Park (eds.). Play, Games, and Sports in Cultural Contexts. Champaign, IL: Human Kinetics Publishers, 1983. SYMBOLISM, POLITICS, MYTHS, HEROES, RITUAL, PLAY, SOCIALIZATION, CHILDREN.

24.   Huizinga, Johan. Homo Ludens: A Study of the Play-Element in Culture. Boston: Beacon Press, Inc., 1950. NATURE OF PLAY, CULTURE, LANGUAGE, LAW, WAR, POETRY, MYTHOPOIESIS, ART, CIVILIZATION.

25.   Hyland, Drew A. Philosophy of Sport. New York: Paragon House, 1990. IDEAL AND MEANING, VALUES, ETHICAL ISSUES, SEXISM, RACISM, WINNING, PLAY, MIND AND BODY, FREEDOM.

26.   Hyland, Drew A. The Question of Play. Lanham, MD: University Press of America, 1984. SOCIOLOGY, PSYCHOLOGY, HISTORY, COMPETITION, FRIENDSHIP.

27.   Jones, Michael E. (ed.). Current Issues in Professional Sports. Durham, NH: Whittemore School of Business and Economics, University of New Hampshire, 1980. CONTRACTUAL RELATIONSHIPS, NCAA, AGENTS, MEDIA, RESERVE CLAUSE, INJURIES, SPORTS MEDICINE.

28.   Kaplan, Max. Leisure in America: A Social Inquiry. New York: John Wiley and Sons, Inc., 1960. CULTURE, WORK, SOCIAL CLASSES, SUBCULTURES, POLITICS, RELIGION.

29.   Keating, James W. Competition and Playful Activities. Washington, D.C: University Press of America, 1978. JEAN PAUL SARTRE ON SPORT AND PLAY, GAMES, DISTINCTION BETWEEN PLAY AND COMPETITION, DEFINITION OF PLAY AND SPORT, DEFINITION OF SPORTSMANSHIP, NATURE OF ATHLETICS.

30.   Kelly, John R. Leisure Identities and Interactions. London: Allen and Unwin, 1983. DEFINITION OF LEISURE, FREEDOM, STRUCTURE, PLAY AND WORK, LEISURE AND SPORT, LEISURE AND FAMILY.

31.   Klausner, Samuel Z. (ed.). Why Man Takes Chances: Studies in Stress Seeking. Garden City, NY: Anchor Books, 1968. PSYCHOLOGY, SOCIOLOGY, ANTHROPOLOGY, COMPETITION.

32.   Knight, James Allen and Ralph Slovenko (eds.). Motivations in Play, Games and Sports. Springfield, IL: Charles C. Thomas Publishers, 1967. DEFINITION, IDEAL AND MEANING, RELIGION, SIN IN SPORTS, MEANING OF THE SELF.

33.   Lancy, David F. and B. Allan Tindall (eds.). The Study of Play: Problems and Prospects. West Point, NY: Leisure Press, 1977. CHILDREN, EXPRESSIVE ASPECTS OF PLAY, SOCIO-PSYCHOLOGICAL ASPECTS.

34.   Landers, Daniel M. (ed.). Social Problems in Athletics: Essays in the Sociology of Sport. Urbana, IL: University of Illinois Press, 1976. MINORITIES, RACISM, DISCRIMINATION, COMPETITION, SOCIOLOGY, PSYCHOLOGY, SOCIAL MOBILITY THROUGH SPORTS, CHILDREN, THE NEW LEFT AND THE ATHLETIC ESTABLISHMENT.

35.   Lapchick, Richard Edward and John Brooks Slaughter. The Rules of the Game: Ethics in College Sport. New York: American Council on Education, 1989. HISTORY, STUDENT-ATHLETES, WOMEN, RACISM, RECRUITING, PLAYER PAYOFFS, DRUGS, AGENTS, MEDIA, COACHES, ATHLETIC DIRECTORS, NCAA, COLLEGE PRESIDENTS.

36.   Lee, Mabel. A History of Physical Education and Sports in the U.S.A. New York: John Wiley and Sons, Inc., 1983. PROFESSIONAL ORGANIZATIONS, AMATEURISM.

37.   Lenk, Hans (ed.). Topical Problems of Sport Philosophy. Schriftenreihe Des Bundesinstituts Fur Sportwissenschaft, 1980. PLAY, ART, CREATIVITY, PEACE, ABUSIVE BEHAVIOR.

38.   Lowe, Benjamin. The Beauty of Sport: A Cross-Disciplinary Inquiry. Englewood Cliffs, NJ: Prentice-Hall, Inc., 1977. AESTHETICS, RELATIONSHIP OF SPORT AND ART, SPORT AND THE PERFORMING ARTS, SYMBOLS.

39.   Loy, John W. Jr. and Gerald S. Kenyon (eds.). Sport, Culture and Society: A Reader on the Sociology of Sport. New York: Macmillan Publishing Company, 1969. SOCIOLOGY OF SPORT, SPORT AS A VEHICLE FOR SOCIAL MOBILITY, POLITICS.

40.   Lucas, John A. and Ronald A. Smith. The Saga of American Sports. Philadelphia: Lea and Febiger, 1978. HISTORY, SPORT AS A REFLECTION OF SOCIETY, RELIGION, WOMEN, OLYMPICS, REFORM.

41.   Michener, James. Sports in America. New York: Random House, Inc., 1976. CHILDREN, WOMEN, EXPLOITATION, MONEY, RELIGION, POLITICS, GOVERNMENT INTERVENTION, VIOLENCE, MEDIA, BIG TIME COLLEGE SPORTS, REFORM, RECRUITING, INTERCOLLEGIATE ATHLETICS, BENEFIT AND HARM.

42.   Mihalich, Joseph C. Sports and Athletics: Philosophy in Action. Totowa, NJ: Rowman and Littlefield Publishers, Inc., 1982. PURSUIT OF EXCELLENCE, EXISTENTIALISM, STUDENT-ATHLETES, COLLEGE SPORTS, WINNING, FUTURE.

43.   Moltmann, Jurgen (Translated by Reinhard Ulrich). Theology of Play. New York: Harper and Row Publishers, Inc., 1972. TRANSCENDENCE, THEOLOGY, MEANING OF PLAY AND RELIGION, DOCTRINE OF CREATION, PLAY AND FREEDOM.

44. Morgan, William John (ed.). Sport and the Humanities: A Collection of Original Essays. Knoxville, TN: University of Tennessee Press, 1979. WINNING, RITUAL AND ITS USE IN SPORTS, LANGUAGES OF SPORT, SPORT AS HUMANIZING EXPERIENCE.

45. Morgan, William John and Klaus V. Meier (eds.). Philosophic Inquiry in Sport. Champaign, IL: Human Kinetics Publisher, 1988. NATURE OF SPORT, PLAY, GAMES, MIND-BODY PROBLEM, GENDER EQUALITY, DRUGS, METAPHYSICS, IDEAL AND MEANING.

46. Murray, J. Alex (ed.). Sports or Athletics: A North American Dilemma. Windsor, Ont: University of Windsor Press, 1974. OLYMPICS, CHILDREN, BIG BUSINESS, MEDIA, FUTURE.

47. Ortega y Gasset, Jose. Meditations on Hunting. New York: Charles Scribner's Sons, 1972. ETHICS OF HUNTING, ESSENCE OF HUNTING, RELIGION, HAPPINESS, EXISTENTIALISM.

48. Osterhoudt, Robert G. An Introduction to the Philosophy of Physical Education and Sport. Champaign, IL: Stipes Publishing Company, 1978. METAPHYSICS, NATURALISM, IDEALISM, REALISM, PRAGMATISM, EXISTENTIALISM, PHENOMENOLOGY.

49. Osterhoudt, Robert G. Sport: A Humanistic Overview. Tempe: Arizona State University, 1982. ANTHROPOLOGY, HISTORY, HUMANIZING EXPERIENCE OF SPORT, RELIGION, ART, COMMERCIAL ROLE OF SPORT.

50. Osterhoudt, Robert G. (ed.). The Philosophy of Sport: A Collection of Original Essays. Springfield, IL: Charles C. Thomas, Publisher, 1973. ONTOLOGY OF SPORT, SPORT AND PLAY, EXISTENTIALISM, PHENOMENOLOGY, RELIGION, ETHICS OF COMPETITION, KANTIAN ETHIC, GAMBLING, AESTHETICS.

51. Piaget, Jean. Play, Dreams and Imitation in Childhood. New York: William Norton and Company, Inc., 1962. PSYCHOLOGY, CHARACTER, CHILDREN, RULES, MORALS.

52. Potter, Stephan. The Theory and Practice of Gamesmanship Or, the Art of Winning Games Without Actually Cheating. New York: Bantam Books Inc., 1965. NATURE OF PLAY, LEISURE, GAMES AND SPORT, MORALITY.

53. Rahner, Hugo. Man at Play. New York: Herder and Herder, 1967. THEOLOGY, DOCTRINE OF CREATION, GOD AND FREEDOM, MEANINGFUL PLAY.

54. Rees, C. Roger and Andrew W. Miracle (eds.). Sport and Social Theory. Champaign, IL: Human Kinetics Publishers, 1986. NATURE OF SPORT, PLAY, IDEALIZATION OF PLAY.

55. Riess, Stevan A. (ed.). The American Sporting Experience: A Historical Anthology of Sport in America. West Point, NY: Leisure Press, 1984. HISTORY, BOXING, CORRUPTION, RACISM, BIG TIME COLLEGE SPORTS, TITLE IX.

56.   Rigauer, Bero (translated by Allen Guttmann). Sport and Work. New York: Columbia University Press, 1981. SPORT AS DISGUISED WORK, SPECIALIZATION, BUREAUCRATIZATION, REPRESSION, PLAY, COMPETITION, SPORT AS AN AVENUE OF UPWARD MOBILITY.

57.   Ryan, Bob. The Pro Game: The World of Professional Basketball. New York: McGraw-Hill Book Company, 1975. HISTORY, REFEREES, COACHES, PLAYING POSITIONS.

58.   Salter, Michael A. (ed.). Play: Anthropological Perspectives. West Point, NY: Leisure Press, 1978. ANTHROPOLOGY, CULTURE, VALUES, CHILDREN, WORK AND PLAY.

59.   Shea, Edward J. Ethical Decisions in Physical Education and Sport. Springfield, IL: Charles C. Thomas, 1978. NORMATIVE ETHICS, RULES, REGULATIONS, FAIR PLAY, SPORTSMANSHIP.

60.   Sheehan, George. Running and Being: The Total Experience. New York: Warner Books, Inc., 1978. METAPHYSICS, SELF REALIZATION, IDENTITY, EXISTENTIALISM.

61.   Stevens, Phillips Jr. (ed.). Studies in the Anthropology of Play. West Point, NY: Leisure Press, 1977. WORK, DEFINITION OF SPORT, LEISURE, RECREATION.

62.   Stone, Gregory P. (ed.). Games, Sport and Power. New Brunswick, NJ: E. P. Dutton, 1972. COMPETITION, PLAY, VALUES, DEFINITION OF SPORT.

63.   Thomas, Carolyn E. Sport in a Philosophic Context. Philadelphia: Lea and Febiger, 1983. METAPHYSICS, EPISTEMOLOGY, PLAY, COMPETITION, IDEAL AND MEANING, AESTHETICS, ETHICS OF COMPETITION.

64.   Tunis, John Roberts. The American Way in Sport. New York: Duell, Sloan, and Pearce, 1958. BIG BUSINESS, PROFIT MOTIVE, EMPHASIS ON COMPETITION, VALUES.

65.   Vanderwerken, David L. and Spencer K. Wertz (eds.). Sport Inside Out: Readings in Literature and Philosophy. Fort Worth, TX: Texas Christian University Press, 1985. SPECTATORS, SPORTSMANIA, VIOLENCE, EQUALITY, SPORTS AND SOCIETY, MYTHS, IDEAL AND MEANING, RELIGION, AESTHETICS.

66.   VanderZwaag, Harold J. Toward a Philosophy of Sport. Reading, MA: Addison-Wesley Publishing Company, Inc., 1972. SPORTS AND PHYSICAL EDUCATION; WOMEN; SPORTS CONTRASTED WITH PLAY, GAMES, AND ATHLETICS; AGGRESSION; VALUES.

67.   Weiss, Paul. Sport: A Philosophic Inquiry. Carbondale, IL: Southern Illinois University Press, 1969. PLAYERS, COACHES, FANS, CONCERN FOR EXCELLENCE, METAPHYSICS, COMPETITION, COMMERCIALIZATION, WOMEN, CHARACTER BUILDING.

68.   Wertz, Spencer K. Talking a Good Game: Inquiries Into the Principles of Sport.
Dallas: Southern Methodist University Press, 1988. TEXTUALITY OF SPORT,
RULES, REGULATIONS, SOCIAL ASPECTS, MORAL DIMENSION.

69.   Wind, Herbert Warren. The Realm of Sport: A Classic Collection of the
World's Great Sporting Events and Personalities As Recorded by the Most
Distinguished Writers. New York: Simon and Schuster, Inc., 1966. NON-
FICTION SPORTS WRITING, MEANING OF SPORTS, VALUES, SPORTS REPORTING.

70.   Young, David C. The Olympic Myth of Greek Amateur Athletics. Chicago:
Ares Publishers, Inc., 1984. AMATEURISM, GREEK OLYMPICS, HISTORY,
PROFESSIONALISM, EXCELLENCE IN SPORTS.

71.   Zeigler, Earle F. Ethics and Morality in Sport and Physical Education: An
Experiential Approach. Champaign, IL: Stipes Publishing Company, 1984.
VIOLENCE, COACHES, DRUGS, ELITISM, ACADEMICS, CASE STUDIES, RECRUITING,
SPORTSMANSHIP.

72.   Zeigler, Earle F. Philosophical Foundations for Physical, Health, and Recreation
Education. Englewood Cliffs, NJ: Prentice Hall, 1964. CHALLENGE OF THE
BODY, GAMES, SPORT ENDURANCE, COORDINATION, METAPHYSICS.

73.   Zeigler, Earle F. Physical Education and Sport Philosophy. Englewood Cliffs,
NJ: Prentice-Hall, Inc., 1977. IDEAL AND MEANING OF SPORT, HEALTH,
FUNCTIONS OF SPORT, BENEFIT OF SPORT.

74.   Zeigler, Earle F. Problems in the History and Philosophy of Physical Education
and Sport. Englewood Cliffs, NJ: Prentice-Hall, Inc., 1968. VALUES, POLITICS,
NATIONALISM, ECONOMICS, RELIGION.

75.   Zeigler, Earle F. (ed.). History of Physical Education and Sport. Champaign,
IL: Stipes Publishing Company, 1988. HISTORICAL PERSPECTIVES, EARLY
SOCIETIES, MIDDLE AGES, MODERN TIMES, UNITED STATES, CANADA.

Articles

76.   Adler, Peter and Patricia A. Adler. "The Role of Momentum in Sport." Urban
Life: A Journal of Ethnographic Research. 7, No.2 (July 1978), 153-176.
SOCIOLOGY OF SPORT, SPORT AS A MIRROR OF SOCIETY, RISK TAKING,
TERRITORIALITY.

77.   Algozin, Keith. "Man and Sport." Philosophy Today. 20, No.3/4 (Fall 1976),
190-195. DEFINITION, EXCELLENCE, PAUL WEISS, FASCINATION WITH SPORT,
WILL TO POWER.

78.   American Academy of Physical Education. "Position Statement: Moral and
Ethical Judgements and Behavior Associated with Sports Should Receive
Increased Emphasis in Programs of Physical Education in School." The Academy
Papers. 15 (October 1981), 107-108. MORAL VALUES, TEACHING PHYSICAL
EDUCATION, COACHES.

79.   Anderson, Earl R.   "Plato's Lesser Hippias: A Neglected Document in Sport
History."   Journal of Sport History.   8, No.1 (Spring 1981), 102-110. GREEK
VIEW OF ROLE OF ATHLETIC TRAINING, INCLUSION OF WOMEN, SPORTS
METAPHORS.

80.   Arnold, Peter J.   "Competitive Games and Education."   Physical Education
Review.   5, No.2 (Autumn 1982), 126-130. CHARACTER DEVELOPMENT,
COMPETITION, RULES, FREEDOM.

81.   Burke, Richard. "'Work' and 'Play'."   Ethics. 82, No.1 (October 1971), 33-47.
DEFINITION OF WORK AND PLAY, RELATIONSHIP BETWEEN WORK AND PLAY.

82.   Champlin, Nathaniel L.   "Are Sports Methodic?"   Journal of the Philosophy of
Sport.   4 (Fall 1977), 104-116. DEFINITION, SPORTS AS QUALITATIVE METHOD.

83.   Cowan, Ed. "Why Sport?"   The Humanist.   39, No.6 (November/December
1979), 22-28. COMPETITION, WINNING, FAIR PLAY.

84.   Dombrowski, Daniel A.   "Plato and Athletics."   Journal of the Philosophy of
Sport.   6 (Fall 1979), 29-38. ATHLETICS AND SOPHISTRY, STRUCTURE OF
ATHLETIC CONTESTS, ATHLETICS AND THE MILITARY.

85.   Double, Richard.   "Teaching the Philosophy of Sport."   Teaching Philosophy.
4 (January 1981), 47-53. COMPETITIVENESS, AGGRESSION, EXISTENTIALISM,
SPORTSMANSHIP.

86.   Eitzen, D. Stanley. "Ethical Problems in American Sport." The Journal of Sport
and Social Issues.   12, No.1 (Spring 1988), 17-30. FAIR PLAY, SAFETY,
VIOLENCE, SPECTATORS, MEDIA.

87.   Haper, William.   "On Playing Sport."   Physical Education Review.   6, No.1
(Spring 1983), 52-57. OVER-RATIONALIZATION OF SPORTS, SPORTS AS A FORM
OF HUMAN EXPRESSION, PLAY AS INVOLUNTARY RESPONSIBLE THINKING.

88.   Hyland, Drew A.   "Modes of Inquiry of Sports, Athletics, and Play."   Journal
of the Philosophy of Sport.   1 (1974), 123-128. ETHICS, VALUES, MIND AND
BODY IN SPORT, PHENOMENOLOGY, DEFINITION OF SPORT.

89.   Kempton, Murray.   "Jock Sniffing."   The New York Review of Books.   16, No.2
(February 11, 1971), 34-38. VINCE LOMBARDI, WINNING IS THE ONLY THING,
SATURDAY'S AMERICA, CONFESSION OF A DIRTY BALL PLAYER, BALL FOUR, OUT
OF THEIR LEAGUE, PLAYER OF THE YEAR, THE CITY GAME.

90.   Kleinman, Seymour. "Is Sport Experience?" Quest. 19 (January 1973), 93-96.
SPORT AS EXPERIENCE, SPORT AS NON-INTELLECTUAL.

91.   Kleinman, Seymour.   "The Nature of a Self and Its Relation to an 'Other' in
Sport."   Journal of the Philosophy of Sport.   2 (September 1975), 45-50.
MEANING OF SPORT, RELATIONSHIP OF SELF TO OTHER, SPORT ENVIRONMENT.

92. Kleinman, Seymour. "Toward a Non-Theory of Sport." Quest. 10 (May 1968), 29-34. DEFINITION OF SPORT, AESTHETIC THEORY, PHENOMENOLOGY.

93. Kleinman, Seymour. "Will the Real Plato Please Stand Up?" Quest. 14 (June 1970), 73-75. PLATO'S MIND-BODY DUALISM, ORGANISMIC UNITY.

94. Kretchmar, Robert Scott. "At the Heart of Athletics." Journal of Physical Education, Recreation and Dance. 53, No.1 (January 1982), 35-36. FORGETTING AND REMEMBERING, TENSION BETWEEN HEART AND HEAD.

95. Kretchmar, Robert Scott. "Ethics and Sport: An Overview." Journal of the Philosophy of Sport. 10 (1983), 21-32. METAPHYSICS, NONMORAL GOOD, VALUE OF SPORT, PRESCRIPTIVE ETHICS, THE GOOD LIFE.

96. Kretchmar, Robert Scott. "Modes of Philosophic Inquiry and Sport." Journal of the Philosophy of Sport. 1 (1974), 129-131. EPISTEMOLOGY, METAPHYSICS, IDEAL AND MEANING, VALUES, ACADEMIC STUDY.

97. Kunstler, Robin (ed.). "Ethics Courses Offered." Parks and Recreation. 20, No.4 (April 1985), 28-30+. VALUES, SURVEY OF ETHICAL TRAINING, RIGHTS, MEDICAL AND LEGAL ASPECTS.

98. Lenk, Hans. "Notes Regarding the Relationship Between the Philosophy and the Sociology of Sport." International Review for the Sociology of Sport. 21 (1986), 83-91. ACADEMIC STUDY, DEFINITION OF SPORT.

99. Lenk, Hans. "Presidential Address--1981: Tasks of the Philosophy of Sport: Between Publicity and Anthropology." Journal of the Philosophy of Sport. 9 (1982), 94-106. CONTRIBUTION OF PHILOSOPHY, PLATO, ORTEGA Y GASSET, PYTHAGORAS, PHILOSOPHIC ANTHROPOLOGY, OLYMPICS.

100. Lenk, Hans. "Sport, Achievement, and the New Left Criticism." Man and World. 5, No.2 (May 1972), 179-192. IDEOLOGY, SOCIOLOGY, PHILOSOPHY OF SPORT.

101. Lucas, J. R. "Moralists and Gamesmen." Philosophy: The Journal of the Royal Institute of Philosophy. 34, No.128 (January 1959), 1-11. THEORY OF GAMES, FAIR PLAY, CONCEPTIONS OF MORALITY.

102. McMurtry, John. "The Illusions of a Football Fan: A Reply to Michalos." Journal of the Philosophy of Sport. 4 (Fall 1977), 11-14. SPORT AS A PARADIGM OF SOCIETY, FOOTBALL AS A REINFORCER OF CAPITALISM.

103. Meier, Klaus V. "Presidential Address: Philosophic Society for the Study of Sport--1985. 'Restless Sport'." Journal of the Philosophy of Sport. 12 (1985), 64-77. STATE OF THE ART OF SPORT PHILOSOPHY, CRITIQUE, METAETHICS, NORMATIVE ETHICS, FORMALISM, RULES.

104. Michalos, Alex C. "The Unreality and Moral Superiority of Football." Journal of the Philosophy of Sport. 3 (September 1976), 22-24. INTELLECTUALITY IN FOOTBALL, RULES, CHARACTER, DISCIPLINE, STRATEGY.

105.   Midgley, Mary. "The Game Game." Philosophy: The Journal of the Royal Institute of Philosophy. 49, No.189 (July 1974), 231-253. DEFINITION OF GAMES, RULES.

106.   Miller, Donna Mae. "Ethics in Sport: Paradoxes, Perplexities, and a Proposal." Quest. 32, No.1 (1980), 3-7. MEDIA, COACHES, VALUES, PROFESSIONAL PREPARATION.

107.   Morgan, William John. "An Analysis of the Sartrean Ethic of Ambiguity As the Moral Ground for the Conduct of Sport." Journal of the Philosophy of Sport. 3 (September 1976), 82-96. EXISTENTIALISM, FREEDOM, CONTEXT, RELATIVITY, AMBIGUITY, METAETHICS, JEAN PAUL SARTRE.

108.   Morgan, William John. "Presidential Address: Philosophic Society for the Study of Sport. 'The Impurity of Reason: A Reflection on the Social Critique of the Philosophy of Sport'." Journal of the Philosophy of Sport. 15 (1988), 69-90. STRUCTURALISM, TALCOTT PARSONS, SOCIOLOGY, MARX, DEFENSE OF PHILOSOPHY OF SPORT.

109.   Oberlander, Susan. "New North Carolina Chancellor Has Record of Strong Views on Integrity in Sports." The Chronicle of Higher Education. 34, No.32 (April 20, 1988), A41-42. BIG TIME COLLEGE SPORTS, ACADEMIC EXCELLENCE, PAUL HARDIN, UNIVERSITY OF NORTH CAROLINA AT CHAPEL HILL, INTEGRITY, SOUTHERN METHODIST UNIVERSITY, PLAYER PAYOFFS.

110.   Ogilvie, Bruce C. and Maynard A. Howe. "Beating Slumps at Their Own Game." Psychology Today. 18, No.7 (July 1984), 28-32. STRESS, AROUSAL LEVEL, VARIATION IN PERFORMANCE.

111.   Osterhoudt, Robert G. "In Praise of Harmony: The Kantian Imperative and Hegelian Sittlichkeit as the Principle and Substance of Moral Conduct in Sport." Journal of the Philosophy of Sport. 3 (September 1976), 65-81. METAETHICS, NORMATIVE ETHICS, CONTEXT, FAIR PLAY, MORAL RULES, PHILOSOPHY, EMANUEL KANT, FREIDRICH HEGEL, MORAL CONDUCT.

112.   Osterhoudt, Robert G. "Modes of Philosophic Inquiry Concerning Sport: Some Reflections On Method." Journal of the Philosophy of Sport. 1 (1974), 137-141. ACADEMIC STUDY, EPISTEMOLOGY, IDEAL AND MEANING, METHODOLOGY.

113.   Osterhoudt, Robert G. "The History and Philosophy of Sport: The Re-unification of Once Separated Opposites." Journal of the Philosophy of Sport. 5 (Fall 1978), 71-76. DEVELOPMENT OF HISTORIC AND PHILOSOPHIC DIMENSION OF SPORT.

114.   Osterhoudt, Robert G. "The Kantian Ethic as a Principle of Moral Conduct in Sport." Quest. 19 (January 1973), 118-123. KANT'S CATEGORICAL IMPERATIVE, IDEAL CONDUCT IN SPORT.

115. Rader, Benjamin G. "Modern Sports: In Search of Interpretations." Journal of Social History. 13, No.2 (Winter 1979), 307-321. REVIEW OF THE JOY OF SPORTS, RIP OFF THE BIG GAME, FROM RITUAL TO RECORD, THE SAGA OF AMERICAN SPORT.

116. Ralls, Anthony. "The Game of Life." The Philosophical Quarterly. 16, No.62 (January 1966), 23-34. RULES, MORAL COMMITMENT, JOHN RAWLS, PRINCIPLES.

117. Reddiford, Gordon. "Morality and the Games Player." Physical Education Review. 4, No.1 (Spring 1981), 8-16. FAIR PLAY, VIOLENCE, MORALITY, JOHN RAWLS, COOPERATION.

118. Roochnik, David L. "Play and Sport." Journal of the Philosophy of Sport. 2 (September 1975), 36-44. EXISTENTIALISM, DEFINITION OF PLAY, GAME AND SPORT, PLAY AS PRESENT IN SPORT.

119. Russell, Bill and Taylor Branch. "How Sports Fit Into the Grand Scheme of Things." Scholastic Coach. 50, No.8 (March 1981), 13+. RULES; RELATIONSHIP OF SPORTS TO RELIGION, POLITICS, AND ART; HUMOR; LONG RANGE VIEW.

120. Simon, Irving. "A Humanistic Approach to Sports." The Humanist. 43, No.4 (July/August 1983), 25-26+. OPPONENT VS. ASSOCIATE, FRIENDLY COMPETITION, WINNING AT ALL COSTS.

121. Slusher, Howard S. "Sport: A Philosophical Perspective." Law and Contemporary Problems. 38, No.1 (Winter-Spring 1973), 129-134. FUNCTION OF RULES, INSTITUTIONAL CONTROL OF ATHLETICS, REASON FOR SPORT, RIGHT TO EXPRESSION IN SPORT.

122. Stoll, Sharon Kay. "What is Ethical and What is Not: A Philosophical Stance for the Physical Educator of the 80's." The Physical Educator. 39, No.4 (December 1982), 181-184. DEFINITION OF ETHICS, RULES, TEACHING, FAIR PLAY.

123. Suits, Bernard. "Sticky Wickedness: Games and Morality." Dialogue: Canadian Philosophical Review. 21, No.4 (1982), 755-759. MORAL EGOISM, RELATIONSHIP BETWEEN GAMES AND MORALITY, ENDS VS. MEANS, GAME METAPHORS.

124. Suits, Bernard. "What Is A Game?" Philosophy of Science. 34, No.2 (June 1967), 148-156. PENALTIES, CHEATING, IDEAL AND MEANING, DEFINITION, COMPETITION, FUN, PLAY, PHILOSOPHY.

125. Wenz, Peter S. "Human Equality in Sports." The Philosophical Forum. 12, No.3 (Spring 1981), 238-250. SOCIAL JUSTICE, WOMEN, VALUES, PROFESSIONALIZATION, REFORM, UTILITARIAN, EGALITARIAN, RAWLSIAN ETHICS.

126. Wertz, Spencer K. "Novak's Analogies." Journal of the Philosophy of Sport. 6 (Fall 1979), 79-86. MICHAEL NOVAK'S, THE JOY OF SPORTS, WOMEN, FANS, ANALOGIES BETWEEN SPORTS AND RELIGION.

127.   Wertz, Spencer K.   "Teaching Sport Philosophy Analytically."   <u>Teaching Philosophy</u>.   9, No.2 (June 1986), 121-146.   ETHICS, AESTHETICS, GENDER, POLITICS, METAPHYSICS.

128.   Zaner, Richard M.   "Sport and the Moral Order."   <u>Journal of the Philosophy of Sport</u>.   6 (Fall 1979), 7-18.   DEFINITION OF SPORT, PLAY AND GAMES, MORAL DEVELOPMENT, CULTURE, IDEAL AND MEANING, RULES, MORAL DIMENSION.

129.   Zeigler, Earle F.   "Application of a Scientific Ethics Approach to Sport Decisions."   <u>Quest</u>.   32, No.1 (1980), 8-21.   AMATEUR-PROFESSIONAL CONTROVERSY IN SPORT.

130.   Zeigler, Earle F.   "Basic Considerations About a Philosophy of Sport (and its Possible Relationship With Success in Competitive Sport)."   <u>Canadian Journal of Applied Sport Sciences</u>.   3, No.1 (March 1978), 35-42.   DEFINITION OF TERMS, STATUS OF ATHLETICS, RELATIONSHIP TO PREVAILING SOCIAL FORCES.

The Team, Players, and Coaches

AGENTS, MANAGERS, AND OWNERS

Books

131.   Allen, George Herbert and Charles Maher. <u>Merry Christmas--You're Fired!</u> New York: Simon and Schuster, Inc., 1982. PRO FOOTBALL, WINNING, MONEY, OWNERS.

132.   Dark, Alvin and John Underwood. <u>When in Doubt, Fire the Manager: My Life and Times in Baseball</u>. New York: E. P. Dutton, 1980. INSIDE STORY, MANAGERS' RELATIONSHIPS WITH PLAYERS, OWNERS, FANS, MEDIA.

133.   Garvey, Edward B. <u>The Agent Game: Selling Players Short</u>. Washington, D.C: Federation of Professional Athletes, AFL-CIO, 1984. RECRUITING, MONEY NEGOTIATIONS, OWNERS AND UNIONS, JUSTICE, PLAYER ABUSE.

134.   Trope, Mike with Steve Delsohn. <u>Necessary Roughness</u>. Chicago: Contemporary Books, Inc., 1987. RECRUITING, AGENTS, COLLEGE ATHLETES, MONEY, AUTHOR IS AN AGENT, NCAA RULES, FOOTBALL, COMPETITION.

Articles

135.   "Agents: What's the Deal?" <u>Sports Illustrated</u>. 67, No.17 (October 19, 1987), 74-78+. AGENTS, ABUSE, MONEY.

136.   Deford, Frank. "The Guard Who Would Be Quarterback." <u>Sports Illustrated</u>. 67, No.12 (September 14, 1987), 64-69+. GENE UPSHAW, NFL PLAYERS UNION, BATTLE WITH OWNERS, UNRESTRICTED FREE AGENCY, WAGE SCALES, GUARANTEED CONTRACTS.

137.   Farrell, Charles S. "Player Who Accepted Money Reinstated; Colleges Weigh Appeals in Similar Cases." The Chronicle of Higher Education. 34, No.2 (September 9, 1987), A34. PAYMENTS TO ATHLETES, AGENT SCANDALS, TERYL AUSTIN, NORBY WALTERS, LLOYD BLOOM, COACHES.

138.   Garvey, Edward B. "From Chattel to Employee: The Athlete's Quest for Freedom and Dignity." The Annals of the American Academy of Political and Social Science. 445 (September 1979), 91-101. AUTONOMY, MONEY, FREEDOM, DIGNITY.

139.   Hartley, Charles J. "Controlling Unscrupulous Agents: State Legislatures Come to Colleges' Aid." The Chronicle of Higher Education. 34, No.13 (November 25, 1987), A33-34. MIKE ARCHER, LOUISIANA STATE UNIVERSITY FOOTBALL COACH, AGENTS, IMPROPER PAYMENTS.

140.   Johnson, William Oscar and Ron Reid. "Some Offers They Couldn't Refuse." Sports Illustrated. 50, No.21 (May 21, 1979), 28-35. CORRUPTION, COLLEGE FOOTBALL, PLAYER PAYOFFS, AGENTS, CASH LOANS, SIGNING "OFFER" SHEETS, NCAA RULES VIOLATIONS, MIKE TROPE.

141.   Kirshenbaum, Jerry. "Sports Agents: Raising Ethical Questions That Run From A (Armas) to Z (Zadora)." Sports Illustrated. 56, No.15 (April 12, 1982), 21. BASEBALL PLAYER AGENTS, CONFLICT OF INTEREST, TINO BARZIE, EXPLOITATION OF PLAYERS.

142.   Kurkjian, Tim. "The Boss Strikes Again." Sports Illustrated. 72, No.25 (June 18, 1990), 48-50+. GEORGE STEINBRENNER, OWNER, BUCKY DENT, FIRING MANAGER, PRO BASEBALL.

143.   Lederman, Douglas. "Grand Jury Will Call 60 College Athletes in a Probe of Alleged Payments by Agents." The Chronicle of Higher Education. 33, No.38 (June 3, 1987), 35-36. EXTORTION, FRAUD, RACKETEERING, NORBY WALTERS, LLOYD BLOOM.

144.   Lederman, Douglas. "Universities Probe Published Allegations That Players Received Money From Agents." The Chronicle of Higher Education. 33, No.30 (April 8, 1987), 35+. AGENTS, PAYMENTS TO ATHLETES, NORBY WALTERS, LLOYD BLOOM, THREATS TO PLAYERS.

145.   Looney, Douglas S. "Jack Be Nimble: A Day in the Life of An Agent." Sports Illustrated. 67, No.17 (October 19, 1987), 100-101. JACK MILLS, PLAYERS' AGENT, CREDIBILITY, REPUTATION, SELF REFLECTION.

146.   Lupica, Mike. "In New York, Another Sad Tale of a Rich Man in Trouble Unfolds." The National Sports Daily. (July 5, 1990), 2. GEORGE STEINBRENNER, DAVID WINFIELD, PAY-OFF TO HOWIE SPIRA, OWNER, PRO BASEBALL.

147.   Milverstedt, Fred. "Colleges Tackle Unethical Agents." Athletic Business. 11, No.9 (September 1987), 24-26+. EDUCATING ATHLETES, NCAA RULES, GOVERNMENT INTERVENTION.

148. Neff, Craig. "Agents of Turmoil." <u>Sports Illustrated</u>. 67, No.5 (August 3, 1987), 34-51. PLAYER AGENTS, POWER, ABUSE, CASE STUDIES, MONEY.

149. Neff, Craig. "Den of Vipers." <u>Sports Illustrated</u>. 67, No.17 (October 19, 1987), 76-78+. PLAYER AGENTS, MANAGEMENT ABUSE, SCANDALS, MISUSE OF PLAYERS' MONEY, KICKBACKS, EXCESSIVE FEES.

150. Oberlander, Susan. "Agents Who Were Indicted For Racketeering and Fraud Expected to Challenge Integrity of College Sports." <u>The Chronicle of Higher Education</u>. 35, No.2 (September 7, 1988), A30. NORBY WALTERS, LLOYD BLOOM, SIGNING COLLEGE ATHLETES TO CONTRACTS, RACKETEERING, MAIL FRAUD, WIRE FRAUD, CONSPIRACY TO COMMIT EXTORTION.

151. Papanek, John. "A Lot of Hurt: Inaction Got Kareem Creamed." <u>Sports Illustrated</u>. 67, No.17 (October 19, 1987), 89-92+. KAREEM ABDUL-JABBAR, NBA, LOS ANGELES LAKER BASKETBALL PLAYER, AGENT, LAWSUIT, IMPROPRIETIES, AGENT LOST MILLIONS.

152. Ruxin, Robert H. "Unsportsmanlike Conduct: The Student-Athlete, the NCAA, and Agents." <u>The Journal of College and University Law</u>. 8, No.3 (1981/1982), 347-367. NCAA RULES, EDUCATION AND ATHLETES, AGENTS, AMATEURISM.

153. Selcraig, Bruce. "Agents of Violence?" <u>Sports Illustrated</u>. 66, No.14 (April 6, 1987), 25. PAYMENTS TO ATHLETES, NORBY WALTERS, LLOYD BLOOM, RECRUITING, AGENTS, THREATS TO PLAYERS.

154. Selcraig, Bruce. "The Deal Went Sour." <u>Sports Illustrated</u>. 69, No.10 (September 5, 1988), 32-33. AGENTS, NORBY WALTERS, LLOYD BLOOM, RACKETEERING, EXTORTION, INDICTMENT, MAIL FRAUD.

155. Wulf, Steve. "This Time George Went Overboard." <u>Sports Illustrated</u>. 56, No.19 (May 10, 1982), 40-42+. NEW YORK YANKEES, GEORGE STEINBRENNER, REGGIE JACKSON, OWNER TRASHING PLAYERS, FIRING MANAGERS, BOB LEMON, GENE MICHAEL.

CHARACTER AND VALUES

Books

156. <u>Development of Human Values Through Sports</u>. Reston, VA: American Alliance for Health, Physical Education and Recreation, 1974. CULTURE, OUTWARD BOUND, LEADERSHIP.

157. Ross, Saul and Leon Charette (eds.). <u>Persons, Minds and Bodies: A Transcultural Dialogue Amongst Physical Education, Philosophy and the Social Sciences</u>. North York, Ontario: University Press of Canada, 1988. PHILOSOPHY, ALTRUISM IN SPORT, ARISTOTLE'S TELEOLOGY, AESTHETICS, ETHICAL STANDARDS.

Articles

158.   Allen, E. John B.   "Values and Sport: The Development of New England Skiing, 1870-1940." The Oral History Review. 13 (1985), 55-76. SECULARISM, EQUALITY, SPECIALIZATION, RATIONALIZATION, BUREAUCRATIC ORGANIZATION, QUANTIFICATION, RECORDS.

159.   Arnold, Peter J.   "Sport, Moral Education and the Development of Character." Journal of Philosophy of Education.   18, No.2 (1984), 275-281. SPORT AS FAIRNESS, BELIEFS, ATTITUDES, BEHAVIORS, VALUES.

160.   Barkovich, Cheryl.   "What About Values in Competition?"   The Journal of Physical Education.   76, No.1 (September/October 1978), 21.   FAIR PLAY, SPORTSMANSHIP, YMCA, COMPETITION, COACHES.

161.   Bishop, Thelma.   "Values in Sports." Journal of Health, Physical Education and Recreation.   33, No.6 (September 1962), 45-47+.   DRUGS, COMPETITION, CONFLICT, COOPERATION.

162.   Bozzi, Vincent.   "You Are What You Play." Psychology Today.   23 (October 1989), 69.   IMAGE, GOLF, TENNIS, BOWLING, SKIING.

163.   Bueter, Robert J.   "Sports, Values and Society." The Christian Century.   89, No.14 (April 5, 1972), 389-398.   SOCIETY IN TRANSITION, VINCE LOMBARDI, FOOTBALL, VALUES, CHANGE.

164.   Congdon, Paul U.   "An Examination of Values in Sports."   The Journal of Physical Education and Program.   79, No.6 (September 1982), F21-22. DEVELOPING VALUES THROUGH SPORTS CONFERENCE, AGGRESSION, ROLE OF COACHES.

165.   Cosentino, Frank.   "Sports, Awareness, Values and Education."   Canadian Association for Health, Physical Education and Recreation Journal.   45, No.2 (November/December 1978), 6-8+.   SPORTS AS PREPARATION FOR LIFE, ROLE OF SPORT IN SOCIETY, DEFINITION OF SPORT, NATURE OF SPORT.

166.   Crawford, Scott A. G. M.   "Values in Disarray: The Crisis of Sport's Integrity." Journal of Physical Education, Recreation, and Dance.   57, No.9 (November/December 1986), 41-44.   CURTIS STRONG, TEXAS CHRISTIAN UNIVERSITY, VALUES, TEACHING PHYSICAL EDUCATION, EXCELLENCE.

167.   Dannehl, Wayne E. and Jack E. Razor.   "The Values of Athletics: A Critical Inquiry."   The Bulletin of the National Association of Secondary School Principals.   55, No.356 (September 1971), 59-65.   OVEREMPHASIS ON WINNING, EXPLOITATION, VALUES OF SCHOOL SPORTS, SELF DISCIPLINE, PHYSICAL FITNESS, SPORTSMANSHIP, SCHOOL SPIRIT, SELF RELIANCE, COOPERATION.

168.   Davis, Howard and Glen D. Baskett.   "Do Athletes and Non-Athletes Have Different Values?" Athletic Administration.   13, No.3 (Spring 1979), 17-19. TERMINAL VALUES, INSTRUMENTAL VALUES.

169. Deford, Frank. "'A Little Lower Than the Angels'." Sports Illustrated. 67, No.27 (December 21, 1987), 12-15. SALUTE TO EIGHT ATHLETES, HONORABLE SERVICE, DALE MURPHY, JUDY BROWN KING, CHIP RIVES, RORY SPARROW, KIP KEINO, BOB BOURNE, PATTY SHEEHAN, REGGIE WILLIAMS.

170. Dubois, Paul E. "Gender Differences in Value Orientation Toward Sports: A Longitudinal Analysis." Journal of Sport Behavior. 13, No.1 (March 1990), 3-14. CHILDREN, SOCCER, EMPIRICAL STUDY, MALES EMPHASIZE WINNING, SOCIALIZATION, WOMEN AND SPORTS.

171. Fimrite, Ron. "Triumph of the Spirit." Sports Illustrated. 73, No.13 (September 24, 1990), 94-100+. PROFESSIONAL BASEBALL, DR. ROY CAMPANELLA, CATCHER FOR THE BROOKLYN DODGERS, AUTOMOBILE ACCIDENT, SPINAL INJURY, REHABILITATION, DETERMINATION, VIRTUE.

172. Galvin, Richard. "Are 'Sport Values' Real Values?" Momentum: A Journal of Human Movement Studies. 12, No.2 (Autumn 1987), 39-46. ETHICS, MORALITY, BENEFIT AND HARM OF SPORT, MEANING OF SPORT.

173. Gray, Marv. "Character Building in Sports. Myth or Fact." The Indiana IAHPER Journal. 7 (February 1978), 9-10. BENEFIT AND HARM OF SPORT, COACHES AND PLAYERS, COMPETITION, WINNING.

174. Greene, Robert Ford. "Tennis Values and Human Values." Journal of Physical Education and Recreation. 48, No.6 (June 1977), 33. SOCIAL DEVELOPMENT, PSYCHOLOGICAL DEVELOPMENT, TEACHING PHYSICAL EDUCATION, INTERCOLLEGIATE ATHLETICS.

175. Kew, Francis C. "Values in Competitive Games." Quest. 29 (Winter 1978), 103-112. RADICAL ETHIC, LOMBARDIAN ETHIC, COUNTER CULTURE.

176. Lumpkin, Angela. "Sport and Human Values." Journal of Popular Culture. 16, No.4 (Spring 1983), 4-10. VALUE DEVELOPMENT, COMPETITION, BIG BUSINESS, PRESSURE TO WIN, BENEFIT AND HARM, FAIR PLAY, COOPERATION, DISCIPLINE, TEAMWORK, SELF ESTEEM, COMMERCIALIZATION.

177. O'Connor, Gerry. "Bernard Malamud's The Natural: 'The Worst There Ever Was in the Game'." Arete: The Journal of Sport Literature. 3, No.2 (Spring 1986), 37-42. RULES, MYTHS, CHARACTER DEVELOPMENT.

178. Obertueffer, Delbert. "On Learning Values Through Sport." Quest. 1 (December 1963), 23-29. SPORTSMANSHIP, VALUES, RULES, TEACHING ETHICS.

179. Ogilvie, Bruce C. and Thomas A. Tutko. "Sport: If You Want to Build Character, Try Something Else." Psychology Today. 5, No.5 (October 1971), 61-63. NEED FOR ACHIEVEMENT, WOMEN, EMPHASIS ON WINNING, CHANGE.

180. Ostro, Harry. "Ethical Values: Does the Rhetoric Exceed the Practice?" Scholastic Coach. 56, No.7 (February 1987), 4+. MORAL STANDARDS, LITIGATION, ROLE MODELS, TEACHING ETHICS, SPORTSMANSHIP.

181.   Paul, John. "Sport, A School for Human Virtue." Olympic Review. 144 (October 1979), 576-577. CHARACTER, VALUES, COOPERATION, DISCIPLINE, SPORTSMANSHIP.

182.   Podeschi, Ronald. "The Farther Reaches of Physical Activity." Quest. 21 (January 1974), 12-18. EXCELLENCE, THIRD FORCE MOVEMENT, ABRAHAM MASLOW, UNIVERSAL VALUES, WOMEN.

183.   Potter, Mitch, Rich Pein, and Archie Harris.   "Values in Competitive Swimming." Swimming World and Junior Swimmer. 20, No.6 (June 1979), 28-29. VALUE DEVELOPMENT, ROLE OF COACHES, RULES, SEXUAL EQUALITY, INDIVIDUAL WORTH, PARENTS.

184.   Roberts, John E. "Sports and Values: Integrity Is Most Critical Issue Facing High School Athletics Today." Interscholastic Athletic Administration. 15, No.2 (Winter 1988), 4-5. VIRTUE, CHARACTER, BENEFIT AND HARM OF SPORT, WINNING, CHEATING.

185.   Sage, George H. "American Values and Sport: Formation of a Bureaucratic Personality." Journal of Physical Education and Recreation. 49, No.8 (October 1978), 42-44. SPORT AS A MICROCOSM OF SOCIETY, SPORT SOCIOLOGY, RECIPROCAL RELATIONSHIP BETWEEN SPORT AND AMERICAN VALUES, CULTURE, AMERICAN CHARACTER, RELIGION, DEMOCRACY.

186.   Segal, Erich. "'To Win or Die': A Taxonomy of Sporting Attitudes." Journal of Sport History. 11, No.2 (Summer 1984), 25-31. PLAY AS A REFLECTION OF SOCIETY, WINNING AT ALL COSTS, COMPETITION, GREEK ATHLETICS.

187.   Townshend, Philip. "On American Games and Values." Current Anthropology. 20 (March 1979), 188. CONSERVATISM OF ATHLETES, REPLY TO MUNROE AND CONROY.

188.   Tuckett, Glen. "Athletic Values: More Than Winning." Interscholastic Athletic Administration. 8 (Spring 1982), 22-23, 29. OVEREMPHASIS ON WINNING, INTEGRITY, CHARACTER, FAIRNESS, COMPETITION.

189.   Turnbull, I. "Value of Interschool Activities." Pacer. 62 (January/February 1977), 2-3. CHARACTER, DISCIPLINE, HEALTH, ACADEMICS, COOPERATION, TEAMWORK.

190.   Wandzilak, Thomas. "Values Development Through Physical Education and Athletics." Quest. 37, No.2 (1985), 176-185. ROLE MODELS, LAWRENCE KOHLBERG, MORAL REASONING.

191.   Wandzilak, Thomas and Glenn Potter. "Teaching Values Through the Athletic Experience." National Association of Secondary School Principals Bulletin. 70, No.487 (February 1986), 61-65. VALUES EDUCATION, ROLE MODELS, VALUES IDENTIFICATION, COACHES, DECISION MAKING.

192.   Williams, Roger M. "The U.S. Open Character Test." Psychology Today. 22 (September 1988), 60+. MENTAL TOUGHNESS, COMPETITIVE PRESSURE.

COACHES, PLAYERS, AND TEAM

Books

193.   Allen, Maury. Damn Yankee: The Billy Martin Story. New York: Times
        Books, 1980. MANAGERS, OWNERS, GEORGE STEINBRENNER, MANAGER-OWNER
        RELATIONSHIPS, MANAGER-PLAYERS RELATIONSHIPS, PRO BASEBALL.

194.   Armstrong, Robert. The Coaches. Mankato, MN: Creative Education, Inc.,
        1977. TEACHING AND MENTORING, DISCIPLINE, FAIRNESS, EXCELLENCE,
        CHARACTER, SKILLS.

195.   Bleier, Rocky with Terry O'Neil. Fighting Back. New York: Stein and Day,
        1975. HEROISM, EXCELLENCE, PRO FOOTBALL, ROCKY BLEIER, PITTSBURGH
        STEELERS, OVERCOMING ADVERSITY.

196.   Brondfield, Jerry. Woody Hayes and the 100 Yard War. New York: Random
        House, Inc., 1974. VIOLENCE, BENEFIT AND HARM, BIG TIME NCAA, WOODY
        HAYES, COLLEGE FOOTBALL, COACHES, UNSPORTSMANLIKE CONDUCT.

197.   Clarke, Kenneth S. (ed.). Drugs and the Coach. Washington, D.C: American
        Association for Health, Physical Education and Recreation, 1972. DRUGS,
        COACHES AND PLAYERS, BLOOD DOPING.

198.   Cousy, Robert and John Devaney. The Killer Instinct. New York: Random
        House, Inc., 1975. PRO BASKETBALL, COMPETITION, WINNING.

199.   Curry, George E. Jake Gaither, America's Most Famous Black Coach. New
        York: Dodd, Mead and Company, 1977. ALONZO GAITHER, COLLEGE
        FOOTBALL, FLORIDA A&M, BLACK ATHLETES, ATHLETIC DIRECTORS.

200.   Dailey, Joseph Michael. A Measurement of Machiavellian Personality Traits of
        Football and Wrestling Coaches in Small Colleges and Universities. PhD Thesis,
        University of New Mexico, 1986. COACH AND PLAYER RELATIONSHIP, VALUES,
        COMPETITION, HARM AND BENEFIT OF SPORT.

201.   Gallon, Arthur J. Coaching Ideas and Ideals. Boston: Houghton Mifflin
        Company, 1974. WINNING AT ALL COSTS, MOTIVATION, COMPETITION, DRUGS,
        FANS.

202.   Hahn, James and Lynn Hahn. Bill Walton: Maverick Cager. St. Paul: EMC
        Corp, 1978. POLITICAL RADICAL, INTEGRITY, LIFESTYLE, OPINIONS ABOUT
        ATHLETES' PRIVATE AND PUBLIC LIVES, PRO BASKETBALL, PORTLAND
        TRAILBLAZERS.

203.   Hill, Grant Michael. A Study of Sport Specialization in Midwest High Schools and Perception of Coaches Regarding the Effects of Specialization on High School Athletes and Athletic Programs. Doctoral Dissertation, University of Iowa, 1987. BASEBALL, BASKETBALL, FOOTBALL, POLICIES.

204.   Johnson, Spencer. The Value of Courage: The Story of Jackie Robinson. La Jolla, CA: Value Communications, 1977. DISCRIMINATION, BLACK BASEBALL PLAYERS, MINORITIES, RACISM, SOCIALIZATION.

205.   Jordan, Pat. Black Coach. New York: Dodd, Mead and Company, 1971. MINORITIES, BASEBALL.

206.   Madden, John with Dave Anderson. Hey, Wait A Minute, I Wrote a Book! New York: Villard Books, 1984. MEDIA, LOS ANGELES RAIDERS, PRO FOOTBALL.

207.   Maravich, Pete and Darrel Campbell. Heir to a Dream. Nashville, TN: Thomas Nelson Publishers, 1987. MEDIA, COLLEGE BASKETBALL, PRO BASKETBALL, DISCIPLINE, INTEGRITY, CHARACTER, LOUISIANA STATE UNIVERSITY.

208.   May, Julian. Roy Campanella, Brave Man of Baseball. Mankato, MN: Crestwood House, Inc., 1974. BLACK BASEBALL PLAYERS, BROOKLYN DODGERS, HEROISM, MINORITIES, OVERCOMING ADVERSITY, BIOGRAPHY.

209.   Miller, Donna Mae. Coaching the Female Athlete. Philadelphia: Lea and Febiger, 1974. HISTORY, MOTIVATION, INJURIES.

210.   O'Brien, Michael. Vince: A Personal Biography of Vince Lombardi. New York: William Morrow and Company, Inc., 1987. PRO FOOTBALL, WINNING, COMPETITION.

211.   Ogilvie, Bruce C. and Thomas A. Tutko. Problem Athletes and How to Handle Them. London: Pelham Books, Ltd., 1966. SUCCESS PHOBIA, INJURY-PRONE ATHLETES, WITHDRAWN ATHLETES, DEPRESSED ATHLETES, HYPER-ANXIOUS ATHLETES.

212.   Phelps, Richard "Digger" and Larry Keith. A Coach's World. New York: Thomas Y. Crowell Company, 1974. BASKETBALL, BIG TIME COLLEGE SPORTS, NOTRE DAME UNIVERSITY.

213.   Ralbovsky, Martin. Lords of the Locker Room: The American Way of Coaching and Its Effect on Youth. New York: P. H. Wyden, Inc., 1974. YOUTH, COACH AND PLAYER RELATIONSHIPS, INTERSCHOLASTIC COMPETITION, HIGH SCHOOL SPORTS, BENEFIT AND HARM OF SPORTS.

214.   Ralbovsky, Martin. The Namath Effect. Englewood Cliffs, NJ: Prentice-Hall, 1976. JOE NAMATH, NEW YORK JETS, EXCELLENCE, LEADERSHIP, PRO FOOTBALL, CONTRIBUTION TO THE GAME.

215. Schoor, Gene. Football's Greatest Coach: Vince Lombardi. Garden City, NY: Doubleday and Company, Inc., 1974. PRO FOOTBALL, WINNING, EXCELLENCE.

216. Scott, Jack. Bill Walton: On the Road with the Portland Trail Blazers. New York: Crowell, 1978. PRO BASKETBALL, RENEGADE, POLITICAL RADICAL, INTEGRITY, SOCIAL JUSTICE, COURAGE.

217. Shecter, Leonard. The Jocks. New York: The Bobbs-Merrill Company, 1969. "DUMB JOCKS", GAME-FIXING, POINT SHAVING, SPORTS WRITING, HEROES, PROFESSIONALISM.

218. Stambler, Irwin. Bill Walton, Super Center. New York: Putnam Publishing Group, 1976. COLLEGE BASKETBALL, PRO BASKETBALL, RADICAL POLITICS, SOCIAL JUSTICE, EXCELLENCE, LIFESTYLE, UNIVERSITY OF CALIFORNIA AT LOS ANGELES, PORTLAND TRAILBLAZERS.

219. Temple, Ed with B'Lou Carter. Only the Pure in Heart Survive. Nashville, TN: Broadman Press, 1980. WOMEN, TRACK AND FIELD, MOSCOW OLYMPICS, TENNESSEE STATE UNIVERSITY.

220. White, Dan. Play to Win: A Profile of Princeton Basketball Coach Pete Carril. Englewood Cliffs, NJ: Prentice Hall, 1978. COLLEGE BASKETBALL, COMPETITION, WINNING.

221. Wooden, John R. They Call Me Coach. Waco, TX: Word Books, 1972. UNIVERSITY OF CALIFORNIA AT LOS ANGELES BRUINS, COLLEGE BASKETBALL, HISTORY, PLAYERS.

Articles

222. Albinson, J. G. "Professionalized Attitudes of Volunteer Coaches Towards Playing a Game." International Review of Sport Sociology. 8, No.2 (1973), 77-87. ACHIEVEMENT-ORIENTED SOCIETY, SOCIALIZATION, EXCELLENCE, PSYCHOLOGY, COMPETITIVE BEHAVIOR, VALUES, PROFESSIONALISM, COACHES AND PLAYERS.

223. Bain, Linda L. "Differences in Values Implicit in Teaching and Coaching Behaviors." Research Quarterly. 49, No.1 (March 1978), 5-11. TEACHING PHYSICAL EDUCATION, GENDER, PRIVACY, UNIVERSALISM, PEDAGOGY, COACHES AND PLAYERS.

224. Besecker, Irv. "On the Conduct of Coaches." Referee. 3, No.9 (September 1978), 37+. ROLE MODELS, TEMPER, ABUSIVE BEHAVIOR.

225. "Black Head Coaches: Taking Charge on Major Campuses." Ebony. 37, No.7 (May 1982), 57-58+. SPORTS AS A MICROCOSM OF SOCIETY, RACISM.

226.   Bohlig, Mary. "Women Coaches/Administration: An Endangered Species." Scholastic Coach. 57, No.7 (February 1988), 89-90+. EFFECT OF STEREOTYPES ON WOMEN IN LEADERSHIP ROLES, TITLE IX, CAREER AND CONFLICT, GROVE CITY COLLEGE, DECLINE OF WOMEN IN ATHLETIC ADMINISTRATION.

227.   Bonventre, Peter. "Did the Coach Play Too Rough?" Newsweek. 94 (October 29, 1979), 91. FRANK KUSH, ASSAULT BY A COACH, VIOLENCE, PLAYER-COACH RELATIONS.

228.   Chakravarty, Subrata N. "Character is Destiny." Forbes. 132, No.8 (October 10, 1983), 114+. MANAGEMENT, SELF CONFIDENCE, CONSISTENCY, LEADERSHIP, EXCELLENCE, WINNING, FOOTBALL, COACHES, VALUES, VIRTUES.

229.   Cohen, Neil. "And Where Are the Black Head Coaches?" Sport. 78, No.8 (August 1987), 6. BLACKS IN MANAGEMENT, BASEBALL, FOOTBALL, RACISM.

230.   Curtis, Bill, Ronald E. Smith and Frank L. Smoll. "Scrutinizing the Skipper: A Study of Leadership Behaviors in the Dugout." Journal of Applied Psychology. 64, No.4 (August 1979), 391-400. VALUES, PRO BASEBALL, CHARACTER.

231.   Dent, David J. "Black Coaches Remain Scarce in College Ranks." Black Enterprise. 18, No.5 (December 1987), 34. COACHES, EXPLOITATION, RACISM, BOOSTER CLUBS.

232.   Enberg, Dick. "Giving the Athletes a Voice in College Sports." The New York Times. 139 (January 14, 1990), Section 8, Page 8. AUTONOMY, COLLEGE SPORTS, CHANGES AND REFORM, RULES, DEMOCRACY, RIGHTS.

233.   Farney, Bill. "High School Coaches, Players Not Immune From Violations." Tennis Coach. 31 (January 1987), 27. VALUES, ABUSES, FAIRNESS, SPORTSMANSHIP.

234.   Farrell, Charles S. "Memphis State University Fires Basketball Coach Who Was Involved in Controversies." The Chronicle of Higher Education. 33, No.4 (September 24, 1986), 31. DANA KIRK, BASKETBALL COACH, MEMPHIS STATE UNIVERSITY, IMPROPER BENEFITS TO ATHLETES, SPORTS GAMBLING, GRAND JURY PROBE.

235.   Farrell, Charles S. "Women Said to Hold Fewer Coaching Positions and Administrative Jobs Than in the Early 1970's." The Chronicle of Higher Education. 31, No.4 (September 25, 1985), 35+. MERGER OF MEN'S AND WOMEN'S ATHLETIC DEPARTMENTS, REFORM.

236.   "The Football Coach is a Lady." Ebony. 34, No.2 (December 1978), 115-116+. SHIRLEY MCCRAY, FEMALE FOOTBALL COACH, RELIGION.

237.   Franks, Ian M. and Gary Miller. "Eyewitness Testimony in Sport." Journal of Sport Behavior. 9, No.1 (March 1986), 38-45. COACHES, RECALL ABILITY.

238. Good, Paul. "I Feel Betrayed." Sport. 68, No.6 (June 1979), 62-64+.
      WASHINGTON STATE UNIVERSITY, CONTRACT-BREAKING, ROLE MODELS.

239. Good, Paul. "Tarkanian vs. the NCAA: Behind the Congressional Probe That
      May Revamp College Sports." Sport. 66, No.3 (March 1978), 37-38+. JERRY
      TARKANIAN, UNIVERSITY OF NEVADA AT LAS VEGAS, NCAA, CONGRESSIONAL
      PROBE, COLLEGE BASKETBALL.

240. Grimsley, Jimmie R. and Carl King. "Ethics and Values--A Coach's
      Responsibility?" Texas Coach. 33 (November 1988), 16-17. MORAL
      MENTORING, SPORTSMANSHIP, CHARACTER, ROLE OF THE COACH.

241. Herman, Daniel J. "Mechanism and the Athlete." Journal of the Philosophy of
      Sport. 2 (September 1975), 102-110. HISTORY, MECHANISM OF PSYCHOLOGY,
      INFLUENCE OF MECHANISM ON PHYSICAL EDUCATION AND SPORT.

242. Hersch, Hank. "Choosing Sides." Sports Illustrated. 71, No.22 (November 27,
      1989), 42-46+. HIGH SCHOOL FOOTBALL, BIGOTRY, POSITION COMPETITION,
      JUSTICE, BLACK FOOTBALL PLAYERS, COMPETITION BETWEEN BLACK AND WHITE
      QUARTERBACKS, SOCIAL ASPECTS.

243. Hogue, Micki King. "When a Woman Coaches Men." Women's Sports and
      Fitness. 7, No.9 (October 1985), 61. CREDIBILITY GAP, RELATIONSHIP BETWEEN
      PLAYERS.

244. Huffman, Steve with Rick Telander. "I Deserve My Turn." Sports Illustrated.
      73, No.9 (August 27, 1990), 26-28+. COLLEGE FOOTBALL COACH LOU HOLTZ,
      STEVE HUFFMAN BRANDED A QUITTER, COACHING ETHICS, NOTRE DAME
      UNIVERSITY, CHARACTER, FOOTBALL INJURIES.

245. Keller, Richard D. "The Man in Charge: Coaches in Modern Literature."
      Arete: The Journal of Sport Literature. 1, No.2 (Spring 1984), 139-150.
      POETRY, NOVELS, LITERARY VERSIONS OF THE COACH.

246. Knoppers, Annelies. "Gender and the Coaching Profession." Quest. 39, No.1
      (April 1987), 9-22. STRUCTURAL DETERMINANTS OF WORK BEHAVIOR, POWER,
      OPPORTUNITY, PROPORTION, DISCRIMINATION, PREJUDICE.

247. Krasnow, Stefanie and David Elfin. "Survey: Major Colleges Shun Black
      Coaches...Except in Washington, D. C. Area." Sport. 79, No.6 (June 1988),
      11. RACISM, BLACKS IN MANAGEMENT, DISCRIMINATION.

248. Lacy, Alan C. and Phylis D. Goldston. "Behavior Analysis of Male and Female
      Coaches in High School Girls' Basketball." Journal of Sport Behavior. 13, No.1
      (March 1990), 29-39. COACHES AND PLAYERS, GENDER DIFFERENCES, PRAISE
      AND BLAME BEHAVIORS EXAMINED.

249. Leavy, Walter. "Northwestern's New Head Coach: Dennis Green Takes
      Charge." Ebony. 36, No.11 (September 1981), 72-74+. BLACK HEAD COACH,
      RACISM.

250.   Lederman, Douglas. "Black Coaches' Movement Gains Momentum; First Annual Meeting Attracts 300." The Chronicle of Higher Education. 34, No.31 (April 13, 1988), A43-44. BLACK COACHES ASSOCIATION, BLACK REPRESENTATION AND INFLUENCE IN COLLEGIATE COACHING RANKS, BOYCOTTS, EQUAL OPPORTUNITY.

251.   Luxbacher, Joe. "Player Violence and the Coach." Soccer Journal. 30, No.5 (September/October 1985), 41-44. LEADERSHIP, RESPONSIBILITY, AGGRESSION THEORIES, COACH/PLAYER RELATIONSHIPS.

252.   Margolis, Joseph A. "Women Coaches: A Struggle for Equality." Athletic Administration. 12, No.3 (Spring 1978), 8-9. PREJUDICE, INJUSTICE, EXCELLENCE.

253.   Massengale, John D. "Coaching as an Occupational Subculture." Phi Delta Kappan. 56, No. 2 (October 1974), 140-142. COACHES, RECRUITMENT, SOCIALIZATION, FAILURE, AMATEURISM, PROFESSIONALISM, LEADERSHIP.

254.   Massengale, John D. and Steven R. Farrington. "The Influence of Playing Position Centrality on the Careers of College Football Coaches." Review of Sport and Leisure. 2 (June 1977), 107-115. CAREER MOBILITY, STRUCTURE IN COLLEGE FOOTBALL.

255.   Mastruzzi, R. "Sports Philosophy: The Responsibility of the Coach." Audible. (Fall 1985), 21-22. COACH AND PLAYER RELATIONSHIP, DISCIPLINE, SPORTSMANSHIP, VALUES, COOPERATION, WINNING.

256.   Monaghan, Peter. "Take Control of Sports Reform, College Athletic Officials Urged." The Chronicle of Higher Education. 30, No.11 (May 15, 1985), 37. RESPONSIBILITY OF ATHLETIC DIRECTORS AND HEAD COACHES, SUPPORT PROGRAMS, DEFINING RESPONSIBILITY.

257.   Morawetz, Thomas. "The Concept of A Practice." Philosophical Studies. 24, No.4 (July 1973), 209-224. CHESS, BASEBALL, CONSTITUTIVE RULES.

258.   Potera, Carol and Michele Kort. "Are Women Coaches an Endangered Species?" Women's Sports and Fitness. 8, No.9 (September 1986), 34-35. SEX EQUITY, TITLE IX, HOMOPHOBIA, REFORM.

259.   Purcell, J. "Coaches and the War on Drugs." Texas Coach. 26, No.2 (September 1982), 40. COACH AND PLAYER RELATIONSHIP, RULES AND REGULATIONS, VALUES, STEROIDS, DISCIPLINE, MENTORING.

260.   Ravizza, Kenneth and Kathy Daruty. "Paternalism and Sovereignty in Athletics: Limits and Justifications of the Coaches' Exercise of Authority Over the Adult Athlete." Journal of the Philosophy of Sport. 11 (1984), 71-82. INDIVIDUAL FREEDOM, ROLE OF THE COACH, INFORMED CONSENT, PATERNALISM.

261.   Relic, Peter D. "Run-Away Specialization in High School Sports." The Connecticut Interscholastic Activities Bulletin. (January 1986), 2. FUN, BENEFIT AND HARM.

262.   Roberts, Ozzie. "Where Are the Coaches? No Blacks Head Professional Grid Teams; Only Five Have Been Selected As Assistants." Ebony. 29, No.2 (December 1973), 160-169. DISCRIMINATION, BLACKS IN MANAGEMENT, PLAYING POSITIONS.

263.   Rostron, Larry. "Purpose of Sports Tainted When Students Specialize." Illinois Interscholastic. (May 1983), 4. IDEAL AND MEANING, FUN, PLAY, DEMISE OF SPORTS, DEFINITION.

264.   Sage, George H. "The Coach as Management: Organizational Leadership in American Sport." Quest. 19 (January 1973), 35-40. SCIENTIFIC MANAGEMENT, HUMAN RELATIONS MANAGEMENT, LEADERSHIP STYLE.

265.   Sheehan, George. "The Cardinal Sins of Coaching." The Physician and Sportsmedicine. 8, No.11 (November 1980), 29. UNREASONABLE GOALS, SHORT TERM VIEW, MISGUIDED EFFORTS, PATERNALISM, EMPHASIS ON WINNING, INJURIES.

266.   Sperber, Murray A. "The College Coach As Entrepreneur." Academe: Bulletin of the American Association of University Professors. 73 (July/August 1987), 30-33. COACHES, WINNING AT ALL COSTS, NCAA, SUMMER CAMP, PRODUCT PROMOTION.

267.   Staffo, Donald. "Will Sport Specialization Reduce the Number of All-Around Athletes?" The Physical Educator. 34, No.4 (December 1977), 194-196. STUDENT-ATHLETES, INTERSCHOLASTIC ATHLETICS, IDEAL AND MEANING.

268.   Stockton, Leslie. "Schooling the Fan, Player and Coach in Sportsmanship." Washington J.O.H.P.E.R. 37 (Winter 1982), 7+. INTEGRITY, VALUES, SPORTSMANSHIP.

269.   Telander, Rick. "An Open Letter to Alex: It Wasn't Just You, Coach, It Was the Whole System." Sports Illustrated. 71, No.22 (November 27, 1989), 106. COLLEGE FOOTBALL, DIGNITY, NORTHWESTERN UNIVERSITY, ALEX AGASE.

270.   Telander, Rick. "Shamefully Lily-White: NFL Head-Coach Opening? Blacks Need Not Apply." Sports Illustrated. 66, No.8 (February 23, 1987), 80. NFL, LACK OF BLACK COACHES.

271.   Underwood, John. "Fewer is Finer Except for Some Flaws." Sports Illustrated. 47, No.10 (September 5, 1977), 28-31+. COACHES, REFORM, ACADEMICS.

272.   Weiss, Paul. "The Nature of a Team." Journal of the Philosophy of Sport. 8 (1981), 47-54. DEFINITION OF A TEAM, COACHES AND PLAYERS, COMPETITION, TEAM AS UNITARY REALITY.

273.   Welker, William A. "An Ethical Approach for Wrestling Coaches." Scholastic Wrestling News. 14 (February 1, 1979), 4-6. RULES, FAIRNESS, MORAL MENTORING, CHARACTER, VALUES, DISCIPLINE, HONORABLE BEHAVIOR.

274.   Zeigler, Earle F.   "Without Philosophy, Coaches and Physical Educators Are 'Unguided Missiles'."   The Physical Educator.   37, No.3 (October 1980), 122-127.   IDEAL AND MEANING, HISTORY, TEACHING ETHICS AND PHYSICAL EDUCATION.

DRUG USE AND TESTING

Books

275.   Asken, Michael J.   Dying to Win: The Athlete's Guide to Safe and Unsafe Drugs in Sports.   Washington, D.C: Acropolis Books Ltd., 1988.   HISTORY, MYTHS, WHY ATHLETES TAKE DRUGS, PROS AND CONS, SPORTS MEDICINE.

276.   Bertacchi, Gloria M.   Athletes and Drug Use.   Roseville, CA: National Medical Seminars, 1988.   SPORTS MEDICINE, STEROIDS, SCREENING, FAIRNESS, HEALTH, DISCIPLINE, COACHES AND TRAINERS, RESPONSIBILITY.

277.   Bronsen, Hugo H.   Sports and Anabolic Steroids: Index of Modern Information.   Washington, D. C: ABBE Publishers Association of Washington, D. C., 1988.   REFERENCE, TECHNICAL INFORMATION, RESEARCH TOOL.

278.   Di Pasquale, Mauro G.   Drug Use and Detection in Amateur Sports.   Warkworth, Ont: M.G.D. Press, 1984.   STIMULANTS, NARCOTIC ANALGESICS, STEROIDS, HUMAN GROWTH HORMONES, DIURETICS.

279.   Dolan, Edward F. Jr.   Drugs in Sports.   New York: Franklin Watts, 1986.   STEROIDS, AMPHETAMINES, COCAINE, MARIJUANA, JUVENILE LITERATURE, CASE STUDIES, RESPONSE OF SPORTS ORGANIZATIONS, EMPHASIS ON WINNING, RISKS AND HARM.

280.   Donohoe, Tom and Neil Johnson.   Foul Play: Drug Abuse in Sports.   Oxford: Basil Blackwell Ltd., 1986.   HISTORY OF DRUG USE, STIMULANTS, STEROIDS, ANXIOLYTICS, ANALGESICS, WOMEN, FUTURE, TECHNIQUES TO AVOID DETECTION, BLOOD DOPING, COCAINE.

281.   Goldman, Bob.   Death in the Locker Room: Steroids and Sports.   South Bend, IN: Icarus Press, Inc., 1984.   DEATH, WOMEN, SPORTS MEDICINE, ERGOGENIC AIDS, STEROIDS.

282.   Harris, Jonathan.   Drugged Athletes: The Crisis in American Sports.   New York: Four Winds Press, 1987.   CAUSES OF WIDESPREAD DRUG USE, EFFORTS TO CURB ABUSE, RECREATIONAL DRUGS, PERFORMANCE-ENHANCING DRUGS, TESTING, MEDIA, REFORM, EDUCATION, WINNING AT ALL COSTS.

283.   Kerr, Robert.   The Practical Use of Anabolic Steroids with Athletes.   San Gabriel, CA: R. Kerr, 1982.   HARM AND BENEFIT OF STEROID USE, HEALTH, STRENGTH, SPORTS MEDICINE, TRAINERS AND PLAYERS.

284. Mandell, Arnold Joseph The Nightmare Season. New York: Random House, Inc., 1976. VIOLENCE, PRO FOOTBALL, SAN DIEGO CHARGERS.

285. Meer, Jeff. Drugs and Sports. New York: Chelsea House Publishers, 1987. RATIONALE FOR DRUG USE, PHYSIOLOGICAL EFFECTS, TESTING.

286. Mohun, Janet. Drugs, Steroids, and Sports. New York: F. Watts, 1988. RISKS, JUVENILE LITERATURE, OLYMPICS.

287. Morris, Eugene "Mercury" with Steve Fiffer. Against the Grain. New York: McGraw-Hill Book Company, 1988. MIAMI DOLPHINS, NFL, INJURIES, COCAINE, JUSTICE.

288. Sabljak, Mark and Martin J. Greenberg. Sports Babylon: Sex, Drugs and Other Dirty Dealings in the World of Sports. New York: Bell Publishing Company, 1988. INSIDE SPORT REVELATIONS, IMMORALITY, ELITISM, PERMISSIVENESS, ABUSES, CORRUPTION OF SPORTS.

289. Strauss, Richard H. (ed.). Drugs and Performance in Sports. Philadelphia: W. B. Saunders Company, 1987. PERFORMANCE-ENHANCING DRUGS, ETHICS, BLOOD DOPING, STEROIDS, STIMULANTS, DEPRESSANTS, DETECTION.

290. Taylor, William N.   Anabolic Steroids and the Athlete.   Jefferson, NC: McFarland and Company, Inc., Publishers, 1982.   MUSCLE ENHANCEMENT, DETECTION, PROS AND CONS OF STEROIDS, ENDURANCE, WOMEN, HUMAN GROWTH HORMONE.

291. Taylor, William N. Hormonal Manipulation: A New Era of Monstrous Athletes. Jefferson, NC: McFarland and Company, Inc., Publishers, 1985. STEROIDS, RISKS, BLACK MARKET, WINNING, HUMAN GROWTH HORMONE, LAW, MORALITY, TESTING.

292. Thomas, John A. Drugs, Athletes, and Physical Performance. New York: Plenum Medical Book Company, 1988.   STEROIDS, ANALGESICS, ANTI-INFLAMMATORY DRUGS, BLOOD DOPING, HUMAN GROWTH HORMONES, STIMULANTS, ALCOHOL, MARIJUANA, COCAINE, WOMEN.

293. Wadler, Gary I. and Brian Hainline. Drugs and the Athlete. Philadelphia: F. A. Davis Company, 1989. MANAGEMENT OF DRUG ABUSE IN SPORTS, PRESSURES ON ATHLETES, BLOOD DOPING, TESTING, POLICIES.

294. Weiner, Betty. Drug Abuse in Sports: An Annotated Bibliography. Brooklyn, NY: CompuBibs, 1985. REFERENCE.

295. Welch, Bob and George Vecsey. Five O'Clock Comes Early: A Young Man's Battle with Alcoholism. New York: William Morrow and Company, Inc., 1982. LOS ANGELES DODGERS, ROLE MODELS, PRO BASEBALL.

296. Williams, Melvin H. Drugs and Athletic Performance. Springfield, IL: Charles C. Thomas, Publisher, 1974. STIMULANTS, DEPRESSANTS, DOPING, RESEARCH.

297.   Williams, Melvin H. (ed.). Ergogenic Aids in Sport. Champaign, IL: Human Kinetics Publishers, 1983. AMPHETAMINES, CAFFEINE, STEROIDS, BLOOD DOPING, HYPNOSIS.

298.   Woodland, Les. Dope: The Use of Drugs in Sport. Newton Abbot, England: David and Charles, 1980. UPPERS, BUILDERS, DOWNERS, SUPPLIERS, TESTERS, PROS AND CONS, FUTURE.

299.   Wright, James Edward. Anabolic Steroids and Sports. Natick, MA: Sports Science Consultants, 1978. HARM AND BENEFIT OF STEROID USE, ABUSES, FAIRNESS IN COMPETITION, HEALTH RISKS, TECHNICAL INFORMATION.

Articles

300.   "ACLU Sues to Block Mandatory Tests for Drug Use at University of Washington." The Chronicle of Higher Education. 33, No.38 (June 3, 1987), 35. ACLU, UNIVERSITY OF WASHINGTON, MANDATORY DRUG TESTING, UNREASONABLE SEARCH, RIGHT TO PRIVACY, DUE PROCESS.

301.   Allen, Lesley. "HGH: The Dangerous Edge." Women's Sports and Fitness. 7, No.6 (July 1985), 17-18. DETECTION, RISKS.

302.   "American College of Sports Medicine Position Statement on the Use and Abuse of Anabolic-Androgenic Steroids in Sports." Swimming Technique. 15, No.2 (Summer 1978), 46-47. REFERENCE, STEROIDS, FEMALE USE.

303.   "Anabolic Shadows." The Economist. 288, No.7305 (September 3-9, 1983), 26. CIVIL RIGHTS, PAN AM GAMES, DRUG TESTING.

304.   Anderson, Ian. "Drugs and the Olympics." World Press Review. 31, No.3 (March 1984), 61. STEROIDS, HUMAN GROWTH HORMONES, TESTING, SIDE EFFECTS.

305.   "Are Drugs Braking Gymnasts' Growth?" The Physician and Sportsmedicine. 7, No.17 (November 1979), 18-20. WOMEN, USE OF DRUGS BY GYMNASTS.

306.   "The Athletes and Steroids." Maclean's. 96, No.46 (November 14, 1983), 60. CANADIAN WEIGHT LIFTERS, MOSCOW OLYMPICS, PAN AM GAMES, STEROIDS.

307.   Axthelm, Pete. "A Star Flunks His Test." Newsweek. 109, No.1 (January 5, 1987), 48-49. STEROIDS, BRIAN BOSWORTH, PRO FOOTBALL.

308.   Axthelm, Pete. "Baseball's Bad Trip." Newsweek. 106 (September 16, 1985), 64-65. COCAINE TRAFFICKING, CURTIS STRONG TRIAL.

309.   Axthelm, Pete. "Cocaine Crisis in the NFL." Newsweek. 102, No.4 (July 25, 1983), 52-53. REHABILITATION, EDUCATION, INNER CIRCLE.

310. Axthelm, Pete. "The Doped-Up Games." Newsweek. 112, No.15 (October 10, 1988), 54-56. SEOUL OLYMPICS, BEN JOHNSON, STEROIDS, SIDE EFFECTS, REFORM, TESTING.

311. Axthelm, Pete. "Using Chemistry to Get The Gold." Newsweek. 112 (July 25, 1988), 62-63. STEROIDS, BLOOD DOPING, DETECTION, TESTING, FAIR PLAY, OLYMPICS.

312. Baker, Richard H. "A Congressman Looks at Steroids." Athletic Administration. 22, No.5 (November 1987), 13+. LONG TERM HEALTH COSTS, FAIR PLAY, INCONCLUSIVE EVIDENCE, FEDERAL FUNDING, ROLE OF CONGRESS.

313. Barnes, Lan. "Olympic Drug Testing: Improvements Without Progress." The Physician and Sportsmedicine. 8, No.6 (June 1980), 21-24. POLICIES, SEX TESTING, HISTORY.

314. "Baseball: Drugs Come Up to Bat." U. S. News and World Report. 98, No.19 (May 20, 1985), 13. PETER UEBERROTH, MANDATORY DRUG TESTING, REASONABLE CAUSE.

315. Baxley, Robert C. "The Mandell Case." Journal of Psychedelic Drugs. 10, No.4 (October-December 1978), 385-392. AMPHETAMINE USE, PRESCRIPTION OF AMPHETAMINES BY PHYSICIANS, LITIGATION, NEED FOR REFORM, ARNOLD MANDELL.

316. Beckett, A. H. and D. A. Cowan. "Misuse of Drugs in Sports." British Journal of Sports Medicine. 12, No.4 (January 1979), 185-194. HISTORY, TESTING, ADVERSE EFFECTS OF DRUG MISUSE, EFFECTS OF DOPE CONTROL.

317. Beckett, Arnold. "Philosophy, Chemistry and the Athlete." New Scientist. No.1415 (August 2, 1984), 18. DRUGS, DOPE CONTROL, OLYMPIC COMMITTEE MEDICAL COMMISSIONER, STEROIDS.

318. "Behind Drug Crackdown in Pro Sports." U. S. News and World Report. 95, No.6 (August 8, 1983), 8. COCAINE, NFL, BASEBALL, GAME-FIXING.

319. Bell, Jack A. and Theodore C. Doege. "Athletes' Use and Abuse of Drugs." The Physician and Sportsmedicine. 15, No.3 (March 1987), 99-102+. LITERATURE ON DRUG MISUSE, STEROIDS, HARM, BLOOD DOPING, TOBACCO AND ALCOHOL, ANTI-DRUG PROGRAMS.

320. Boyle, Robert H. "Happiness Boys at the Track." Sports Illustrated. 33, No.15 (October 12, 1970), 20-21. RACE FIXING, WHOLESALING, TRANQUILIZATION OF HORSES, TESTING.

321. Boyle, Robert H. "Who and When and Mostly Why." Sports Illustrated. 37, No.10 (September 4, 1972), 12-15. HORSE DRUGGING, RIVA RIDGE, KENTUCKY DERBY, BELMONT, MONMOUTH INVITATIONAL, TRANQUILIZERS.

322.   Brown, W. Miller. "Ethics, Drugs and Sport." Journal of the Philosophy of Sport. 7 (Fall 1980), 15-23. OLYMPICS, BLOOD DOPING, CONSTITUTIVE RULES, FAIRNESS.

323.   Brown, W. Miller. "Paternalism, Drugs, and the Nature of Sports." Journal of the Philosophy of Sport. 11 (1984), 14-22. PERSONHOOD, SOFT AND HARD FAIRNESS, JUSTIFICATION OF PATERNALISM, VALUES, HONESTY, FAIRNESS, AUTONOMY, RULES.

324.   Brubaker, Bill. "A Pipeline Full of Drugs." Sports Illustrated. 62, No.3 (January 21, 1985), 18-21. CLEMSON UNIVERSITY, PHENYLBUTAZONE, DRUG TRAFFICKING.

325.   Bueter, Robert J. "The Use of Drugs in Sports: An Ethical Perspective." The Christian Century. (April 5, 1972), 394-397. PAIN KILLERS, THERAPEUTIC USE OF DRUGS, STEROIDS, AMPHETAMINES, FAIR PLAY, HARM TO THE BODY.

326.   Burt, John J. "Drugs and the Modern Athlete: The Legacy of Lenny Bias and Don Rogers." Journal of Physical Education, Recreation and Dance. 58, No.5 (May/June 1987), 74-79. ATHLETE RIGHTS, DRUG TESTING.

327.   Burwell, Bryan. "Branded." Sport. 77, No.8 (August 1986), 39-40. DRUG TESTS, LEAKS TO PRESS, NFL, PRO FOOTBALL.

328.   Buterbaugh, Gary G. "The Use of Drugs in Athletics." Maryland State Medical Journal. 19, No.8 (August 1970), 69-70. RESTORATIVE DRUGS, VALID AND INVALID REASONS FOR PRESCRIBING.

329.   Caldwell, Frances. "Education, Not Testing, May Cut Athlete Drug Use." The Physician and Sportsmedicine. 9, No.2 (February 1981), 22-24. HOSTILITY, PERFORMANCE, EDUCATION.

330.   Callahan, Tom. "A Heady Mix: Booze and Baseball." Time. 131, No.21 (May 23, 1988), 69-70. ALCOHOL, SPECTATOR AND PLAYER DRINKING.

331.   Callahan, Tom. "Larger and Darker by the Day." Time. 126, No.14 (October 7, 1985), 64. VOLUNTARY DRUG TESTING, BASEBALL, PETER UEBERROTH.

332.   Carpenter, Betsy. "A Game of Cat and Mouse." U. S. News and World Report. 105, No.14 (October 10, 1988), 38-39. SEOUL OLYMPICS, STEROIDS, TESTING, PEER PRESSURE.

333.   Chaikin, Tommy with Rick Telander. "The Nightmare of Steroids." Sports Illustrated. 69, No.18 (October 24, 1988), 82-102. TOMMY CHAIKIN, STEROIDS, AGGRESSION, VIOLENCE, ROLE OF THE COACH, ANXIETY, UNIVERSITY OF SOUTH CAROLINA.

334.   Chu, Daniel. "A California Sports Doctor Defends the Controlled Use of a Fad Drug by Olympic Athletes." People Weekly. 22, No.3 (July 16, 1984), 53-54+. HUMAN GROWTH HORMONE, SIDE EFFECTS.

335. Clarke, Kenneth S. "Drugs, Sports, Doping." The Journal of the Maine Medical Association. 61, No.3 (March 1970), 55-58. PURPOSES OF DRUGS, EFFECTS OF DRUGS, CONTROLS, CONCEPT OF DOPING, AMPHETAMINES, STEROIDS.

336. Clarke, Kenneth S. "The Dope on Drug Control." Women's Sports and Fitness. 6, No.7 (July 1984), 126. OLYMPICS, PAN AM GAMES, TESTING.

337. Cohen, Neil. "Just Say No...To Mandatory Drug Testing." Sport. 78, No.5 (May 1987), 6. RIGHT TO PRIVACY, REFORM.

338. "Coke and a Pitching Ace." Maclean's. 100, No.15 (April 13, 1987), 26. DWIGHT GOODEN, DRUGS, BRAWLS, PRO BASEBALL, NEW YORK METS.

339. Connolly, Pat. "Who Needs Male Hormones?" Women's Sports and Fitness. 7, No.3 (April 1985), 88. DRUG AND SEX TESTING, STEROID ABUSE.

340. Cooper, Donald L. "Drugs and the Athlete." The Journal of the American Medical Association. 221, No.9 (August 28, 1972), 1007-1011. LOSER VS WINNER DRUG USE, EDUCATION, RISKS, STEROIDS.

341. Cooter, G. Rankin. "Amphetamines and Sports Performance." Journal of Physical Education and Recreation. 51, No.8 (October 1980), 63-64. HAZARDS OF AMPHETAMINES, DRUG TESTING, LEGAL RAMIFICATIONS.

342. Courson, Steve. "Steroids: Another View." Sports Illustrated. 69, No.21 (November 14, 1988), 106. BLAMING THE ATHLETES, PRESSURE TO WIN, HEALTH HAZARDS, TESTING.

343. Cowart, Virginia S. "Athletes and Steroids: The Bad Bargain." The Saturday Evening Post. 259, No.3 (April 1987), 56-59. STEROIDS, BENEFIT AND HARM, SIDE EFFECTS.

344. Creamer, Robert W. (ed.). "The Cocaine Crisis: Baseball or Sleezeball?" Sports Illustrated. 63, No.13 (September 16, 1985), 13. KEITH HERNANDEZ, COCAINE USE, DEALER CURTIS STRONG, BASEBALL, REFORM.

345. Creamer, Robert W. (ed.). "Tranquility." Sports Illustrated. 33, No.20 (November 16, 1970), 15. DOPING OF HORSES, RACE FIXING.

346. Cumming, Candy. "Sports and Spirits." Women's Sports. 6, No.4 (April 1984), 73. EFFECT OF ALCOHOL ON ABILITY, ALCOHOLISM.

347. Darden, Ellington. "The Facts About Anabolic Steroids." Athletic Journal. 63, No.8 (March 1983), 100-101. SIDE EFFECTS, EDUCATION FOR PREVENTION.

348. "A Decision Made For America." America. 154, No.10 (March 15, 1986), 199. COCAINE TRIALS, "PITTSBURGH 21," PETER UEBERROTH, PLAYER AND OWNER RIGHTS, PRIVACY.

349. Dirix, Albert. "The Doping Problem." Olympic Review. 187 (May 1983), 288. U.S. TEAM, FAIRNESS IN COMPETITION, HEALTH, RULES AND REGULATIONS.

350. Dishman, Rod K. "Overview of Ergogenic Properties of Hypnosis." Journal of Physical Education and Recreation. 51, No.2 (February 1980), 53-54. MOTIVATION, METHODOLOGY.

351. "Doping and Cyclists." Bike World. 7, No.6 (November/December 1978), 58. SCANDALS, STIMULANTS, TOBACCO.

352. "Doping Control at Montreal." Track Technique. 69 (September 1977), 2213. MONTREAL OLYMPICS, COMPUTERIZED TESTING.

353. "The Doping of Amateur Sport." Maclean's. 96, No.36 (September 5, 1983), 36-38. PAN AM GAMES, STEROIDS, SIDE EFFECTS, TESTING.

354. "Doping Scandals Mar Tour History." Bike World. 7, No.6 (November/December 1978), 16-17. MICHEL POLLENTIER, HISTORY, OLYMPICS, TOM SIMPSON, TOUR DE FRANCE, TESTING.

355. "Doping: Standardizing Sanctions." Olympic Review. 247 (June 1988), 216-217. ANTI-DOPING CAMPAIGN, CODE OF ETHICS, TESTING, SECURITY.

356. "Doping: The Tide is Coming." Swimming World and Junior Swimmer. 20, No.4 (April 1979), 118+. SCANDALS, OLYMPICS, TESTING, WINNING.

357. "Drug Abuse at the Race Track." Chemistry. 52, No.3 (March 1979), 24-25. SUBLIMAZE-TESTING, HORSE RACING.

358. "Drug Abuse in Sports: Denial Fuels the Problem." The Physician and Sportsmedicine. 10, No.4 (April 1982), 114+. AMATEUR DRUG USE, WOMEN, POLICIES, EMOTIONAL CONSEQUENCES.

359. "Drug Deaths: A Killer Stalks the Locker Room." U. S. News and World Report. 101, No.2 (July 14, 1986), 6. LEN BIAS, DON ROGERS, DRUG TESTING, CIVIL RIGHTS.

360. "The Drug Factor at the Derby." Business Week. No.2585 (May 14, 1979), 36. LEGAL AND ILLEGAL DRUG USE ON HORSES.

361. "Drug Patrol: Olympic Watchdogs Are Ready." Time. 115, No.4 (January 28, 1980), 70-71. LAKE PLACID OLYMPICS, WIDESPREAD USE OF DRUGS, TESTING.

362. "Drug Testing in Sports." The Physician and Sportsmedicine. 13, No.12 (December 1985), 69-82. EFFECTIVENESS OF TESTING, PROS AND CONS OF TESTING, OLYMPICS.

363. "Drugs and Athletes: The Fault Is Not In Our Stars." Current Health 2. 7, No.7 (March 1981), 12-13. AMPHETAMINES, STEROIDS, PAIN KILLERS, FANS, SOCIETY, BENEFIT AND HARM OF SPORTS.

364. "Drugs in Athletics." Current Health 2. 10, No.3 (November 1983), 10-11. DRUG ABUSE, EXTENT OF USE, TESTING.

365. "Drugs in Sports: Schools are Responding." <u>Athletic Business</u>. 8, No.9 (September 1984), 12+. TESTING, EDUCATION, COUNSELING, PURDUE UNIVERSITY, NOTRE DAME UNIVERSITY, NCAA, HIGH SCHOOLS, ARKADELPHIA SCHOOL DISTRICT, HAZELDON FOUNDATION, OPERATION CORK.

366. Duda, Marty. "Female Athletes: Targets for Drug Abuse." <u>The Physician and Sportsmedicine</u>. 14, No.6 (June 1986), 142-146. PRESSURES TO WIN, SOCIALIZATION, STEREOTYPES, EATING DISORDERS, STEROIDS, ALCOHOL.

367. Dyment, Paul G. "Drug Misuse by Adolescent Athletes." <u>The Pediatric Clinics of North America</u>. 29, No.6 (December 1982), 1363-1368. STEROIDS, NUTRITIONAL AIDS, MARIJUANA, ANTI-INFLAMMATORY DRUGS, NARCOTIC ANALGESICS, FAIR PLAY, CHEATING, LOCAL ANESTHETIC AGENTS.

368. Dyment, Paul G. "Drugs and the Adolescent Athlete." <u>Pediatric Annals</u>. 13, No.8 (August 1984), 602-604. PSYCHOMOTOR STIMULANTS, STEROIDS, DIURETICS, DMSO, RISKS.

369. Edwards, Harry. "Sport's Tragic Drug Connection: Where Do We Go From Here?" <u>Journal of Sport and Social Issues</u>. 10, No.2 (Summer/Fall 1986), 1-5. LEN BIAS, DON ROGERS, WINNING, REFORM, DRUG RELATED DEATHS, RECOMMENDATIONS FOR PREVENTION AND RESOLUTION.

370. Fackelmann, K. A. "Male Teenagers at Risk of Steroid Abuse." <u>Science News</u>. 134, No.25 (December 17, 1988), 391. LONG TERM USE, RISKS, COACHES, ETHICS.

371. Fahey, Thomas D. "Anabolic Steroids and Athletics." <u>The Physical Educator</u>. 30, No.1 (March 1973), 40. MEDICAL PROBLEMS, SPORTSMANSHIP, WINNING.

372. Fairchild, David L. "Sport Abjection: Steroids and the Uglification of the Athlete." <u>Journal of the Philosophy of Sport</u>. 16 (1989), 74-88. STEROIDS, EXCELLENCE, IDEAL AND MEANING, BEN JOHNSON, OLYMPIC GAMES, BODY BUILDING.

373. "Fake Horse Hormones." <u>FDA Consumer</u>. 22, No.4 (May 1988), 35-36. COUNTERFEIT STEROIDS, EQUIPOISE, FDA CENTER FOR VETERINARIAN MEDICINE.

374. Farrell, Charles S. "Colleges Eye Limit on Time Players Give to Sports, Tougher Tests for Drug Abuse." <u>The Chronicle of Higher Education</u>. 32, No.19 (July 9, 1986), 23-24. DRUG TESTING, TIME DEVOTED TO SPORTS, ACADEMICS, DEMANDS ON ATHLETES.

375. Farrell, Charles S. "Drug Education to Play Major Role in Ending Abuse, NCAA Believes." <u>The Chronicle of Higher Education</u>. 33, No.24 (February 25, 1987), 36. EDUCATION, DRUG ABUSE CLINIC, TELEVISION COMMERCIALS.

376. Farrell, Charles S. "Drug Use and Academic Rules are Probed After Death of Maryland Basketball Player." <u>The Chronicle of Higher Education</u>. 32, No.18 (July 2, 1986), 17-18. LEN BIAS, UNIVERSITY OF MARYLAND, DRUG USE, COCAINE, DEATH.

377.   Farrell, Charles S. "From Big Man on Campus to Prison Inmate: Tragedy of an Athlete Turned Cocaine Addict." The Chronicle of Higher Education. 33, No.4 (September 24, 1986), 1+. MIKE HELMS, WAKE FOREST UNIVERSITY, DRUG TRAFFICKING, BASKETBALL, COCAINE CONNECTION CONFERENCE.

378.   Farrell, Charles S. "NCAA Panel Refining Drug-Testing Plan, Hopes to Begin Checking Athletes in 1986." The Chronicle of Higher Education. 30, No.18 (July 3, 1985), 19. COST OF TESTING, EMPHASIS ON DIVISION ONE, PENALTIES FOR POSITIVE TESTS.

379.   Farrell, Charles S. "Professor Has Final Say on Winner of Kentucky Derby." The Chronicle of Higher Education. 30, No.9 (May 1, 1985), 33. TESTING OF HORSES, UNIVERSITY OF KENTUCKY, STIMULANTS.

380.   Farrell, Charles S. "Temple's Model Drug-Education Program Includes Tests But Emphasizes Counseling." The Chronicle of Higher Education. 33, No.24 (February 25, 1987), 35-36. TEMPLE UNIVERSITY, MIKE GREEN, CONSULTANT, COST OF PROGRAM, EDUCTION.

381.   Farrell, Charles S. and Douglas Lederman. "Lawsuit, High Costs, and Low Failure Rate Keep Drug Testing of Athletes in Headlines." The Chronicle of Higher Education. 33, No.18 (January 14, 1987), 41-42. LAWSUITS, TESTING, AVOIDANCE OF DETECTION.

382.   Feinstein, Charles D. "Analysis of a Drug-Testing Program for Intercollegiate Athletes." Journal of Policy Analysis and Management. 7, No.3 (Spring 1988), 548-550. COST-BENEFITS ANALYSIS, DECISION MAKING.

383.   Figone, Albert J. "Drugs in Professional Sport: External Control of Individual Behavior." Arena Review. 12, No.1 (May 1988), 25-33. SOCIALIZATION, ROLE PRESSURES.

384.   Fimrite, Ron. "Don't Knock the Rock." Sports Illustrated. 60, No.26 (June 25 1984), 48-56. TIM (ROCK) RAINES, MONTREAL EXPOS, BASEBALL.

385.   Forsyth, Adrian. "Strong Medicine." Saturday Night. 99, No.5 (May 1984), 15-17. STEROIDS, LONG-TERM EFFECTS, ILLEGALITY, REFORM.

386.   Fost, Norman. "Banning Drugs in Sports: A Skeptical View." The Hastings Center Report. 16, No.4 (August 1986), 5-10. MANDATORY DRUG TESTING, RESTORATIVE DRUGS, ADDITIVE DRUGS, PAIN KILLERS, RECREATIONAL DRUGS, LOSS OF INNOCENCE, FDA, BENEFIT AND HARM.

387.   Fost, Norman. "Let 'Em Take Steroids." The New York Times. 132 (September 9, 1983), A19. STEROIDS, UNFAIR ADVANTAGE, POTENTIAL HARM, EXPLOITATION OF ATHLETES, UNNATURAL MEANS TO SUCCESS.

388.   Fraleigh, Warren P. "Performance-Enhancing Drugs in Sport: The Ethical Issue." Journal of the Philosophy of Sport. 11 (1984), 23-29. RULES, HARM, COERCION, FAIRNESS, VIOLATION, PATERNALISM, AUTONOMY, DEHUMANIZATION, SELF HARM.

389. Fuller, John R. and Marc J. LaFountain. "Performance-Enhancing Drugs in Sport: A Different Form of Drug Abuse." Adolescence. 22, No.88 (Winter 1987), 969-976. STEROIDS, RATIONALES FOR DRUG USE, HEALTH PROBLEMS OF STEROID USE.

390. Furlong, William Barry. "How 'Speed' Kills Athletic Careers." Today's Health. 49, No.2 (February 1971), 30-33+. AMPHETAMINES, COACH RESPONSIBILITY, CASE STUDIES.

391. Gall, Sarah L., Marty Duda, Debra Giel, and Cindy Christian Rogers. "Who Tests Which Athletes for What Drugs?" The Physician and Sportsmedicine. 16, No.2 (February 1988), 155-161. ORGANIZATIONS WHICH TEST, BANNED DRUGS, TESTING METHODS, WHY ATHLETES TAKE DRUGS.

392. Gallmeier, Charles P. "Juicing, Burning and Tooting: Observing Drug Use Among Professional Hockey Players." Arena Review. 12, No.1 (May 1988), 1-12. ETHICAL CONSIDERATIONS AND METHODOLOGICAL PROBLEMS ENCOUNTERED WHEN OBSERVING DRUG USE.

393. Gardner, Roger. "On Performance-Enhancing Substances and the Unfair Advantage Argument." Journal of the Philosophy of Sport. 16 (1989), 59-73. PERFORMANCE ENHANCING DRUGS, STANOZOLOL, BEN JOHNSON, SPRINTER, PHILOSOPHY, EQUALITY, INEQUALITY, UNFAIR ADVANTAGE.

394. Garrett, Kelly. "Frankenstein Athletes?" Muscle & Fitness. 46, No.9 (September 1985), 105. HUMAN GROWTH HORMONES, ETHICS OF COMPETITION, EXPERIEMENTATION, CONTROL.

395. Gelband, Myra (ed.). "Banned: Use of Drugs Butazolidin and Lasix at Maryland Race Tracks." Sports Illustrated. 51, No.23 (December 3, 1979), 11. MARYLAND RACING COMMISSION, BANNING OF BUTAZOLIDIN AND LASIX, PROS AND CONS OF LEGALIZATION.

396. Gilbert, Bil. "Problems in a Turned-On World." Sports Illustrated. 30, No.25 (June 23, 1969), 64-72. DRUGS AS A MEANS TO PERFORMANCE IMPROVEMENT, ROLE OF THE ESTABLISHMENT, DRUG CULTURE, REFORM, SCANDAL.

397. Gilbert, Bil. "Something Extra On the Ball." Sports Illustrated. 30, No.26 (June 30, 1969), 30-42. RESTORATIVE AND ADDITIVE DRUGS, SIDE EFFECTS, AMPHETAMINES, STEROIDS.

398. Gleason, Tim. "Drugs and the College Athlete." Athletic Administration. 18, No.2 (Winter 1983), 15-17. DRUG CLINICS, MEDIA, TESTING, GAMBLING, STEROIDS.

399. Goldman, Bob, Patricia Bush and Ronald Klatz. "Steroids For Women, A Reversal of Nature." The Globe and Mail. 141 (July 24, 1984), S3. HEALTH RISKS, FAIRNESS IN COMPETITION.

400. Greenberg, Joel. "When is a Drug a Drug?" Science News. 126, No.5 (August 4, 1984), 72. OLYMPICS, HERBS, CAFFEINE, TESTOSTERONE, STEROIDS.

401.   Greenspan, Edward L. and George Jonas.   "The Case For the Defense."
       Maclean's. 100, No.42 (October 19, 1987), 48-52. FERGUSON JENKINS, LAW,
       BASEBALL.

402.   Grupe, Ommo. "The Problem of Doping or the Influence of Pharmaceutics on
       Performance in Sports From the Standpoint of Sport Ethics." SNIPES Journal.
       8 (January 1985), 51-56. SPORTS MEDICINE, FAIRNESS IN COMPETITION, HEALTH
       RISKS, ROLE OF COACHES AND TRAINERS.

403.   Gunby, Phil. "Olympics Drug Testing: Basis for Future Study." The Journal
       of the American Medical Association. 252, No.4 (July 27, 1984), 454-455+.
       ONGOING U.S. OLYMPIC COMMITTEE EFFORT, BENEFITS, ATHLETES RIGHTS.

404.   Haas, Robert. "One For the Road." World Tennis. 32, No.2 (July 1984), 100-
       101. ALCOHOL, NUTRITION.

405.   Hamilton, Jonathan. "Who Are the Steroid Pushers?" Women's Sports. No. 10
       (October 1983), 76. CHEATING, COMPETITIVE DRIVE, PAN AM GAMES, TESTING.

406.   Haupt, Herbert A. and George D. Rovere. "Anabolic Steroids: A Review of the
       Literature."   The American Journal of Sports Medicine.   12, No.6
       (November/December 1984), 469-484. EFFECT ON ATHLETIC PERFORMANCE,
       SIDE EFFECTS, INCONCLUSIVE EVIDENCE, REVIEW OF LITERATURE.

407.   Hecht, Annabel. "Anabolic Steroids: Pumping Trouble." FDA Consumer. 18,
       No.7 (September 1984), 12-15. SIDE EFFECTS, MASCULINIZATION OF WOMEN,
       DRUGS, HISTORY.

408.   Heitzinger, Ron. "Getting Serious About Steroids." Athletic Business. 11, No.9
       (September 1987), 32-35. RISKS, TESTING, WINNING AT ALL COSTS.

409.   Henderson, Joe. "The Side Effects of Drug Testing." Runner's World. 22,
       No.5 (May 1987), 12. MANIA, PROS AND CONS OF TESTING.

410.   "Heroes Are Made..." The Nation. 241, No.9 (September 28, 1985), 267-268.
       BASEBALL, DRUGS, HEROES, SPORT IN SOCIETY.

411.   Hill, James A., Jacob R. Suker, Kalman Sachs, and Craig Brigham.   "The
       Athletic Polydrug Abuse Phenomenon: A Case Report." The American Journal
       of Sports Medicine. 11, No.4 (July/August 1983), 269-271. CASE STUDY,
       INCONCLUSIVE EVIDENCE, COMPLICATIONS OF LONG TERM USE.

412.   Hopkins, Harold. "Drugs Used to Soup Up Racehorses." FDA Consumer. 18,
       No.5 (June 1984), 40-41. MAIL ORDER DRUGS, BIG BUSINESS, DRUGGING
       HORSES, HORSE RACING.

413.   Hopkins, Thomas. "Playing Football Under a Snowdrift." Maclean's. 95,
       No.25 (June 21, 1982), 41. DON REESE, SAN DIEGO CHARGERS, COCAINE, NFL.

414.   "The Hormone Olympics." The Economist. 276, No.7144 (August 2, 1980), 65.
       MOSCOW OLYMPICS, DRUGS, TESTING.

415.   Horn, Jack C. "A Dangerous Edge." Psychology Today. 17, No.11 (November 1983), 68. WOMEN'S BODYBUILDING, STEROIDS, FEMALE USE.

416.   Horn, Jack C. "Drug Control at the Olympics." Psychology Today. 10, No.3 (August 1976), 19. MONTREAL OLYMPICS, WINNING AT ANY COST, DRUGS, TESTING.

417.   "How Many Athletes Are High?" Women's Sports And Fitness. 9, No.4 (April 1987), 26. ALCOHOL, WOMEN.

418.   "How Pro Teams Abuse Drug-Abuse Programs." Discover. 7, No.4 (April 1986), 13. SUCCESS/FAILURE RATES, MICHAEL RAY RICHARDSON, NEW JERSEY NETS, PRO BASKETBALL.

419.   "Hypnosis: New Road to Victory for Talented Athletes." Ebony. 35, No.6 (April 1980), 44-46+. HYPNOTHERAPY CLINICS, MENTAL PREPARATION.

420.   Ingersoll, Robert. "Defector Says GDR Uses Steroids." The Physician and Sportsmedicine. 7, No.3 (March 1979), 24-25. RENATE NEUFELD-SPASSOV, GERMANY, STEROIDS.

421.   "Inside Baseball: Drugs, Money and Expansion (Interview With P. Ueberroth)." U. S. News and World Report. 99, No.18 (October 28, 1985), 68-69. DRUG TESTING, TELEVISION, FRANCHISE RELOCATION.

422.   "International Olympic Charter Against Doping in Sport." Olympic Review. 253 (Novmeber 1988), 628-631. ROLE OF THE SPORTS COMMUNITY, RULES, DOPE, ROLE OF GOVERNMENT, EDUCATION.

423.   "Is This the End of Chuck Muncie's Road?" Sports Illustrated. 61, No.15 (September 24, 1984), 65. DRUG PROBLEMS, SAN DIEGO CHARGERS, MIAMI DOLPHINS.

424.   "It's Not Nice to Fool Mother Nature." Maclean's. 92, No.2 (January 8, 1979), 31. STEROIDS, MEXICO OLYMPICS, EAST GERMANY, RENATE NEUFELD.

425.   Ivy, J. L. "Amphetamines in Sports: Are They Worth the Risk?" Sportsmedicine Digest. 6, No.3 (March 1984), 1-2. HEALTH RISKS, UNFAIR COMPETITION, SPORTS MEDICINE.

426.   Johns, Malini. "The Inside Dope." Runner's World. 23, No.9 (September 1988), 78-80+. OLYMPICS, TRACK AND FIELD, HISTORY, EASY ACCESS, TESTING.

427.   Johnson, William Oscar. "Hit for a Loss." Sports Illustrated. 69, No.13 (September 19, 1988), 50-53. NFL DRUG USE, SUSPENSIONS, TESTING, STEROIDS, INEQUITABLE PUNISHMENTS.

428.   Johnson, William Oscar. "Steroids: A Problem of Huge Dimensions." Sports Illustrated. 62, No.19 (May 13, 1985), 38-42+. BLACK MARKET, STEROID USE, HEALTH HAZARDS, ILLEGALITY, ETHICAL ISSUES.

429.   Johnson, William Oscar and Kenny Moore. "The Loser." Sports Illustrated. 69, No.15 (October 3, 1988), 20-27. OLYMPIC TRACK AND FIELD, BEN JOHNSON, TESTED POSITIVE FOR STEROIDS, GOLD MEDAL TAKEN AWAY, CARL LEWIS, SHAME.

430.   Kaplan, Jim. "Taking Steps to Solve the Drug Dilemma." Sports Illustrated. 60, No.21 (May 28, 1984), 36-45. COCAINE POSSESSION, KANSAS CITY ROYALS, WILLIE WILSON, WILLIE AIKENS, JERRY MARTIN, BASEBALL.

431.   Keteyian, Armen and Bruce Selcraig. "A Killer Drug Strikes Again." Sports Illustrated. 65, No.1 (July 7, 1986), 18-19. DON ROGERS, COCAINE, DEATH, CLEVELAND BROWNS FOOTBALL, FREE SAFETY, EIGHT DAYS AFTER THE LEN BIAS DEATH.

432.   King, Peter. "We Can Clean It Up." Sports Illustrated. 73, No.2 (July 9, 1990), 34+. BILL FRALIC, ATLANTA FALCONS, PRO FOOTBALL, STEROIDS, CLEANING UP DRUGS IN NFL, NFL PLAYERS ASSOCIATION.

433.   Kinnard, William J. "The Use of Drugs in Athletics." Maryland State Medical Journal. 19, No.8 (August 1970), 67-68. PERFORMANCE ENHANCING DRUGS, JUDICIOUS USE OF DRUGS, POLICIES.

434.   Kirshenbaum, Jerry. "Steroids: The Growing Menace." Sports Illustrated. 51, No.20 (November 12, 1979), 33. INTERNATIONAL AMATEURS ATHLETIC FEDERATION, STEROIDS, BANNING OF WOMEN FROM TRACK AND FIELD COMPETITION.

435.   Kirshenbaum, Jerry. "The Golden Moment." Sports Illustrated. 51, No.8 (August 20, 1979), 60-64+. RICK DEMONT, MUNICH OLYMPICS, ASTHMA MEDICATION, DISQUALIFICATION.

436.   Kirshenbaum, Jerry. "Uppers in Baseball: A Downer for the National Pastime." Sports Illustrated. 53, No.4 (July 21, 1980), 11. AMPHETAMINES, PHILADELPHIA PHILLIES, DR. PATRICK MAZZA, BASEBALL.

437.   Kirshenbaum, Jerry (ed.). "Back to the Dark Ages." Sports Illustrated. 59, No.2 (July 11, 1983), 15. COCAINE ABUSES, REHABILITATION VS PUNISHMENT, STEVE HOWE, FINES AND PROBATION FOR USE OF DRUGS.

438.   Kirshenbaum, Jerry (ed.). "The Continuing Saga of Dr. Mazza and His 'Good Friends'." Sports Illustrated. 54, No.8 (February 16, 1981), 11. PHILADELPHIA PHILLIES, BASEBALL, AMPHETAMINES, DR. PATRICK MAZZA.

439.   Kitman, Jane. "The Owner's Moral Grandstanding." The Nation. 242, No.16 (April 26, 1986), 581-583. HYPOCRISY, MANDATORY DRUG TESTING, ALCOHOL SALES AT GAMES, HOOLIGANISM.

440.   Kontor, Ken. "Curbing the Use of Steroids in American Football." National Strength and Conditioning Association Journal. 10, No.3 (June/July 1988), 72. STEROIDS, EDUCATION, RULES, REFORM.

441. Kreiter, Marcella S. "Steroids: The Stuff of Synthetic Supermen?" Current Health 2. 14, No.4 (December 1987), 14-16. EFFECT ON MALES AND FEMALES, ILLEGALITY.

442. Lamar, Jacob V. Jr. "Scoring Off the Field." Time. 128, No.8 (August 25, 1986), 52-55. LEN BIAS, DRUGS, ANTIDRUG CRUSADE, TESTING.

443. Lamb, David R. "Anabolic Steroids and Strength and Power Related Athletic Events." Journal of Physical Education and Recreation. 51, No.2 (February 1980), 58-59. RATIONALE FOR USE, POTENTIAL HEALTH HAZARDS, EDUCATION.

444. Lamb, David R. "Anabolic Steroids in Athletics: How Well Do They Work and How Dangerous Are They?" The American Journal of Sports Medicine. 12, No.1 (January/February 1984), 31-38. EFFECT ON MUSCULAR DEVELOPMENT, RED BLOOD CELL PRODUCTION AND CENTRAL NERVOUS SYSTEM, EXTENT OF USE, ANIMAL AND HUMAN STUDIES, ATHLETIC PERFORMANCE, SIDE EFFECTS.

445. Lambert, Mike. "Strength: How Do They Beat the Drug Tests?" Muscle & Fitness. 47, No.2 (February 1986), 31+. ESCAPING DETECTION, POWER LIFTING, AMERICAN DRUG FREE POWERLIFTING ASSOCIATION.

446. Lavin, Michael. "Sports and Drugs: Are the Current Bans Justified?" Journal of the Philosophy of Sport. 14 (1987), 34-43. RATIONALE FOR REGULATING DRUG USE BY ATHLETES, FAIRNESS, DANGERS OF DRUG USE, IDEAL OF SPORT, THREE CLASSES OF DRUGS, RECREATIONAL DRUGS, RESTORATIVE DRUGS, ADDITIVE DRUGS.

447. Leach, Robert E. "Drug Testing and the Games." Skiing. 36, No.6 (February 1984), 30-31+. PAN AM GAMES, BANNED SUBSTANCES, STEROIDS, BLOOD DOPING, NEGATIVE EFFECTS.

448. Lederman, Douglas. "California Judge Bars NCAA From Testing Athletes at Stanford for Drugs." The Chronicle of Higher Education. 34, No.13 (November 25, 1987), A1+. PRELIMINARY INJUNCTION BARRING NCAA, DRUG TESTING, LAWSUITS, STANFORD UNIVERSITY.

449. Lederman, Douglas. "California Judge Hears Arguments in Challenge to NCAA Drug-Test Program." The Chronicle of Higher Education. 34, No.8 (October 21, 1987), A1+. MANDATORY DRUG TESTING, STANFORD UNIVERSITY, LAWSUITS, CONSENT FORM.

450. Lederman, Douglas. "Stanford University Asks Court to Curb Enforcement of Drug Tests Until Their Legality is Decided." The Chronicle of Higher Education. 33, No.42 (July 1, 1987), 23. LAWSUITS, SIMONE LEVANT, JENNIFER HALL, ATHLETE REFUSAL TO SUBMIT TO DRUG TESTING.

451. Leerhsen, Charles. "Olympian Drug Scandal." Newsweek. 102, No.10 (September 5, 1983), 36-41. LOS ANGELES OLYMPICS, PAN AM GAMES, DRUG TESTING, DETECTION.

452. Leggett, William. "Experiment in Drugs at Santa Anita." Sports Illustrated. 34, No.4 (January 25, 1971), 18-19. LEGALIZATION OF BUTAZOLIDIN, CALIFORNIA, HORSE RACING.

453. Legwold, Gary. "Have We Learned a Lesson About Drugs in Sports?" The Physician and Sportsmedicine. 12, No.3 (March 1984), 175-178+. OLYMPICS, TESTING, POLICY, STEROIDS.

454. Leistner, Ken. "Drugs: A Statement." Athletic Journal. 65, No.9 (April 1985), 31-33+. COACH RESPONSIBILITY, STEROIDS, TEACHING PHYSICAL EDUCATION.

455. Lipsyte, Robert. "Baseball and Drugs." The Nation. 240, No.20 (May 25, 1985), 613. TESTING, DRUGS, PETER UEBERROTH.

456. "The Long Season." Commonweal. 112, No.17 (October 4, 1985), 517-518. DOCK ELLIS, DRUG TESTING, SPORTS AND SOCIETY.

457. Looney, Douglas S. "A Test With Nothing But Tough Questions." Sports Illustrated. 57, No.6 (August 9, 1982), 24-29. PRO FOOTBALL, REACTION TO TESTING BY MANAGEMENT AND PLAYERS, PRIVACY, PLAYERS UNION, GENE UPSHAW.

458. Looney, Douglas S. "He Has Seen the Light." Sports Illustrated. 58, No.16 (April 18, 1983), 48-54. JOHN REAVE, DRUGS, ALCOHOL, TAMPA BAY BANDITS, PRO FOOTBALL.

459. Looney, Douglas S. "New Uproar Over a Controversial Drug." Sports Illustrated. 48, No.22 (May 22, 1978), 20-27. DEATH, ACCIDENTS, BUTAZOLIDIN, HORSE RACING.

460. Lucking, M. T. "Experimental Random Spot Testing for Drugs in Sportsmen." British Journal of Sports Medicine. 15, No.1 (March 1981), 33-38. RANDOM TESTING, COLLECTION RATES, COOPERATION OF ATHLETES.

461. Magnuson, Ed. "Baseball's Drug Scandal." Time. 126, No.11 (September 16, 1985), 26-28. COCAINE, ROLE MODELS, VOLUNTARY DRUG TESTING.

462. Mandell, Arnold Joseph. "Pro Football Fumbles the Drug Scandal." Psychology Today. 9, No.1 (June 1975), 39-47. SAN DIEGO CHARGERS, PAIN PILLS, AGGRESSION, STIMULANTS, MARIJUANA, DRUG EDUCATION.

463. Mandell, Arnold Joseph. "The Sunday Syndrome." Journal of Psychedelic Drugs. 10, No.4 (October-December 1978), 379-383. AMPHETAMINE ABUSE, DRUG WORKSHOPS, CASE STUDIES.

464. Mann, Carol. "Let's Talk About Drugs--Honestly." Women's Sports and Fitness. 8, No.6 (June 1986), 60. GOLFING, AMPHETAMINES, EXPOSE.

465. Marshall, Eliot. "Drugging of Football Players Curbed by Central Monitoring Plan, NFL Claims." Science. 203, No.4381 (February 16, 1979), 626-628. AMPHETAMINES, ARNOLD MANDELL, NFL, SAN DIEGO CHARGERS.

466. Marshall, Eliot. "The Drug of Champions." Science. 242, No.4876 (October 14, 1988), 183-184. STEROIDS, BLACK MARKET, OLYMPICS, TESTING, AGGRESSION.

467. McCallum, Jack. "'The Cruelest Thing Ever'." Sports Illustrated. 64, No.26 (June 30, 1986), 20-22+. LEN BIAS, COCAINE, DEATH, UNIVERSITY OF MARYLAND, ALL-AMERICAN BASKETBALL PLAYER.

468. McCallum, Jack. "Life Was Sweet...But the Sugar Ran Out." Sports Illustrated. 64, No.2 (January 13, 1986), 26-28. MICHAEL RAY RICHARDSON, RELAPSE, NEW JERSEY NETS.

469. McDonald, Kim. "Experts Say Steroids Offer Few Benefits, Pose Great Risks." The Chronicle of Higher Education. 30, No.10 (May 8, 1985), 27+. BENEFITS OF USE, RISKS, IRRITABILITY, AGGRESSIVENESS, WOMEN.

470. McDonald, Kim. "Testing Athletes for Drugs Now Common as Colleges Try to Deter Experimentation." The Chronicle of Higher Education. 29, No.3 (September 12, 1984), 31-32. STREET DRUGS, PERFORMANCE ENHANCING DRUGS, TESTING, DETERENCE, COST OF TESTING.

471. McDonald, Kim and N. Scott Vance. "Colleges Urged to Teach Athletes, Coaches the Dangers of Drug Abuse and 'Doping'." The Chronicle of Higher Education. 25, No.1 (September 1, 1982), 25+. BLOOD DOPING, STEROIDS, DRUG EDUCATION, ROLE OF THE COACH.

472. McLain, Gary as told to Jeffrey Marx. "The Downfall of a Champion." Sports Illustrated. 66, No.11 (March 16, 1987), 42-46+. GARY MCLAIN, VILLANOVA UNIVERSITY, COLLEGE BASKETBALL, NCAA CHAMPIONS, COCAINE, SENIOR YEAR.

473. Mellion, Morris B. "Anabolic Steroids in Athletics." American Family Physician. 30, No.1 (July 1984), 113-118. EMPHASIS ON WINNING, STEROIDS, INCONCLUSIVE EVIDENCE, POTENTIAL RISKS, WOMEN.

474. Miller, Roger W. "Athletes and Steroids: Playing a Deadly Game." FDA Consumer. 21, No.9 (November 1987), 16-21. SIDE EFFECTS, BENEFITS, WOMEN, TESTING, EDUCATION.

475. Mitchell, Freddie. "Anabolic Steroids for Christian Ironmen?" Iron Man. 42 (February/March 1983), 43. UNFAIR COMPETITION, SPORTSMANSHIP, MORALITY, WINNING.

476. Mofenson, Howard and Joseph Greensher. "Drug Use in Sports: Facts and Fallacies." Drug Therapy: The Journal of Clinical Therapeutics. 12, No.3 (March 1982), 77-78+. HAZARDS AND BENEFITS, MISUSE, STEROIDS, DMSO, DIURETICS, ANESTHETICS, OPIATES, ANTI-INFLAMMATORY DRUGS, PSYCHOMOTOR STIMULANTS, SEDATIVES.

477. Monaghan, Peter. "Colleges Learn That Testing Athletes for Steroids Won't Be Easy or Cheap." The Chronicle of Higher Education. 30, No.10 (May 8, 1985), 27-28. EXPENSE OF STEROID TESTING, DEPENDABILITY OF TESTING.

478.   Monaghan, Peter. "Colleges Unable to Agree on Anti-Drug Program." The Chronicle of Higher Education. 29, No.19 (January 23, 1985), 34. NCAA ANTI-DRUG INITIATIVE, TESTING, BANNED DRUGS, STREET DRUGS.

479.   Monaghan, Peter. "Federal Court Rules NCAA's Drug-Testing Program Does Not Violate College Athletes' Privacy Right." The Chronicle of Higher Education. 34, No.26 (March 9, 1988), A37+. MANDATORY DRUG TESTING, UNIVERSITY OF WASHINGTON, ELIZABETH O'HALLORAN, VIOLATION OF CONSTITUTIONAL RIGHTS, RIGHT TO PRIVACY.

480.   Monaghan, Peter. "How To Avoid Legal Pitfalls in Setting Up Drug Tests for Athletes." The Chronicle of Higher Education. 30, No.1 (March 6, 1985), 33. SUSPENSIONS, PENALTIES, NCAA, CHEATING.

481.   Monaghan, Peter. "Members of Small-College Sports-Governing Body Told to Begin Screening Their Athletes For Drugs." The Chronicle of Higher Education. 32, No.22 (July 30, 1986), 30. NCAA, DRUG TESTING, POLICY.

482.   Monaghan, Peter. "NCAA Approves Drug Testing of Players at Football Bowl Games, Championships." The Chronicle of Higher Education. 31, No.19 (January 22, 1986), 29+. RANDOM TESTING, PROS AND CONS OF TESTING.

483.   Monaghan, Peter. "Psychologists, Counselors Cite Complex Drug-Test Problems." The Chronicle of Higher Education. 30, No.1 (March 6, 1985), 32-33. LITIGATION, CIVIL RIGHTS, DUE PROCESS, PRIVACY, DEFAMATION, INFORMED CONSENT.

484.   Monaghan, Peter. "Testing Athletes For Drug Use: Debate Raises Questions." The Chronicle of Higher Education. 31, No.17 (January 8, 1986), 32. DEPENDABILITY OF TESTS, LEGALITY OF TESTS, ROLE OF NCAA, EXPENSE OF TESTING.

485.   Monaghan, Peter. "Three Men Are Indicted for Conspiracy to Distribute Drugs to Athletes." The Chronicle of Higher Education. 30, No.9 (May 1, 1985), 31+. CLEMSON UNIVERSITY, COLGATE UNIVERSITY, VANDERBILT UNIVERSITY, 'DOC' KREIS, TENNESSEE BUREAU OF INVESTIGATION.

486.   Monaghan, Peter. "Vanderbilt to Tell Athletic Officials About Its Drug Testing Facilities." The Chronicle of Higher Education. 31, No.4 (September 25, 1985), 35-36. MARKETING OF DRUG TESTING, EXPENSE OF TESTING.

487.   Monmaney, Terence. "The Insanity of Steroid Abuse." Newsweek. 111 (May 23, 1988), 75. MENTAL HARM, MENTAL DISORDERS.

488.   Moore, Mary L. and Thomas Hanney. "Performance Enhancing Drugs." Strategies: A Journal for Physical and Sport Educators. 1, No.6 (June 1988), 27-28. MORALITY, RIGHTS, RESTRICTIONS AGAINST DRUG USE, FAIR COMPETITION, FREEDOM OF CHOICE.

489. Moore, Mike. "Hazelden: Putting Athletes' Drug Abuse In Perspective." The Physician and Sportsmedicine. 11, No.12 (December 1983), 37-40. HAZELDEN FOUNDATION, NFL, YOUTH, TREATMENT CENTER.

490. Moore, Mike. "Use of Anabolic Steroids by Elite Athletes Studied." The Physician and Sportsmedicine. 9, No.7 (July 1981), 22. TESTOSTERONE LEVELS, SIDE EFFECTS, OBTAINING STEROIDS.

491. Murray, Thomas H. "Drug Tests: Just One More Instance of Treating College Athletes Like Children." The Chronicle of Higher Education. 33, No.22 (February 11, 1987), 42-43. MORAL CASE AGAINST DRUG USE, CHEATING, FAIR COMPETITION, MASS TESTING UNFAIR.

492. Murray, Thomas H. "The Coercive Power of Drugs in Sports." The Hastings Center Report. 13, No.4 (August 1983), 24-30. STEROIDS, RISKS, FREE CHOICE, REFORM.

493. Nack, William. "The Disgrace of Lasix." Sports Illustrated. 68, No.3 (January 25, 1988), 66. ALYSHEBA, HORSE OF THE YEAR, LASIX, DRUGGING HORSES.

494. "NCAA Recommendations." The Chronicle of Higher Education. 25, No.1 (September 1, 1982), 28. DRUG EDUCATION COMMITTEE, DRUG AND ALCOHOL AWARENESS COURSE, TREATMENT OF STUDENTS WITH PROBLEMS, COACHES' ROLE, TRAINING FOR COACHES.

495. Neff, Craig. "Bosworth Faces the Music." Sports Illustrated. 66, No.1 (January 5, 1987), 20-25. STEROIDS, TESTING, PHYSICIAN PRESCRIBING DRUGS, BARRY SWITZER, OKLAHOMA FOOTBALL.

496. Neff, Craig. "Caracas: A Scandal and A Warning." Sports Illustrated. 59, No.11 (September 5, 1983), 18-23. PAN AM GAMES, DRUGS, DISQUALIFIED ATHLETES, TRACK AND FIELD, STEROIDS, COACH-PLAYER RELATIONS.

497. Neff, Craig. "Time to Rise and Shine." Sports Illustrated. 67, No.23 (November 23, 1987), 30-32+. PHOENIX SUNS BASKETBALL, DEATH, NICK VANOS-VICTIM, POINT SHAVING, GAMBLING, PRO BASKETBALL.

498. Neff, Craig and Robert Sullivan. "The NFL and Drugs: Fumbling For a Game Plan." Sports Illustrated. 64, No.6 (February 10, 1986), 82-89. TESTING, PLAYERS' UNION, STEROIDS.

499. Newman, Bruce. "Another NCAA Fumble." Sports Illustrated. 67, No.25 (December 7, 1987), 100. MANDATORY DRUG TESTING, LAW, PROS AND CONS, SIMONE LEVANT.

500. Norris, William. "The Guys Who Won't Play Ball." The Times Higher Education Supplement. 716 (July 25, 1986), 10. LEN BIAS, COCAINE, UNIVERSITY OF MARYLAND.

501.   Novich, Max M. "Drug Abuse and Drugs in Sports." New York State Journal of Medicine. 73, No.21 (November 1, 1973), 2597-2600. AMPHETAMINES, STEROIDS, ANTI-PAIN MEDICATION, MUSCLE RELAXANTS, BARBITUATES, ADVANTAGES AND HARM.

502.   Olson, O. Charles. "The Use of Drugs, Alcohol, and Tobacco by High School Athletes in Washington State." Athletic Training. 9, No.3 (September 1974), 137+. AMPHETAMINES, STEROIDS, MARIJUANA.

503.   "Olympic Testing." SciQuest. 52, No.9 (November 1979), 10. MOSCOW OLYMPICS, STEROIDS, DETECTION.

504.   "On the Track of Doped Horses." Business Week. No.2194 (September 18, 1971), 85. DRUG TESTING OF HORSES, RESEARCH ON EFFECTS OF DRUGGING HORSES, CORNELL UNIVERSITY.

505.   Ostro, Harry. "Drug Abuse and What You Can Do About It." Scholastic Coach. 52, No.5 (December 1982), 4-6+. ROLE OF ATHLETIC DIRECTORS AND COACHES, RULES, ROLE MODELS, ALCOHOL, TESTING.

506.   Ostro, Harry. "Drugs and Sports: A Symbiotic Relationship?" Scholastic Coach. 56, No.3 (October 1986), 4+. TESTING, LEGALITY, HOWARD COSELL, REFORM.

507.   Ostro, Harry. "Handling the Drug-Abusing Colleague." Scholastic Coach. 57, No.6 (January 1988), 4+. ALCOHOL, DRUGS, TESTING.

508.   Ostro, Harry. "The Problem That Won't Go Away." Scholastic Coach. 54, No.6 (January 1985), 4+. DRUG AND ALCOHOL ABUSE, STEROIDS, SUICIDE REFORM, ROLE OF THE ATHLETIC DIRECTOR, DISCIPLINE.

509.   Padwe, Sandy. "Drugs in Sports: Symptoms of a Deeper Malaise." The Nation. 243, No.9 (September 27, 1986), 276-279. MEDIA ROLE, SPORTS CULTURE, HEROES, ROLE MODELS.

510.   Papanek, John. "Athletes or Role Models? Demanding Higher Standards From Players is Unrealistic." Sports Illustrated. 66, No.24 (June 15, 1987), 84. ROLE MODELS, EXCELLENCE, SECOND CHANCES.

511.   Pate, Russell. "Does the Sport Need New Blood?" Runner's World. 11, No.11 (November 1976), 25-27. OLYMPICS, BLOOD DOPING, PERFORMANCE ENHANCEMENT, SIDE EFFECTS.

512.   Penn, Stanley. "Muscling In: As Ever More People Try Anabolic Steroids, Traffickers Take Over." Wall Street Journal. 212, No.66 (October 4, 1988), 1+. SMUGGLED DOPE, ILLICIT STEROIDS, BLACK MARKET.

513.   Perry, Arlette. "The Distinction Between Drug Use and Abuse." Athletic Training. 20, No.2 (Summer 1985), 114-116. STEROIDS, LACK OF EDUCATION, RISKS AND BENEFITS, HAZARDS OF USE, DETECTION.

514. Perry, Clifton. "Blood Doping and Athletic Competition." International Journal of Applied Philosophy. 1 (1983), 39-45. COMPETITIVE ADVANTAGE, OLYMPICS, JUSTICE, BLOOD DOPING, COMPETITION.

515. Pietschmann, Richard J. "Drugs and Athletics." Runner's World. 18, No.6 (June 1983), 47+. ANTI-INFLAMMATORY DRUGS, SPORTS MEDICINE, STEROIDS, AMPHETAMINES, PERFORMANCE IMPROVEMENT.

516. Pipe, Andrew. "The Making of a Champion--Chemistry or Coaching?" Track and Field Quarterly Review. 88, No.3 (Fall 1988), 4-8. DRUGS, RESPONSIBILITY OF COACHES, NUTRITION, ALCOHOL, DMSO, DIURETICS, BLOOD DOPING, STEROIDS.

517. Pipes, Thomas V. "A.C.T.: The Steroid Alternative." Scholastic Coach. 57, No.6 (January 1988), 106+. INCREASE OF MUSCLE MASS, BENEFIT OF STEROIDS, ANTI-CATABOLIC TRAINING.

518. Quinn, Hal. "Baseball's Looming Drug Scandal." Maclean's. 98, No.20 (May 20, 1985), 40. PRO BASEBALL, MANDATORY DRUG TESTING, ALAN WIGGINS, SAN DIEGO PADRES.

519. Quinn, Hal. "Drawing the Line on Cocaine Abuse." Maclean's. 95, No.28 (July 12, 1982), 36. COCAINE USE, NFL, CANADIAN FOOTBALL LEAGUE, DON REESE, GEORGE ROGERS.

520. Quinn, Hal. "Drugs in Sports." Maclean's. 98, No.24 (June 17, 1985), 40-43. SALARIES, STEROIDS, MEDIA COVERAGE, TESTING.

521. Quinn, Hal. "Getting Tough on Drugs." Maclean's. 100, No.40 (October 5, 1987), 46-47. CALGARY GAMES, DRUG TESTING, BANNED SUBSTANCES.

522. Quinn, Hal. "Head Winds and Scandals." Maclean's. 100, No.35 (August 31, 1987), 39. DRUG USE, STEROIDS, TESTING, PAN AM GAMES.

523. Quinn, Hal. "Innocence or Guilt and a Larger Problem." Maclean's. 93, No.38 (September 22, 1980), 40. FERGUSON JENKINS, TEXAS RANGERS, PLAYER GRIEVANCES, PRO BASEBALL.

524. Quinn, Hal. "The Science of Winning." Maclean's. 94, No.1 (January 12, 1981), 38. DRUG ABUSE, STEROIDS, RULES, EFFECT ON FEMALES.

525. Reed, J. D. "A Miracle! Or Is It a Mirage?" Sports Illustrated. 54, No.17 (April 20, 1981), 71-75. USE OF DMSO, RISKS AND BENEFITS, STATUS OF LEGALIZATION.

526. Reed, William F. "Just the Prescription the Doctors Needed: Use of Hypnotism on University of Louisville Basketball Players." Sports Illustrated. 50, No.6 (February 12, 1979), 12-13. HYPNOTISM, UNIVERSITY OF LOUISVILLE, BASKETBALL.

527.   Reed, William F. "Use a Little Horse Sense: Let's Rid the Triple Crown of Bonuses and Lasix." Sports Illustrated. 72, No.24 (June 11, 1990), 90. HORSE RACING, BONUS ARRANGEMENT QUESTIONED, LASIX MEDICATION, DRUGGING HORSES.

528.   Reilly, Rick. "When the Cheers Turned to Tears." Sports Illustrated. 65, No.2 (July 14, 1986), 28-30+. DON ROGERS, COCAINE, DEATH, CLEVELAND BROWNS FOOTBALL, FREE SAFETY, DRUG GENOCIDE, JESSE JACKSON, LEN BIAS.

529.   Remensky, Carl. "The Baseball Drug Scandal." Maclean's. 98, No.23 (June 10, 1985), 58. PRO BASEBALL, DRUG INDICTMENTS, PITTSBURGH PIRATES.

530.   Riley, Dan B. "Danger! Athletes Who Are Dying to Win." Scholastic Coach. 54, No.4 (November 1984), 48-50+. SPORTS MEDICINE, STEROIDS, LAWSUITS, MEDIA, PROS AND CONS, ROLE OF COACHES.

531.   Rolfe, John. "New Triple Crown Threat." Sport. 78, No.6 (June 1987), 16. BUTAZOLIDIN, DMSO, STEROIDS, TESTING, HORSE RACING.

532.   Ryan, Allan J. "Causes and Remedies for Drug Misuse and Abuse by Athletes." The Journal of the American Medical Association. 252, No.4 (July 27, 1984), 517-519. REASONS FOR DRUG USE, CONTROL MEASURES, REFORM.

533.   Ryan, Allan J. "Drugs and Corinthian Sportsmanship." The Physician and Sportsmedicine. 1, No.2 (September 1973), 97. AMPHETAMINES, STEROIDS, ABUSE CONTROL, TESTING, FAIR PLAY.

534.   Ryan, Allan J. "More Hormone Abuse." The Physician and Sportsmedicine. 12, No.8 (August 1984), 31. INCONCLUSIVE EVIDENCE, SELF CONFIDENCE, STEROIDS.

535.   Ryan, Jeff. "Boxing Slips the Drug Punch." Sport. 78, No.8 (August 1987), 19. DRUG TESTING, PRO BOXING.

536.   Sanders, Joseph L. "The Racer's Edge." The Progressive. 38, No.10 (October 1974), 47-50. DRUGS, PAINKILLERS, AMPHETAMINES, STEROIDS, REFORM.

537.   Sanoff, Alvin P. "Baseball's Drug Menace." U. S. News and World Report. 100, No.10 (March 17, 1986), 57. PETER UEBERROTH, DRUG TESTING, UNION PROTEST, PREVENTION PROGRAM.

538.   Sanoff, Alvin P. "Drug Problem in Athletics: It's Not Only the Pros." U. S. News and World Report. 95, No.16 (October 17, 1983), 64-66. STEROIDS, SIDE EFFECTS, BLACK MARKET, FAIR PLAY, REFORM.

539. Sanoff, Alvin P. "Drugs Take a Big Swing at Baseball." U. S. News and World Report. 99, No.11 (September 9, 1985), 60. COCAINE, TESTING, PRIVACY RIGHTS.

540.   Sanoff, Alvin P. "How Drugs Threaten to Ruin Pro Sports." U. S. News and World Report. 95, No.11 (September 12, 1983), 64-65. NFL, BASKETBALL, FINANCIAL RESULTS, REFORM.

541.   Sanoff, Alvin P. "How They're Keeping the Olympics Honest." U. S. News and World Report. 97, No.6 (August 6, 1984), 25-26. TESTING, PRESSURE TO WIN, SEX TESTING.

542.   Scott, Jack. "It's Not How You Play the Game, But What Pill You Take." The New York Times Magazine. (October 17, 1971), 40-41+. STEROIDS, AMPHETAMINES, PAINKILLERS, SEX TESTING, EMPHASIS ON WINNING.

543.   Selcraig, Bruce. "The NCAA Goes After Drugs." Sports Illustrated. 65, No.15 (October 6, 1986), 75. PARANOIA, NCAA TESTING PROGRAM, CIVIL LIBERTIES.

544.   Shapiro, Barry. "Why Spot Drug Testing Can't Work." Sport. 77, No.1 (January 1986), 9. BASEBALL, TECHNICAL PROBLEMS, INACCURACY.

545.   Shapiro, Michael. "I'm At the Edge of A Cliff." Sport. 75, No.4 (April 1984), 102-103+. MICHAEL RAY RICHARDSON, NBA, COCAINE, BASKETBALL.

546.   Shuer, Marjorie. "The Truth About Steroids." Women's Sports. 4 (April 1982), 17-22+. LONG TERM SIDE EFFECTS, FAIRNESS, RULES.

547.   Simon, Robert L. "Good Competition and Drug-Enhanced Performance." Journal of the Philosophy of Sport. 2 (1984), 6-13. DEFINITION OF PERFORMANCE-ENHANCING DRUGS, COERCION, HARM, INFORMED CONSENT, IDEAL OF COMPETITIVE SPORT, COMPETITION, RESPECT FOR PERSON, STEROIDS, FAIRNESS, HARM.

548.   Smith, James C. "An Administrator's View of Use and Misuse of Drugs Among Athletes." The Journal of School Health. 42, No.3 (March 1972), 170-171. KANAWHA COUNTY SCHOOLS, CHARLESTON, WEST VIRGINIA, PRESSURE ON COACHES, ROLE OF SCHOOL ADMINISTRATOR.

549.   Solomon, Harold. "Drugs in Tennis?" World Tennis. 28, No.7 (December 1980), 9. ROLE MODELS, STEROIDS.

550.   Spencer, Diane. "Drugs Warning to Young Athletes." The Times Higher Education Supplement. 3363 (December 5, 1980), 14. AVAILABILITY OF DRUGS, PUNISHMENT, BENEFIT AND HARM.

551.   Sperryn, Peter N. "Drugged and Victorious: Doping in Sport." New Scientist. No.1415 (August 2, 1984), 16-19. DRUGS, AMPHETAMINES, STEROIDS, SIDE EFFECTS, FAIR PLAY.

552.   Stehlin, Dori. "For Athletes and Dealers, Black Market Steroids Are Risky Business." FDA Consumer. 21, No.7 (September 1987), 24-25. ILLEGAL STEROIDS, RISKS, FDA.

553.   Stern, Robert. "Who Me, Addicted?" Health Education. 12, No.2 (March/April 1981), 36. SOCIAL DEPENDENCY, PSYCHOLOGICAL DEPENDENCY, PHYSICAL DEPENDENCY, DRUG DEPENDENCY INVENTORY.

554.   "Steroids Stir Mental Backlash." Science News. 133, No.18 (April 30, 1988), 284. PSYCHIATRIC COMPLICATIONS, DEPRESSION, MANIA.

555.   "Steroids: Great Risk to Young Athletes." USA Today. 112, No.2465 (February 1984), 10-11. EFFECT ON YOUTH, SIDE EFFECTS, GIRLS, RISKS.

556.   Stifler, Glori. "Drug Testing: Helping or Hurting Our Athletes?" International Gymnast. 29, No.9 (September 1987), 33. NCAA, DRUG TESTING, RULES.

557.   Stodghill, Ron. "Athletes, Drugs and Very Nervous Advertisers." Business Week. No.3074 (October 17, 1988), 36. ADVERTISERS, SCREENING JOCKS, CONTRACT CLAUSES.

558.   Stoler, Peter. "The Toughest Test for Athletes: Olympic Officials Are Vowing to Catch Steroid Users." Time. 123, No.26 (June 25, 1984), 61-62. LOS ANGELES OLYMPICS, DANGERS OF STEROID USE.

559.   "The Substances Athletes Use." The Chronicle of Higher Education. 25, No.1 (September 1, 1982), 26. ALCOHOL, AMPHETAMINES, STEROIDS, ANTI-INFLAMMATORY DRUGS, CAFFEINE, NICOTINE, TRANQUILIZERS, VITAMINS.

560.   Sullivan, Robert. "Groping For a Drug Plan That Will Work." Sports Illustrated. 64, No.10 (March 10, 1986), 7-8. COCAINE USE, NEW JERSEY NETS, MICHAEL RAY RICHARDSON, PETER UEBERROTH, ANTI-DRUG PROGRAM, KEITH HERNANDEZ.

561.   Taylor, William N. "Drug Testing Dilemma." Strength and Health. 53, No.3 (April/May 1985), 54-56. TESTING, PARANOIA, CAT AND MOUSE APPROACH, STEROIDS, GENETIC ENGINEERING.

562.   Taylor, William N. "Gigantic Athletes: The Dilemma of Human Growth Hormone." The Futurist. 19, No.4 (August 1985), 8-12. INCONCLUSIVE EVIDENCE, GIGANTISM, WOMEN, ADVERSE EFFECTS.

563.   Taylor, William N. "Growth Hormone: Preventing Its Abuse in Sports." Technology Review. 88, No.7 (October 1985), 14-15+. ADVANTAGES, POTENTIAL ABUSE, EXPERIMENTATION.

564.   Taylor, William N. "Super Athletes Made to Order." Psychology Today. 19, No.5 (May 1985), 62-66. WIN AT ANY COST PHILOSOPHY, HUMAN GROWTH HORMONE, PHYSICAL AND PSYCHOLOGICAL EFFECTS, CHILDREN, REFORM.

565.   Telander, Rick. "A Peril for Athletes." Sports Illustrated. 69, No.18 (October 24, 1988), 114. TOMMY CHAIKIN, EFFECT OF STEROID USE.

566.   Thompson, Paul. "Dope and Glory." Runner's World. 23, No.12 (December 1988), 47. BEN JOHNSON, STEROIDS, STANOZOLOL, DETECTION, SIDE EFFECTS.

567.   Thompson, Paul B. "Privacy and the Urinalysis Testing of Athletes." Journal of the Philosophy of Sport. 9 (1982), 60-65. DRUGS, BANNED SUBSTANCES, RULE ENFORCEMENT, PRIVACY RIGHTS.

568.   Todd, Terry. "Anabolic Steroids: The Gremlins of Sport." Journal of Sport History. 14, No.1 (Spring 1987), 87-107. CHRONOLOGY OF STEROID USE, RULES, REFORM, DRUG TESTING, FANATICISM, CASE STUDIES, NCAA, LEGISLATION.

569.   Todd, Terry. "The Steroid Predicament." Sports Illustrated. 59, No.5 (August 1, 1983), 62-78. WIDESPREAD USE, PERFORMANCE-ENHANCING DRUGS, NFL, RUSSIAN ATHLETES, BENEFIT AND HARM, MEDICAL DEFINITION OF STEROIDS, DIANOBOL, WEIGHT LIFTERS, PERSONAL REFLECTIONS OF STEROID USERS, IOC TESTING.

570.   Ullyot, Joan. "The Steroid Stand." Women's Sports and Fitness. 7, No.9 (October 1985), 10. VARIETIES OF STEROIDS, RISKS.

571.   Underwood, John. "Speed is All the Rage." Sports Illustrated. 49, No.9 (August 28, 1978), 30-41. FOOTBALL, BRUTALITY, ARNOLD MANDELL, SPEED, VIOLENCE.

572.   Unger, Norman O. "Should Baseball Players Be Forced to Take Drug Tests?" Jet. 68, No.14 (June, 1985), 46-48. MANDATORY DRUG TESTING, INVASION OF PRIVACY, ACLU, PUBLICITY, RACIAL BIAS, EXPOSING BLACK DRUG USERS ONLY.

573.   Vecsey, Peter. "Inside the Drug Scandal With Dr. J." Sport. 71, No.6 (December 1980), 16+. NBA, JULIUS ERVING, PRO BASKETBALL.

574.   Wade, Nicholas. "Anabolic Steroids: Doctors Denounce Them, But Athletes Aren't Listening." Science. 176, No.4042 (June 30, 1972), 1399-1403. WIDE SPREAD USE OF STEROIDS, PROS AND CONS, FADDISM.

575.   "Waging War on Drugs on the Sports Front." Athletic Business. 9, No.9 (September 1985), 20+. ATHLETICS AS A VEHICLE TO SPREAD THE ANTI-DRUG MESSAGE, DRUG PREVENTION, COACHES, DRUG EDUCATION.

576.   Walsh, David. "Drugs on Tour." Bicycling. 28, No.6 (July 1987), 24-26+. HISTORY, CASE STUDIES, TOUR DE FRANCE.

577.   Watman, Mel. "Doping Allegations." Women's Track World. 2, No.1 (January 1979), 32-33. EAST GERMANY, STEROIDS, SIDE EFFECTS.

578.   Weider Research Group. "Drug Testing: The Odds Against Steroids: A Billion to One." Muscle & Fitness. 48, No.8 (August 1987), 122-124. STEROID TESTING TECHNOLOGY, ATTEMPTS TO ESCAPE DETECTION, HUMAN GROWTH HORMONES.

579.   Weiskopf, Herman. "High-Ho, High-Ho, It's Off to Lift We Go." Sports Illustrated. 33, No.13 (September 28, 1970), 63-66. DRUG SCANDALS, DISQUALIFICATION, AMPHETAMINES, WORLD WEIGHTLIFTING CHAMPIONSHIPS.

580.   "Why Next Olympics May Be Drug-Free." U. S. News and World Report. 95, No.10 (September 5, 1983), 10. LOS ANGELES OLYMPICS, TESTING, STEROIDS, DETECTION.

581.   Williams, Melvin H. "Drugs and Sport." Arena Review. 4, No.4 (December 1980), 16-18. EDUCATION AS A SOLUTION TO DRUG ABUSE, FUTURE.

582.   Wood, Chris. "The Drug Busters." Maclean's. 101, No.4 (February 1988), 122-126. PERFORMANCE ENHANCING DRUGS, TESTING, OLYMPICS, FAIR PLAY, POLITICS.

583.   Woolf, Norma Bennett. "Recruit Coaches and Athletes to Help Battle Drugs." The American School Board Journal. 173, No.2 (February 1986), 36. DRUG PREVENTION PROGRAMS, FOREST HILLS, OHIO SCHOOL DISTRICT, ROLE MODELS, COACHES.

584.   Wulf, Steve. "A Crash Landing for An Ace." Sports Illustrated. 66, No.15 (April 13, 1987), 32-34. DWIGHT GOODEN, NEW YORK METS, COCAINE, REHABILITATION.

585.   "Young Athletes, Drinking and Drugs: In Search of a Cure." Athletic Business. 9, No.9 (September 1985), 14+. EDUCATION VS. INTERVENTION, APPROACHES FOR USERS, ABUSERS, AND ABSTAINERS, STANDARDS, MIDDLE GROUND.

RECRUITING

Books

586.   Kerrane, Kevin. Dollar $ign on the Muscle: The World of Baseball Scouting. New York: Beaufort Books, Inc., 1984. PRO BASEBALL, SCOUTING.

587.   Nuwer, Hank. Recruiting in Sports. New York: Franklin Watts, 1989. BUSINESS, ACADEMICS, RECRUITING, HIGH SCHOOL COACHES, WOMEN, SCANDALS.

588.   Rooney, John F. The Recruiting Game: Toward a New System of Intercollegiate Sports. Lincoln: The University of Nebraska Press, 1980. CHANGES AND REFORM, COMPETITION, COLLEGE SPORTS.

589.   Sutton, William Anthony. The Blue Chip Quest: A Geographical Analysis of Collegiate Football Recruiting, 1972-1981. Ed.D. Thesis, Oklahoma State University, 1983. ORIGIN AND MIGRATION PATTERNS, HIGH SCHOOL ALL-AMERICAN FOOTBALL PLAYERS, RELATIONSHIP OF RECRUITING AND WINNING, COMMUNITY SPORTS, SPECIALIZATION, TRADITION.

590.   Upshaw, Gene and E. R. Garvey. Institutional Discrimination: A Study of Managerial Recruitment in Professional Football. Report Prepared for the NFL Players Association, 1980. JUSTICE, DISCRIMINATION, UNIONS, NFL, MONEY, CONSTITUTIONAL RIGHTS.

Articles

591. Axthelm, Pete. "Scandal on the Court." Newsweek. 94 (December 24, 1979), 77. UNIVERSITY OF NEW MEXICO, COLLEGE BASKETBALL, ACADEMICS.

592. "Boosters Barred From Recruiting; Coaches Incomes to be Watched." The Chronicle of Higher Education. 33, No.19 (January 21, 1987), 34-35. NCAA RULES, OUTSIDE INCOME OF COLLEGE COACHES, BOOSTERS BANNED FROM RECRUITING.

593. Chu, Donald B. and Jeffrey O. Segrave. "Leadership Recruitment and Ethnic Stratification in Basketball." Journal of Sport and Social Issues. 5, No.1 (Spring/Summer 1981), 13-22. PLAYING POSITION, RACISM, DISCRIMINATION, CAREER SUCCESS.

594. DuPree, David. "Playing the Game: Sports-Crazy Colleges Continue to Lure Stars With Improper Offers." Wall Street Journal. 176, No.71 (October 8, 1970), 1+. WHISTLEBLOWING, COACHES, IMPROPER OFFERS, NCAA RULES.

595. Evans, Arthur S. "Differences in the Recruitment of Black and White Football Players at a Big Eight University." Journal of Sport and Social Issues. 3, No.2 (Fall/Winter 1979), 1-10. SPORT AS AN AVENUE OF SOCIAL MOBILITY, KANSAS STATE UNIVERSITY, INEQUALITY.

596. Farrell, Charles S. "Football Powers Endorse Reforms in Recruiting." The Chronicle of Higher Education. 32, No.15 (June 11, 1986), 1+. COLLEGE FOOTBALL ASSOCIATION, BAN ON RECRUITING BY BOOSTERS, REDUCTION IN TIME COACHES CAN SPEND RECRUITING OFF CAMPUS, REDUCTION OF SCHOLARSHIPS.

597. Farrell, Charles S. "NCAA Admits Difficulty in Catching Violators of Recruiting And Financial-Aid Regulations." The Chronicle of Higher Education. 29, No.2 (September 5, 1984), 29+. NCAA STUDY, SAT SCORES, PROPOSITION 48, DISCRIMINATION.

598. Farrell, Charles S. "Recruiting Violations in Women's Basketball Said to Be Up, Despite NCAA Investigations." The Chronicle of Higher Education. 29, No.23 (February 20, 1985), 31-32. PRESSURE TO WIN, CHEATING, ABUSES, WOMENS' SPORTS.

599. Hult, Joan S. "Recruiting the Female Student-Athlete." Journal of Physical Education and Recreation. 49, No.8 (October 1978), 18-20. AIAW, DISCRIMINATION, EQUAL OPPORTUNITY, STUDENT-ATHLETES, HIGH SCHOOL COACHES, FINANCIAL AID.

600. Kirshenbaum, Jerry (ed.). "How Top-Ranked Clemson Made Some Bad News Worse." Sports Illustrated. 55, No.25 (December 14, 1981), 13-16. PAYMENTS TO ATHLETES, CLEMSON UNIVERSITY, RECRUITING ABUSES.

601. Layne, Pat. "Recruiting an Athlete Academically." Women's Varsity Sports. 4, No.1 (November/December 1982), 24+. COACHES, ACADEMICS, STUDENT-ATHLETES.

602. Leifsen, Marian A. "House Divided." Sports Illustrated. 50, No.10 (March 5, 1979), 60-64+. COLLEGE BASKETBALL, PARENTS.

603. Myers, Willie. "Recruiting or Selling?" Coaching Clinic. 20, No.3 (March 1982), 15-16. COACH RECOMMENDATIONS, HIGH SCHOOL COACHES, COLLEGE ATHLETICS.

604. Odenkirk, James E. "The Three R's: Revenues, Recruiting and Reputation." The Center Magazine. 15, No.1 (January/February 1982), 26-28. TELEVISION, ATHLETIC BUDGETS, SCANDALS, BIG TIME COLLEGE SPORTS, ROLE OF UNIVERSITY PRESIDENTS, REFORM.

605. Sabock, Ralph J. "Preventing Recruiting Violations." Athletic Journal. 67, No.1 (August 1986), 22-23. HIGH SCHOOL COACHES, PREVENTION OF RECRUITING ABUSES.

606. Selleck, George A. "Effective Recruiting Without Cheating." Athletic Business. 8 (October 1984), 10+. RULES, EDUCATING RECRUITERS.

607. Telander, Rick. "The Shark Gets a Ruling With Bite." Sports Illustrated. 47, No.15 (October 10, 1977), 26-27. RECRUITING VIOLATIONS, UNIVERSITY OF NEVADA AT LAS VEGAS, COACH JERRY TARKANIAN, REINSTATEMENT BY COURT, NCAA RULES, NCAA REBUFFED, COLLEGE BASKETBALL.

608. "Women's Basketball Team in Louisiana Penalized for Recruitment Violations." The Chronicle of Higher Education. 31, No.19 (January 22, 1986), 29. RULE VIOLATIONS, WOMENS' BASKETBALL, NORTHEAST LOUISIANA UNIVERSITY, PENALTIES, NCAA, ROLE OF THE COACH.

RIGHTS, RULES, AND ETHICAL STANDARDS

Articles

609. Center for Athletes' Rights and Education. "Athletes' Bill of Rights." Arena Review. 6, No.1 (May 1982), 58. DISCRIMINATION, ACADEMICS, DUE PROCESS, WOMEN, UNIONS, DIGNITY, RULES, ETHICS.

610. Childs, Alan W. "Athletic and Academic Policy in the Context of a New League." Academe: Bulletin of the American Association of University Professors. 73 (July/August 1987), 34-38. ACADEMIC EXCELLENCE, COLONIAL LEAGUE, COACHES, ABUSES IN INTERCOLLEGIATE ATHLETICS, ACADEMICS AS A PRIORITY, ELIGIBILITY, AMATEURISM.

611.   Clear, Delbert K. "Participation in Interscholastic Athletics: They Fight--Fight--Fight for the Right--Right--Right." Phi Delta Kappan. 64, No.3 (November 1982), 166-171. LITIGATION, INSTITUTIONAL CONTROL OF ATHLETIC PROGRAMS, RIGHTS, ETHICS, RESPONSIBILITY, HIGH SCHOOL SPORTS.

612.   "Code of Ethics." Texas Coach. 23 (August 1979), 29+. RULES, RIGHTS, RESPONSIBILITY, DISCIPLINE, SPORTSMANSHIP, HONORABLE PLAY.

613.   "Code of Ethics." Soccer Journal. 27, No.3 (May/June 1982), 17+. RULES, RIGHTS, RESPONSIBILITY, OFFICIALS AND PLAYERS, PUBLIC RELATIONS, RECRUITING.

614.   Criley, Dick. "A Bill of Rights for Athletes." International Gymnast. 19, No.9 (September 1977), 10. AMATEURISM, RIGHT TO COMPETE, RULES, RESPONSIBILITIES.

615.   Crowl, John A. "Quest for Ethical Standards Will Dominate Sports This Year: Tough Penalties Face Test." The Chronicle of Higher Education. 31, No.1 (September 4, 1985), 71-72. BIG TIME COLLEGE SPORTS, REFORM, RULE VIOLATIONS.

616.   Edwards, Harry. "The Collegiate Athletic Arms Race: Origins and Implications of the 'Rule 48' Controversy." Journal of Sport and Social Issues. 8, No.1 (Winter/Spring 1984), 4-22. ELIGIBILITY, NCAA.

617.   Erffmeyer, Elizabeth S. "Rule-Violating Behavior on the Golf Course." Perceptual and Motor Skills. 59, No.2 (October 1984), 591-596. CHEATING, SOCIAL CONTEXT, NORMATIVE PRESSURE, DEINDIVIDUATION, MOTIVATION, RULES, HONOR, HONESTY, COURTESY, ETHICS.

618.   Espinosa, Dana S. "Is No Pass/No Play Doing What It Was Intended to Do?" Journal of Physical Education, Recreation and Dance. 59, No.2 (February 1988), 21. HOUSE BILL 72, COACHES, TEACHERS, PARENTS.

619.   Farrell, Charles S. "Sports Departments Overseen Closely By Presidents Have Fewer Rule-Breaking Problems, Study Finds." The Chronicle of Higher Education. 31, No.18 (January 15, 1986), 37-38. ROLE OF COLLEGE PRESIDENTS, EXEMPLARY PROGRAMS, INTERNAL CONTROL.

620.   Finneran, Carolyn A. "Code of Conduct for Swimming." Coaching: Women's Athletics. 5, No.4 (September/October 1979), 72-73. OLYMPICS, CURFEWS, ALCOHOL, DRUGS, SEX, UNIFORMS.

621.   Gilbert, Bil. "High Time to Make Some Rules." Sports Illustrated. 31, No.1 (July 7, 1969), 30-35. CHANGES AND REFORM, DRUGS, RULES.

622.   Greenberg, Jerald, Melvin M. Mark, and Darrin R. Lehman. "Justice In Sports and Games." Journal of Sport Behavior. 8, No.1 (March 1985), 18-33. DISTRIBUTIVE, RETRIBUTIVE AND PROCEDURAL JUSTICE, JUSTICE RELATED THEORY.

623.   Horn, Stephen. "Ethics, Due Process, Diversity and Balance." Vital Speeches of the Day. 43, No.15 (May 15, 1977), 463-468. INTERCOLLEGIATE ATHLETICS, AMATEURISM, RULES, CODE OF ETHICS, AGENTS, MEDIA, RISING COSTS.

624.   Jurenas, Albert C. "No-Pass, No-Play: An Issue That Won't Go Away." American Secondary Education. 15, No.4 (1987), 29-30. REFORM, LINKING CLASSROOM PERFORMANCE TO ELIGIBILITY FOR SPORTS, BENEFIT AND HARM, CONSTITUTIONALITY OF RULE 48.

625.   Keerdoja, Eileen. "The NCAA Drops the Ball." Newsweek. 103, No.15 (April 9, 1984), 99. IMPACT OF RULE 48.

626.   Keith, Dwight. "On Sportsmanship." Coach and Athlete. 43, No.6 (April 1981), 7. COMPROMISE OF PRINCIPLES TO WIN, RULES, REFORM.

627.   Langerman, Samuel and Noel Fidel. "Responsibility Is Also Part of the Game." Trial: The National Legal Newsmagazine. 13, No.1 (January 1977), 22-25. ASSUMED RISK THEORY, DUTY OF COACHES, INJURIES.

628.   McNatt, Robert. "Debate Grows Over Rule 48." Black Enterprise. 13, No.10 (May 1983), 18. NCAA, EXPLOITATION, ACADEMIC STANDARDS.

629.   Middleton, Lorenzo. "NCAA Tightens Rules on Academic Records and Off-Campus Courses to Limit Abuses." The Chronicle of Higher Education. 20, No.14 (June 2, 1980), 2. CORRESPONDENCE COURSES, FORGED TRANSCRIPTS, SCANDALS.

630.   Middleton, Lorenzo. "NCAA to Vote on Tougher Academic Rules for Athletes." The Chronicle of Higher Education. 21, No.17 (December 15, 1980), 1+. FORGED TRANSCRIPTS, ACADEMIC STANDARDS, REFORM.

631.   Middleton, Lorenzo. "New Group Pushes Bill of Rights for Athletes." The Chronicle of Higher Education. 23, No.6 (October 7, 1981), 4. RIGHT TO FORM UNIONS, CENTER FOR ATHLETES' RIGHTS AND EDUCATION, MULTI-YEAR SCHOLARSHIPS, LEGAL ASSISTANCE, EQUAL ACCESS, ALAN SACK, BIG BUSINESS.

632.   Moore, Kenny. "The Campaign for Athletes' Rights." The Annals of the American Academy of Political and Social Science. 445 (September 1979), 59-65. AMATEURISM, PLAYER RIGHTS, NCAA, AMATEUR ATHLETIC UNION, REFORM.

633.   "'No Pass/No Play'." America. 152, No.14 (April 13, 1985), 294. REFORM, TEXAS, ELIGIBILITY, EXCELLENCE, RULES, ACADEMICS.

634.   "No-Pass No-Play and Other Vital Issues of the Day Straight From the S. C. Blue-Ribbon Panel of A. D.'s." Scholastic Coach. 55, No.8 (March 1986), 50-53+. ELIGIBILITY STANDARDS, DRUGS, SEX DISCRIMINATION, LAWSUITS, VIOLENCE, CROWD CONTROL.

635.   "Not Sporting." The Economist. 307, No.7549 (May 7, 1988), 68. EUROPEAN ECONOMIC COMMUNITY, PROTECTIONISM, SOCCER.

636. Ostro, Harry. "Due Process." Scholastic Coach. 50, No.1 (August 1980), 6+.
      LITIGATION, PLAYER AND COACHES RIGHTS, DISCIPLINARY ACTION, CONTRACTS,
      CODE OF CONDUCT, RESPONSIBILITY OF ATHLETIC DIRECTORS.

637. Ostro, Harry. "Team Rules and Personal Freedom." Scholastic Coach. 54,
      No.1 (August 1984), 10+. PLAYER GROOMING, LITIGATION, PLAYER RIGHTS,
      RULES, ROLE MODELS, COACHES.

638. Ostro, Harry. "The New, Tough Eligibility Rules: Good Points and 'Red
      Flags'." Scholastic Coach. 53, No.9 (April 1984), 10+. REFORM, RULE 48,
      INEQUITIES, RULES, BENEFIT AND HARM, EXPLOITATION, ROLE OF THE ATHLETIC
      DIRECTOR.

639. "A Potpourri of Athletics Concerns: Top 10, Best Coach, New Rules, New NIT-
      -and a Venerable Bowl." The Chronicle of Higher Education. 31, No.1
      (September 4, 1985), 73-74. COLLEGE BASKETBALL, ELIGIBILITY, FINANCIAL
      AID.

640. Press, Aric with Donna Foote. "Do Athletes Have a Right To Play?"
      Newsweek. 99 (January 25, 1982), 91. ACADEMICS, RIGHT TO DUE PROCESS,
      MARK HALL.

641. Reddiford, Gordon. "Constitutions, Institutions, and Games." Journal of the
      Philosophy of Sport. 12 (1985), 41-51. CONSTITUTIVE RULES, REGULATIVE
      RULES, COMPETITION, SPORTING INSTITUTIONS.

642. Rivello, J. Roberta. "Rules and Ethical Actions." Aitia. 3, No.2 (1975), 9-12.
      COMMONALITY BETWEEN GAMES AND ACTS, ETHICS OF COMPETITION.

643. Sack, Allen L. "Proposition 48: A Masterpiece in Public Relations." Journal
      of Sport and Social Issues. 8, No.1 (Winter/Spring 1984), 1-3. BIG TIME NCAA
      COLLEGE SPORT, ACADEMICS AND ATHLETICS.

644. Shults, Fredrick D. "Freedom Issues in Sport." Journal of Physical Education,
      Recreation and Dance. 53, No.2 (February 1982), 57-61. DRAFT SYSTEM,
      OPTION CLAUSE, ROLE OF COLLEGE PRESIDENTS, RULES, REFORM.

645. Stahr, Jack. "Jack Stahr's 10 Commandments." World Tennis. 26, No.8
      (January 1979), 36. COURT COURTESY, SPECTATORS, PLAYERS.

646. Staton, Richard. "Recent Cases Concerning the Rights of Student Athletes." The
      Journal of College and University Law. 10, No.2 (Fall 1983/1984), 209-224.
      LAW, STUDENT-ATHLETES, AGENTS, TRANSFER RULE, WORKER'S COMPENSATION,
      COACHES, FREEDOM OF INFORMATION.

647. "Stringent Standards." America. 153, No.13 (November 9, 1985), 290-291. NO
      PASS/NO PLAY, TEXAS, REFORM, ADULT ABUSES.

648. Sullivan, Robert. "A New Law Cuts Deep in the Heart of Texas." Sports
      Illustrated. 63, No.20 (November 4, 1985), 17. HOUSE BILL 72, NO PASS/NO
      PLAY, FOOTBALL, PROS AND CONS.

649.   Utz, Stephan G.   "The Authority of the Rules of Baseball: The Commissioner as Judge." Journal of the Philosophy of Sport. 16 (1989), 89-99. FUNCTION OF RULES, AUTHORITY OF OFFICIALS, BARTLETT GIAMATTI, PETE ROSE, PRO BASEBALL, LAW.

650.   Vance, N. Scott.   "Modifications of New NCAA Rules Weighed By College Presidents." The Chronicle of Higher Education. 26, No.2 (March 9, 1983), 1+. ACADEMIC REQUIREMENT REVISIONS, DISCRIMINATION, SAT SCORES, GRADE POINT AVERAGES.

651.   Vance, N. Scott.   "Testing-Service Head Hits NCAA's Academic Rules." The Chronicle of Higher Education. 25, No.21 (February 2, 1983), 1+. GREGORY ANRIG, EDUCATIONAL TESTING SERVICE, DISCRIMINATION, TIGHTENING STANDARDS, SAT SCORES.

652.   von Weizsaecker, Richard.   "A Clear and Binding Sport Ethic." Olympic Review. 219 (January 1986), 29-30. IMPORTANCE OF SPORT, OLYMPICS, POLITICS, AMATEUR QUESTION, COMMERCIALIZATION, VIOLENCE, DRUGS.

The Game, Competition, and Contestants

CHANGE, REFORM, AND DEMISE

Books

653. Andreano, Ralph. No Joy in Mudville: The Dilemma of Major League Baseball. Cambridge, MA: Schenkman Publishing Company, 1965. BIG LEAGUE BASEBALL, DEMISE, HISTORY, HEROES, BIG BUSINESS.

654. Dickey, Glenn. The Jock Empire: Its Rise and Deserved Fall. Radnor, PA: Chilton Book Company, 1974. BUSINESS, DISCRIMINATION, WINNING AT ALL COSTS, SPORTS WRITING, GAME-FIXING, COLLEGE SPORTS, PRO SPORTS, OLYMPICS.

655. Jaworski, Ron. Excellence Now--and For the Future. Medford, NJ: Beyond Athletics, 1986. BENEFIT AND HARM, COMPETITION, NFL FOOTBALL, PHILADELPHIA EAGLES.

656. Kramer, Jerry. Farewell to Football. New York: The World Publishing Company, 1969. INJURIES, PURSUIT OF EXCELLENCE, WINNING.

657. Scott, Jack. The Athletic Revolution. New York: Free Press, 1971. COLLEGE SPORTS, NCAA, OVEREMPHASIS ON WINNING, COACHES, PSYCHOLOGICAL TESTING, DRUGS, POLITICS.

658. Underwood, John. The Death of An American Game: The Crisis in Football. Boston: Little, Brown and Company, 1979. HISTORY, BIG BUSINESS, MEDIA, INFLUENCE, MONEY, ACADEMICS, FOOTBALL.

659. Voigt, David Quentin. America's Leisure Revolution: Essays in the Sociology of Leisure and Sport. Reading, PA: Albright College, 1974. ANTHROPOLOGY, FUTURE, SPORT AND SOCIETY, POLITICS, CHANGE.

660.   Voigt, David Quentin. <u>American Baseball: From Postwar Expansion to the Electronic Age</u>. University Park, PA: The Pennsylvania State University Press, 1983. AMERICAN LEAGUE, NATIONAL LEAGUE, JACKIE ROBINSON, FANS, OWNERS, FUTURE, TECHNOLOGY.

661.   Voigt, David Quentin. <u>American Baseball: From the Commissioners to Continental Expansion</u>. University Park, PA: The Pennsylvania State University Press, 1983. AMERICAN LEAGUE, NATIONAL LEAGUE, HEROES, NEW YORK YANKEES.

662.   Voigt, David Quentin. <u>American Baseball: From Gentleman's Sport to the Commissioner System</u>. University Park, PA: The Pennsylvania State University Press, 1983. COMMERCIALISM, HEROES, PLAYER REVOLT, BASEBALL.

Articles

663.   Allison, Maria T. "Kaleidoscope on Prism: The Study of Social Change in Play, Sport and Leisure." <u>Sociology of Sport Journal</u>. 4, No.2 (June 1987), 144-155. SOCIAL CHANGE, UNDIRECTIONALITY, DEVIANCE AND SEMANTIC ILLUSION.

664.   Ariel, Gideon B. "Physical Education: 2001?" <u>Quest</u>. 21 (January 1974), 49-52. TEACHING PHYSICAL EDUCATION, YOUTH, TECHNOLOGY.

665.   Axthelm, Pete. "How to Reform the System." <u>Newsweek</u>. 96 (September 22, 1980), 59. REFORM, SCHOLARSHIPS, ACADEMICS, COACHES, PENALTIES, CHEATING.

666.   Axthelm, Pete. "The Sickness of College Sports." <u>Newsweek</u>. 105, No.16 (April 22, 1985), 74. SCANDALS, REFORM, ROLE OF THE COLLEGE PRESIDENT, BOOSTERS, PENALTIES.

667.   Becker, Gary S. "College Athletes Should Get Paid What They're Worth." <u>Business Week</u>. No.2914 (September 30, 1985), 18. NCAA RULES, PROFESSIONALISM, OPEN COMPETITION.

668.   Benenson, Robert. "Changing Environment in College Sports." <u>Editorial Research Reports</u>. 1, No.14 (April 15, 1983), 275-292. ACADEMICS, NCAA RULES, MONEY, WOMEN, REFORM, PROFESSIONALIZATION, BILL OF RIGHTS.

669.   Boyle, Robert H. "The Bizarre History of American Sport." <u>Sports Illustrated</u>. 16, No.1 (January 8, 1962), 54-63. RISE OF SPORT, TECHNOLOGY, WINNING AT ALL COSTS, SPORTSMANSHIP, FUTURE.

670.   "Council Head Chief Cries Foul as Campus Brawn Triumphs." <u>The Times Higher Education Supplement</u>. 795 (January 29, 1988), 11. REFORM, ACADEMICS, SCHOLARSHIP, MONEY.

671.   Crase, Darrell. "The Continuing Crises in Athletics." Phi Delta Kappan. 56, No.2 (October 1974), 99-101. WINNING AT ALL COSTS, INTERCOLLEGIATE ATHLETICS, PLAYER APATHY, RECRUITING, MEDIA, SPECTATOR VIOLENCE, WOMEN.

672.   Dickinson, Vern. "The Cool and the Lonely: Conformity in Changing American Sport." Quest. 27 (Winter 1977), 97-105. CONFORMITY, DAVID RIESMAN, COMPETITION, FANS.

673.   Farrell, Charles S. "Colleges Must Clean Up Their Athletics Programs or Face Professionalization, NCAA President Says." The Chronicle of Higher Education. 33, No.37 (May 27, 1987), 27-28. WILFORD S. BAILEY, PRESIDENT OF NCAA, DRUG TESTING, ACADEMIC STANDARDS, ROLE OF COLLEGE PRESIDENTS, COMMERCIALIZATION.

674.   Farrell, Charles S. "Drugs and Gambling Said to 'Threaten Very Existence' of College Sports." The Chronicle of Higher Education. 32, No.12 (May 21, 1986), 36. AVOIDANCE OF DETECTION, LEGAL PROBLEMS OF DRUG TESTING.

675.   Farrell, Charles S. "Notre Dame's Father Joyce: Tireless Campaigner for Honesty in Sports." The Chronicle of Higher Education. 33, No.39 (June 10, 1987), 34+. FATHER EDMUND P. JOYCE, UNIVERSITY OF NOTRE DAME, CHEATING, SCANDALS.

676.   Figler, Stephen K. "Measuring Academic Exploitation of College Athletes and a Suggestion for Sharing Data." Sociology of Sport Journal. 1, No.4 (December 1984), 381-388. EXPLOITATION, ACADEMICS, DATA POOL.

677.   Frey, James H. "Boosterism, Scarce Resources and Institutional Control: The Future of American Intercollegiate Athletics." International Review of Sport Sociology. 17, No.2 (1982), 53-70. INSTITUTIONAL CONTROL OF ATHLETICS, INTERCOLLEGIATE ATHLETICS.

678.   Gilley, J. Wade. "College Athletics Reform: Losing Through Intimidation." The Education Digest. 52 (March 1987), 57-59. INTERCOLLEGIATE ATHLETICS, ACADEMICS, DRUGS, GAMBLING AND POINT SHAVING, NCAA VIOLATIONS, ROLE OF THE COLLEGE PRESIDENT, LEADERSHIP, REFORM.

679.   Gilley, J. Wade. "The Intimidated College President: A Bar to Sports Reform." The Chronicle of Higher Education. 33, No.11 (November 12, 1986), 104. ROLE OF THE COLLEGE PRESIDENT, STUDY OF INTERCOLLEGIATE ATHLETICS, REFORM.

680.   Gladwell, Malcolm. "Fumbling on Reform." The Washington Monthly. 18, No.8 (September 1986), 45-49. NCAA, REFORM, EXCELLENCE, GRADUATION RATES.

681.   Goodger, John M. "Pluralism, Transmission and Change in Sport." Quest. 38, No.2 (1986), 135-147. SOCIAL STRUCTURE, CULTURE.

682.   Greene, John B. "Blitzing Athletic Abuses." Community and Junior College
        Journal. 52, No.6 (March 1982), 32-35. CHEATING, COACHES, STUDENT-
        ATHLETES, ACADEMICS, VALUE-ORIENTED PROGRAMS, WINNING AT ALL COSTS,
        RULES, REFORM.

683.   Greer, H. Scott. "The Future of Olympism as a Social Movement." Arena
        Review. 6, No.2 (December 1982), 22-25. REFORM, SOCIAL ORDER, CHANGE.

684.   Hammel, Bob. "Student-Athletes: Tackling the Problem." Phi Delta Kappan.
        62, No.1 (September 1980), 7-13. SCANDALS, ACADEMICS, RESPONSIBLITY OF
        THE COLLEGE PRESIDENT, JOHN WOODEN, JOE PATERNO, DARRELL MUDRA, BOB
        HAMMEL.

685.   Hanford, George H. "Controversies in College Sports." The Annals of the
        American Academy of Political and Social Science. 445 (September 1979), 66-
        79.   REVENUE PRODUCING SPORTS, EQUAL OPPORTUNITY FOR WOMEN,
        RECRUITMENT, SUBSIDIZATION OF ATHLETES, FINANCING COLLEGE SPORTS, BIG
        TIME COLLEGE ATHLETICS, WINNING AT ANY COST, TITLE IX.

686.   Herrmann, Donald E. and Vern Seefeldt. "What is the Future of Sports for High
        School-Age Youth?" Athletic Purchasing & Facilities. 6, No.10 (October 1982),
        14+.   STATE HIGH SCHOOL ASSOCIATIONS, POTENTIAL CONFLICT BETWEEN
        SCHOOLS AND AGENCIES, NON-SCHOOL GROUPS, COOPERATION BETWEEN SCHOOLS
        AND AGENCIES, RULES, CHANGE.

687.   "How Colleges Voted on Revisions in Academic Standards for Athletes (Table)."
        The Chronicle of Higher Education. 31, No.19 (January 22, 1986), 31.
        DIVISION ONE, NCAA, RULE CHANGES, SAT SCORES.

688.   Ivey, Mark. "How Educators Are Fighting Big-Money Madness in Athletics."
        Business Week. No.2970 (October 27, 1986), 136+.   REFORMS, MONEY,
        ALUMNI, RACISM, PROPOSITION 48, BOOSTERISM, GAME FIXING.

689.   Jewett, Ann E. "Who Knows What Tomorrow May Bring?" Quest. 21 (January
        1974), 68-72. FUTURE, PHYSICAL EDUCATION, TEACHING PHYSICAL EDUCATION.

690.   Kirshenbaum, Jerry (ed.). "Restating the Case for Reform." Sports Illustrated.
        53, No.10 (September 1, 1980), 7+. BENEFITS OF FOOTBALL, BIG TIME COLLEGE
        ATHLETICS, CHEATING, REFORMS.

691.   Korobkov, Anatoli. "Sport in the Year 2000." The Journal of Sports Medicine
        and Physical Fitness. 12, No.2 (June 1972), 129-130. NECESSITY OF SPORT,
        TECHNOLOGY, FUTURE.

692.   Lawson, Hal A. "Looking Back From the Year 2082." Journal of Physical
        Education, Recreation and Dance. 53, No.4 (April 1982), 15-17. DEFINING
        STUDENT NEEDS, SELF-HELP, SCHOOL PROGRAMS, TEACHING PHYSICAL
        EDUCATION.

693.   Lawson, Hal A. "Physical Education and Sport: Alternatives for the Future."
        Quest. 21 (January 1974), 19-29. SOCIOLOGY, TECHNOLOGY, LEISURE, VALUES.

694.   Lawson, Hal A.   "Physical Education and the Reform of Undergraduate Education."   Quest.   40, No.1 (April 1988), 12-32.   REFORM IN THE EIGHTIES, RELATIONSHIP BETWEEN GENERAL, LIBERAL AND PROFESSIONAL EDUCATION.

695.   Lederman, Douglas.   "Small-College Sports Association Adopts Sweeping Package of Reforms."   The Chronicle of Higher Education.   34, No.29 (March 30, 1988), A37-38.   NATIONAL ASSOCIATION OF INTERCOLLEGIATE ATHLETICS, REFORMS, RULE CHANGES.

696.   Lederman, Douglas.   "Sports Reform Catches on Among Smaller Colleges, But Grinds to a Halt Among Big-Time Universities."   The Chronicle of Higher Education.   34, No.20 (January 27, 1988), A39-40.   REFORM, BAR ON CONSIDERATION OF ATHLETIC ABILITY FOR FINANCIAL AID, REJECTION OF PROPOSED INCREASE IN FOOTBALL SCHOLARSHIPS.

697.   Lederman, Douglas.   "Trustees' Role in Cleaning Up Sports Abuses Seen Crucial."   The Chronicle of Higher Education.   33, No.38 (June 3, 1987), 35-36.   GOVERNING BOARD INVOLVEMENT IN ATHLETICS, DEFINING THE ROLE OF THE BOARD.

698.   McCarthy, Eugene J.   "Bad Calls."   The New Republic.   189, No.9 (August 29, 1983), 9-11.   BASEBALL, CHANGES AND DEMISE, UMPIRES.

699.   McGrath, Ellie.   "Blowing the Whistle on Johnny."   Time.   123, No.5 (January 30, 1984), 80.   REFORM, TEXAS, H. ROSS PEROT, NO PASS/NO PLAY, ACADEMICS.

700.   Monaghan, Peter.   "Unethical Behavior Said to Permeate Sports; Scholars, Athletic Officials Call for Reforms."   The Chronicle of Higher Education.   30, No.13 (May 29, 1985), 27-28.   ROLE OF COACHES, ASSAULT ON PLAYERS, ILLEGAL INDUCEMENTS, WHISTLEBLOWING.

701.   Moore, Clarence A.   "Future Trends and Issues in Physical Education and Athletics."   Journal of Physical Education and Recreation.   51, No.1 (January 1980), 20-21.   CERTIFICATION, BUDGETS, UNIONS, CURRICULUM, FUTURE, WOMEN, TITLE IX.

702.   Morikawa, Sadao.   "Amateurism--Yesterday, Today, and Tomorrow."   International Review of Sport Sociology.   12, No.2 (1977), 61-72.   IDEOLOGY, MODERN SPORTS.

703.   Naison, Mark.   "Scenario for Scandal."   Commonweal.   109, No.16 (September 24, 1982), 493-496.   COLLEGE ATHLETICS, SCANDALS, ROLE OF SPORT IN HIGHER EDUCATION, REFORM, PROFESSIONALIZATION, ALUMNI, TELEVISION.

704.   Naison, Mark.   "The Perversion of the Dream."   Southern Exposure.   7, No.2 (Fall 1979), 112-116.   WORKING CLASS ENTERTAINING MIDDLE CLASS, EXCESSIVE INJURIES, DRUGS, ACADEMICS, DISCRIMINATION, RACISM.

705.   Oberlander, Susan.   "Two-Year Colleges Expected to Vote to Strengthen
        Academic-Eligibility Rules for Athletes." The Chronicle of Higher Education.
        34, No.28 (March 23, 1988), A35-36. NATIONAL JUNIOR COLLEGE ATHLETIC
        ASSOCIATION, ACADEMIC ELIGIBILITY REQUIREMENT, SEMESTER BASED
        ELIGIBILITY, GRADE POINT AVERAGES.

706.   Odenkirk, James E.   "Make 'Em All Pros."   College Teaching.   34, No.2
        (Spring 1986), 42.   BIG TIME COLLEGE SPORTS, SCANDALS, INADEQUATE
        CONTROL,   RESPONSIBILITY   OF   COLLEGE   PRESIDENTS,   REMOVAL   OF
        INTERCOLLEGIATE ATHLETICS FROM THE ACADEMIC SETTING.

707.   "A Plan For Cleaning Up College Sports."   Sports Illustrated.   63, No.15
        (September 30, 1985), 36-37.   ADMISSIONS, ELIGIBILITY OF FRESHMEN,
        ACADEMICS, SCHOLARSHIP, ATHLETIC DORMS, STEROIDS, BOOSTERS.

708.   Purdy, Dean A.   "Current and Future Orientations: The Sociology of Sport."
        Journal of Sport and Social Issues.   4, No.1 (Spring/Summer 1980), 46-55.
        FUTURE, SOCIOLOGY, SPECIALIZATION.

709.   Rosenbloom, Steve. "NHL to Kayo Goons." Sport. 79, No.6 (June 1988), 16.
        NHL, SPORTSMANSHIP, VIOLENCE.

710.   Sack, Allen L.   "Yale 29--Harvard 4:   The Professionalization of College
        Football."   Quest.   19 (January 1973), 24-34.   AMATEURISM, COLLEGE
        FOOTBALL, PRO FOOTBALL, SOCIAL CLASSES, VALUES.

711.   Sage, George H. "Blaming the Victim: NCAA Responses to Calls for Reform
        in Major College Sports."   Arena Review.   11 (November 1987), 1-11.
        STRUCTURAL PROBLEMS, BIG TIME COLLEGE SPORTS, STUDENT-ATHLETES,
        PROPOSITION 48.

712.   Scully, Malcolm G. "26 University Presidents to Probe Sports Abuses." The
        Chronicle of Higher Education. 25, No.1 (September 1, 1982), 27. AMERICAN
        COUNCIL ON EDUCATION, PAYMENTS TO ATHLETES, TRANSCRIPT MANIPULATION,
        ABUSES.

713.   Scully, Malcolm G. and Lorenzo Middleton.   "Moves to Control Abuses in
        Sports Eyed by Major Universities." The Chronicle of Higher Education. 24,
        No.15 (June 9, 1982), 1+. RECRUITING VIOLATIONS, CORRUPTION, TRANSCRIPT
        MANIPULATION.

714.   Seurin, Pierre. "The Future of the Olympic Games and Tomorrow's Sport."
        The FIEP Bulletin. 50, No.2 (April/June 1980), 7-16. MOSCOW OLYMPICS,
        BOYCOTT, POLITICS, HISTORY, REFORM.

715.   "Should College Athletes Be Paid Salaries?" U. S. News and World Report. 99,
        No.26 (December 23, 1985), 56.   PROFESSIONALISM, SALARIES, ACADEMICS,
        EXPLOITATION, GRADUATION RATES, CHEATING.

716. Shults, Fredrick D. "Toward Athletic Reform." Journal of Physical Education and Recreation. 50, No.1 (January 1979), 18-19+. PHILOSOPHY, BILL OF RIGHTS, POLICY.

717. Stokvis, R. "Conservative and Progressive Alternatives in the Organization of Sport." International Social Science Journal. 34, No.2 (1982), 197-208. HISTORY, ACHIEVEMENT MOTIVE, NATIONAL INTEGRATION, CONSERVATIVE AND PROGRESSIVE ATTITUTES, AMATEURISM AND PROFESSIONALISM.

718. Telander, Rick. "Dollars and Change." Sports Illustrated. 71, No.27 (January 1, 1990), 166. HIGH PLAYERS' SALARIES, GREED, BIG BUSINESS OF NCAA SPORT, PETE ROSE, GAMBLING, BLACK QUARTERBACKS.

719. Vance, N. Scott. "Raising Academic Standards for Athletes Tops Agenda of Sports-Reform Panel." The Chronicle of Higher Education. 25, No.7 (October 13, 1982), 17-18. TIGHTENING STANDARDS, IMPORTANCE OF INTERCOLLEGIATE ATHLETICS, ROLE OF THE COLLEGE PRESIDENT, RECRUITING ABUSES.

720. Watterson, John S. "Inventing Modern Football." American Heritage. 39, No.6 (September/October 1988), 102-113. SCANDALS, FOOTBALL SCANDAL OF 1905, HISTORICAL, REFORM.

721. Weistart, John C. "College Sports Reform: Where Are the Faculty?" Academe: Bulletin of the American Association of University Professors. 73 (July/August 1987), 12-17. BIG TIME COLLEGE SPORT, COMMERCIALIZATION, COMPETITION, SCANDALS, REVENUE SHARING.

722. Weistart, John C. "The Role of Faculty in College Sports Reform." The Education Digest. 53 (February 1988), 56-59. NCAA, BIG TIME COLLEGE SPORTS, STUDENT-ATHLETES, GRADUATION RATES.

723. Wells, Christine L. "The Game of 2084: A Doomsday Fantasy." Quest. 21 (January 1974), 46-48. FUTURE, TECHNOLOGY, POLITICS, LIFESTYLE.

724. White, Gordon. "How to Save Intercollegiate Athletics." Phi Delta Kappan. 56, No.2 (October 1974), 106-109. JOE PATERNO, REFORM, NCAA, RULES.

725. Zeigler, Earle F. "Past, Present and Future Development of Physical Education and Sport." The Academy Papers. 13 (November 1979), 9-19. HISTORY, FUTURE, SPORTS AS A PROFESSION, PHILOSOPHY, AMATEURS.

726. Ziegler, Susan G. "A Futurist Approach to Sport Sociology." Journal of Sport and Social Issues. 4, No.1 (Spring/Summer 1980), 56-59. YOUTH, COACHES AND PLAYERS.

CHEATING AND CORRUPTION

Books

727.   Allison, Dean B. and Bruce B. Henderson. Empire of Deceit. London: Columbus Books, 1986. MUHAMMAD ALI PROFESSIONAL SPORTS ORGANIZATION, HAROLD SMITH--EMBEZZLER, PRO BOXING, SCANDALS.

728.   Bowyer, J. Barton. Cheating: Deception in War and Magic, Games and Sports, Sex and Religion, Business and Con Games, Politics and Espionage, Art and Science. New York: St. Martin's Press 1982. RULES, DECEIT, CHANCE, LYING, BLUFFING, GAMBLING, GAME-FIXING, HORSE RACING.

729.   Golenbock, Peter. Personal Fouls: The Broken Promises and Shattered Dreams of Big Money College Basketball. New York: Carroll and Graf Publishers, 1989. BIG TIME COLLEGE SPORTS, MONEY.

730.   Hoch, Paul. Rip Off The Big Game: The Exploitation of Sports by the Power Elite. Garden City, NY: Anchor Books, 1972. SPORTS AND SOCIETY, CAPITALISM, MONOPOLIES, MILITARISM, SOCIALIZATION, SEXISM, RACISM, SOCIALISM, FASCISM.

731.   Kirby, James. Fumble: Bear Bryant, Wally Butts and the Great College Football Scandal. San Diego, CA: Harcourt Brace Jovanovich, Inc., 1986. GAME-FIXING, LITIGATION.

732.   Nash, Bruce and Allan Zullo. Baseball Confidential. New York: Pocket Books, Inc., 1988. RITUALS, CHEATING, CORKED BATS, DOCTORED BALLS, SPORTSMANSHIP.

733.   New Jersey State Commission of Investigation. Organized Crime in Boxing. Trenton, NJ: The Commission, 1985. CORRUPTION, GAMBLING, FIXED FIGHTS, AGENT ABUSE OF FIGHTERS, HEALTH RISKS.

Articles

734.   Alexander, Charles. "The Wells Fargo Stickup." Time. 117, No.7 (February 16, 1981), 64-65. MUHAMMAD ALI PROFESSIONAL SPORTS, HAROLD SMITH, COMPUTER SWINDLE, EMBEZZLEMENT.

735.   "Another Year, Another Scandal." Scholastic Coach. 50, No.3 (October 1980), 6+. COLLEGE FOOTBALL, NCAA, CHEATING, BIG BUSINESS.

736.   Axthelm, Pete. "A Short Cut to Glory?" Newsweek. 95 (May 5, 1980), 98. ROSIE RUIZ, BOSTON MARATHON, RUNNING.

737.   Axthelm, Pete. "A Winner by Any Name." Newsweek. 90 (November 7, 1977), 73. SWITCHING HORSES, HORSE RACING, BELMONT.

738.   Axthelm, Pete. "Psst, Somebody May Be Cheating." Newsweek. 102, No.6 (August 8, 1983), 74. RULES, BREAKING RULES, FAN REACTION, PINE TAR BATS, DOCTORED EQUIPMENT.

739.   Axthelm, Pete. "The High Price of Cheating." Newsweek. 100 (August 9, 1982), 43. REV. JOHN LOSCHIAVO, UNIVERSITY OF SAN FRANCISCO, PAYMENT TO PLAYERS.

740.   Blagden, Nellie. "Beset By A Foul Claim and Rumors of Bribery, Preakness Winner Angel Cordero Claims Innocence." People Weekly. 13, No.22 (June 2, 1980), 30-31. RACE-FIXING, SCANDAL.

741.   Boyle, Robert H. "Mud Flies All Over the Track." Sports Illustrated. 35, No.18 (November 1, 1971), 30-31. RALPH WILSON, BUFFALO BILLS OWNER, FRAUD, HORSE RACING.

742.   Bruning, Fred. "Sticky Thoughts for Sultry Days." Maclean's. 96, No.34 (August 22, 1983), 9. KANSAS CITY ROYALS, GEORGE BRETT, PINE TAR BATS.

743.   Callahan, Tom. "Batty Balls: Unkindest Cuts of All." Time. 130, No.8 (August 24, 1987), 45. CORKED BATS, EMERY BOARDS, SLIPPERY PITCHES.

744.   Crowl, John A. "Coaches Ask Penalties for Colleagues Caught Cheating." The Chronicle of Higher Education. 24, No.16 (June 16, 1982), 1+. STIFF PENALTIES FOR VIOLATIONS, PAYMENTS TO ATHLETES, COACHES.

745.   Dreisell, Charles G. "Cracking Down on Cheaters: A Coach's View." The Chronicle of Higher Education. 32, No.2 (March 12, 1986), 44. RECRUITING VIOLATIONS, BOOSTERS, OFF CAMPUS RECRUITING, NCAA, REFORM.

746.   Enarson, Harold. "Cheating, Not Professionalism, Is The Problem." The Center Magazine. 15, No.1 (January/February 1982), 13-15. TELEVISION, BIG BUSINESS, COLLEGE AS A TRAINING GROUND FOR THE PROS, ENTERTAINMENT, REFORM.

747.   Farrell, Charles S. "Big Jump in Money and Prestige Spurs Cheating in Women's Basketball, Coaches and Players Say." The Chronicle of Higher Education. 31, No.20 (January 29, 1986), 25. INCENTIVES FOR CHEATING, PENALTIES, NORTHEAST LOUISIANA UNIVERSITY.

748.   Farrell, Charles S. "Big-Time College Football Powers Eye Monitoring System to Prevent Cheating." The Chronicle of Higher Education. 33, No.39 (June 10, 1987), 34+. NATIONWIDE MONITORING SYSTEM, AUDITORS, REFORM.

749.   Feezell, Randolph M. "On the Wrongness of Cheating and Why Cheaters Can't Play the Game." Journal of the Philosophy of Sport. 15 (1988), 57-68. GAYLORD PERRY, SPITBALLS, PRO BASEBALL, KANT, INTEGRITY, RULES.

750.   Feinstein, John. "Cheating in Football is a Matter of Degrees." Maclean's. 93, No.2 (January 14, 1980), 40. BIG BUSINESS, RECRUITING VIOLATIONS, LOWERED ADMISSION STANDARDS.

751.   Footlick, Jerrold K. "Boxing's Biggest Scam." Newsweek. 97 (February 16, 1981), 98. MUHAMMAD ALI PROFESSIONAL SPORTS, BOXING, FRAUD.

752.   Frayne, Trent. "Of Doctored Balls and Apple Pie." Maclean's. 94, No.21 (May 25, 1981), 38. DOCTORED PITCHES, OAKLAND A'S, PRO BASEBALL.

753.   Gammon, Clive. "This Isn't Cricket...But It Is." Sports Illustrated. 54, No.15 (April 6, 1981), 36. UNSEEMLY BEHAVIOR, INTERNATIONAL CRICKET, WEST INDIES, ENGLAND, AUSTRALIA, NEW ZEALAND, UNFAIR PITCH, UNRULY FANS, VIOLENCE, PROFANITY, ROWDYISM.

754.   Gammons, Peter. "O.K., Drop That Emery Board." Sports Illustrated. 67, No.7 (August 17, 1987), 34-37. DOCTORED BALLS, CORKED BATS, BASEBALL, CHEATING.

755.   "The Great Belmont Park Sting." Time. 110, No.21 (November 21, 1977), 122. HORSE SWAPPING, SCANDAL, HORSE RACING.

756.   Gutman, Dan. "The Physics of Foul Play." Discover. 9, No.4 (April 1988), 70-77. CORKED BATS, BASEBALL, TECHNOLOGY.

757.   Harper, Donald D. and John Hammon. "The Hyprocrisy of Amateurism." Quest. 27 (Winter 1977), 121-130. DEFINITION OF AMATEUR, PROFESSIONALISM, OLYMPICS, SUBSIDIES TO AMATEURS, REFORM.

758.   Hertzel, B. "Cheating Frowned On, But Still a Part of Baseball." Baseball Digest. 43, No.9 (September 1984), 34-36. DIRTY TRICKS, FAIRNESS IN COMPETITION, DISHONESTY AND DECEPTION, CORRUPTION.

759.   Hitzges, Norm. "Dirty Tricks: A Guidebook to Sneaky Baseball." Sport. 73, No.8 (August 1982), 58-59. SPITTERS, CUT BALLS, LOADED BATS, INFIELD TAILORING.

760.   Johnson, Diane H. "MAPSCAM's Hidden Costs." Black Enterprise. 12, No.9 (April 1982), 15. HAROLD SMITH, MUHAMMAD ALI PROFESSIONAL SPORTS, COMPUTER SCAM.

761.   Jones, J. G. and John C. Pooley. "Cheating in Sport: An International Problem." International Journal of Physical Education. 19, No.3 (1982), 19-23. INDIVIDUAL, COACH, OWNER, MANAGEMENT, AND OFFICIAL RESPONSIBILITY FOR GROWTH IN CHEATING, DEVIANCE.

762.   "Jugoslavia: If You Can't Beat 'Em, Bribe 'Em." The Economist. 249, No.6801 (December 29, 1973), 25-26. CORRUPTION, FOOTBALL, SCANDALS.

763.   Katz, Michael. "See Harold Run: Of Boxing, Banks and Beating It." Rolling Stone. No.343 (May 14, 1981), 14-15+. PRO BOXING, MUHAMMAD ALI PROFESSIONAL SPORTS, HAROLD SMITH, EMBEZZLEMENT.

764.   Kiersh, Edward. "The Man Who Tried To Take Over Boxing." Sport. 72, No.4 (April 1981), 66-70. MUHAMMAD ALI PROFESSIONAL SPORTS, SCANDAL, WELLS FARGO BANK, HAROLD SMITH.

765.   Kirshenbaum, Jerry. "The Loneliness of the Long-Distance Subway Rider." Sports Illustrated. 52, No.19 (May 5, 1980), 11. ROSIE RUIZ, BOSTON MARATHON, WOMEN, FRAUD.

766.   Kirshenbaum, Jerry (ed.). "Making Cost-of-Living and Other Allowances for Cheating at USC." Sports Illustrated. 56, No.19 (May 10, 1982), 27. PROBATION, UNIVERSITY OF SOUTHERN CALIFORNIA TROJAN FOOTBALL, ACADEMIC ABUSES, PAYMENTS TO PLAYERS.

767.   Lasch, Christopher. "The Corruption of Sports." The New York Review of Books. 24, No.7 (April 28, 1977), 24-30. SPECTATORS, SPORT IN SUBJECTION TO PROFIT, PATRIOTISM, HEALTH OR MORALITY, SECULARIZATION OF SPORTS, HISTORY, URGE TO AVOID DEFEAT.

768.   Leggett, William. "Is This Horse That Horse?" Sports Illustrated. 47, No.20 (November 14, 1977), 28-31. LEBON, CINZANO, URUGUAYAN RACEHORSES, FRAUD, BELMONT.

769.   Lehman, Craig K. "Can Cheaters Play the Game?" Journal of the Philosophy of Sport. 8 (Fall 1981), 41-46. RULES, VIOLATION OF RULES, COMPETITION, SPORTSMANSHIP, FAIR PLAY, MORAL RULES, CHEATING AND COMPETING, LOGICAL INCOMPATIBILITY.

770.   Levy, Michael. "Cheating." Women's Sports. 4, No.9 (September 1982), 18-20. CLOSE CALLS, RATIONALIZATIONS, COVER-UPS, INADEQUACY.

771.   Looney, Douglas S. "Deep In Hot Water in Stillwater." Sports Illustrated. 49, No.1 (July 3, 1978), 18-20+. STILLWATER, COLLEGE FOOTBALL, OKLAHOMA STATE UNIVERSITY, NCAA PROBATION, PLAYER PAYOFFS, BOOSTERISM.

772.   Meschery, Tom. "There Is a Disease in Sports Now...." Sports Illustrated. 37, No.14 (October 2, 1972), 56-63. BIG BUSINESS, BASKETBALL, CORPORATIONS, RELATIONSHIP OF PLAYERS AND OWNERS, EMPHASIS ON MONEY AND WINNING.

773.   Middleton, Lorenzo. "Former Player is Convicted in College Basketball Fix." The Chronicle of Higher Education. 23, No.14 (December 2, 1981), 10. GAMBLING, GAME-FIXING, BOSTON COLLEGE, RICHARD KUHN, POINT SHAVING.

774.   Monaghan, Peter. "NCAA to Get Tough With Chronic Cheaters, Perhaps Cancel Entire Seasons, Byers Warns." The Chronicle of Higher Education. 30, No.1 (March 6, 1985), 31. JEOPARDIZING TEAM SPIRIT, DEMEANING, RATIONALE FOR TAKING DRUGS.

775.   Putnam, Pat. "Fighting the Rulers of the WBA." Sports Illustrated. 54, No.13 (March 23, 1981), 30-39. WORLD BOXING ASSOCIATION, DUBIOUS RATINGS, SELF AGGRANDIZEMENT, BOXERS EXPLOITED, CORRUPT PROMOTERS, MONEY, CHAMPIONSHIP CREDIBILITY.

776.   Putnam, Pat. "Time to Clean Up Boxing Again." Sports Illustrated. 54, No.12 (March 16, 1981), 36-53. WORLD BOXING COUNCIL, DUBIOUS RATINGS, SELF AGGRANDIZEMENT, BOXERS EXPLOITED, CORRUPT PROMOTERS, MISMATCHES, MONEY, CHAMPIONSHIP CREDIBILITY.

777.   Quinn, Hal. "Fat, Old Friends and An Empty Ring." Maclean's. 95 (August 30, 1982), 40. BENNY MITCHELL, IMPOSTERS, BOXING.

778.   Quinn, Hal. "The Longest Home Run." Maclean's. 96, No.32 (August 8, 1983), 37. PINE TAR BAT, GEORGE BRETT, KANSAS CITY ROYALS, TARGATE.

779.   "Racing on Trial: Did Top Jockeys Take Bribes?" Time. 115, No.21 (May 26, 1980), 89. CON ERRICO, RACE-FIXING, TRIAL.

780.   Scobie, William. "A Scandalous Blow to Boxing." Maclean's. 94, No.7 (February 16, 1981), 29-30. BOXING, FRAUD, MUHAMMAD ALI PROFESSIONAL SPORTS.

781.   Seligman, Daniel. "The Meaning of It All." Fortune. 108, No.4 (August 22, 1983), 79. PINE TAR BATS, RULES, KANSAS CITY ROYALS, GEORGE BRETT.

782.   Sharnik, Morton. "This Saint Has Been Called A Sinner." Sports Illustrated. 32, No.22 (June 1, 1970), 18-23. ERNIE WHEELWRIGHT, NEW ORLEANS SAINTS FOOTBALL, CO-OWNERSHIP OF BAR WITH MAFIA ASSOCIATES.

783.   Slote, John. "Getting Away With It." Esquire. 98, No.6 (December 1982), 29-30. RULES, CHEATING, BASKETBALL, TENNIS, SQUASH, BASEBALL, FOOTBALL.

784.   Smith, Dean. "The Black Sox Scandal." American History Illustrated. 11, No.9 (January 1977), 16-24. CHICAGO WHITE SOX, BASEBALL, GAMBLING, HISTORICAL.

785.   Solomon, Harold. "The Cancer Within Tennis." World Tennis. 29, No.7 (December 1981), 8-9. GUARANTEES, RULES, REFORM.

786.   Sullivan, Robert and Craig Neff. "Shame on you, SMU." Sports Illustrated. 66, No.10 (March 9, 1987), 18-23. SOUTHERN METHODIST UNIVERSITY, FOOTBALL, SCANDALS, SUSPENSION, PLAYER PAYOFFS, RECRUITING VIOLATIONS, METHODIST CHURCH.

787.   Surface, Bill. "Racing's Big Scandal." Sports Illustrated. 49, No.19 (November 6, 1978), 26-31. GAMBLING, TONY CIULLA, FIXED RACES, BRIBERY, JOCKEYS, ORGANIZED CRIME, HORSE RACING, FBI INVESTIGATION.

788.   Tarshis, Barry. "How to Protect Yourself Against the Tennis Cheater." Tennis. 14, No.11 (March 1979), 71-74. TENNIS, RULES, SELF REGULATION, FAIRNESS.

789.   Tatz, Colin. "The Corruption of Sport." Current Affairs Bulletin. 59, No.4 (September 1982), 4-16. DISHONESTY AND DECEPTION, UNFAIRNESS IN COMPETITION, RESPONSIBILITY OF COACHES.

790. "That Bat!: The Dirty End of the Stick." Time. 122, No.6 (August 8, 1983), 71. BASEBALL, CUSTOMIZED BATS, PINE-TAR BATS.

791. Thompson, James G. "The Intrusion of Corruption Into Athletics: An Age-old Problem." The Journal of General Education. 38, No.2 (1986), 144-153. INTERCOLLEGIATE ATHLETICS, ACADEMICS, HISTORY, RECRUITING, ROLE OF THE COLLEGE PRESIDENT.

792. Vance, N. Scott. "Deterring Cheaters in College Sports: Tougher Penalties vs. Better Policing." The Chronicle of Higher Education. 25, No.8 (October 20, 1982), 15+. EXPANSION OF ENFORCEMENT STAFF, BIG BROTHER PROGRAM, SUSPENSIONS.

793. Vance, N. Scott. "How the NCAA's Investigators Catch College Rule Breakers." The Chronicle of Higher Education. 25, No.8 (October 20, 1982), 15+. INVESTIGATION REGARDING VIOLATIONS, DAVID BERST, NCAA ENFORCEMENT DEPARTMENT, PENALTIES.

794. Vance, N. Scott. "NCAA May Soon Permit Investigations of Cheating in Women's Athletics." The Chronicle of Higher Education. 25, No.7 (October 13, 1982), 17. RULE VIOLATIONS, IMPROPER OFFERS, CHEATING, ENFORCEMENT, GRACE PERIOD.

795. Voigt, David Quentin. "The Chicago Black Sox and the Myth of Baseball's Single Sin." Journal of the Illinois State Historical Society. 62, No.3 (Autumn 1969), 293-306. SCANDALS, CHICAGO WHITE SOX SCANDAL OF 1919, MYTHS, CORRUPTION, ORIGIN OF BASEBALL, GAMBLING.

796. Wertz, Spencer K. "The Varieties of Cheating." Journal of the Philosophy of Sport. 8 (Fall 1981), 19-40. CHEATING, SELF CHEATING, INTENTIONALITY, EVIL, WINNING, REGULATION, DEFINITION OF CHEATING, REGULATORY RULES, CONSTITUTIVE RULES.

797. Wulf, Steve. "Minnesota's Mess." Sports Illustrated. 69, No.3 (July 18, 1988), 13. UNIVERSITY OF MINNESOTA, LUTHER DARVILLE, SWINDLING, IMPROPER PAYMENTS TO ATHLETES, PAUL GIEL, ATHLETIC DIRECTOR, ACADEMICS.

798. Wulf, Steve. "Pine-Tarred and Feathered." Sports Illustrated. 59, No.9 (August 29, 1983), 48-49. PINE TAR BATS, GEORGE BRETT, KANSAS CITY ROYALS, NEW YORK YANKEES.

799. Wulf, Steve. "Tricks of the Trade." Sports Illustrated. 54, No.16 (April 13, 1981), 92-108. PRO BASEBALL, LOADED BATS, DOCTORED BALLS.

800. Ziegel, Vic. "The Man Who Would Be King." New York. 14, No.9 (March 2, 1981), 47-48. MUHAMMAD ALI PROFESSIONAL SPORTS, FRAUD, BOXING, HAROLD SMITH, CORRUPTION.

ETHICS OF COMPETITION

Books

801. Barry, Mike and Bob Buck. <u>Playing Dirty</u>. New York: St. Martin's Press, Inc., 1983. LAW, SPORTSMANSHIP.

802. Braine, Tim and John Stravinsky. <u>The Not-So-Great Moments in Sports</u>. New York: Quill, 1986. PLAYING DIRTY, SCANDALS, SPORTSMANSHIP, FANS.

803. Cromartie, Bill. <u>Clean Old-Fashioned Hate</u>. Huntsville, AL: Strode Publishers, 1977. VIOLENCE, AGGRESSION, BENEFIT AND HARM OF SPORTS, WINNING, MORAL DIMENSION.

804. Fraleigh, Warren P. <u>Right Actions in Sport: Ethics for Contestants</u>. Champaign, IL: Human Kinetics Publishers, Inc., 1984. MORAL BASIS, ENDS VS MEANS, WINNING AND LOSING, RULES, RELATIONSHIP BETWEEN OPPONENTS, VALUES.

805. Jordan, Pat. <u>Chase the Game</u>. New York: Dodd, Mead and Company, 1979. BASKETBALL, VIOLENCE, DEHUMANIZATION, INEQUALITY, FAILURE, FRANK OLEYNICK, BARRY MCLEOD, WALTER LUCKETT.

806. Kohn, Alfie. <u>No Contest: The Case Against Competition</u>. Boston: Houghton Mifflin Company, 1986. PSYCHOLOGY OF COMPETITION, RATIONALIZATIONS FOR COMPETITION, CHARACTER BUILDING, SELF ESTEEM, WINNING AT ALL COSTS, SOCIOLOGY, AGGRESSION.

807. Kramer, Jerry (ed.). <u>Lombardi: Winning Is the Only Thing</u>. New York: The World Publishing Company, 1970. WINNING AT ALL COSTS, PRO FOOTBALL, COACHES.

808. Nideffer, Robert M. <u>The Ethics and Practice of Applied Sport Psychology</u>. Ithaca, NY: Mouvement Publications, 1981. SPORTS PSYCHOLOGY, ETHICAL STANDARDS, TESTING, CASE HISTORIES, INJURIES.

809. Tutko, Thomas A. and William Bruns. <u>Winning is Everything and Other American Myths</u>. New York: Macmillan Publishing Company, Inc., 1976. WINNING, CHARACTER BUILDING, MYTHS, COMPETITION, CHILDREN, INJURIES, COACHES, BILL OF RIGHTS.

810. Warner, Gary. <u>Competition</u>. Elgin, IL: David C. Cook Publishing Company, 1979. BENEFIT AND HARM, WINNING AND LOSING, HEROES, CREED, EXPLOITATION, VIOLENCE, CHILDREN, COLLEGE SPORTS, COACHES, SPECIALIZATION.

Ethics of Competition   71

Articles

811. Alapack, Rich. "The Distortion of a Human Value." The Journal of Physical
Education. 72, No.4 (March/April 1975), 118-119. COMPETITION, WINNING,
VIOLENCE, CHILDREN, VALUES.

812. Axthelm, Pete. "Bring Back the Pedestal." Newsweek. 100 (July 19, 1982),
43. FAN EXPECTATIONS, COCAINE, RAPE, ROLE MODELS.

813. Ball, Donald W. "Failure in Sport." American Sociological Review. 41, No.4
(August 1976), 726-739. REACTIONS TO FAILURE, PRO BASEBALL, PRO
FOOTBALL, UNCERTAINTIES AND ANXIETIES OF FAILURE.

814. Bauslaugh, Gary. "Ethics in Professional Sports." The Humanist. 46, No.6
(November/December 1986), 30-31. BIG BUSINESS, HEROES, WINNING AT ALL
COSTS, HONESTY, COMPETITION.

815. Bennet, Brother. "Morals and Ethics in Powerlifting." Muscular Development.
19, No.4 (July/August 1982), 44+. MORALITY, VIRTUE, DRUGS, FAIRNESS,
RELIGION.

816. Callahan, Tom. "Spilling Over Into the Streets." Time. 132, No.10 (September
5, 1988) 47. VIOLENCE, IMPROPER PAYMENTS TO ATHLETES, GAMBLING.

817. "Color Me Venal." America. 153, No.9 (October 12, 1985), 210. NCAA,
TEXAS CHRISTIAN UNIVERSITY, GREED, DRUGS, BIG BUSINESS, FANS.

818. Delattre, Edwin J. "Some Reflections on the Success and Failure in Competitive
Athletics." Journal of the Philosophy of Sport. 2 (September 1975), 133-139.
BENEFIT AND HARM, WINNING, IDEAL AND MEANING.

819. Elsom, John. "A Way of Life." Contemporary Review. 240, No.1392 (January
1982), 27-31. NATIONAL HONOR, BOOKS ABOUT CRICKET, SCANDALS, ETHICS OF
THE GAME.

820. Flink, Steve. "Men's Tennis and the Ethics of Sport?" World Tennis. 29, No.8
(January 1982), 38-42. POOR DEPORTMENT, JOHN MCENROE, ROLE MODELS,
RULES.

821. Fraleigh, Warren P. "Why the Good Foul is Not Good." Journal of Physical
Education, Recreation and Dance. 53, No.1 (January 1982), 41-42. RULES,
PURSUIT OF THE GOOD SPORTS CONTEST, SELF INTEREST, FOULS, SOCIALIZATION,
REGULATIONS, SPORTSMANSHIP.

822. Gamson, William A. and Norman A. Scotch. "Scapegoating in Baseball." The
American Journal of Sociology. 70, No.1 (July 1964), 69-72. OSCAR GRUSKY,
EFFECT OF THE FIELD MANAGER ON TEAM PERFORMANCE, MANAGERIAL
SUCCESSION.

823.   Gilbert, Bil. "Competition: Is It What Life's All About?" Sports Illustrated. 68, No.20 (May 16, 1988), 86-90+. DEFINITION, DEBATE CONCERNING BENEFIT AND HARM OF COMPETITION, PSYCHOLOGICAL PERSPECTIVES, DEMISE OF SPORTSMANSHIP.

824.   Hult, Joan S. and Rosalie Gershon. "Intercollegiate Ethics and Eligibility." Coaching: Women's Athletics. 4, No.3 (May/June 1978), 70-73. INTERCOLLEGIATE ATHLETICS, ETHICS, ELIGIBILITY, AIAW REGULATIONS, RECRUITING RESPONSIBILITY FOR COLLEGIATE COACHES, HIGH SCHOOL COACHES, AMATEURISM, HISTORY.

825.   Hyland, Drew A. "Opponents, Contestants and Competitors: The Dialectic of Sport." Journal of the Philosophy of Sport. 11 (1984), 63-70. DEFINITION OF COMPETITION, HEGEL, AGGRESSION, VIOLENCE, ALIENATION, FRIENDSHIP, COOPERATION.

826.   Keating, James W. "The Ethics of Competition and Its Relation to Some Moral Problems in Athletics." Philosophic Exchange. 1, No.4 (Summer 1973), 5-20. SPORTSMANSHIP, AMATEURISM, DRUGS, DEFINITION OF COMPETITION.

827.   Keating, James W. "Winning in Sport and Athletics." Thought: A Review of Culture and Ideas. 38, No.149 (Summer 1963), 201-210. DIFFERENCE BETWEEN SPORTS AND ATHLETICS, WINNING, DEFINITION OF SPORT, IMPORTANCE OF VICTORY, EXCELLENCE.

828.   Knoppers, Annelies, Jayne Schuiteman, and Bob Love. "Winning Is Not the Only Thing." Sociology of Sport Journal. 3, No.1 (March 1986), 43-56. SITUATION SPECIFITY AND MAGNITUDE OF GAME ORIENTATION IN TEENS, GENDER, ETHNICITY.

829.   Kohn, Alfie. "Why Competition?" The Humanist. 40, No.1 (January/February 1980), 14-15+. COMPETITION AS UNHEALTHY, REALM OF THE INTERHUMAN.

830.   Kretchmar, Robert Scott. "From Test to Contest: An Analysis of Two Kinds of Counterpoint in Sport." Journal of the Philosophy of Sport. 2 (September 1975), 23-30. SPORT AND THE TEST, SPORT AND THE CONTEST, DIVERSITY OF SPORT.

831.   Leonard, George Burr. "Winning Isn't Everything. It's Nothing." Intellectual Digest. 4, No.2 (October 1973), 45-47. WINNING AT ALL COSTS, OBSESSION WITH VICTORY, COMPETITION, REFORM.

832.   McMurtry, John. "Philosophy of a Corner Linebacker." The Nation. 212, No.3 (January 18, 1971), 83-84. SPORT AS RELIGION, BELLICOSE AMERICANS, PRO FOOTBALL, POSSESSION, AGGRESSION, COMPETITION, AUTHORITY, HIERARCHY, RELATIONSHIP BETWEEN FOOTBALL AND POLITICS, FACISM.

833.   Miller, Donna Mae. "Scoring Ethically In Sport." Strategies: A Journal for Physical and Sport Educators. 1 (January 1988), 5-7. WINNING, HONESTY AND DECEPTION, FAIRNESS IN COMPETITION, ETHICS OF WINNING.

834.   Monaghan, Peter. "Tulane University, Beset by Recruiting Violations, Gambling Allegations, To Drop Basketball." The Chronicle of Higher Education. 30, No.6 (April 10, 1985), 31. ABOLITION OF BASKETBALL TEAM, MEN'S BASKETBALL, SCHOLARSHIPS HONORED, TULANE UNIVERSITY.

835.   Moore, Alan C. "Nobody Goes Through Life 10-0-0." The Physical Educator. 30, No.2 (May 1973), 69. WINNING, LOSING, REALITY, BEAUTY IN ATHLETICS, BIG BUSINESS.

836.   Narancic, V. "The Dynamic Training and Integrity of Sportsmen." International Journal of Sport Psychology. 9, No.3 (1978), 227-230. INTEGRITY, EXCELLENCE, CHARACTER.

837.   Neely, Jess. "Ethics." Texas Coach. 30 (November 1985), 12-13. RESPONSIBILITY OF COACHES, SPORTSMANSHIP, CHEATING, UNFAIR COMPETITION.

838.   Nelson, Mariah Burton. "What's More Important Than Winning?" Women's Sports. 6, No.3 (March 1984), 60. WINNING AT ALL COSTS, BIG BUSINESS, MEN'S RULES AND VALUES.

839.   Ostro, Harry. "A Course in Ethical Behavior?" Scholastic Coach. 52, No.4 (November 1982), 6+. ATHLETIC DIRECTORS, MORALITY, CHARACTER, LOYALTY, ROLE MODELS.

840.   Pelton, Barry C. "Moral and Ethical Issues in Sport." The Physical Educator. 44, No.1 (Late Winter 1986), 273-277. RECIPROCAL RELATIONSHIP OF SPORTS AND RELIGION, SPORTSMANSHIP, COMPETITION.

841.   Ray, Ralph. "Baseball or Beanball? What's the Game Coming To?" The Sporting News. 198, No.11 (September 10, 1984), 3+. VIOLENCE, SPORTSMANSHIP, RULES.

842.   Reiger, George. "Competition vs. Sport." Field and Stream. 88, No.3 (July 1983), 27+. WINNING AS PARAMOUNT, CONFLICT, COMPETITIVENESS.

843.   Sadler, William A. Jr. "Competition Out of Bounds: Sport in American Life." Quest. 19 (January 1973), 124-132. COUNTER CULTURE, SPIRIT OF COMPETITION, SPORT AS AN INSTITUTION, SPIRIT OF PLAY, VALUES.

844.   Scott, Jack. "Sport: Scott's Radical Ethic." Intellectual Digest. 2, No.11 (July 1972), 49-50. COMPETITION DEFINED, DEFENSE OF COMPETITION, BENEFIT OF SPORT.

845.   Shames, Laurence. "Heels and Heroes." Esquire. 99, No.1 (January 1983), 26-27. GEORGE STEINBRENNER, HOLMES-COONEY FIGHT, DON REESE, MASTERS TENNIS.

846.   Shelton, Frank W. "Sports and the Competitive Ethic: Death of a Salesman and That Championship Season." Arete: The Journal of Sport Literature. 1, No.2 (Spring 1984), 182. PURSUIT OF ECONOMIC SELF INTEREST, MATERIAL SUCCESS.

847.   Spander, Art. "Blame Civilization for Win At All Costs Code." The Sporting News. 199, No.11 (March 18, 1985), 11. CHARACTER BUILDING, WINNING AT ALL COSTS, SPORTS AS A REFLECTION OF SOCIETY, RECRUITING.

848.   Thuma, Cynthia. "Batter Up! Ethics in School Athletics." Momentum. 11, No.4 (December 1980), 34. CATHOLIC SCHOOL ETHICS, FAIR PLAY, SELF DISCIPLINE, TEACHING PHYSICAL EDUCATION, PRAYER, MASS, RECOGNITION, COACHES.

849.   Underwood, John. "Punishment is a Crime." Sports Illustrated. 49, No.8 (August 21, 1978), 32-38+. FOOTBALL, COACHING PRACTICES, INTIMIDATION NOT SPORTSMANSHIP, AGGRESSION, VIOLENCE, INTENTIONAL INJURIES, REFEREES, CHEAP SHOTS, DIRTY PLAY.

850.   Watterson, John S. III. "The Football Crisis of 1909-1910: The Response of the Eastern 'Big Three'." Journal of Sport History. 8, No.1 (Spring 1981), 33-49. FOOTBALL REFORM, INJURIES, ACADEMICS.

851.   Zeigler, Earle F. "A Reappraisal of Freedom in Competitive Sport." Philosophy in Context. 9 (1979), 54-63. COMPETITION, ACADEMICS, COMMERCIALIZATION.

FAIR PLAY AND SPORTSMANSHIP

Books

852.   Brown, Catherine L. Attitudes Towards Fair Play in Women's Lacrosse. PhD Thesis, The Ohio State University, 1983. FOLLOWING THE SPIRIT OF RULES, MOTIVATION, WINNING, SELF CONCEPT.

853.   Chambers, Robin L. Sportsmanship in a Sporting America: Tradition, Ideal, Reality. Ed.D. Thesis, Temple University, 1984. AMERICAN CULTURE, BASIS FOR SPORTING IDEALS, REFORM.

854.   Dickey, Glenn. Champs and Chumps: An Insider's Look at America's Sports Heroes. San Francisco, CA: Chronicle Books, 1976. JIMMY CONNERS, BILL WALTON, BILLIE JEAN KING, WOODY HAYES, AL DAVIS, HOWARD COSELL, CHARACTER, INTEGRITY, BENEFIT AND HARM, GOOD AND BAD IN SPORTS.

855.   Evans, Richard. Nasty: Ilie Nastase vs. Tennis. New York: Stein and Day, 1979. PRO TENNIS, VERBAL ABUSE, TEMPERMENTAL OUTBURSTS, ABUSE OF OFFICIALS, TENNIS SULLIED.

856.   French Committee for Fair Play. Fair Play. Paris: ICSPE/UNESCO, 1976. DEFINITION OF FAIR PLAY, CHARACTER, INTEGRITY, HONORABLE BEHAVIOR.

857.   McIntosh, Peter C. Fair Play: Ethics in Sport and Education. London: Heinemann Educational Books, 1979. ANCIENT GREEKS, MUSCULAR CHRISTIANITY, GERMANY, UNITED STATES, POLITICS, MORALITY, MORAL EDUCATION, CHILDREN, CHEATING, COMPETITION, VIOLENCE.

858. Morrow, Ellen Ruth. <u>Latitude of Sportsmanship Behavior Deemed Acceptable</u> <u>by Spectators of Basketball Games</u>. PhD Thesis, Texas Woman's University, 1981. CHILDREN, BASKETBALL, COLLEGE SPORTS, CHARACTER DEVELOPMENT, BENEFIT AND HARM, RULES, FANS.

859. Riggs, Doug. <u>Keelhauled: Unsportsmanlike Conduct and the America's Cup</u>. Newport, RI: Seven Seas Press, Inc., 1986. SAILING, ALCOHOL, BUSINESS.

860. Stein, Joe and Diane Clark. <u>Don Coryell, 'Win With Honor'</u>. San Diego, CA: Joyce Press, 1976. PRO FOOTBALL, SAN DIEGO CHARGERS, CHARACTER, INTEGRITY, COACH AND PLAYER RELATIONSHIP.

861. Stokes, Lynette and Fawn Duchaine (eds.). <u>Unsportsmanlike Conduct</u>. Montreal: Eden Press, 1985. NHL, TELEVISION, FOOTBALL, RACISM, BASEBALL, VIOLENCE, RUNNING.

862. Underwood, John. <u>Spoiled Sport: A Fan's Notes on the Troubles of Spectator</u> <u>Sports</u>. Boston: Little Brown and Company, 1984. ACADEMICS, BIG TIME COLLEGE SPORTS, AMATEURISM, OWNERS, VIOLENCE, FANS, TELEVISION.

Articles

863. Adams, Susan B. "Let's Temper the Tantrums." <u>World Tennis</u>. 31, No.8 (January 1984), 6. DISRESPECT, ROLE MODELS, PENALTIES, REFORM, RULES.

864. Adams, Susan B. "The Players and the Powers That Be: They Can Work It Out." <u>World Tennis</u>. 29, No.12 (May 1982), 7. BORG RULE, TELEVISION, POOR CONDUCT.

865. Allison, Maria T. and Thomas J. Templin. "Sportsmanship Dilemma." <u>Physical</u> <u>Education</u>. 39, No.4 (December 1982), 204-207. FAIR PLAY, ETHICS OF COMPETITION, WINNING, ROLE OF COACHES AND PLAYERS, CHARACTER.

866. Arnold, Peter J. "Sport as Fairness." <u>Canadian Association for Health, Physical</u> <u>Education and Recreation Journal</u>. 51, No.1 (September/October 1984), 10-12. DEFINITION, MORAL DIMENSION, EQUITY.

867. Arnold, Peter J. "Three Approaches Toward an Understanding of Sportsmanship." <u>Journal of the Philosophy of Sport</u>. 10 (1983), 61-70. NATURE OF SPORT, FAIR COMPETITION, SPORT AS A FORM OF SOCIAL UNION, SPORT AS A MEANS OF PROMOTION OF PLEASURE, SPORT AS A FORM OF ALTRUISM, KANT.

868. Aspin, David N. "Ethical Aspects of Sports and Games, and Physical Education." <u>Proceedings of the Philosophy of Education Society of Great Britain</u>. 9 (July 1975), 49-71. NATURE OF SPORT, PLAY AND LEISURE, PLEASURE, EXCELLENCE, EGO EXPANDING FUNCTION OF PLAY.

869. Axthelm, Pete. "New Scratch on Athletics." <u>Vogue</u>. 157, No.7 (April 1, 1971), 163. JACK SCOTT, INDIVIDUALISM, JOCK LIBERATION.

870.   Axthelm, Pete. "The Lousy Losers." Newsweek. 85 (June 2, 1975), 50.
       WINNING AT ALL COSTS, LOSING WITH DIGNITY.

871.   "Bad News Boys." World Tennis. 28, No.9 (February 1981), 39. DENNIS
       RALSTON, PANCHO GONZALEZ, EARL COCHELL, CLIFF RICKEY, ILIE NASTASE.

872.   Baker, Russell. "Good Bad Sports." The New York Times Magazine.
       (February 1, 1976), 6. VINCE LOMBARDI, WINNING AT ALL COSTS.

873.   "Baseball Manners." The Economist. 268, No.7039 (July 29, 1978), 31. BILLY
       MARTIN, REGGIE JACKSON, MANAGERS.

874.   Bellamy, Rex. "The Last Word on McEnroe: Cool It." World Tennis. 29,
       No.9 (February 1982), 15. JOHN MCENROE, REFORM, UMPIRE CALLS.

875.   Bodo, Peter. "Sportsmanship: Has It Vanished From the Game?" Tennis. 19,
       No.4 (August 1983), 48+. GOOD BEHAVIOR, CODE OF CONDUCT, TENNIS,
       MORAL DIMENSION OF SPORTSMANSHIP.

876.   Borotra, Jean. "A Plea for Sporting Ethics." The FIEP Bulletin. 48, No.3
       (July-September 1978), 7-10. VALUES, FAIR PLAY, RESPECT.

877.   Chambers, Robin L. "Sportsmanship In a Sporting America: Tradition, Ideal,
       Reality." Journal of Sport History. 14, No.2 (Summer 1987), 252.
       TECHNOLOGY AND SPORTING IDEALS, WINNING.

878.   Costello, Joan. "On Being a Good Sport." Parents. 58, No.3 (March 1983),
       96.   GAMES AS A VEHICLE FOR SOCIAL LEARNING, OBSTACLES TO
       SPORTSMANSHIP, WINNING, FAIR PLAY.

879.   D'Ormesson, Jean. "Fair Play." Olympic Review. 134 (December 1978), 688-
       689. SPORTSMANSHIP, AWARDS, HONORABLE PLAY, CHARACTER.

880.   Dickie, Matthew W. "Fair and Foul Play in the Funeral Games in the Iliad."
       Journal of Sport History. 11, No.2 (Summer 1984), 8-17. WINNING VS. THE
       SPIRIT OF COMPETITION, GREEK ATHLETICS.

881.   Drysdale, Jean. "Understanding the Barnyard Etiquette Syndrome." World
       Tennis. 26, No.3 (August 1978), 74. CHANGE, POINT PENALTY SYSTEM, SPORTS
       WRITING.

882.   Exley, Frederick. "Football '83." Rolling Stone. No.404 (September 15,
       1983), 20-22+. UNSPORTSMANLIKE CONDUCT, DRUGS, GAMBLING, STRIKES.

883.   Feezell, Randolph M. "Sportsmanship." Journal of the Philosophy of Sport. 13
       (1986), 1-14. VIRTUE, CHARACTER, THE VIRTUE OF SPORTSMANSHIP, CHEATER
       AS BAD SPORT, CRITIQUE OF JAMES KEATING, DEFINITION OF SPORTSMANSHIP,
       ARISTOTLE, GOLDEN MEAN.

884.   Grimsley, Jimmie R. "Sportsmanship: An Official Problem." Texas Coach.
       31 (February 1987), 59-61. COMPETITION AND MORALITY, FAIR PLAY, WINNING.

885. Harris, Janet C., Kimberly Blankenship, Marie E. Cawley, Ken R. Crouse, Michael D. Smith, and William A. Winfrey. "Ethical Behavior and Victory in Sport: Value Systems at Play." Journal of Physical Education, Recreation and Dance. 53, No.4 (April 1982), 37+. PROCESS VS. GOAL ORIENTATION TO SPORT, RULES, REFORM.

886. Holsberry, J. "Sportsmanship Athletic Directors Influence Establishment of Code." Interscholastic Athletic Administration. 8, No.4 (Summer 1982), 10-11+. FAIR PLAY, CHARACTER, ROLE OF CODES AND RULES.

887. Horrocks, Robert Norman. "Sportsmanship." Journal of Physical Education and Recreation. 48, No.9 (November/December 1977), 20-21. MORAL REASONING, TEACHING PHYSICAL EDUCATION, YOUTH.

888. Horrocks, Robert Norman. "Sportsmanship: Moral Reasoning." The Physical Educator. 37, No.4 (December 1980), 208-212. TEACHING STRATEGIES, GAME CREATING, MORAL DEVELOPMENT.

889. Hunter, Maxine Grace. "Fair Play: The Girl Athlete in Young Adult Fiction, 1900-1980." North American Society for Sport History Proceedings and Newsletter. (1982), 16-17. AGE OF GENTILITY, AGE OF METAMORPHIS, AGE OF NEW REALISM, CHANGE OF ATTITUDES OF FEMALES TOWARD SPORT.

890. "Is Sportsmanship Dead?" World Tennis. 29, No.5 (October 1981), 41-43. VALUES, CODE OF CONDUCT, FAIRNESS.

891. Kalyn, Wayne. "The Young Challenger Brings a Dark and Brooding Presence." World Tennis. 30, No.2 (July 1982), 54-57. JOHN MCENROE, JUSTICE, PENALTIES.

892. Keating, James W. "Sportsmanship as a Moral Category." Ethics. 75, No.1 (October 1964), 25-35. ATTITUDE AND CONDUCT PROPER TO SPORTS, ESSENCE OF GENUINE SPORTSMANSHIP.

893. Keenan, Francis W. "Justice and Sport." Journal of the Philosophy of Sport. 2 (September 1975), 111-123. EQUALITY, DIGNITY, SPORTSMANSHIP, FAIRNESS, JUSTICE.

894. Keith, Dwight. "Sportsmanship and Honesty." Coach and Athlete. 44, No.5 (March 1982), 10. COACHES, BENEFIT AND HARM, HARRY MEHRE, "OLE MISS".

895. Kirkby, Roy. "Competition and Sportsmanship." Sports Coach. 8 (March 1985), 58-59. FAIR PLAY, WINNING, VALUES, ETHICS, MORAL PRIORITIES.

896. Loehr, Jim E. "Temper Your Tantrums on Court." World Tennis. 32, No.6 (November 1984), 71. TEMPER, COMPETITIVE PLAYERS, WINNING.

897. Lorge, Barry. "Some Thorns Among the Roses." World Tennis. 28, No.12 (May 1981), 63-67. CORRUPTION, INFLATION, DISORDER ON AND OFF THE COURT, PEER PRESSURE, POSITIVE LEADERSHIP.

898.   Marks, Sharon. "Get Out There and Kill 'Em Sportsmanship?" CAHPER Journal. 40 (May 1978), 27. OVEREMPHASIS ON WINNING, FAIRNESS, ETHICS OF COMPETITION.

899.   McAfee, Robert A. "Sportsmanship Attitudes of Sixth, Seventh, and Eighth Grade Boys." The Research Quarterly. 26, No.1 (March 1955), 120. RULES, TEACHING PHYSICAL EDUCATION.

900.   Mills, Joyce. "Will Sportsmanship Strike Out?" Coaching: Women's Athletics. 5, No.4 (September/October 1979), 30-33. SPORTSMANSHIP DEFINED, COACHES AND PLAYERS, FAIR PLAY, WINNING AT ALL COSTS, SPECTATORS.

901.   Neff, Craig. "Booted Out Down Under." Sports Illustrated. 72, No.4 (January 29, 1990), 30-31. JOHN MCENROE, UNSPORTSMANLIKE CONDUCT, OBSCENITIES, CODE VIOLATION, PRO TENNIS.

902.   Nelson, Katherine and Carolyn Cody. "Competition, Cooperation, and Fair Play." International Review of Sport Sociology. 1, No.14 (1979), 97-103. DISHONESTY, VIOLENCE, DEHUMANIZATION.

903.   "No Medals for Good Manners." The Economist. 244, No.6734 (September 16, 1972), 27. MARY PETERS, NATIONALISM, COMPETITION, WINNING.

904.   O'Hare, Joseph A. "Of Many Things." America. 146, No.7 (February 20, 1982), 120. SPORTSMANIA, BRAWLS, VIOLENCE, POINT SHAVING, COACHING.

905.   Paratore, Jean. "Controlling Unsportsmanlike Conduct in Intramural Sports." NIRSA: Journal of the National Intramural-Recreational Sports Association. 3, No.1 (October 1978), 34-36. ABUSE OF OFFICIALS, FIGHTING, COMMUNICATION AS KEY, RULES AND REGULATIONS.

906.   Parsons, Terry W. "Gamesmanship and Sport Ethics." Coaching Review. 7 (July/August 1984), 28-30. MORAL CODE, BENEFIT OF SPORTS, CHARACTER EDUCATION, VALUES.

907.   Pearson, Kathleen M. "Deception, Sportsmanship and Ethics." Quest. 19 (January 1973), 115-118. DEFINITIONAL DECEPTION, STRATEGIC DECEPTION, DELIBERATE FOUL, RULES, FAIR PLAY, COMPETITION.

908.   Scott, Ian. "Setting Standards of Sportsmanship." Action: British Journal of Physical Education. 12, No.1 (January 1981), 4. STANDARDS, CONDUCT ON AND OFF THE FIELD.

909.   "Sportsmanship and Self-Respect." UNESCO Features. No. 574/575 (May 1970), 23-24. INTERNATIONAL FAIR PLAY TROPHY, FRANCISCO BUSCATO, DIGNITY AND SELF RESPECT.

910.   "Teaching Sportsmanship and Values in Athletics." Physical Education Newsletter. No.154 (December 1983), 8. GUIDELINES FOR PLAYERS, SPECTATORS, COACHES, VALUES OF ATHLETICS.

911. Templin, Thomas J. and Maria T. Allison. "The Sportsmanship Dilemma." The Physical Educator. 39, No.4 (December 1982), 204-207. COACHES, WINNING AT ALL COSTS, RULES, OFFICIALS.

912. Voy, Robert O. "The Science of Fair Play." Technology Review. 87, No.6 (August/September 18, 1984), 34+. DRUGS, SPORTS MEDICINE, HUMAN GROWTH HORMONE, BLOOD PACKING, TESTING.

913. Will, George F. "Through Hoops For a Column." Newsweek. 99 (March 15, 1982), 88. EXCELLENCE, STANDARDS OF FAIRNESS, ETHICS OF COMPETITION, CODE OF CONDUCT.

914. Witherell, Mary. "Sportsmanship: Lost and Found?" World Tennis. 36, No.3 (August 1988), 60-63. UNITED STATES TENNIS ASSOCIATION, JUNIOR CHAMPIONSHIPS, PENALTIES, PRESSURE TO WIN, OFFICIALS, PARENTS, CHILDREN.

FANS AND SUPPORTERS

Books

915. Andelman, Eddie. Sports Fans of the World, Unite! New York: Dodd, Mead and Company, 1974. VIOLENCE, MINORITIES, FUN, SPECTATORS.

916. Cohen, Stanley. The Man in the Crowd: Confessions of a Sports Addict. New York: Random House, Inc., 1981. NEW YORK SPORTS SCENE, YANKEES, JETS, NEW YORK KNICKS, MUHAMMAD ALI, TELEVISION.

917. Colton, Larry. Idol Time: Profile in Blazermania. Forest Grove, OR: Timber Press, 1978. PRO BASKETBALL, SPORT AND SOCIETY, PORTLAND TRAILBLAZERS.

918. Dunning, Eric, Patrick Murphy and John Williams. The Roots of Football Hooliganism: An Historical and Sociological Study. New York: Routledge and Kegan Paul, Ltd., 1988. SOCIAL CLASSES, ALIENATION, BRUSSELS RIOT, MYTHS, ALCOHOL, SOCIOLOGY, HISTORY, GOVERNMENT.

919. Guttmann, Allen. Sports Spectators. New York: Columbia University Press, 1986. HISTORY, CIVILIZATION, RIOTS, FAIR PLAY, SPORTSMANSHIP, VIOLENCE, SOCIOLOGY, PSYCHOLOGY.

920. Ingham, Roger (ed.). Football Hooliganism: The Wider Context. London: Inter-Action, Imprints, 1978. SOCCER, EUROPE, ENGLAND, CROWD CONTROL.

921. Johnson, William Oscar. Super Spectator and the Electric Lilliputians. Boston: Little, Brown and Company, 1971. EFFECT OF TELEVISION ON SPORTS, HISTORY, BIG BUSINESS.

922.   Kleinman, Seymour.   A Study to Determine the Factors That Influence the
       Behavior of Sport Crowds.   Unpublished Doctoral Dissertation, Ohio State
       University, 1960. PSYCHOLOGY, SOCIOLOGY, COLLECTIVE BEHAVIOR, COACHES,
       HIGH SCHOOL SPORTS, REFORM.

923.   Roberts, Michael.   Fans! How We Go Crazy Over Sports.   Washington, D.C:
       New Republic Books, 1976. COMMERCIALIZATION, WORSHIP OF SPORT HEROES,
       EXPLOITATION, BIG TIME COLLEGE SPORTS.

924.   Vinnai, Gerhard.   Football Mania: The Players and the Fans: The Mass
       Psychology of Football.   London: Orbach and Chambers Ltd., 1973.
       SPORTSMANIA, PSYCHOLOGY.

925.   White, Cyril Marigo Desmond.   An Analysis of Hostile Outbursts in Spectator
       Sports.   Ph.D. Dissertation, University of Illinois, 1970. AMATEUR FOOTBALL,
       SOCCER, RUGBY, COLLECTIVE BEHAVIOR, INDUSTRIALIZATION, URBANIZATION,
       ECONOMICS, POLITICS.

926.   Williams, John, Eric Dunning and Patrick Murphy.   Hooligans Abroad: The
       Behavior and Control of English Fans in Continental Europe.   London:
       Routledge and Kegan Paul, 1984. SOCCER, ENGLAND, FANS, HISTORY, SOCIAL
       CLASSES.

927.   Wright, Sam.   Crowds and Riots: A Study in Social Organization.   Beverly
       Hills, CA: Sage Publication, Inc., 1978. ROWDYISM, HOOLIGANISM.

       Articles

928.   "Agenda for Europe's Polecats." The Economist. 295, No.7397 (June 8, 1985),
       15-16. CLASS, BRITAIN, FOOTBALL RIOTS.

929.   Anderson, Dean F.   "Sport Spectatorship: Appropriation of An Identity or
       Appraisal of Self." Review of Sport and Leisure. 4, No.2 (Winter 1979), 115-
       127. FAN BEHAVIOR, EVOLUTION OF THE EMPIRICAL SELF.

930.   Arms, Robert L., Gordon W. Russell and Mark L. Sandilands. "Effects on the
       Hostility of Spectators of Viewing Aggressive Sports." Social Psychology
       Quarterly. 42, No.3 (September 1979), 275-279. HOSTILITY, PLAYER AND FAN
       VIOLENCE, HOOLIGANISM, AGGRESSION.

931.   Banerjee, Shib Sanatan. "Violence in Football Stadiums Must Be Stamped Out."
       Olympic Review. 182 (December 1982), 741-743. SOCCER, EUROPE, VIOLENCE,
       FAN SPORTSMANSHIP, SPORTSMANIA, CRIMINAL ACTS, CROWD CONTROL.

932.   Birchall, Heather. "The Hostile Sports Fan." Maclean's. 95, No.1 (January 4,
       1982), 46. VERBAL ABUSE, HOCKEY FANS, TENNIS FANS, VIOLENCE.

933.   "Britain's Shame in Brussels." The Economist. 295, No.7396 (June 1, 1985),
       51-52. VIOLENCE, BRITAIN, BRUSSELS, SPORTSMANSHIP.

934. Bryant, Jennings, Dan Brown, Paul W. Comisky and Dolf Zillmann. "Sports and Spectators: Commentary and Appreciation." Journal of Communication. 32, No.1 (Winter 1982), 109-119. SPECTATORS, CONFLICT, COMPETITION, RELATIONSHIP BETWEEN PLAYERS, TELEVISION.

935. Canter, David. "Football in Its Place." New Statesman. 1, No.2 (June 17, 1988), 29-30. ENGLISH HOOLIGANS, SPECTATORS, REFORM.

936. Case, Bob, H. Scott Greer, and Michael G. Lacourse. "Moral Judgement Development and Perceived Legitimacy of Spectator Behavior In Sport." Journal of Sport Behavior. 10, No.3 (September 1987), 147-156. STAGES OF MORAL JUDGMENT, SPORTSMANSHIP, SPECTATOR BEHAVIOR, REST'S DEFINING ISSUES TEST.

937. Case, Robert W. "Spectator Violence in Sport: An Examination of North American Research Trends." Abstracts of Research Papers. (1983), 117. SPECTATOR VIOLENCE, RESEARCH TRENDS, AGGRESSION LEVELS, COLLECTIVE BEHAVIOR THEORIES, CONFLICT THEORY, FUNCTIONALISM.

938. Case, Robert W. and Robert L. Boucher. "Spectator Violence in Sport: A Selected Review." Journal of Sport and Social Issues. 5, No.2 (Fall/Winter 1981), 1-14. CROWD VIOLENCE, AGGRESSION.

939. Collie, Ashley. "The Centennial of a Troubled Game." Maclean's. 100, No.33 (August 17, 1987), 36-37. BRUSSELS RIOT, FANS, VIOLENCE, REFORMS.

940. Deford, Frank. "Fans to Press: Drop Dead." Sports Illustrated. 45, No.24 (December 13, 1976), 24-27. TICKET SCALPING, SPORTSWRITER'S EXPOSE, FAN RESENTMENT, OKLAHOMA FOOTBALL.

941. Duncan, Margaret Carlisle. "The Symbolic Dimensions of Spectator Sport." Quest. 35, No.1 (1983), 29-36. AESTHETICS, RELIGION, POLITICS, RECURRING LIFE ISSUES, TRANSCENDENCE OF HUMAN LIMITATIONS, INDUSTRIALIZED SOCIETY.

942. Duncan, Margaret Carlisle and Barry Brummett. "The Mediation of Spectator Sport." Research Quarterly for Exercise and Sport. 58, No.2 (June 1987), 168-177. TELEVISION, MEDIA, SPECTATOR SPORT, MEDIATION, SOCIOLOGY OF SPORT.

943. Dunning, Eric, Patrick Murphy and John Williams. "Spectator Violence at Football Matches: Towards a Sociological Explanation." The British Journal of Sociology. 37, No.2 (June 1986), 221-244. FOOTBALL HOOLIGANISM AS A SOCIAL PHENOMENON, AGGRESSIVE MASCULINITY, FORMS OF HOOLIGANISM, OFFICIAL EXPLANATIONS FOR HOOLIGANISM, ACADEMIC EXPLANATIONS, CLASSES, HISTORY, MEDIA.

944. "Football Fanimals: Hooliganism Wreaks Havoc with Soccer." Time. 111, No.16 (April 17, 1978), 43. SOCCER, FOOTBALL, HOOLIGANISM, VIOLENCE, SPORTSMANSHIP.

945.   Gary, Allen. "Code of Conduct for Soccer Spectator." Soccer Journal. 25, No.3 (September 1980), 15-16. BOOING, YELLING AT OFFICIALS AND PLAYERS, ABUSIVE LANGUAGE, GOOD LOSERS, PHILOSOPHY OF ATHLETICS.

946.   Gilbert, Bil and Lisa Twyman. "Violence: Out of Hand in the Stands." Sports Illustrated. 58, No.4 (January 31, 1983), 62-74. ROWDYISM, ALCOHOL, PRO SPORTS, SPORTSMANIA.

947.   Glasser, Brian. "All Boys Together: A New Angle on Soccer Hooliganism." Sport and Leisure. 25, No.6 (January/February 1985), 33. SOCCER HOOLIGANISM, CLASS ISSUES, VIOLENCE, MACHO VALUES.

948.   Greenberg, Peter S. "Wild In the Stands." New Times. 9, No.10 (November 11, 1977), 25-30+. VIOLENCE, SPORTSMANIA, TELEVISION, CROWD CONTROL.

949.   Greer, Donald L. "Spectator Booing and the Home Advantage: A Study of Social Influence in the Basketball Arena." Social Psychology Quarterly. 46, No.3 (September 1983), 252-261. COLLEGE BASKETBALL, FANS, HOME ADVANTAGE, TEAM PERFORMANCE CHANGES, SOCIAL INFLUENCE AND PLAYER PERFORMANCE, SOCIAL INFLUENCE AND REFEREE PERFORMANCE.

950.   Guttmann, Allen. "On the Alleged Dehumanization of the Sports Spectator." Journal of Popular Culture. 14, No.2 (Fall 1980), 275-282. NEO-MARXISM, SPORT VS. POLITICAL ACTIVISM, SPORT AS AN EMOTIONAL SAFETY VALVE FOR CAPITALISM, VIOLENCE, DIVISION OF LABOR IN SPORTS.

951.   Guttmann, Allen. "Sports Spectators from Antiquity to the Renaissance." Journal of Sport History. 8, No.2 (Summer 1981), 5-27. FANS, SPECTATORS, VIOLENCE.

952.   Harrell, W. Andrew. "Verbal Aggressiveness in Spectators at Professional Hockey Games: The Effects of Tolerance of Violence and Amount of Exposure to Hockey." Human Relations. 34, No.8 (1981), 643-655. TOLERANCE OF VIOLENCE AND IRRITABILITY, VERBAL HOSTILITY.

953.   Hearn, Thomas K. "Fans Passions May Be Too Strong for Colleges." The National Sports Daily. (July 11, 1990), 38. SPORTSMANIA, FANATICISM, RELIGION, RITUAL, INTERCOLLEGIATE SPORTS, MEANING OF GAME.

954.   Hill, Dave. "Blighty's Bulldogs." New Statesman. 1, No.2 (June 17, 1988), 15. VIOLENT FANS, LAW AND ORDER, ENGLISH FOOTBALL, CHAUVINISM.

955.   Horn, Jack C. "Fan Violence: Fighting the Injustice of It All." Psychology Today. 19, No.10 (October 1985), 30-31. SPECTATOR VIOLENCE, PERCEIVED INJUSTICE, EQUITY-BASED JUSTICE, RULE CHANGES.

956.   "Is There Any Sport in Rowdyism?" Senior Scholastic. 107, No.2 (September 9, 1975), 25. SPORTSMANSHIP, FANS, PETE ROSE.

957.   Jacobs, Helen Hull. "Spectators Should Behave Themselves Better." Tennis. 14, No.12 (April 1979), 26+. PARTISANSHIP, ITALIAN OPEN, SHOUTING, TENNIS.

958. Kennedy, Carol. "Mob Violence Stalks British Football." Maclean's. 91, No.31 (December 11, 1978), 44-45. SOCCER HOOLIGANS, LEGAL CRACKDOWNS.

959. Kennedy, Ray and Nancy P. Williamson. "Money in Sports: The Fans: Are They Up in Arms?" Sports Illustrated. 49, No.5 (July 31, 1978), 34+. COMMERCIALIZATION, SPECTATOR ATTITUDES, SPORTSMANIA, ATTENDANCE, REVENUES, MONEY, CHANGE, WOMEN AS FANS.

960. Kiersh, Edward. "Controlling Violence in the Grandstands." Police Magazine. 4, No.1 (January 1981), 44-48+. BIG TIME COLLEGE SPORTS, INCREASE IN SPORTS VIOLENCE, SECURITY, FAN VIOLENCE, CROWD CONTROL, ALCOHOL, OVERCROWDING, EGOISM.

961. Kirshenbaum, Jerry. "It's Time for the NHL to Stop the Hooliganism." Sports Illustrated. 54, No.11 (March 9, 1981), 9. NHL, HOCKEY, REFORM, SPORTSMANSHIP.

962. Lacayo, Richard. "Blood in the Stands." Time. 125, No.23 (June 10, 1985), 38-41. ENGLISH SOCCER FANS, BRUSSELS, RIOTS, STADIUM DESIGN, REFLECTION OF SOCIETY.

963. Lamon-Famaey, Annie. "Some Social Status Aspects of Spectators of Sports Events." International Review of Sport Sociology. 16, No.1 (1981), 87-96. EDUCATION LEVEL, DEGREE OF URBANIZATION, WOMEN, CLASSES.

964. Lederman, Douglas. "Citing a 'Disturbing Increase' in Dangerous Incidents, NCAA Backs Penalties for Teams with Unruly Fans." The Chronicle of Higher Education. 34, No.24 (February 24, 1988), A45. THROWING DEBRIS ON THE COURT, PENALTIES, PUNISHMENT, FANS.

965. Lee, Martin J. "From Rivalry to Hostility Among Sports Fans." Quest. 37, No.1 (1985), 38-49. GROUP CONSCIOUSNESS, GROUP DIFFERENTIATION, CONFLICT THEORY, SOCIAL CATEGORIZATION THEORY, SOCIAL COMPETITION THEORY.

966. Leerhsen, Charles. "When Push Comes to Shove." Newsweek. 111 (May 16, 1988), 72-73. ALCOHOL, CROWD CONTROL, BASEBALL, VIOLENCE, BRAWLS.

967. Lejeune, Anthony. "Soccer Madness." National Review. 37, No.13 (July 12, 1985), 31+. BRUSSELS RIOT, BRITISH NATIONAL IMAGE, RESPONSIBILITY OF BRITISH PROFESSIONAL FOOTBALL, HOOLIGANISM, UNDERCLASS, CHAUVINISM.

968. Lennon, Joseph X. and Frederick C. Hatfield. "The Effects of Crowding and Observation of Athletic Events on Spectator Tendency Toward Aggressive Behavior." Journal of Sport Behavior. 3, No.2 (May 1980), 61-68. SPECTATOR VIOLENCE, ZAKS-WALTERS AGGRESSION SCALE, MEDIA.

969. Levy, Linda. "A Study of Sports Crowd Behavior: The Case of the Great Pumpkin Incident." Journal of Sport and Social Issues. 13, No.2 (Fall 1989), 69-91. PRO FOOTBALL, COLLECTIVE BEHAVIOR, NEW JERSEY JETS, ROWDYISM, SPECTATORS.

970.   Lodato, Francis J. "A View on Sports: Vicarious Conflict Resolution. That's What It's All About." International Journal of Sport Psychology. 10, No.1 (1979), 52-53. AGGRESSION, VIOLENCE.

971.   Maguire, Joe. "The Emergence of Football Spectating As a Social Problem 1880-1985: A Figurational and Developmental Perspective." Sociology of Sport Journal. 3, No.3 (September 1986), 217-244. FOOTBALL HOOLIGANISM, CLASS CULTURAL CONTEXT, ENGLAND, PROFESSIONALIZATION, DEMOCRATIZATION, HISTORY.

972.   Meier, Klaus V. "The Ignoble Sports Fan." Journal of Sport and Social Issues. 13, No.2 (Fall 1989), 111-119. SPECTATORS, GARRY SMITH.

973.   Melnick, Merrill J. "The Mythology of Football Hooliganism: A Closer Look at the British Experience." International Review of Sport Sociology. 21, No.1 (1986), 1-21. FAN BEHAVIOR, EMPIRICAL STUDY.

974.   Mewshaw, Michael. "Soccer Italian Style." Sports Illustrated. 72, No.24 (June 11, 1990), 72-76+. SOCCER, EUROPE, SPORTSMANIA, ROWDYISM, VIOLENCE, BIG BUSINESS.

975.   Miller, Stuart. "Personality Correlates of Football Fandom." Psychology: A Journal of Human Behavior. 13, No.4 (November 1976), 7-13. DYNAMICS OF FANDOM, FOOTBALL, FANS AS SENSATION SEEKERS, AGGRESSION, WINNING.

976.   Monaghan, Peter. "Controlling Crowds at Basketball Games: Persistent Problem for Coaches, Officials." The Chronicle of Higher Education. 29, No.24 (February 27, 1985), 33+. LARGER ARENAS, CROWD CONTROL, COACHES INCITING CROWDS.

977.   Neff, Craig. "Can It Happen in the U. S?" Sports Illustrated. 62, No.23 (June 10, 1985), 27. SPECTATOR VIOLENCE, EUROPEAN SOCCER FANS, CLASS DIFFERENCES, ALCOHOL, OPEN SEATING.

978.   Ostro, Harry. "Crowd Control, A Top Priority." Scholastic Coach. 52, No.10 (May/June 1983), 4+. INTERSCHOLASTIC SPORTS, ROWDYISM, SPECTATOR CONTROL, RULES, ROLE OF COACHES, PLAYERS AND DIRECTORS.

979.   Pearton, R. E. and G. Gaskell. "Youth and Social Conflict: Sport and Spectator Violence." International Review of Sport Sociology. 2, No.16 (1981), 57-67. VALUES, VIOLENCE.

980.   Petryszak, Nicholas. "Spectator Sports as an Aspect of Popular Culture--An Historical View." Journal of Sport Behavior. 1, No.1 (February 1978), 14-27. HISTORY OF SPORTS IN NORTH AMERICA, MASS SPECTATOR SPORTS, DEVELOPMENT OF THE SPORTS SPECTACLE, BIG BUSINESS.

981.   "The Price of Brussels." The Economist. 295, No.7397 (June 8, 1985), 57. BRUSSELS, VIOLENCE, SPORTSMANSHIP.

982.   Reston, Jay. "Crisis in American Education: The Threat to School Athletics."
        Coach and Athlete. 43, No.6 (April 1981), 24-25. ECONOMIC BASE OF SCHOOL
        ATHLETICS, BOOSTER CLUBS.

983.   Richards, Jeffrey. "The Hooligan Culture: Violence and the Ethic of the
        Undermass." Encounter. 65, No.4 (November 1985), 15-23. BRUSSELS SOCCER
        RIOT, MOTIVATION OF RIOTERS, CULTURAL CHANGES, REFORM.

984.   "Seeking a Cure for Hooliganitis." The Economist. 307, No.7555 (June 18,
        1988), 56+. SOCIOLOGY, WEST GERMANY, ALCOHOL, REFORM.

985.   Smith, Garry J. "The Noble Sports Fan." The Journal of Sport and Social
        Issues. 12, No.1 (Spring 1988), 54-65. SOCIALIZATION, AESTHETICS, VALUES.

986.   "Soccer Match Riot Mars Image." Beijing Review. 28, No.22 (June 3, 1985),
        7-8. CHINA, WORLD CUP, ADMINISTRATIVE RESPONSIBILITY, REFORM, VIOLENCE.

987.   "Soccer Rioters Sentenced to Jail." Beijing Review. 28, No.26 (July 1, 1985),
        8-9. CHINA, WORLD CUP, SPORTSMANSHIP, VIOLENCE.

988.   Staples, Brent. "Where are the Black Fans?" The New York Times Magazine.
        (May 17, 1987), 26+. BLACK ATTENDANCE, PRO SPORTS, RACISM IN BASEBALL,
        PLAYING POSITIONS.

989.   Taylor, Ian. "Hooligans: Soccer's Resistance Movement." New Society. 14,
        No.358 (August 7, 1969), 204-206. WORKING CLASSES, SOCCER, CROWD
        CONTROL.

990.   Taylor, Ronald A. "For Sports Fans, A Season of Discontent." U. S. News and
        World Report. 93, No.9 (August 30, 1982), 49. DRUGS, UNION PROTESTS, POOR
        PLAY, SCANDAL, FREE AGENT RULES, MEDIA.

991.   Thirer, Joel and Mark S. Rampey. "Effects of Abusive Spectators' Behavior on
        Performance of Home and Visiting Intercollegiate Basketball Teams." Perceptual
        and Motor Skills. 48, No.3 (June 1979), 1047-1053. SPECTATOR BEHAVIOR,
        AGGRESSION, EFFECT ON HOME TEAM.

992.   "The Ugly Sports Fan." Newsweek. 83 (June 17, 1974), 93-94. ROWDYISM,
        FANS, CROWD CONTROL.

993.   Vecsey, George. "A Nation of Sports Fans." The New York Times. 132
        (March 16, 1983), B11. PERVASIVE CHARACTER OF SPORTS IN THE UNITED
        STATES, MILLER LITE REPORT ON AMERICAN ATTITUDES TOWARD SPORTS.

994.   Vulliamy, Edward. "Live by Aggro, Die by Aggro." New Statesman. 109,
        No.2829 (June 7, 1985), 8-10. ITALIAN FOOTBALL, ENGLISH FOOTBALL
        CULTURE, ALCOHOL, VALUES, SPORTS IN SOCIETY.

995.   "Why Are Soccer Fans So Violent?" Discover. 6, No.8 (August 1985), 8-9.
        ENGLISH SOCCER FANS, BELGIUM SOCCER MATCH, WORKING CLASSES, ALCOHOL,
        VERBAL AGGRESSION.

996.   Yaffe, Maurice. "Saving Soccer From Its Supporters." New Statesman. 87, No.2255 (June 7, 1974), 792. WORLD CUP, HOOLIGANISM, ANONYMITY, SELF IDENTITY.

GAMBLING AND POINT SHAVING

Books

997.   Abt, Vicki, James F. Smith, and Eugene Martin Christiansen. The Business of Risk: Commercial Gambling in Mainstream America.   Lawrence, KS: University Press of Kansas, 1985. CULTURE, CONTEXT OF SPORTS, BIG BUSINESS, OFF-TRACK BETTING.

998.   Asinof, Eliot. Eight Men Out: The Black Sox and the 1919 World Series. New York: Holt, Rinehart and Winston, Inc., 1963. CHICAGO WHITE SOX, SCANDAL, HISTORY, PRO BASEBALL.

999.   Cohen, Stanley. The Game They Played. New York: Farrar, Straus and Giroux, Inc., 1977. BASKETBALL, GAMBLING, BRIBERY, POINT SHAVING.

1000.   Rosen, Charles. Scandals of '51: How the Gamblers Almost Killed College Basketball.   New York: Holt, Rinehart and Winston, 1978.   BRIBES, PROFESSIONALISM, AMATEURISM, REFORM.

Articles

1001.   Adams, Susan B.   "Something Should and Can Be Done About Guarantees." World Tennis. 29, No.9 (February 1982), 6. KICKBACKS, RULES, CODE OF CONDUCT, REFORM.

1002.   Axthelm, Pete. "All-American in Trouble." Newsweek. 101 (April 25, 1983), 81-82. ART SCHLICHTER, GAMBLING, BASEBALL.

1003.   Axthelm, Pete. "It's No Sweat for the Angel." Newsweek. 95 (June 2, 1980), 91. ANGEL CORDERO, PREAKNESS, HORSE RACING.

1004.   Axthelm, Pete.   "Lowdown On a High Roller."   Newsweek.   97 (April 20, 1981), 74.   HAROLD SMITH, MUHAMMAD ALI PROFESSIONAL SPORTS, EMBEZZLEMENT, COMPUTER SCAM.

1005.   Axthelm, Pete. "Slap on the Wrist." Newsweek. 75, No.15 (April 13, 1970), 48. DENNY MCLAIN, BASEBALL, GAMBLING, BOWIE KUHN, VALUES.

1006.   Axthelm, Pete. "The Good Doctor." Newsweek. 84, No.10 (September 2, 1974), 63-64. NEW YORK GIANTS, SPORTS MEDICINE, GAMBLING, ANTHONY PISANI, NFL.

1007. Axthelm, Pete. "The Guy With The Edge." Newsweek. 90 (October 3, 1977), 57. DICK SORKIN, GRAND LARCENY, GAMBLING.

1008. Axthelm, Pete. "The Sport of Suckers?" Newsweek. 95 (May 26, 1980), 66. JOSE AMY, HORSE RACING, RACE-FIXING, CON ERRICO, TRIALS.

1009. Axthelm, Pete. "The Wages of Sin." Newsweek. 83 (January 28, 1974), 55. GAMBLING, ATLANTIC COAST CONFERENCE.

1010. "Bookmaker's Dream." Time. 104, No.10 (September 2, 1974), 86-87. ANTHONY PISANI, NEW YORK GIANTS, SPORTS MEDICINE, DOCTORS.

1011. Breen, T. H. "Horses and Gentlemen: The Cultural Significance of Gambling Among the Gentry of Virginia." The William and Mary Quarterly. 34, No.2 (April 1977), 239-257. GAMBLING, RACISM, VALUES, CLASSES, MATERIALISM, CULTURAL DOMINANCE, INDIVIDUALISM, COMPETITION.

1012. Callahan, Tom. "When Scandals Do Not Scandalize." Time. 118, No.22 (November 30, 1981), 99. POINT SHAVING, RICK KUHN, COLLEGE BASKETBALL, TRIAL, RECRUITING EXCESSES, CORRUPTION, SPORTS AND SOCIETY.

1013. Cotton, Anthony. "New Floor for Las Vegas." Sports Illustrated. 59, No.24 (December 5, 1983), 70-75. NBA, LEGALIZED BETTING ON GAMES PLAYED IN LAS VEGAS, SPORTS BETTING, UTAH JAZZ.

1014. D'Angelo, Raymond. "Sports Gambling and the Media." Arena Review. 11 (May 1987), 1-4. DEVIANCE, POINT SPREADS, ODDS.

1015. Dowie, William. "Sport, Gambling, and Death: Bill Barich's Laughing in the Hills." Aethlon. 5, No.2 (Spring 1988), 25-36. HORSE RACING, BETTING, AUTOBIOGRAPHY, EXPOSE, POWER, CONTROL.

1016. Drury, Bob. "Beating the Odds." Sport. 75, No.11 (November 1984), 33-34. GAMBLING, GAME-FIXING, PRO FOOTBALL.

1017. Farrell, Charles S. "NCAA's Council Weighs Policies to Curb Campus Gambling and Drug Use." The Chronicle of Higher Education. 31, No.2 (September 11, 1985), 45. POINT SHAVING, GAMBLING, TULANE UNIVERSITY, DRUG TESTING, COACHES.

1018. Farrell, Charles S. "New Woes at Memphis State: NAACP Blasts Coach, Official Testifies in Gambling Probe." The Chronicle of Higher Education. 30, No.12 (May 22, 1985), 31+. MEMPHIS STATE UNIVERSITY, GAMBLING, DISCRIMINATION.

1019. Figone, Albert J. "Gambling and College Basketball: The Scandal of 1951." Journal of Sport History. 16, No.1 (Spring 1989), 44-61. BIG TIME COLLEGE SPORTS, CORRUPTION, QUEST FOR PROFITS, HISTORY OF SCANDALS, LONG ISLAND UNIVERSITY, MANHATTAN COLLEGE, CITY COLLEGE OF NEW YORK, NEW YORK UNIVERSITY.

1020. "The Fixer: A Hood Sings of Point Shaving." Time. 117, No.8 (February 23, 1981), 102. POINT SHAVING, HENRY HILL, BOSTON COLLEGE.

1021. Flower, Joe. "Betting the Rent." Sport. 75, No.11 (November 1984), 39-40. GAMBLING, PRO FOOTBALL, BILLY YOUNG.

1022. Frey, James H. "Gambling and College Sports: Views of Coaches and Athletic Directors." Sociology of Sport Journal. 1, No.1 (1984), 36-45. GAMBLING, POINT SPREADS, IMPACT OF LEGALIZATION, COLLEGE GAMBLING POLICIES.

1023. Frey, James H. and I. Nelson Rose. "The Role of Sports Information Services in the World of Sports Betting." Arena Review. 2, No.1 (May 1987), 44-51. BETTING, PROFESSIONALIZATION.

1024. Furlong, William Barry. "Out in the Bleachers, Where the Action Is." Harper's. 233, No.1394 (July 1966), 49-53. ANALYSTS, BALL PARK BETTING.

1025. Gammon, Clive. "Tales of Self Destruction." Sports Illustrated. 64, No.10 (March 10, 1986), 64-66+. GAMBLERS ANONYMOUS, RECOVERING GAMBLERS, COMPULSIVE GAMBLERS, LOAN SHARKS.

1026. Grossmann, John. "The Gamble." Esquire. 102, No.3 (September 1984), 25-26. SPORTING WAGES, SUBVERSION OF SPORTS, CAPITALISM VS. PLAY.

1027. Hickman, Dennis P. "Should Gambling Be Legalized for the Major Sport Events?" Journal of Police Science and Administration. 4, No.2 (June 1976), 203-212. REVENUE CONSIDERATIONS, EFFECT ON ORGANIZED CRIME, EFFECT ON OFFICIAL CORRUPTION.

1028. Hill, Henry (ed. by Douglas S. Looney). "How I Put the Fix In." Sports Illustrated. 54, No.8 (February 16, 1981), 14-21. GAME-FIXING, BOSTON COLLEGE BASKETBALL, RIGGED GAMES, POINT SHAVING, PLAYER PAYOFFS, SCANDAL.

1029. Ignatin, George. "Sports Betting." The Annals of the American Academy of Political and Social Science. 474 (July 1984), 168-177. REASONS FOR GAMBLING, HORSE RACING, FOOTBALL, BASKETBALL, BASEBALL, POLICY IMPLICATIONS.

1030. Kaplan, H. Roy. "Sports, Gambling, and Television: The Emerging Alliance." Arena Review. 7, No.1 (February 1983), 1-11. TELEVISION, MONEY, BETTING.

1031. Kaplan, H. Roy. "The Convergence of Work, Sport, and Gambling in America." The Annals of the American Academy of Political and Social Science. 445 (September 1979), 24-38. MEANINGFUL WORK, GAMBLING, BOREDOM, ESCAPISM.

1032. Keteyian, Armen. "The Straight-Arrow Addict." Sports Illustrated. 64, No.10 (March 10, 1986), 74-77+. ART SCHLICHTER, PRO FOOTBALL PLAYER, COMPULSIVE GAMBLER, BIOGRAPHY, STRAIGHT ARROW.

1033. Koppett, Leonard. "Sticky Questions Surround Gambling Issue." The Sporting News. 179, No.5 (February 8, 1975), 6. LEGALIZATION OF GAMBLING, MORALITY OF GAMBLING, ECONOMIC CONSEQUENCES OF GAMBLING, AMATEUR SPORTS.

1034. Leggett, William. "Denny McLain: Ready For His Comeback Try." Sports Illustrated. 32, No.26 (June 29, 1970), 20-21. DETROIT TIGERS, DENNY MCLAIN, SUSPENSION, PRO FOOTBALL, GAMBLING.

1035. Leggett, William. "Judgment at Brooklyn." Sports Illustrated. 52, No.23 (June 2, 1980), 54-58. CON ERRICO, CONVICTIONS, RACE-FIXING, BRIBES, HORSE RACING, GAMBLING.

1036. Looney, Douglas S. "A Big Loss For A Gambling Quarterback." Sports Illustrated. 58, No.22 (May 30, 1983), 30-31. PRO FOOTBALL, NFL SANCTIONS, BALTIMORE COLTS, ART SCHLICHTER, QUARTERBACK, GAMBLING, ADDICTION, SUSPENSION, PETE ROZELLE.

1037. Looney, Douglas S. "Big Trouble at Tulane." Sports Illustrated. 62, No.14 (April 8, 1985), 36-39. TULANE BASKETBALL, POINT SHAVING, SCANDAL, BRIBERY.

1038. Looney, Douglas S. "The Line is Pulled Out of a Hat." Sports Illustrated. 64, No.10 (March 10, 1986), 58-60+. POINT SPREADS, LAS VEGAS, LINE MAKERS.

1039. Looney, Douglas S. "Troubled Times at Memphis State." Sports Illustrated. 62, No.25 (June 24, 1985), 36-38+. MEMPHIS STATE UNIVERSITY, COLLEGE BASKETBALL, COACHES, DANA KIRK, GAMBLING, PLAYER PAYOFFS, POINT SHAVING.

1040. Merwin, John and David Whitford. "Betting Football." Sport. 75, No.11 (November 1984), 26-28. GAMBLING, ILLEGALITY, LEGALIZATION, REFORM.

1041. Middleton, Lorenzo. "FBI Investigating Possible 'Point Shaving' in Big Eight Basketball." The Chronicle of Higher Education. 22, No.9 (April 20, 1981), 7. FBI, POINT SHAVING, OKLAHOMA STATE UNIVERSITY, UNIVERSITY OF NEBRASKA, EXAMINATION OF FILMS OF GAMES.

1042. Middleton, Lorenzo. "Justice Department Looks into Charges of Point Shaving by Former Members of Boston College Basketball Team." The Chronicle of Higher Education. 21, No.20 (January 26, 1981), 5. POINT SHAVING, BOSTON COLLEGE, EXTORTION, GAME-FIXING.

1043. Monaghan, Peter. "Jury Acquits Former Tulane University Basketball Star of Charges He 'Shaved Points' to Aid Gamblers." The Chronicle of Higher Education. 32, No.17 (June 25, 1986), 26. JOHN (HOT ROD) WILLIAMS, FORMER TULANE BASKETBALL STAR, GAMBLING, POINT SHAVING, SPORTS BRIBERY.

1044. Neugeboren, Jay. "Say It Ain't So!" Commonweal. 109, No.5 (March 12, 1982), 143-146. POINT SHAVING, RICK KUHN, BOSTON COLLEGE, COLLEGE BASKETBALL, SCANDALS.

1045. Pascarelli, Peter. "Hustled Off to Prison." The National Sport Daily. (July 20, 1990), 4-5. GAMBLING, PETE ROSE, PRO BASEBALL, PRISON.

1046. Paul, Angus. "Gambling on College Games Said to Be Up Dramatically." The Chronicle of Higher Education. 26, No.1 (March 2, 1983), 1+. ANTI-GAMBLING RESOLUTION, ROLE MODELS, EDUCATION.

1047. Paul, Angus. "Growth of Gambling on College Sports Laid to Publicizing of Point Spreads." The Chronicle of Higher Education. 26, No.6 (April 6, 1983), 17-18. INCREASE IN GAMBLING, SPORTS SERVICES, CAMPAIGN AGAINST GAMBLING.

1048. Paul, Angus. "How Coaches Warn Players of the Dangers of Gambling." The Chronicle of Higher Education. 26, No.1 (March 2, 1983), 17. SPORTS GAMBLING, POINT SHAVING, SCANDALS.

1049. Quinn, Hal. "The Mob, a Death and the NFL." Maclean's. 96, No.5 (January 31, 1983), 41. GAME-FIXING, CARROLL ROSENBLOOM, REFORM.

1050. Rosecrance, John. "The Social World of Sports Betting." Arena Review. 11, No.1 (May 1987), 15-24. SOCIAL WORLD OF GAMBLERS, LAKE TAHOE CASINOS, SOCIOLOGY, TECHNOLOGY.

1051. Samuels, Howard J. "Legalization of Gambling on Sports Events." New York Law Forum. 18, No.4 (Spring 1973), 897-914. SOCIETAL CONTEXT, SOCIAL ACCEPTABILITY, GAME-FIXING.

1052. Sharnik, Morton. "Downfall of a Hero." Sports Illustrated. 32, No.8 (February 23, 1970), 16-21. DETROIT TIGERS, DENNY MCLAIN, BOOKMAKING, MOBSTERS.

1053. Smith, Garry J. "Gambling and Sport." Arena Review. 7, No.1 (February 1983), i-iii. GAMBLING AS A VICTIMLESS CRIME, GAMBLING CONDONED BY THE MASS MEDIA.

1054. Toperoff, Sam. "'Arthur? What Did You Do?'" Sports Illustrated. 64, No.10 (March 10, 1986), 78-80+. 1961 BASKETBALL SCANDAL, POINT SHAVING, BRIBERY, FIXING GAMES, ART HICKS, POINT SHAVER, CONFRONTED BY TEAMMATES, AL SENAVITIS.

1055. Underwood, John. "The True Crisis." Sports Illustrated. 18, No.20 (May 20, 1963), 16-19+. CORRUPTION, VALUES, RECRUITING.

1056. Underwood, John and Morton Sharnik. "The Setting Was Ripe for Scandal." Sports Illustrated. 43, No.23 (December 8, 1975), 36-45. COLLEGE FOOTBALL, SCANDAL, POINT SHAVING, GAMBLING, UNIVERSITY OF KENTUCKY, SONNY COLLINS.

1057. Weiskopf, Herman. "Now It's Yanqui Si, Cuba No." Sports Illustrated. 58, No.24 (June 13, 1983), 58-61. GAME-FIXING, BARBARA GARBEY, PROBATION, CUBA, DETROIT TIGERS.

1058. "Willie's Farewell: Mays Is Now In The Chips." Time. 114, No.20 (November 12, 1979), 122. GAMBLING CASINO, WILLIE MAYS, BASEBALL.

1059. Ziegel, Vic. "The Belmont's Muddy Track." New York. 13, No.23 (June 9, 1980), 56-57. RACE-FIXING, BRIBES, CON ERRICO, GAMBLING.

1060. Zimmerman, Paul and Douglas S. Looney. "Has It All Been Thrown Away?" Sports Illustrated. 58, No.16 (April 18, 1983), 40-47. GAMBLING, ART SCHLICHTER, FOOTBALL, BALTIMORE COLTS.

IDEAL AND MEANING

Books

1061. Allen, Dorothy J. and Brian W. Fahey (eds.). Being Human in Sport. Philadelphia: Lea and Febiger, 1977. TEACHING PHYSICAL EDUCATION, RELIGION, SEXUALITY.

1062. Arnold, Peter J. Meaning in Movement, Sport and Physical Education. London: Heinemann, 1979. PLAY, METAPHYSICS, PHILOSOPHY, AESTHETICS, DEFINITION, VALUE OF SPORT.

1063. Auguet, Roland. Cruelty and Civilization: The Roman Games. London: George Allen and Unwin Ltd., 1972. GLADIATORIAL COMBATS, CHARIOT RACES.

1064. Bradley, Bill. Life on the Run. New York: Quadrangle/New York Times Book Company, 1976. HEROES, MONEY.

1065. Brasch, R. How Did Sport Begin? A Look at the Origins of Man at Play. New York: David McKay Company, Inc., 1972. GENESIS OF SPORTS, MYTHS, HISTORY, DEFINITION, ROLE OF SPORT IN SOCIETY.

1066. Daley, Robert. Only a Game. New York: New American Library, 1967. PRO FOOTBALL, WALLACE CRAIG, SEX.

1067. Fuller, Peter. The Champions: The Secret Motives in Games and Sport. London: Allen Lane, 1978. BOBBY FISCHER, MUHAMMAD ALI, EL CORDOBES, JACKIE STEWART, ALBERTO ASCARI, MALCOLM CAMPBELL, DONALD CAMPBELL, COMPETITION, FANS, PSYCHOLOGY, FREUDIAN ANALYSIS.

1068. Gallwey, W. Timothy. The Inner Game of Tennis. New York: Random House, Inc., 1974. COMPETITION, WINNING.

1069. Halberstam, David.   The Amateurs.   New York: William Morrow and Company, 1985.   AMERICAN SPORTS MYTHOLOGY, COURAGE, SACRIFICE, COMPETITION, ROWERS, HARVARD, YALE.

1070. Hans, James S.   The Play of the World.   Amherst, MA: The University of Massachusetts Press, 1981.   PLAY, DESIRE, LANGUAGE, AESTHETICS, SOCIOLOGY, ETHICAL ISSUES.

1071. Harris, Harold Arthur.   Greek Athletes and Athletics.   Bloomington, IN: Hutchinson, 1964.   WOMEN, HISTORY, OLYMPICS.

1072. Hemery, David.   The Pursuit of Sporting Excellence: A Study of Sport's Highest Achievers.   Champaign IL: Human Kinetics Publishers, 1986.   SPECIALIZATION, COACH-ATHLETE RELATIONS, COMPETITION, GAMESMANSHIP, DRUGS, RELIGION.

1073. Herrigel, Eugen.   Zen in the Art of Archery.   New York: Vintage Books, 1971. STATE OF UNCONSCIOUSNESS.

1074. Koppett, Leonard.   The Essence of the Game is Deception: Thinking About Basketball.   Boston: Little, Brown and Company 1973.   RULES, COACHES, PLAYERS, REFEREES, FANS, SPORTS WRITERS, MEDIA, GAME-FIXING.

1075. Kretchmar, Robert Scott.   A Phenomenological Analysis of the Other in Sport. Unpublished Thesis, University of Southern California, 1971.   PHENOMENOLOGY, OPPONENTS, TEAMMATES, OFFICIALS, COACHES, SPECTATORS, BASEBALL, BASKETBALL, CROSS COUNTRY.

1076. Leonard, George Burr.   The Ultimate Athlete: Re-visioning Sports, Physical Education and the Body.   New York: Viking Press, 1975.   IMPORTANCE OF NON-COMPETITIVE PLAY, EXISTENTIALISM, PHILOSOPHY, CHANGE, REFORM.

1077. Metheny, Eleanor.   Movement and Meaning.   New York: McGraw-Hill Book Company, 1968.   DANCE, SPORTS, EXERCISE.

1078. Miller, Donna Mae and Kathryn R. E. Russell.   Sport: A Contemporary View. Philadelphia: Lea and Febiger, 1971.   SPECTATORS, HEROES, INTERNATIONAL SPORTS, CULTURE, ARTS, WOMEN, BIG BUSINESS, PHYSICAL EDUCATION, ACADEMICS.

1079. Molloy, John W. Jr. and Richard C. Adams (eds.).   The Spirit of Sport: Essays About Sport and Values.   Bristol, IN: Wyndham Hall Press, 1987.   DEFINITION OF SPORT, IDEAL AND MEANING, BENEFIT OF SPORT.

1080. Rosen, Charles.   God, Man and Basketball Jones: The Theory and Practice of Professional Basketball.   New York: Holt, Rinehart and Winston, Inc., 1979. COACHES, REFEREES, MEDIA, FANS.

1081. Rozin, Skip.   One Step From Glory: On the Fringe of Professional Sports.   New York: Simon and Schuster, Inc., 1979.   BASEBALL, BASKETBALL, FOOTBALL, MARGINAL ATHLETES, BIG BUSINESS, EXPLOITATION.

1082. Sabo, Donald F. Jr. and Ross T. Runfola. Jock: Sports and Male Identity. Englewood Cliffs, NJ: Prentice Hall, 1980. RELATIONSHIP BETWEEN SPORTS AND MASCULINITY, SPORT AS A SOCIALIZING AGENT, VIOLENCE, WOMEN, FANS, REFORM.

1083. Simon, Robert L. Sports and Social Values. Englewood Cliffs, NJ: Prentice Hall, 1985. EQUALITY, REWARDS, EXCELLENCE, VIOLENCE, ETHICAL ISSUES, ROLE OF SPORTS IN SOCIETY.

1084. Slovenko, Ralph and James Allen Knight (eds.). Motivations in Play, Games and Sports. Springfield, IL: Charles C. Thomas, Publisher, 1967. PLAY AND HUMAN DEVELOPMENT, CHILDREN, RELIGION, COACHES.

1085. Stanford, Derek. The Arts of Sport and Recreation. London: Thomas Nelson and Sons, 1967. AESTHETICS, FOOTBALL, POETRY, PHILOSOPHY.

1086. Suits, Bernard. The Grasshopper: Games, Life and Utopia. Toronto: University of Toronto Press, 1978. CHEATING, AMATEURISM, PROFESSIONALISM, REFORM.

1087. Whiting, H. T. A. and Don W. Masterson (eds.). Readings in the Aesthetics of Sport. London: Lepus Books, 1974. ART, DANCE, IDEAL AND MEANING, MOVEMENT.

1088. Will, George F. Men at Work: The Craft of Baseball. New York: Macmillan Publishing Company, 1990. BASEBALL, EXCELLENCE, VALUES, TONY LA RUSSA, OREL HIRSHISER, TONY GWYNN, CAL RIPKIN JR., WORK HABITS, VIRTUE.

Articles

1089. Aldrich, Virgil C. "A Theory of Ball-Play." Psychological Review. 44, No.5 (September 1937), 395-403. MARKSMANSHIP, DEFINITION OF BALL-PLAY, NATURE OF PLAY.

1090. Anchor, Robert. "History and Play: Johan Huizinga and His Critics." History and Theory: Studies in the Philosophy of History. 17, No.1 (1978), 63-93. PLAY'S CONTRIBUTION TO CULTURE, DEFINITION OF PLAY, MEANING OF EXISTENCE.

1091. Arnold, Peter J. "Aesthetic Aspects of Sports." International Review of Sport Sociology. 13, No.3 (1978), 45-63. RELATIONSHIP OF SPORT AND ART, NATURE OF SPORT, AESTHETIC PERCEPTION OF SPORT, PHENOMENOLOGY.

1092. Arnold, Peter J. "Agency, Action and Meaning 'In' Movement: An Introduction to Three New Terms." Journal of the Philosophy of Sport. 6 (Fall 1979), 49-57. MORAL RESPONSIBILITY, DEFINITIONS: MOVISTRUCT, MOVICEPT, AND MOVISYMBOL.

1093. Aspin, David N. "On the Nature and Purposes of a Sporting Activity: The Connection Between Sport, Life and Politics." Physical Education Review. 9, No.1 (Spring 1986), 5-13. VALUES, ROWING, RELATIONSHIP BETWEEN SPORTS AND GAMES.

1094. Baumbach, Jonathan. "The Aesthetics of Basketball." Esquire. 73, No.1 (January 1970), 140-146. MOVEMENT, AESTHETICS. FANATICS, FANS, PRO BASKETBALL, NEW YORK KNICKS.

1095. Binkley, Luther J. "Presidential Address: From the Point of View of Sport." Journal of the Philosophy of Sport. 6 (Fall 1979), 101-116. DEFINITION OF SPORT, AESTHETICS, LEGITIMACY OF SPORT, SPORTS POINT OF VIEW, RULES.

1096. Bredemeier, Brenda Jo and David L. Shields. "Divergence In Moral Reasoning About Sport and Everyday Life." Sociology of Sport Journal. 1, No.4 (December 1984), 348-357. MORAL ADAPTATIONS OF SPORTS PARTICIPANTS, HAAN'S INTERACTIONAL MODEL OF MORAL DEVELOPMENT, INTERACTIONAL MORALITY.

1097. Chastel, Andre. "The Element of Play in Twentieth Century Art." Diogenes. 50 (Summer 1965), 1-12. AESTHETICS, PLAY, ART.

1098. Coleman, James S. "Athletics in the High School." The Annals of the American Academy of Political and Social Science. 338 (November 1961), 33-43. VALUES OF HIGH SCHOOL STUDENTS, DEMOCRATIZING EFFECTS OF SPORTS, MOTIVATION, IDENTITY WITH SCHOOL THROUGH SPORTS, ATHLETICS IN THE STATUS SYSTEM.

1099. Cook, Tom. "Some Typologies Relevant to the Philosophic Study of Sport." Journal of the Philosophy of Sport. 5 (Fall 1978), 63-70. GAMESTERS, PLAYERS, COMPETITORS, JOCKS.

1100. Cordner, Christopher. "Differences Between Sport and Art." Journal of the Philosophy of Sport. 15 (1988), 31-47. AESTHETICS, DEFINITION, WINNING.

1101. Coutts, Curtis A. "Freedom in Sport." Quest. 10 (May 1968), 68-71. FREEDOM, MOTIVATION, VALUES.

1102. D'Agostino, Fred. "The Ethos of Games." Journal of the Philosophy of Sport. 8 (Fall 1981), 7-18. MORAL RULES, SPORTSMANSHIP, DEFINITION, PENALTIES.

1103. Doherty, Kenneth J. "Why Men Run." Quest. 2 (April 1964), 60-66. PHYSIOLOGY, HISTORY, SOCIOLOGY, PSYCHOLOGY, CULTURE.

1104. Eggerman, Richard W. "Games and the Action-Guiding Force of Morality." Philosophical Topics. 13, No.2 (Spring 1985), 31-36. CATEGORICAL IMPERATIVE, KANT, RULES OF MORALITY, CRITIQUE OF PHILIPPA FOOT.

1105. Fairchild, David L. "Prolegomena to an Expressive Function of Sport." Journal of the Philosophy of Sport. 14 (1987), 21-33. SPORTS EXPRESS VALUES, MEANING OF PLAY, NEGATIVE AND POSITIVE VALUES, PHENOMENOLOGY, EXCELLENCE.

1106. Feezell, Rudolph M. "Play, Freedom, and Sport." Philosophy Today. 25, No.2/4 (Summer 1981), 166-175. DEFINITION OF PLAY AND SPORTS, JOHAN HUIZINGA, THEORIES OF FREEDOM, SPORTS AS A FORM OF PLAY.

1107. Fetters, Jan L. "Sport, Myth and the Courage of Self-Creation." Quest. 30 (Summer 1978), 36-45. COURAGE, SELF CREATION, WINNING, OBJECTIVE MEASUREMENT, ABSTRACTION AND GENERALIZATION, MYTH OF SEPARATENESS, MYTH OF CONTROL AND POWER OVER OTHERS, MYTH OF UNCHANGING SELF.

1108. Fink, Eugen. "The Ontology of Play." Philosophy Today. 4, No.2/4 (Summer 1960), 95-109. DEFINITION OF PLAY, ELEMENTS OF PLAY, TYPES OF PLAY, CHARACTER OF PLAY.

1109. Fox, Richard M. "The Honorific Meaning of Sport." Philosophical Context. 9 (1979), 84-94. IDEAL AND MEANING, DEFINITION OF SPORT, VALUES, BENEFIT OF SPORTS.

1110. Fox, Richard M. "The So-Called Unreality of Sport." Quest. 34, No.1 (1982), 1-11. SPORT AS UNPRODUCTIVE, CONSTITUTIVE RULES.

1111. Fraleigh, Warren P. "Different Educational Purposes: Different Sport Values." Quest. 42, No.1 (April 1990), 77-92. VALUES, DISCIPLINE, SELF ACTUALIZATION.

1112. Fraleigh, Warren P. "Sport-Purpose." Journal of the Philosophy of Sport. 2 (September 1975), 74-82. PROBLEMS IN DISCUSSING PURPOSE OF SPORT, DIVERSITY OF IDEAS.

1113. Fraleigh, Warren P. "The Sports Contest and Value Priorities." Journal of the Philosophy of Sport. 13 (1986), 65-78. VALUES, FUN, THE GOOD SPORTS CONTEST, KNOWLEDGE AS A VALUE, VALUE THEORY FOR SPORT, NATURE OF THE SPORT CONTEST, MOVING MASS IN SPACE AND TIME--PRIME VALUE.

1114. Garrett, Roland. "The Metaphysics of Baseball." Philosophy Today. 20, No.3/4 (Fall 1976), 209-226. MEANING OF BASEBALL, BASEBALL'S LINK TO AMERICAN HISTORY.

1115. Hardy, Stephen H. "The Medieval Tournament: A Functional Sport of the Upper Class." Journal of Sport History. 1, No.2 (Fall 1974), 91-105. JOUSTING, RELATIONSHIP OF SPORTS AND WAR, SOCIAL EXCLUSIVENESS.

1116. Harper, William. "Literature: A Messenger of Truth." Journal of Physical Education, Recreation and Dance. 53, No.2 (February 1982), 37-39. INSTRUCTIVE CAPACITY OF LITERATURE, MEANING OF SPORT.

1117. Hinman, Lawrence M. "Nietzsche's Philosophy of Play." Philosophy Today. 18, No.2/4 (1974), 106-124. NIETZSCHE'S IDEAL MAN, GREEK CULTURE, NIHILISM, WILL TO POWER, CREATIVE PLAY.

1118. Hoffman, Shirl J. "The Athletae Dei: Missing the Meaning of Sport." Journal of the Philosophy of Sport. 3 (September 1976), 42-51. THEOLOGY OF PLAY, FELLOWSHIP OF CHRISTIAN ATHLETES, MOTIVATION.

1119. Hyland, Drew A. "And That Is the Best Part of Us: Human Being and Play." Journal of the Philosophy of Sport. 4 (Fall 1977), 36-49. DEFINITION OF PLAY, PLATO, PLAY AS RESPONSIVE OPENNESS.

1120. Jeu, Bernard. "What is Sport?" Diogenes. 80 (Winter 1972), 150-163. DEFINITION OF SPORT, POLITICS, COMPETITION, WAR AND SPORT, SPORT AS A REFLECTION OF CIVILIZATION, ECONOMY, CLASS, SOCIAL CHANGE.

1121. Kaelin, E. F. "The Well-Played Game: Notes Toward an Aesthetics of Sport." Quest. 10 (May 1968), 16-28. COMPETITION, BENEFIT OF SPORT, EXCELLENCE.

1122. Keating, James W. "The Urgent Need for Definitions and Distinctions." The Physical Educator. 28 (March 1971), 41-42. LEISURE, GAMES, PLAY, SPORT, DEFINITION, WINNING, AMATEURS, SPORTSMANSHIP, ATHLETES AS ENTERTAINERS.

1123. Keenan, Francis W. "The Athletic Contest As a 'Tragic' Form of Art." International Review of Sport Sociology. 10, No.1 (1975), 39-54. ART, COMPETITION, BENEFIT AND HARM, AESTHETICS.

1124. Kidd, Thomas R. "Applying Sartre's Existential Psychoanalysis to Sport." The Physical Educator. 35, No.3 (October 1978), 134-136. EXISTENTIALISM, SOCIAL PRESSURE, PERSONAL CONTROL.

1125. Kretchmar, Robert Scott. "On Beautiful Games." Journal of the Philosophy of Sport. 16 (1989), 34-43. DEFINITION, GAME, PLAY, SPORT, DIVING, GYMNASTICS, AESTHETICS.

1126. Kretchmar, Robert Scott. "Ontological Possibilities: Sport as Play." Philosophic Exchange. 1, No.3 (Summer 1972), 113-124. DEFINITION OF SPORT AND PLAY, ESSENCE, MEANING OF SELF, PLAY AND CULTURE.

1127. Kretchmar, Robert Scott. "The Strange Supremacy of Knowledge in Sport From the Moral Point of View: A Response to Fraleigh." Journal of the Philosophy of Sport. 13 (1986), 79-88. VALUES, CRITIQUE OF KNOWLEDGE AS A VALUE IN SPORT, MORAL POINT OF VIEW, EXCELLENCE, PRODUCING GOOD, NON-MORAL VALUE.

1128. Kuntz, Paul Grimley. "Paul Weiss on Sports as Performing Arts." International Philosophical Quarterly. 17, No.2 (June 1977), 147-165. PHILOSOPHY, AESTHETICS, ART, COMPARISON OF SPORT AND ART, EXCELLENCE, MOTIVATION, MIND AND BODY, RULES, PROFESSIONALISM.

1129. Kupfer, Joseph. "Purpose and Beauty in Sport." Journal of the Philosophy of Sport. 2 (1975), 83-90. DEFINITION, MEANING, AESTHETICS, COMPETITION.

1130. Lenk, Hans. "Herculean 'Myth' Aspects of Athletics." Journal of the Philosophy of Sport. 3 (September 1976), 11-21. FASCINATION WITH SPORT, TECHNOLOGY, MYTHS.

1131. Lenk, Hans. "Toward a Philosophical Anthropology of the Olympic Athlete and as the Achieving Being. Can and/or How Can a Philosopher Understand Athletes and Olympic Athletes?" Report of the 22nd Session of the International Olympic Academy. (1985), 163-177. EPISTEMOLOGY, ACADEMIC STUDY, PHILOSOPHICAL INQUIRY INTO SPORT, CONCEPT OF THE SELF.

1132. Lowe, Benjamin. "The Aesthetics of Sport: The Statement of a Problem." Quest. 16 (June 1971), 13-17. DEFINITION OF SPORTS, PHILOSOPHY.

1133. Loy, John W. Jr. "The Nature of Sport: A Definitional Effort." Quest. 10 (May 1968), 1-15. SPORT AS A SOCIAL SITUATION, SPORT AS A SOCIAL INSTITUTION, SPORT AS AN INSTITUTIONALIZED GAME, SPORT AS A GAME OCCURRENCE.

1134. McBride, Frank. "Toward a Non-Definition of Sport." Journal of the Philosophy of Sport. 2 (September 1975), 4-11. NATURE OF SPORT, RULES, DEFINITION OF SPORT.

1135. Meier, Klaus V. "A Meditation on Critical Mass in the Philosophy of Sport." Journal of the Philosophy of Sport. 10 (1983), 8-20. LITERATURE ON THE PHILOSOPHY OF SPORT, FUTURE, RESEARCH METHODS, QUALITATIVE INVESTIGATION.

1136. Meier, Klaus V. "Cartesian and Phenomenological Anthropology: The Radical Shift and Its Meaning for Sport." Journal of the Philosophy of Sport. 2 (September 1975), 51-73. CHANGES, ANTHROPOLOGY, PHENOMENOLOGY.

1137. Meier, Klaus V. "Performance Prestidigitation." Journal of the Philosophy of Sport. 16 (1989), 13-33. DEFINITION OF GAME, PLAY, SPORT, COMPETITION, CONSTITUTIVE RULES, REGULATORY RULES, DIVING, PRELUSORY GOALS.

1138. Meier, Klaus V. "Triad Trickery: Playing with Sport and Games." Journal of the Philosophy of Sport. 15 (1988), 11-30. DEFINITION, GAMES, PLAY, SPORT, INSTITUTIONALIZATION, RULES, BERNARD SUITS.

1139. Meridith, Lawrence. "The Sensuous Sportsman: An Interpretation of Athletics." 75th Proceedings of the National College Physical Education Association for Men, Annual Meeting, New Orleans. (January 9-12, 1987), 39-45. NATURE OF ATHLETICS, NATURE OF SPORT, ACADEMIC STUDY OF SPORT, CONCEPT OF ATHLETIC SELF.

1140. Mitchell, Robert. "Sport As Experience." Quest. 24 (Summer 1975), 28-33. PHILOSOPHY, PHENOMENOLOGY, AESTHETICS.

1141. Morgan, William John. "On the Path Towards an Ontology of Sport." Journal of the Philosophy of Sport. 3 (September 1976), 25-34. JOHAN HUIZINGA, ELLEN GERBER.

1142. Morgan, William John. "Social Philosophy of Sport: A Critical Interpretation." Journal of the Philosophy of Sport. 10 (1983), 33-51. RADICAL SOCIAL PHILOSOPHY OF SPORT LITERATURE, CRITICAL THEORY.

1143. Morgan, William John. "Some Aristotelian Notes on the Attempt to Define Sport." Journal of the Philosophy of Sport. 4 (Fall 1977), 15-35. DEFINITION OF SPORT, NON-ESSENTIALIST THEORY, ARISTOTLE'S "FOCAL MEANING."

1144. Morgan, William John. "The Logical Incompatibility Thesis and Rules: A Reconsideration of Formalism as an Account of Games." Journal of the Philosophy of Sport. 14 (1987), 1-20. LOGICAL INCOMPATIBILITY BETWEEN WINNING AND CHEATING, FORMALISM THEORY, CHEATING, WINNING, ANTIFORMALISM, DEFINITION OF GAMES.

1145. Novak, Michael. "The Game's the Thing: A Defense of Sports as Ritual." Columbia Journalism Review. 15, No.1 (May/June 1976), 33-38. SPORTS REPORTERS, TELEVISION, CULTURE, FUNCTION OF SPORTS.

1146. Osterhoudt, Robert G. "The Term Sport--Some Thoughts on a Proper Name." International Journal of Physical Education. 14, No.12 (Summer 1977), 11-16. DEFINITION, GAME, PLAY, COMPETITION, DISTINCTION BETWEEN SPORT AND DANCE, EXERCISE, MOVEMENT, PHYSICAL EDUCATION, PLAY AND RECREATION.

1147. Roberts, Terence J. "Sport, Art, and Particularity: The Best Equivocation." Journal of the Philosophy of Sport. 13 (1986), 49-63. FUNCTION OF SPORT, NATURE OF SPORT, PURPOSES OF ART AND SPORT COMPARED, WINNING, SCORING, AESTHETICS.

1148. Shainberg, Lawrence. "Finding 'The Zone'." The New York Times Magazine. 88 (April 9, 1989), 35-39. PSYCHOLOGICAL ABILITY, MOTIVATION.

1149. Steel, Margaret. "What We Know When We Know a Game." Journal of the Philosophy of Sport. 4 (Fall 1977), 96-103. LEARNING GAMES, TEACHING PHYSICAL EDUCATION.

1150. Stone, Roselyn E. "Human Movement Forms as Meaning-Structures: Prolegomenon." Quest. 23 (January 1975), 10-17. SKIING, MEANING-BEARERS, PERCEIVERS, RELATEDNESS, RULES.

1151. Suits, Bernard. "The Trick of the Disappearing Goal." Journal of the Philosophy of Sport. 16 (1989), 1-12. DEFINITION OF GAME, PLAY, SPORT, DIVING, CONSTITUTIVE RULES, GYMNASTICS, PRELUSORY GOALS.

1152. Suits, Bernard. "Tricky Triad: Games, Play, and Sport." Journal of the Philosophy of Sport. 15 (1988), 1-9. DEFINITION, GAMES, PLAY, SPORT, PERFORMANCE, AMATEURISM, PROFESSIONALISM.

1153. Tangen, Jan Ove. "Defining Sport: A Pragmatic-Contextual Approach." International Journal of Physical Education. 22, No.2 (1985), 17-24. DEFINITION OF SPORT, HISTORY, SOCIOLOGY.

1154. Thomas, Carolyn E. "Injury As Alienation in Sport." Journal of the Philosophy of Sport. 16 (1989), 44-58. ESSENTIAL UNITY, EXISTENTIAL ESTRANGEMENT, JEAN PAUL SARTRE, PAUL TILLICH, EXCELLENCE, ANOMIE, SELF ESTRANGEMENT.

1155. Thomas, Carolyn E. "The Sport Contest As Drama." Journal of Physical Education, Recreation and Dance. 53, No.1 (January 1982), 39-40. COMPETITION, DEFINITION, AESTHETICS, SPORT AS ARTISTIC AND AESTHETIC, MASTERY OF TECHNIQUE, ATHLETIC COMMITMENT, PURSUIT OF EXCELLENCE, DESIRE TO WIN.

1156. Thomas, Carolyn E. "Thoughts on the Moral Relationship of Intent and Training in Sport." Journal of the Philosophy of Sport. 10 (1983), 84-91. STAGES IN SPORT PARTICIPATION, INTENT, PREPARATION, INVOLVEMENT, COMMITMENT, RESOLUTION.

1157. Thomas, Duane L. "A Definitional Context For Some Socio-Moral Characteristics of Sport." Journal of the Philosophy of Sport. 6 (Fall 1979), 39-47. PHILOSOPHY, DEFINITION, MORAL DIMENSION, SOCIOLOGICAL.

1158. Thomas, Duane L. "Sport: The Conceptual Enigma." Journal of the Philosophy of Sport. 3 (September 1976), 35-41. SPORT AS A DISCIPLINE, DEFINITION OF SPORT, GAMES, RULES, COMPETITION, INSTITUTIONALIZATION OF SPORT, MOTIVATION.

1159. Umphlett, Wiley Lee. "The Dynamics of Fiction on the Aesthetics of the Sport Film." Arete: The Journal of Sport Literature. 1 (Spring 1984), 113-121. SELF FULFILLMENT, FILM TECHNIQUE.

1160. VanderZwaag, Harold J. "Sport: Existential or Essential." Quest. 12 (May 1969), 47-56. GROUP CONFORMITY, INDIVIDUALISM, ESSENTIALISM, PHILOSOPHY, EXISTENTIALISM.

1161. VanderZwaag, Harold J. "The Four Cornerstones and Gestalt of the Institutionalized Game of Sport." Philosophy in Context. 9 (1979), 76-83. ROLES OF ATHLETES, COACH, OFFICIAL, SPECTATOR.

1162. Voigt, David Quentin. "Myths After Baseball: Notes on Myths in Sports." Quest. 30 (Summer 1978), 46-57. BASEBALL AS A REFLECTION OF SOCIETY, OWNER OPPRESSION, CORRUPTION.

1163. Watson, Scott B. "The Legitimation of Sport: Pindar and Weiss." Quest. 35, No.1 (1983), 37-45. RECORDS, GREEK ATHLETES, MODERN ATHLETICS, PAUL WEISS, PINDAR, ALLEN GUTTMANN, EXCELLENCE, IMMORTALITY.

1164. Wenkart, Simon. "The Meaning of Sports for Contemporary Man." Journal of Existential Psychiatry. 3, No.12 (Spring 1963), 397-404. TIME, HUMAN ACTIVITY, ALIENATION.

1165. Wertz, Spencer K. "Sports: VanderZwaag's View Appraised." Journal of Thought. 13, No.2 (November 1978), 300-309. KNOWLEDGE ACQUIRED THROUGH SPORT, HAROLD VANDERZWAAG.

1166. Zeigler, Earle F. "In Sport, As In All of Life, Man Should Be Comprehensible to Man." Journal of the Philosophy of Sport. 3 (1976), 121-126. FREEDOM, AUTONOMY, NATURE OF MAN, INTERDEPENDENCE OF SPORT AND CULTURE, INTERCOLLEGIATE ATHLETICS.

1167. Ziff, Paul. "A Fine Forehand." Journal of the Philosophy of Sport. 1 (1974), 92-109. TENNIS, AESTHETICS, PLAY, ART.

REFEREES, UMPIRES, AND OFFICIALS

Books

1168. Holst, Art. Sunday Zebras. Lake Forest, IL: Forest Publishings, 1980. OFFICIALS, PRO FOOTBALL, NFL, VALUES.

1169. Honig, Donald. The Man in the Dugout: Fifteen Big League Managers Speak Their Minds. Chicago: Follett Publishing Company, 1977. MANAGERS, BASEBALL, WINNING, RELATIONSHIP OF PLAYERS AND COACHES.

1170. Powers, Richie. Overtime! An Uninhibited Account of a Referee's Life in the NBA. New York: David McKay and Company, Inc., 1975. SPECTATORS, PLAYERS, COACHES, RULES.

1171. Schachter, Norm. Close Calls: The Confessions of a NFL Referee. New York: William Morrow and Company, Inc. 1981. VINCE LOMBARDI, JOHN MADDEN, TOM LANDRY, PAUL BROWN, DON SHULA, COACHES, PRO FOOTBALL.

Articles

1172. Bell, Tommy. "Some Honest Men Wear Stripes." The Saturday Evening Post. 246, No.9 (December 1974), 68-69+. NFL, PRO FOOTBALL, COACHES, JUSTICE, FUNCTIONAL EXCELLENCE, OBJECTIVITY.

1173. "Black Officials In Professional Sports." Ebony. 37, No.9 (July 1982), 83-86. NFL, NBA, PRO BASEBALL, PRO FOOTBALL, BLACKS IN SPORTS MANAGEMENT.

1174. Deford, Frank. "Nobody Loves the Ruling Class." Sports Illustrated. 45, No.15 (October 11, 1976), 126-138. PERSONALITIES OF OFFICIALS, RULES ENFORCEMENT, CHEATING, MISSED CALLS, FUNCTIONAL EXCELLENCE, FAIRNESS.

1175. Johnson, William Oscar. "It's Open Season on the Zebras." Sports Illustrated. 49, No.15 (October 9, 1978), 38-45. REFEREE CREDIBILITY, BOTCHED CALLS, PRO FOOTBALL, QUICK WHISTLES, UNIVERSITY OF REFEREES, SANCTIONS.

1176. Keenan, Sandy. "The Umpress Strikes Back." Sports Illustrated. 61, No.6 (July 30, 1984), 44-45. GENDER DIFFERENCES, WOMEN, UMPIRES.

1177. "Doing Right By Sport: The Treatment of Sport Officials and Referees." A Paper Read at the American Alliance for Health, Physical Education, Recreation and Dance National Convention, New Orleans, 1979. SPORTSMANSHIP, FAIRNESS, SPECTATOR BEHAVIOR, COACHES' BEHAVIOR.

1178. Lesko, Patricia. "Blowing the Whistle on Ref Sexism." Women's Sports and Fitness. 6, No.12 (December 1984), 60. FEMALE SPORTS OFFICIALS, DISCRIMINATION, LAWSUITS, COMPETENCE.

1179. McCallum, Jack. "Disorder on the Court." Sports Illustrated. 68, No.6 (February 8, 1988), 72-76. VIOLENCE, PLAYER SUSPENSIONS, FIGHTING, NBA SUGGESTS THREE REFEREES.

1180. Mitchell, John S., Wilbert Marcellus Leonard II, and Raymond L Schmitt. "Sports Officials' Perceptions of Fans, Players, and Their Occupations: A Comparative Study of Baseball and Hockey." Journal of Sport Behavior. 5, No.2 (June 1982), 83-95. PRO BASEBALL, PRO HOCKEY, COMMUNICATION NETWORK, SPORT OCCUPATIONS AS SUBCULTURES.

1181. Moore, Kenny. "Not on the Up and Up." Sports Illustrated. 43, No.17 (October 27, 1975), 16-19. PAN AM GAMES, BIASED OFFICIATING, HOSTILITY TOWARD THE U.S. CONTINGENT.

1182. Narol, Melvin S. and Stuart Dedopoulos. "Kill the Umpire: A Guide to Referees' Rights." Trial: The National Legal Newsmagazine. 15, No.3 (March 1979), 32-34+. WORKER'S COMPENSATION, NEGLIGENCE, INTENTIONAL TORT, SLANDER, FAN BEHAVIOR.

1183. Newhouse, Dave. "Woman in Blue." The Sporting News. 195, No.18 (May 2, 1983), 49. PAM POSTEMA, FEMALE UMPIRES, BASEBALL.

1184. Putnam, Pat. "A Sad Day in Seoul." Sports Illustrated. 69, No.15 (October 3, 1988), 48-49. BOXING, REFEREE ATTACKED, KOREAN COACH AND TRAINER, BRUTALIZED REFEREE, VIOLENCE.

1185. Radford, Colin. "The Umpire's Dilemma." Analysis. 45, No.2 (March 1985), 109-111. CRICKET, CERTAINTY OF THE UMPIRE, INTUITIONIST, LEGALIST CASE STUDY.

1186. Rainey, David W., Gerald Schweickert, Vincent Granito, and Joseph Pullella. "Fans' Evaluations of Major League Baseball Umpires' Performances and Perceptions of Appropriate Behavior Towards Umpires." Journal of Sport Behavior. 13, No.2 (June 1990), 122-129. FAN VERBAL HOSTILITY, "KILL THE UMP," SOCIAL SCIENCE STUDY, GENDER ATTITUDE DIFFERENCES, FANS, SPECTATORS.

1187. Rainey, David W., Janet D. Larsen, Alan Stephenson, and Sean Coursey. "Accuracy and Certainty Judgments of Umpires and NonUmpires." Journal of Sport Behavior. 12, No.1 (March 1989), 12-22. EMPIRICAL STUDY, INEXPERIENCED PERSONS JUST AS ACCURATE AS PROFESSIONAL UMPIRES, BASEBALL.

1188. Voigt, David Quentin.   "America's Manufactured Villain: The Baseball Umpire."   Journal of Popular Culture.   4, No.1 (Summer 1970), 1-21. BASEBALL, UMPIRES, HISTORY, PROFESSIONALIZATION, SCAPEGOATING.

1189. Wulf, Steve. "30 Days." Sports Illustrated. 68, No.19 (May 9, 1988), 22-25. PETE ROSE SHOVING UMPIRE, 30 DAY SUSPENSION, BART GIAMATTI, FANS RIOT, CINCINNATI REDS, DAVE PALLONE, UMPIRE.

SPORTS MEDICINE

Books

1190. Haycock, Christine E. (ed.). Sports Medicine for the Athletic Female. New York: Perigee Books, 1984. INJURIES, DRUGS, LAW, FUTURE.

1191. Hughston, Jack C. and Kenneth S. Clarke. A Bibliography of Sports Medicine. Park Ridge, IL: American Academy of Orthopaedic Surgeons, 1970. BIBLIOGRAPHY, REFERENCE.

1192. Jokl, Ernst. Medical Sociology and Cultural Anthropology of Sport and Physical Education. Springfield, IL: Charles C. Thomas, Publisher, 1964. SPORTS AND CULTURE, MYTHS, PLAY, SOCIOLOGY OF SPORT, WOMEN, OLYMPICS, MOTIVATION.

1193. Jokl, Ernst. What is Sportsmedicine? Springfield IL: Charles C. Thomas, Publisher, 1964. INJURIES, DEFINITION.

1194. Pacheco, Ferdie. Fight Doctor. New York: Simon and Schuster, Inc., 1976. MUHAMMAD ALI, INJURIES, SPORTS MEDICINE, BOXING.

1195. Wells, Christine L.   Women, Sport and Performance: A Physiological Perspective. Champaign, IL: Human Kinetics Publishers, 1985. GENDER DIFFERENCES, INJURIES.

Articles

1196. American College of Sports Medicine.   "Position Statement on The Use of Alcohol in Sports." Medicine and Science in Sports and Exercise. 14, No.6 (1982), ix-xi. RESEARCH, HARM OF USE, EDUCATION.

1197. American College of Sports Medicine. "Position Statement on the Use and Abuse of Anabolic-Androgenic Steroids in Sports." Medicine and Science in Sports. 9, No.4 (Winter 1977), xi-xiii. RESEARCH, WOMEN, SIDE EFFECTS.

1198. Barnes, Lan. "Blood Boosting: Success and Controversy." The Physician and Sportsmedicine. 6, No.7 (July 1978), 16-17. ABUSE, DANGERS, ETHICS OF FAIR PLAY.

1199. Barry, John M. "It's All a Part of the Game." Sports Illustrated. 43, No.14 (October 6, 1975), 40-51. SPORTS INJURIES, PLAYING WITH PAIN, COACH'S RESPONSIBILITY, TRAINER'S RESPONSIBILITY.

1200. "Blood Doping as an Ergogenic Aid." The Physician and Sportsmedicine. 16, No.1 (January 1988), 131-134. APPLICATIONS, ERGOGENIC EFFECT, REINFUSION.

1201. Brodie, D. A. and K. Stopani. "Experimental Ethics in Sports Medicine Research." Sports Medicine. 9, No.3 (March 1990), 143-149. RESEARCH WITH HUMANS, CONSENT, RISK.

1202. "Controversial 'Blood Doping' Revisited." Science News. 131, No.22 (May 30, 1987), 344. BENEFITS OF BLOOD DOPING, IMPROVEMENT OF PERFORMANCE, SIDE EFFECTS, ETHICS AND FAIR PLAY.

1203. Cramer, Richard Ben. "Olympic Cheating." Rolling Stone. No.441 (February 14, 1985), 25-26+. BLOOD DOPING, OLYMPICS, CHEATING.

1204. Dial, Gilbert. "A Former Dallas Cowboy Learns to Fight the Pain That Once Ruled His Life." People Weekly. 19, No.2 (January 17, 1983), 35-36. BUDDY DIAL, INJURIES, ADDICTION TO PAINKILLERS, DALLAS COWBOYS.

1205. "Docs for Jocks." Ebony. 39, No.5 (March 1984), 51-54. BLACK PHYSICIANS, CAREER OPPORTUNITIES.

1206. Duda, Marty. "Do Anabolic Steroids Pose An Ethical Dilemma For U. S. Physicians?" The Physician and Sportsmedicine. 14, No.11 (Novmeber 1986), 173-175. RESPONSIBILITY OF PHYSICIANS, MONITORING, CONFLICT OF INTEREST.

1207. Ford, P. G. T. "Ethics in Sports Medicine--Some Medico-Legal Considerations." British Journal of Sports Medicine. 14, Nos.2&3 (July 1980), 90-91. LITIGATION, STANDARDS.

1208. Hyland, Drew A. "Playing to Win: How Much Should It Hurt?" The Hastings Center Report. 9, No.2 (April 1979), 5-8. RISK TAKING, EXCELLENCE, SPORTS INJURIES, DRUG USE, PLAYING WITH PAIN, WINNING AT ALL COSTS, REFORMS.

1209. "Is Blood Boosting Fair Game?" Science Digest. 90, No.11 (November 1982), 90. RED BLOOD CELL INCREASES, DETECTION, ADVANTAGES.

1210. "Legal, Moral and Ethical Questions in Sports Medicine." The Physician and Sportsmedicine. 3, No.3 (March 1975), 71-84. DISCLOSURE, PRIMARY OBLIGATIONS, LAWSUITS.

1211. McKeag, Douglas B., Howard Brody, and David O. Hough. "Medical Ethics in Sport." The Physician and Sportsmedicine. 12, No.8 (August 1984), 145-150. CASE STUDIES, CONFLICT OF INTEREST, PHYSICIAN RESPONSIBILITIES, REFORM.

1212. Miller, John M. "Ethical Issues in College Health: Athletic Medicine." Journal of American College Health. 34, No.4 (February 1986), 195-196. CONFIDENTIALITY, MEDIA, SPORTS MEDICINE RESEARCH, RISK ASSUMPTION, INFORMED CONSENT, DRUGS.

1213. Nack, William. "Playing Hurt--The Doctors' Dilemma." Sports Illustrated. 50, No.24 (June 11, 1979), 30-36. TEAM PHYSICIANS, LOYALTY TO THE TEAM OR TO THE PLAYER, CARLTON FISK, DR. ARTHUR PAPPAS, BOSTON RED SOX.

1214. Papanek, John. "Off on a Wronged Foot." Sports Illustrated. 49, No.8 (August 21, 1978), 18-23. BILL WALTON QUIT PORTLAND TRAILBLAZERS, INJURED FOOT, MEDICAL DIAGNOSIS PROBLEMS, PAIN KILLER INJECTIONS, COUNTER CULTURE LIFE STYLE.

1215. Pine, Devera. "Endurance by the Pint." Women's Sports and Fitness. 9, No.7 (July 1987), 56. RISKS, AIDS, FAIR PLAY.

1216. Rein, Richard K. "Colgate's Merrill Miller Plays a New Position: Woman Doc to Male Jocks." People Weekly. 18, No.2 (November 15, 1982), 125-126. COLGATE UNIVERSITY, FEMALE HEAD PHYSICIAN, DIVISION ONE COLLEGE FOOTBALL.

1217. Rostaing, Bjarne and Robert Sullivan. "Triumphs Tainted With Blood." Sports Illustrated. 62, No.3 (January 21, 1985), 12-17. LOS ANGELES OLYMPICS, BLOOD DOPING, CYCLING SCANDALS.

1218. Ruhling, Robert O. "Blood Reinfusion: A Chronological Review of the Controversy." Utah Journal of Health, Physical Education and Recreation. 9 (Fall 1978), 5+. HEALTH RISKS, UNFAIR COMPETITION, BENEFIT AND HARM.

1219. Ryan, Allan J. "Medical Practices in Sports." Law and Contemporary Problems. 38, No.1 (Winter-Spring 1973), 99-111. EDUCATIONAL PROGRAMS, TRAINERS, INJURIES.

1220. Sherman, Mark F. "The Team Doctor in the Computer Age." Scholastic Coach. 54, No.1 (August 1984), 46-47+. DEHUMANIZATION, TECHNOLOGY.

1221. Sperryn, Peter N. "Ethics in Sports Medicine - The Sports Physician." British Journal of Sports Medicine. 14, Nos.2&3 (July 1980), 84-89. FITNESS TESTING, COMMERCIAL ASPECTS, SPORTS CLINICS, ROLE OF THE TEAM DOCTOR, SAFETY, SEX TESTING, DRUGS.

1222. Stiles, Merritt H. "Olympic Doctors Face Controversial Problems: Sex Testing and Drug Use by Athletes." Modern Medicine. (September 9, 1968), 60-64. VISUAL INSPECTION, MEN WHO POSE AS WOMEN.

1223. Thevoz, Francis. "At the Athlete's Side: A Doctor?" Olympic Message. 18 (August 1987), 63-69. ROLE OF DOCTORS, ADVICE, NUTRITION, TRAINING, DRUGS, INJURIES.

1224. Todaro, Gerald J. "Sports Medicine Malpractice: Informed Consent and the Recreational Athlete." Trial: The National Legal Newsmagazine. 21, No.5 (May 1985), 34-38. DOCTRINE OF INFORMED CONSENT, FULL DISCLOSURE, NEGLIGENCE, MOTIVATION, LAW.

1225. Toon, Peter D. "Boxing Clever." Journal of Medical Ethics. 14, No.2 (June 1988), 69. DOCTOR-PATIENT RELATIONSHIPS, DEONTOLOGICAL, UTILITARIAN AND LINGUISTIC ANALYSIS.

1226. Underwood, John. "Just an Awful Toll." Sports Illustrated. 63, No.7 (August 12, 1985), 48-50+. ARTIFICIAL TURF, INJURIES, FOOTBALL, NFL FAILINGS, TURF VICTIMS.

1227. Webb, James L. "Blood Doping: Help or Hinderance?" The Physical Educator. 35, No.4 (December 1978), 187-190. ERGOGENIC AIDS, HARM, INCONCLUSIVE RESEARCH.

1228. Whorton, James C. "'Athlete's Heart': The Medical Debate Over Athleticism, 1870-1920." Journal of Sport History. 9, No.1 (Spring 1982), 30-52. DEBATE AMONG PHYSICIANS CONCERNING THE BENEFITS OF EXERCISE, MORAL BENEFIT OF SPORT, FOOTBALL, SPORTS MEDICINE.

1229. Yesalis, Charles E. III, James E. Wright, and Michael S. Bahrke. "Epidemiological and Policy Issues in the Measurement of Long Term Health Effects of Anabolic-Androgenic Steroids." Sports Medicine. 8, No.3 (September 1989), 129-138. SHORT TERM EFFECTS, FUTURE, STEROIDS.

VIOLENCE

Books

1230. Atyeo, Don. Blood and Guts: Violence in Sports. New York: Paddington Press, 1979. HISTORY, FOOTBALL, BOXING, HUNTING, BULLFIGHTING, COCKFIGHTING, MOTOR RACING, RUGBY, LEGITIMIZATION AND ACCEPTABILITY OF VIOLENCE IN SPORTS, WAR.

1231. Bridges, John Charles. Social Policy, Changing Legal Attitudes and Violence in American Sport, 1875-1980. PhD Thesis, University of Notre Dame, 1984. LAW, POWER, SOCIAL STRUCTURE, LEGITIMIZATION OF VIOLENCE.

1232. Chandler, Bob and Norm Chandler Fox. Violent Sundays. New York: Simon and Schuster, Inc., 1984. BUFFALO BILLS, OAKLAND RAIDERS, PRO FOOTBALL, NFL, INJURIES, PLAYER STRIKES, FANS.

1233. Goldstein, Jeffrey H. (ed.). Sports Violence. New York: Springer-Verlag New York, Inc., 1983. HISTORY, IDEAL AND MEANING, AGGRESSION, SOCIOLOGY.

1234. Gorn, Elliott J. The Manly Art: Bare-Knuckle Prize Fighting in America. Ithaca, NY: Cornell University Press, 1986. ENGLISH BOXING, EVOLUTION OF PUGILISM, WORKING CLASS CULTURE, FAIR PLAY, POLITICAL CONNECTIONS, AESTHETICS.

1235. Hauser, Thomas. The Black Lights: Inside the World of Professional Boxing. New York: McGraw-Hill Publishing Company, 1986. EXPLOITATION, BILL COSTELLO, SAOUL MAMBY.

1236. Holovak, Mike and Bill McSweeny. Violence Every Sunday: The Story of a Professional Football Coach. New York: Coward-McCann, 1967. PRO FOOTBALL, NEW ENGLAND PATRIOTS, COLLEGE FOOTBALL, COACHES, PLAYERS.

1237. Horrow, Richard B. Sports Violence: The Interaction Between Private Lawmaking and the Criminal Law. Arlington, VA: Carrollton Press, Inc., 1980. HOCKEY, FOOTBALL, BASKETBALL, BASEBALL, CASE STUDIES.

1238. Kaye, Ivan N. Good Clean Violence: A History of College Football. Philadelphia: J. B. Lippincott Company, 1973. HARVARD UNIVERSITY, HEROES, BENEFIT AND HARM.

1239. McMurtry, William R. Investigation and Inquiry Into Violence in Amateur Hockey. Toronto: Ministry of Community and Social Services, 1974. SOCIALIZATION, PSYCHOLOGY, COACHES AND OFFICIALS, RULES, REFEREES, PARENTS, REFORM.

1240. Smith, Michael D. Violence and Sport. Toronto: Butterworths, 1983. TYPOLOGY OF SPORTS VIOLENCE, LEGITIMATION OF VIOLENCE, VIOLENT SUBCULTURE, GENDER DIFFERENCES, SOCIAL CLASSES, AGE, FANS, MEDIA, AGGRESSION.

1241. Stingley, Darryl with Mark Mulvoy. Darryl Stingley: Happy to Be Alive. New York: Beaufort Books, Inc., 1983. PROFESSIONAL FOOTBALL, NEW ENGLAND PATRIOTS, WIDE RECEIVER DARRYL STINGLEY, SPINAL INJURY, HIT FROM OAKLAND'S JACK TATUM, RECOVERY.

1242. Tatum, Jack with Bill Kushner. They Call Me Assassin. New York: Everest House, 1979. RULES, CHANGES AND REFORM, DARRELL STINGLEY, NEW ENGLAND PATRIOTS.

1243. Yeager, Robert C. Seasons of Shame: The New Violence in Sports. New York: McGraw-Hill Publishing Company, 1979. HISTORY, STANDARDS OF FAIR PLAY, RULES, PENALTIES, COMPETITION, WINNING, SPORTS AS A MIRROR OF LIFE, REFORM.

Articles

1244. Albrecht, Dirk. "Sport Specific Aggression in Competition." International Journal of Sport Psychology. 10, No.2 (1979), 139. HANDBALL, FOULS, VERBAL ABUSE.

1245. Annas, George J. "Boxing: Atavistic Spectacle or Artistic Sport?" American Journal of Public Health. 73, No.7 (July 1983), 811-812. ABOLITIONIST AND REFORMIST ARGUMENTS, LAW, REFORM, FEDERAL BOXING COMMISSION.

1246. Ardolino, Frank. "Sex, Violence, and Castrated Cowboys in North Dallas Forty." Arete: The Journal of Sport Literature. 4, No.2 (Spring 1987), 107-122. DRUGS, BERTRAND PHILLIP ELLIOTT, SEX, FOOTBALL, MACHISMO.

1247. "The Assassin." Time. 115, No.4 (January 28, 1980), 69. JACK TATUM, DARRYL STINGLEY, INJURIES, OAKLAND RAIDERS.

1248. Axthelm, Pete. "Don't Count Boxing Out." Newsweek. 100 (December 20, 1982), 60. PLUSES OF BOXING, HOWARD COSELL, REFORM, BENEFIT AND HARM.

1249. "Ban Boxing." The New Republic. 199, Nos.6&7 (August 8&15, 1988), 7-8. INNER CITY YOUTH, BLACK ROLE MODELS, VALUES, BOYCOTT.

1250. Berkowitz, Leonard. "Sports, Competition, and Aggression." The Physical Educator. 30, No.2 (May 1973), 59-61. SPECTATORS, BENEFIT AND HARM.

1251. Bianchi, Eugene C. "The Superbowl Culture of Male Violence." The Christian Century. 91, No.31 (September 18, 1974), 842-845. PARENTS, AGGRESSION, SEXISM, CHILDREN, RAPE, WATERGATE.

1252. Bingham, Walter. "Take Me Out of the Ball Game." Sports Illustrated. 32, No.17 (April 27, 1970), 22-23. ROWDYISM, BASEBALL, HOCKEY, FANS.

1253. Blount, Roy Jr. "The Fighting Side of Baseball." Esquire. 88, No.1 (July 1977), 30-32. LENNY RANDLE, FRANK LUCCHESI, TEXAS RANGERS, VIOLENCE, WOODY HAYES.

1254. Bossy, Mike. "Blow the Whistle on Dirty Hockey." Sport. 70, No.6 (June 1980), 8. CHIPPY PLAY, REFORM.

1255. Boucher, Robert L. and Robert W. Case. "Participant Violence in Sport: An Essay Review." Physical Education Review. 3, No.1 (Spring 1980), 8-13. INSTINCTUAL AGGRESSION THEORY, FRUSTRATION-AGGRESSION THEORY, SPORTS AS A MICROCOSM OF SOCIETY.

1256. Bowlsby, Craig. "Playing Dirty." Referee. 7, No.6 (June 1982), 16-20. SUBJECTIVE JUDGING, WINNING AT ALL COSTS, EQUIPMENT REGULATIONS.

1257. Boyle, Robert H. and Wilmer Ames. "Too Many Punches Too Little Concern." Sports Illustrated. 58, No.15 (April 11, 1983), 44-46+. MEDICAL REFORM, PUBLIC SCRUTINY, DEATH, ETHICS, CASE AGAINST BOXING, EMPIRICAL STUDIES.

1258. Brailsford, Dennis. "Morals and Maulers: The Ethics of Early Pugilism." Journal of Sport History. 12, No.2 (Summer 1985), 126-142. PERSONAL INTEGRITY, JUSTICE, RACISM, BOXING, FAIR PLAY.

1259. Bredemeier, Brenda Jo. "Moral Reasoning and the Perceived Legitimacy of Intentionally Injurious Sport Acts." Journal of Sport Psychology. 7, No.2 (June 1985), 110-124. DECISION MAKING.

1260. Bredemeier, Brenda Jo and David L. Shields. "Athletic Aggression: An Issue of Contextual Morality." Sociology of Sport Journal. 3, No.1 (March 1986), 15-28. HAAN'S THEORY OF INTERACTIONAL MORALITY, FRAME ANALYSIS, MORAL REASONING, MORAL AMBIGUITY.

1261. Bredemeier, Brenda Jo and David L. Shields. "The Utility of Moral Stage Analysis in the Investigation of Athletic Aggression." Sociology of Sport Journal. 1, No.2 (1984), 138-149. STAGES OF MORAL REASONING, ATHLETIC AGGRESSION, BASKETBALL, REST'S DEFINING ISSUES TEST.

1262. Bredemeier, Brenda Jo and David L. Shields. "Values and Violence in Sports Today." Psychology Today. 19, No.10 (October 1985), 22-25+. MORAL REASONING, AGGRESSION, SUSPENSION OF USUAL VALUES, COMPETITION.

1263. Bryant, James. "The Business World and Sports Violence." The Physical Educator. 37, No.3 (October 1980), 144-146. PARALLEL BETWEEN BUSINESS AND SPORTS, SPORTS AS A MICROCOSM OF SOCIETY, SYMBOLIC SUPREMACY.

1264. Bryant, Jennings, Paul Comisky, and Dolf Zillmann. "An Appeal of Rough-and-Tumble Play in Televised Professional Football." Communication Quarterly. 29, No.4 (Fall 1981), 256-262. GENDER DIFFERENCES, ENJOYMENT OF TELEVISED PLAYS OF PRO FOOTBALL, MALE ENJOYMENT OF HIGH VIOLENCE PLAYS.

1265. "CAHPER's Position Paper on Violence in Sport." Canadian Journal for Health, Physical Education and Recreation. 46 (November/December 1979), 15-18. RULES, VALUES, ROLE MODELS, SPORTSMANSHIP, SELF DEVELOPMENT, FUTURE.

1266. Carpenter, Linda Jean and R. Vivian Acosta. "Violence in Sport--Is It Part of the Game or the Intentional Tort of Battery?" Journal of Physical Education and Recreation. 51, No.7 (September 1980), 18. NEGLIGENCE, LAWSUITS, LIABILITY, COACHES.

1267. Celozzi, Mathew J., Richard Kazelskis, and Kenneth U. Gutsch. "The Relationship Between Viewing Televised Violence in Ice Hockey and Subsequent Levels of Personal Aggression." Journal of Sport Behavior. 4, No.4 (December 1981), 157-162. MEDIA, TRAIT AGGRESSION.

1268. Cheren, Stanley. "The Psychiatric Perspective: Psychological Aspects of Violence in Sports." Arena Review. 5, No.1 (February 1981), 31-36. ROOTS AND EFFECTS OF VIOLENCE IN SPORTS, SPORTS AS AN OUTLET FOR AGGRESSION, SPORTS AS A STIMULANT OF VIOLENCE, THEORIES OF AGGRESSION, SOCIALIZATION, CHILDREN.

1269. Coakley, Jay J. "The Sociological Perspective: Alternate Causations of Violence in Sport." Arena Review. 5, No.1 (February 1981), 44-56. SOCIOLOGICAL EXPLANATION OF VIOLENCE IN SPORTS, RELATIONSHIP BETWEEN VIOLENCE AND THE SOCIO-STRUCTURAL CONTEXT OF SPORTS, COMMERCIALIZATION OF SPORTS, INSTRUMENT AGGRESSION, SOCIALIZATION.

1270. Cooke, Patrick. "For Whom the Bell Tolls." Science 84. 5, No.10 (December 1984), 88-89. BRAIN DAMAGE, RULES, REFORM.

1271. Cranston, Mary Kate. "Law Would Penalize Violence in Sports." The Physician and Sportsmedicine. 8, No.11 (November 1980), 23. SPORTS VIOLENCE ACT, NFL, SELF POLICING, OFFICIALS, RESPONSIBILITY.

1272. Deford, Frank. "Let's Count Boxing Out." Sports Illustrated. 66, No.6 (February 9, 1987), 222. SUGAR RAY LEONARD, MARVIN HAGLER, EFFECT OF VIOLENCE ON VIEWERS, FUTURE.

1273. Dent, David J. "When Games Become Dangerous." Black Enterprise. 14, No.8 (March 1984), 70+. YOUTH, PARENTS, INJURIES, SPORTS MEDICINE.

1274. Doctorow, E. L. "After the Nightmare." Sports Illustrated. 44, No.26 (June 28, 1976), 72-82. ISRAELI MURDERS IN MUNICH, EFFECT ON SURVIVORS, CASE STUDIES, TERRORISM, MUNICH OLYMPICS.

1275. Dryden, Ken. "Hockey Without Violence: Lesson of U. S. Olympic Victory." U. S. News and World Report. 88, No.9 (March 10, 1980), 64. FUTURE, IMAGE, NHL, ROLE MODELS.

1276. Dunning, Eric (Reviewed by James Peckman). "Social Bonding and Violence in Sport." Journal of Sport History. 12, No.3 (Winter 1985), 293. RUGBY, SOCCER, HOOLIGANISM, HIERARCHICAL RELATIONSHIPS.

1277. Early, Gerald. "'I Only Like it Better When the Pain Comes': More Notes Toward a Cultural Definition of Prizefighting." The Hudson Review. 36, No.4 (Winter 1983-84), 656-676. SEXISM, SUGAR RAY LEONARD, NORMAN MAILER, BLACK MALES.

1278. Edwards, Harry and Van Rackages. "The Dynamics of Violence in American Sport: Some Promising Structural and Social Considerations." Journal of Sport and Social Issues. 1, No.2 (Summer/Fall 1977), 3-31. IDEOLOGY, SPECTATOR VIOLENCE.

1279. Egan, Sean. "Social, Medical, Moral and Legal Aspects of Sport Violence." Momentum: A Journal of Human Movement Studies. 12, No.2 (Autumn 1987), 47-59. SOCIOLOGY, SPORTS MEDICINE, MORAL, LAW.

1280. Evans, Rebecca. "What Price Success? Winning, Aggression and Violence." Ohio. 4 (Fall 1982), 4-5. SPORTSMANSHIP, FAIR PLAY, VALUES.

1281. Fagan, Clifford B.   "Players' Brawls Must Be Eliminated."   The Physical Educator. 29, No.2 (May 1972), 59-60. RESPONSIBILITY OF ADMINISTRATORS, COACHES, AND ATHLETIC DIRECTORS, BRAWLS.

1282. Feigley, David A.   "Is Aggression Justifiable?"   Journal of Physical Education, Recreation and Dance.   54, No.9 (November/December 1983), 63-64. SPORTSMANSHIP, YOUTH, SELF JUSTIFICATION, COGNITIVE DISSONANCE.

1283. Ferreira, Fernando.   "Violence in Sport."   The FIEP Bulletin.   54, No.1 (January/March 1984), 39-41. REFORM, SPORTS EDUCATION, ROLE OF SPORTS IN SOCIETY, RULES.

1284. Figler, Stephen K.   "Aggressive Response to Frustration Among Athletes and Non-Athletes."   International Journal of Physical Education.   15, No.3 (Fall 1978), 29-33. SPORT AS AN OUTLET FOR AGGRESSION, DISTINCTION BETWEEN REACTIVE AND INSTRUMENTAL AGGRESSION.

1285. Fimrite, Ron.   "Take Me Out To the Brawl Game."   Sports Illustrated.   40, No.24 (June 17, 1974), 10-13. ROWDY FANS, ALCOHOL, ANTI-ESTABLISHMENT FEELINGS, ALIENATION.

1286. Fischler, Stan.   "Bad Billy."   Sport.   73, No.2 (February 1982), 49-52. NEW YORK ISLANDERS, PRO HOCKEY, BILLY SMITH.

1287. Fischler, Stan.   "Mean and Nasty."   Sport.   73, No.2 (February 1982), 50-51. PRO HOCKEY.

1288. Flakne, Gary W. and Allan H. Caplan.   "Sports Violence and the Prosecution."   Trial: The National Legal Newsmagazine.   13, No.1 (January 1977), 33-35. IMPLIED CONSENT, HOCKEY, RULES.

1289. Folkenberg, Judy.   "The Boxer: A Deadly Influence."   Psychology Today.   18, No.1 (January 1984), 84. RELATIONSHIP OF HOMICIDES TO VIEWING BOXING, HEAVYWEIGHT CHAMPIONSHIP, MODELING OF AGGRESSION.

1290. Fontana, Andrea.   "Over the Edge: A Return to Primitive Sensations in Play and Games."   Urban Life: A Journal of Ethnographic Research.   7, No.2 (July 1978), 213-229. RISK, SPORT AS A REFLECTION OF SOCIETY, DEFINITION OF PLAY, HEROES, FANS.

1291. Ford, Gerald R. (ed. by John Underwood).   "In Defense of the Competitive Urge."   Sports Illustrated.   41, No.2 (July 8, 1974), 16-23. COMPETITION, INTERNATIONAL, MONEY.

1292. Fotheringham, Allan.   "Fists, Skates and a Games Demise."   Maclean's.   95, No.17 (April 26, 1982), 72. HOCKEY, LOS ANGELES KINGS.

1293. Fotheringham, Allan.   "This Leader of Youth Sent Onto the Ice His Finest Barbarians and Bench Warmers."   Maclean's.   93, No.38 (September 17, 1979), 56. JUNIOR HOCKEY, COACHING.

1294. Fotheringham, Allan. "When Heroes Become Monsters." Maclean's. 96, No.39 (September 26, 1983), 72. PAUL HIGGINS, MAPLE LEAFS, PRO HOCKEY, VIOLENCE, GARY ANDERSON, UNIVERISTY OF ARKANSAS, ILLITERACY, ACADEMICS.

1295. "Foul Players." The Economist. 264, No.6994 (September 17, 1977), 64. CROWD CONTROL, SPECTATOR VIOLENCE, PLAYER VIOLENCE.

1296. Frayne, Trent. "Shake and Come Out Playing." Maclean's. 95, No.8 (February 22, 1982), 64. PRO HOCKEY, SPORTSMANSHIP, VIOLENCE, RULES, REFORM.

1297. Freischlag, Jerry and Charles Schmidke. "Violence in Sports: Its Causes and Some Solutions." The Physical Educator. 36, No.4 (December 1979), 182-185. VALUES, YOUTH, BIG TIME COLLEGE SPORTS, REFORM.

1298. Furlong, William Barry. "Football Violence." The New York Times Magazine. (November 30, 1980), 38-41+. PRO FOOTBALL, INJURIES, EFFECT ON PERSONALITY.

1299. Gammon, Clive. "A Day of Horror and Shame." Sports Illustrated. 62, No.23 (June 10, 1985), 20-30+. SOCCER RIOT, EUROPEAN CUP, BRUSSELS, 38 DEAD, 437 INJURIED, ENGLISH HOOLIGANS.

1300. Gammon, Clive. "Those Thugs Again." Sports Illustrated. 68, No.26 (June 27, 1988), 49-53. EUROPEAN SOCCER CHAMPIONSHIPS, FANS, BAN OF ENGLISH FOOTBALL, ALCOHOL.

1301. Gammon, Clive. "Winning Ugly in Rome." Sports Illustrated. 73, No.3 (July 16, 1990), 26-28+. WORLD CUP SOCCER, FAN ROWDYISM, BRUTALITY, SPORTSMANIA, ARGENTINA, WEST GERMANY.

1302. Gammons, Peter. "Wild Willie Gets A New Lease on Life." Sports Illustrated. 47, No.22 (November 28, 1977), 28-33. WILLIE TROGNITZ, PERMANENT SUSPENSION FROM INTERNATIONAL LEAGUE, WORLD HOCKEY ASSOCIATION, CINCINNATI STINGERS.

1303. Glanville, Brian. "Foul Play." New Statesman. 94, No.2415 (July 1, 1977), 29-30. ENGLAND, ARGENTINA, FOOTBALL.

1304. Hallowell, Lyle and Ronald I. Meshbesher. "Sports Violence and the Criminal Law." Trial: The National Legal Newsmagazine. 13, No.1 (January 1977), 27-32. METHODS OF VIOLENCE CONTROL, SELF DEFENSE, REFORM.

1305. Harrow, Richard B. "Violence in Professional Sports: Is It Part of the Game?" Journal of Legislation. 9, No.1 (Winter 1982), 1-15. INCREASE IN VIOLENCE, RELATIONSHIP OF CIVIL AND CRIMINAL LAW TO SPORTS VIOLENCE, SELF SUPERVISION BY THE SPORTS ESTABLISHMENT, LEGITIMATE AGGRESSIVE PLAY VS. EXCESSIVE ILLEGAL CONDUCT.

1306. Hersch, Hank. "It's War Out There!" Sports Illustrated. 67, No.3 (July 20, 1987), 14-17. PRO BASEBALL, BEANBALLS, RETALIATION, BRAWLS.

1307. "Hit 'em High." Time. 114, No.18 (October 29, 1979), 46-51. FRANK KUSH, COACHES, VIOLENCE TO PLAYER.

1308. Horn, Jack C. "Sir Lancelot of the Rink: The Ritual of Hockey Fights." Psychology Today. 15, No.2 (February 1981), 15-16. HOCKEY, SOCIAL RULES, RITUAL, HONOR.

1309. Horn, Jack C. "The Violent Ones--Male College Athletes." Psychology Today. 11, No.9 (February 1978), 34-36. ATTITUDE TOWARD VIOLENCE, SPORTS ATTRACTING AGGRESSIVE PEOPLE VS. SPORTS INCREASING AGGRESSION.

1310. Horrow, Rick. "Sports Violence: The Prospects for Reform." Arena Review. 5, No.1 (February 1981), 63-65. PRESSURES AND INCENTIVES FOR VIOLENCE, VIOLENCE AS ILLEGAL VS. ENTERTAINING.

1311. Hughes, Robert H. and Jay J. Coakley. "Player Violence and the Social Organization of Contact Sport." Journal of Sport Behavior. 1, No.4 (November 1978), 155-168. TEAM STRUCTURE, MORAL WORTH, PHYSICAL SECURITY, MASCULINITY, SENSE OF ADEQUACY.

1312. Hurford, Daphne. "I'll Do Anything I Can Get Away With." Sports Illustrated. 47, No.4 (July 25, 1977), 30-32+. PRO FOOTBALL, CHEATING, GOUGING, BITING, COMPETITION, DIRTY PLAYERS, ST. LOUIS CARDINALS, CONRAD DOBLER.

1313. "Is Pro Football Too Violent? 'A Clean Shot' Pulverizes a Fullback's Cheek and His Career." People Weekly. 12, No.23 (December 3, 1979), 42-43. NORM BULAICH, STEVE LUKE, INJURIES.

1314. "Is Violence in Sports Getting Out of Control?" Jet. 68, No.15 (June 24, 1985), 52-54. BASKETBALL, BOXING, BRUSSELS SOCCER RIOT, SPORT AS A REFLECTION OF SOCIETY.

1315. Joyce, Randolph. "Another Black Eye For Hockey's Image." Maclean's. 95, No.35 (August 30, 1982), 40-41. PRO HOCKEY, VIOLENCE, WILF PAIEMENT, DENNIS POLONICH, LAWSUIT.

1316. Kamuti, Jeno. "Medical Aspects of Violence at Sports Events." Olympic Review. 195/196 (January/February 1984), 36-41. COACH'S AND TRAINER'S RESPONSIBILITY.

1317. Kennedy, Ray. "Wanted: An End To Mayhem." Sports Illustrated. 43, No.20 (November 17, 1975), 16-21. PRO HOCKEY, ASSAULTING OPPONENTS, BRAWLING, NHL ATTITUDE LEGITIMIZES VIOLENCE.

1318. Kirkpatrick, Curry. "Good Old Violence." Sports Illustrated. 66, No.1 (January 5, 1987), 66. SPORTS AS A MIRROR OF SOCIETY, DESIRE FOR VIOLENCE BY FANS.

1319. Kirkpatrick, Curry. "Shattered and Shaken." Sports Illustrated. 48, No.1 (January 2, 1978), 46-47. NBA, HOUSTON ROCKETS, RUDY TOMJANOVICH, LOS ANGELES LAKERS, KERMIT WASHINGTON.

1320. Kirshenbaum, Jerry (ed.). "A Victory for Kush, Not For His Methods." Sports Illustrated. 54, No.19 (May 4, 1981), 9. KEVIN RUTLEDGE, LAWSUIT, ARIZONA STATE SUN DEVILS, COLLEGE FOOTBALL, COACH PUNCHING A PLAYER, FRANK KUSH.

1321. Kirshenbaum, Jerry (ed.). "Night of Horror." Sports Illustrated. 53, No.16 (October 13, 1980), 29. STABBING OF A FAN, ASSAULT OF A POLICE OFFICER, DRUNKENESS, BRAWLING, HOOLIGANISM, FOXBORO, MASSACHUSETTS, PRO FOOTBALL.

1322. "Knockout for Boxers' Brains." Science News. 123, No.5 (January 29, 1983), 73. RELATIONSHIP BETWEEN BRAIN DAMAGE AND NUMBER OF BOUTS, REFORM, AMERICAN MEDICAL ASSOCIATION.

1323. Kowch, Steve. "Though He Killed One Man In The Ring and Disabled Another, Gaetan Hart Won't Stop Punching." People Weekly. 14, No.4 (July 28, 1980), 22-23. CLEVELAND DENNY, DEATH, INJURIES.

1324. Kram, Mark. "Their Lives Are on the Line." Sports Illustrated. 43, No.7 (August 18, 1975), 32-38. BEANBALL, SPECTER OF DEATH, PITCHERS AND BATTERS, PRO BASEBALL, HISTORY, CASE STUDIES.

1325. LaPoint, James. "Aggression and Violence: Their Effects On Adolescent Female Sports Participants." The KAHPER Journal. 47 (October 1979), 9-11. CHARACTER, VALUES, ETHICS.

1326. Leerhsen, Charles. "The Fall of Billy Don." Newsweek. 99 (April 19, 1982), 86. BILLY DON JACKSON, MANSLAUGHTER, UNIVERSITY OF CALIFORNIA AT LOS ANGELES, ACADEMICS, ILLITERACY.

1327. Leone, Carmen and Dorothy Leone. "Death in the Ring: A Pastoral Dilemma." America. 149, No.4 (August 6-13, 1983), 70-72. PRIESTLY ADVICE TO BOXERS, INTENTION TO HARM.

1328. Levine, Peter and Peter Vinten-Johansen. "The Historical Perspective: Violence and Sport." Arena Review. 5, No.1 (February 1981), 22-30. HISTORICAL, CONTEXT OF REFORMS, RELATIONSHIP BETWEEN SPORTS VIOLENCE AND SOCIETY'S CULTURAL AND POLITICAL VALUES, COMPARATIVE SPORT VALUES, SPORT AS AN AGENT OF SOCIALIZATION.

1329. "The Lowdown on A High-Sticking." Sports Illustrated. 67, No.20 (November 9, 1987), 16. NEW YORK RANGERS, PHILADELPHIA FLYERS, HOCKEY, SUSPENSION.

1330. Lueschen, Guenther. "Sport, Conflict and Conflict Resolution." International Social Science Journal. 34, No.2 (1982), 185-196. ANALOGY OF SPORT AND WAR, SPORT AS A CONTRIBUTION TO PEACE, SOCIO-CULTURAL CONTEXT OF SPORT, CONFLICT THEORY.

1331. Luxbacher, Joe. "Violence in Sport." Coaching Review. 9 (March/April 1986), 14-17. THEORIES OF AGGRESSION, COACHES' INFLUENCE, ROLE MODELS.

1332. Maafe, Ken. "Contact Sports Don't Belong in Catholic Schools." U. S.
Catholic. 50, No.3 (March 1985), 13-14. AGGRESSION, COMPETITIVENESS,
ANGER, TRIUMPHALISM, ELITISM.

1333. McCaghy, Charles H. and Arthur G. Neal. "The Fraternity of Cockfighters:
Ethical Embellishments of an Illegal Sport." Journal of Popular Culture. 8,
No.3 (Winter 1974), 557-569. HISTORY, CRUELTY, DEHUMANIZATION.

1334. McCarthy, Jean. "Sports Violence: Caveat Vendor." Journal of Physical
Education and Recreation. 49, No.9 (November/December 1978), 34+. MEDIA
ATTENTION TO VIOLENCE, EGOISM, ROLE MODELS, RULES.

1335. McCarthy, John F. and Bryan R. Kelly. "Aggressive Behavior and Its Effect on
Performance Over Time in Ice Hockey Athletes: An Archival Study."
International Journal of Sport Psychology. 9, No.2 (1978), 90-96. RELATIONSHIP
BETWEEN AGGRESSION AND ATHLETIC PERFORMANCE, COLLEGE HOCKEY,
AGGRESSION.

1336. McCormack, Thelma. "Hollywood's Prizefight Films: Violence or 'Jock'
Appeal?" Journal of Sport and Social Issues. 8, No.2 (Summer/Fall 1984), 19-
29. AGGRESSION, JOCK APPEAL, MALE NARCISSISM.

1337. McWilliams, Carey. "Out of Kilter." The Nation. 225, No.23 (December 31,
1977), 709. KERMIT WASHINGTON, RUDY TOMJANOVICH, PRO BASKETBALL,
STRUCTURAL VIOLENCE, VALUES, SPORT AS A REFLECTION OF SOCIETY.

1338. Monaghan, Peter.   "Brawls at Several Recent Basketball Games Lead to
Cancellations, Disciplinary Actions." The Chronicle of Higher Education. 31,
No.22 (February 12, 1986), 31+. UNRULY FANS, PENALTIES, REFORM.

1339. Monaghan, Peter.   "Referees Expect Criticism, Not Violence, From College
Fans, Coaches, and Players." The Chronicle of Higher Education. 31, No.18
(January 15, 1986), 37-38. MEMPHIS STATE UNIVERSITY, BASKETBALL, KNIFE
THROWN AT REFEREE.

1340. Monaghan, Peter. "Violence and Aggression at the Olympics: They're Not
New." The Chronicle of Higher Education. 28, No.24 (August 8, 1984), 1+.
RELATIONSHIP BETWEEN WAR AND SPORTS IN ANCIENT GREECE, AGGRESSION AND
VIOLENCE IN SPORTS, VIOLENT SOCIETIES BREED VIOLENT SPORTS.

1341. Moore, Mike. "Fighting NHL Brawling with Suspensions." The Physician and
Sportsmedicine. 8, No.9 (September 1980), 19. RULES, INJURIES, REFORM.

1342. "Morality and Aggression." Psychology Today. 19, No.10 (October 1985), 29.
LAWRENCE KOHLBERG, RELATIONSHIP BETWEEN MORAL REASONING AND
AGGRESSION, NORMA HAAN, CHILDREN.

1343. Mulligan, Jim. "A Very Brutal Show." New Statesman. 106, No.2730 (July
15, 1983), 8-9. BOXING, BRAIN DAMAGE, EYE INJURIES, DEATH.

1344. Mulligan, Jim. "Brain Damage Affects All Boxers." New Statesman. 107, No.2773 (May 11, 1984), 4. BRAIN DAMAGE, BIG BUSINESS, BRITISH MEDICAL ASSOCIATION.

1345. Mulvoy, Mark. "Violence is the Goal." Sports Illustrated. 36, No.19 (May 8, 1972), 20-23. BOSTON BRUINS, NEW YORK RANGERS, STANLEY CUP, HOCKEY.

1346. Narol, Melvin S. and Stuart Dedopoulos. "Violence--A Move in the Right Direction." Referee. 6, No.4 (April 1981), 27. SPORTS VIOLENCE ACT, PROTECTION FOR OFFICIALS, CIVIL AND CRIMINAL LAW.

1347. Naughton, John. "The Apes of Wrath." Channels of Communication. 5, No.2 (July/August 1985), 62. BELGIUM SOCCER RIOT, MEDIA, SPECTATORS, INFLUENCE OF TELEVISION ON VIOLENCE.

1348. Noonan, David. "Boxing and the Brain." The New York Times Magazine. (June 12, 1983), 40+. BRAIN DAMAGE, SPORTS MEDICINE, HEALTH RISKS, REEVALUATION OF BOXING AS A SPORT.

1349. O'Connor, Richard. "My Violence Expert." Sport. 67, No.6 (December 1978), 7. JACK JOYCE, CHIEF OF SECURITY, NBA, DEFINITION OF AN ACT OF VIOLENCE, RACISM, RULES, REFORM.

1350. Oberlander, Susan. "Big East Conference Adopts Rules to Try to Prevent Brawls by Players During Basketball Games." The Chronicle of Higher Education. 34, No.25 (March 2, 1988), A31-32. BASKETBALL, BIG EAST CONFERENCE, BRAWLS, REFORM, SUSPENSION.

1351. Page, Alan. "The Violence Act Comes Up Short." Sport. 72, No.2 (February 1981), 10. NFL, RULES, LAWSUITS, GOVERNMENT CONTROL.

1352. Pilz, Guenter A. "Changes of Violence in Sports." International Review of Sport Sociology. 17, No.4 (1982), 47-71. VIOLENCE AND THE INCREASE OF CIVILIZATION, WOMEN.

1353. Pilz, Guenter A. "Attitudes Toward Different Forms of Aggressive and Violent Behavior in Competitive Sports: Two Empirical Studies." Journal of Sport Behavior. 2, No.1 (February 1979), 3-26. GENDER DIFFERENCES, ATTITUDES TOWARD AGGRESSION, HANDBALL, SOCCER.

1354. "The Punchdrunk Syndrome: What Really Happens to Boxer's Brains?" Science Digest. 75, No.2 (February 1974), 28-31. BRAIN DAMAGE, RULES, REFORM.

1355. Rains, Cameron Jay. "Sports Violence: A Matter of Societal Concern." The Notre Dame Lawyer. 55, No.5 (June 1980), 796-813. SOCIETAL CONTROL, LIABILITY OF NONPLAYERS, INTENTIONAL HARM, NEGLIGENCE.

1356. Ravenhill, Edward. "Aggression and Sport." The FIEP Bulletin. 56, No.2 (April-June 1986), 14-20. AGGRESSION AND VIOLENCE, SPECTATORS, SPORT AS A SPECTACLE.

1357. Redhead, Steve. "Out of Sight, Out of Mind." New Statesman. 111, No.2878 (May 23, 1986), 12-13. GOVERNMENT, FOOTBALL HOOLIGANISM, BANS ON ENGLISH CLUBS, SOCCER, MEDIA, REFORM.

1358. Reed, J. D. "Week of Disgrace on the Ice." Sports Illustrated. 44, No.17 (April 26, 1976), 22-25. PRO HOCKEY, BRAWLS IN TORONTO AND QUEBEC, PLAYER VIOLENCE, ASSUALT CHARGES, HOOLIGANISM.

1359. Reed, William F. "Ugly Affair in Minneapolis." Sports Illustrated. 36, No.6 (February 7, 1972), 18-21. LUKE WITTE, UNIVERSITY OF MINNESOTA, FANS, OHIO STATE UNIVERSITY, COLLEGE BASKETBALL.

1360. Reid, R. Malcolm and Denis Hay. "Aggression in Rugby and Soccer Players." British Journal of Physical Education. 9, No.2 (March 1978), 45-46. INNATE VS. LEARNED AGGRESSION, CATHARTIC THEORY, FRUSTRATION-AGGRESSION.

1361. Richards, Huw. "Understanding Terrace Violence." The Times Higher Education Supplement. 667 (August 16, 1985), 9. LEICESTER UNIVERSITY, STUDY ON HOOLIGANISM, FANS, SOCIAL SCIENCE, STRUCTURAL CHANGE.

1362. Runfola, Ross T. "Violence in Sport: Mirror of American Society?" Vital Issues. 24, No.7 (1975), 1-4. SPORTS AS A REFLECTION OF SOCIETY, SIMILARITY BETWEEN SPORTS AND WAR, CROWD VIOLENCE, PLAYER VIOLENCE, AGGRESSION, REFORM.

1363. Russell, Gordon W. "Does Sports Violence Increase Box Office Receipts?" International Journal of Sport Psychology. 17, No.3 (September 1986), 173-182. PRO HOCKEY, BIG BUSINESS.

1364. Ryan, Jeff. "Boxing's Shame." Sport. 79, No.12 (December 1988), 60-61. RACISM, MEDIA, RULES, MISMATCHES.

1365. Sachs, Michael L. "An Analysis of Aggression in Female Softball Players." Review of Sport and Leisure. 3, No.1 (Fall 1978), 85-97. INSTRUMENTAL AGGRESSION, REACTIVE AGGRESSION, BREDEMEIER ATHLETIC AGGRESSION INVENTORY.

1366. "Should Professional Boxing Be Banned?" Senior Scholastic. 98, No.12 (May 3, 1971), 12-13. DEHUMANIZATION, FRAZIER-ALI MATCH, COMMERCIALIZATION.

1367. Sipes, Richard G. "War, Sports, and Aggression: An Empirical Test of Two Rival Theories." American Anthropologist. 75, No.1 (February 1973), 64-86. RELATIONSHIP BETWEEN WAR, SPORTS AND AGGRESSION, DRIVE DISCHARGE MODEL, CULTURE PATTERN MODEL.

1368. Smith, Gary. "Violence and Sport." Journal of Health, Physical Education and Recreation. 42, No.3 (March 1971), 45-47. CHARACTER DEVELOPMENT, SPORT AS AN AID TO FORMING ETHICAL BEHAVIOR, DEHUMANIZATION, SOCIAL DISORGANIZATION, SPORT AS A FORM OF SOCIAL CONTROL.

1369. Smith, Michael D.   "Hockey Violence: A Test of the Violent Subculture Hypothesis."   Social Problems.   27, No.2 (December 1979), 235-247.   PRE-VIOLENCE ATTITUDES, VALUES, VIOLENT SUBCULTURES.

1370. Smith, Michael D.   "Sport Violence: A Definition."   Arena Review.   5, No.1 (February 1981), 2-8.   SPORTS VIOLENCE AND THE LAW, TYPOLOGY OF SPORTS VIOLENCE, BODY CONTACT, CRIMINAL VIOLENCE.

1371. "Sport and Violence."   International Journal of Physical Education.   19, No.1 (1982), 28-29.   AGGRESSION, SPECTATORS, MEDIA.

1372. Stingley, Darryl.   "Darryl Stingley: Happy to Be Alive."   Ebony.   38, No.12 (October 1983), 68-74.   PARALYSIS, JACK TATUM, INJURY, PRO FOOTBALL, NEW ENGLAND PATRIOTS.

1373. Stingley, Darryl with Mark Mulvoy.   "Facing Up To A New Life."   Sports Illustrated.   59, No.11 (September 5, 1983), 28-33.   PROFESSIONAL FOOTBALL, DARRYL STINGLEY BECOMES A QUADRIPLEGIC, SPORTS MEDICINE, RECOVERY.

1374. Stingley, Darryl with Mark Mulvoy.   "Where Am I?   It Has To Be A Bad Dream."   Sports Illustrated.   59, No.9 (August 29, 1983), 56-60+.   PROFESSIONAL FOOTBALL, NEW ENGLAND PATRIOTS,   WIDE RECEIVER DARRYL STINGLEY, SPINAL INJURY, HIT FROM OAKLAND'S JACK TATUM, RECOVERY.

1375. Sugden, John P.   "The Sociological Perspective: The Political Economy of Violence in American Sport."   Arena Review.   5, No.1 (February 1981), 57-62.   MECHANISMS OF CONTROL, CAPITALISM, AGGRESSION, MARXIST ANALYSIS.

1376. Surface, Bill.   "Pro Football: Is It Getting Too Dirty?"   Reader's Digest.   105, No.631 (November 1974), 151-154.   RULES, STICKING, BRUTALITY, WINNING AT ANY COST, NFL, INJURIES, REFORM.

1377. Swift, E. M.   "Blood and Ice."   Sports Illustrated.   69, No.25 (December 5, 1988), 56-71.   UNSPORTSMANLIKE CONDUCT, NHL, PENALTIES, REFORM.

1378. Swift, E. M.   "The NHL Isn't So Tough."   Sports Illustrated.   67, No.16 (October 12, 1987), 122.   NHL, PENALTIES, FIGHTING, VIOLENCE, RULES, REFORM.

1379. Tandy, Ruth E. and Joyce Laflin.   "Aggression and Sport: Two Theories."   Journal of Health, Physical Education, and Recreation.   44, No.5 (June 1973), 19-20.   AGGRESSION AS INSTINCTIVE, AGGRESSION AS LEARNED.

1380. Terry, Peter C. and John J. Jackson.   "The Determinants and Control of Violence in Sport."   Quest.   37, No.1 (1985), 27-37.   AGGRESSION AS INSTINCT, AGGRESSION AS LEARNED BEHAVIOR, SOCIALIZATION.

1381. Thirer, Joel.   "Aggression Theory Applied to Sport and Physical Activity."   Motor Skills: Theory into Practice.   2, No.2 (Spring 1978), 128-136.   CATHARSIS THEORY AND SOCIAL LEARNING THEORY OF AGGRESSION, VIOLENCE.

1382. Thirer, Joel. "The Effect of Observing Filmed Violence on the Aggressive Attitudes of Female Athletes and Non-Athletes." Journal of Sport Behavior. 1, No.1 (February 1978), 28-36. MEDIA, MENZIES AGGRESSIVE ATTITUDE SCALE.

1383. Thirer, Joel. "The Psychological Perspective: Analysis of Violence in Sport." Arena Review. 5, No.1 (February 1981), 37-43. CATEGORIES OF VIOLENCE, MULTI-FACETED NATURE OF VIOLENCE, SPORTS AS A REFLECTION OF SOCIETY.

1384. Underwood, John. "An Unfolding Tragedy." Sports Illustrated. 49, No.7 (August 14, 1978), 68-72. HARM, FOOTBALL, INJURIES, LAWSUITS, FOOTBALL HELMET AS A WEAPON, CHANGE, NEW TECHNIQUES, SPORTS MEDICINE, COACHING PRACTICES, BRUTALITY.

1385. Unger, Norman O. "Sad Tales Litter Road to Boxing Championship for More Than a Few." Jet. 65, No.18 (January 9, 1984), 46-49. UNFULFILLED DREAMS, INJURIES, BRAIN AND EYE DAMAGE.

1386. "Violence--A Cancer at Hockey's Throat." Maclean's. 92, No.9 (February 26, 1979), 40-41. PRO HOCKEY, REFORM, NHL.

1387. Wehrwein, Austin. "Three Former Minnesota Players Acquitted of Rape, But President Continues to Deplore Their Acts." The Chronicle of Higher Education. 32, No.23 (August 6, 1986), 31-32. MITCHELL LEE, KEVIN SMITH, GEORGE WILLIAMS, UNIVERSITY OF MINNESOTA, ROLE OF THE COLLEGE PRESIDENT.

1388. Williams, John. "The Brutes are Coming." New Statesman and Society. 1, No.1 (June 10, 1988), 19. ENGLISH FANS, EUROPEAN CHAMPIONSHIP, HOOLIGANISM, SOCIAL CLASSES.

1389. Williams, John, Eric Dunning and Patrick Murphy. "Football's Fighting Traditions." History Today. 38 (March 1988), 5-7. ENGLISH SOCCER FANS, RITUALS, HISTORY, RESPECTABILITY.

1390. Woods, Sherwyn M. "The Violent World of the Athlete." Quest. 16 (June 1971), 55-60. ATHLETICS AS A SOCIAL INSTITUTION, COACHES, AGGRESSION.

1391. Wulf, Steve. "Brawl Game!" Sports Illustrated. 73, No.9 (August 27, 1990), 12-17. PROFESSIONAL BASEBALL, BASEBALL RESEMBLING HOCKEY, PITCHERS HITTING BATTERS, BATTERS CHARGING PITCHERS, BENCH CLEARING BRAWLS, NEW RULES.

1392. Ziegel, Vic. "The Boxer." Rolling Stone. No.389 (February 17, 1983), 30-32+. RAY MANCINI, BRAIN DAMAGE, RULE CHANGES.

1393. Zimmerman, Paul. "The Agony Must End." Sports Illustrated. 65, No.20 (November 10, 1986), 16-21. NFL, INJURIES, ARTIFICIAL TURF, STEROIDS, COACHING, SANCTIONS.

Sport and Society

ACADEMICS AND ATHLETICS

Books

1394. Bend, Emil. <u>The Impact of Athletic Participation on Academic and Career Aspiration and Achievement</u>. Pittsburgh: Institute for Performance Technology, American Institutes for Research, 1968. PSYCHOLOGY, SOCIOLOGY, CHARACTER, PERSONALITY, GROWTH AND DEVELOPMENT.

1395. Braddock, Jomills Henry. <u>Academics and Athletics in American High Schools: Some Further Considerations of the Adolescent Subculture Hypothesis</u>. Baltimore: Johns Hopkins University, Center for Social Organization of Schools, 1979. BENEFIT AND HARM OF SPORT, SPORT ETHOS, CHARACTER, VALUES, HIGH SCHOOL SPORTS.

1396. Frey, James H. (ed.). <u>The Governance of Intercollegiate Athletics</u>. West Point, NY: Leisure Press, 1982. HISTORY, INTERCOLLEGIATE ATHLETICS, FUTURE, ATHLETE RIGHTS, ATHLETIC DIRECTORS, NCAA, BIG TIME COLLEGE SPORTS, AIAW, VIOLENCE, LAW.

1397. Lapchick, Richard Edward. <u>Pass to Play: Student Athletes and Academics</u>. Washington, D.C: National Education Association, 1989. FUTURE, NO PASS/NO PLAY, TEXAS, PROPOSITION 48, BLACK ATHLETES.

1398. Lapchick, Richard Edward and Robert Malekoff. <u>On the Mark: Putting the Student Back in Student-Athlete</u>. Lexington, MA: Lexington Books, 1987. DRUGS, ALCOHOL, GAMBLING, RECRUITING, RULES, WOMEN.

1399. Moulton, Phillips P. <u>Enhancing the Values of Intercollegiate Athletics at Small Colleges</u>. Ann Arbor, MI: University of Michigan, Center for the Study of Higher Education, 1978. NCAA DIVISION III, RECRUITING, FINANCIAL AID, REFORM, INTERCOLLEGIATE ATHLETICS.

1400. Slater, Jana Kay. Impact of 'Pass to Play' Legislation. Sacramento, CA: California State Department of Education, 1987. DISCRIMINATION, BLACK ATHLETES, PROPOSITION 48.

1401. Underwood, Clarence. The Student-Athlete: Eligibility and Academic Integrity. East Lansing, MI: Michigan State University Press, 1984. NCAA, BLACK ATHLETE REVOLT, FINANCIAL AID, RECRUITMENT, LAW.

1402. Yaeger, Don. Undue Process: The NCAA's Injustice For All. Champaign, IL: Sagamore Publishing Inc., 1991. CRITIQUE OF NCAA, JUSTICE, TRUTHFULNESS, ABUSE OF POWER, CALL FOR A FAIRER NCAA.

Articles

1403. Adelman, Melvin L. "Academicians and American Athletics: A Decade of Progress." Journal of Sport History. 10, No.1 (Spring 1983), 80-106. REVIEW OF RECENT SCHOLARSHIP ON HISTORY OF AMERICAN SPORT, FUTURE RESEARCH NEEDS, HISTORICAL SURVEYS, SPORT AND THE SOCIAL ORDER, IDEOLOGY OF SPORT, URBAN ORDER AND THE RISE OF SPORT.

1404. Adler, Jerry. "He Can Run, Can He Pass?" Newsweek. 112 (December 26, 1988), 71. GARY EDWARDS, ELIGIBILITY, NO PASS/NO PLAY, RACISM.

1405. Alley, Louis E. "Athletics in Education: The Double-Edged Sword." The Education Digest. 40, No.4 (December 1974), 32-35. BENEFIT AND HARM, SPORTS AS AN EDUCATIONAL TOOL, BEHAVIOR PATTERNS, ATHLETICS AS A DESTRUCTIVE FACTOR, EXCELLENCE.

1406. Arakelian, Greg and Kevin Bashaw. "Beating the Academic Problem." Scholastic Coach. 57, No.5 (December 1987), 92+. RULES, FOOTBALL STUDY HALL, TUTORS.

1407. Banks, Samuel A. "Sport: Academic Stepchild." Journal of Popular Culture. 16, No.4 (Spring 1983), 90-100. ADVERSARY RELATIONSHIP BETWEEN ATHLETICS AND ACADEMICS, REFORM, TEACHING PHYSICAL EDUCATION, VALUES.

1408. Berry, Bill. "They Shot Down the 'Dumb Jock' Label." Ebony. 36, No.7 (May 1981), 82-84+. INDUSTRIALIZATION, BLACK ATHLETES, STEREOTYPES.

1409. Bowen, Ezra. "The Worst of Two Worlds: Academic Double Standard Leave Many Athletes Undereducated." Time. 126, No.17 (October 28, 1985), 64. MISEDUCATION, REFORMS.

1410. Brown, Gwilym S. "Jeepers! Peepers is in Charge Now." Sports Illustrated. 37, No.17 (October 23, 1972), 40-42+. JACK SCOTT, OBERLIN COLLEGE, ATHLETIC DIRECTOR, COMMERCIALIZATION, PRESSURE TO WIN, ELITISM OF SPORTS.

1411. Brubaker, Bill. "It's Not as Simple as A..B..C." Sports Illustrated. 59, No.9 (August 29, 1983), 24-31. GARY ANDERSON, TAMPA BAY BANDITS, PRO FOOTBALL, ILLITERACY, SUITS.

1412. Cramer, Jerome. "Kappan Special Report: Winning or Learning? Athletics and Academics in America." Phi Delta Kappan. 67, No.9 (May 1986), K1-K8. CORRUPTION, REFORM, NCAA, GAMBLING, POINT SHAVING, MONEY.

1413. Crowl, John A. "Sports Figures Urge Higher Entrance Standards for Students Who Get Athletic Scholarships." The Chronicle of Higher Education. 24, No.14 (June 2, 1982), 1+. BIG TIME COLLEGE SPORTS, ACADEMIC STANDARDS, LEGISLATION TO TIGHTEN STANDARDS.

1414. Dalmolen, Albert. "Let's Divorce Competitive Sports From Higher Education." The Chronicle of Higher Education. 31, No.18 (January 15, 1986), 43. TULANE SCANDAL, REFORM.

1415. Edwards, Harry. "Athletic Performance in Exchange for an Education--A Contract Unfulfilled." The Crisis. 90, No.5 (May 1983), 10-14. RECRUITMENT, EXPLOITATION, SCANDALS, BIG TIME COLLEGE SPORTS, SCHOLARSHIP, RULE 48, BILL OF RIGHTS, REFORM.

1416. Eitzen, D. Stanley. "The Educational Experiences of Intercollegiate Student-Athletes." Journal of Sport and Social Issues. 11, Nos.1&2 (December 1987), 15-30. PREPARATION OF STUDENTS, IMPEDIMENTS, WOMEN, MINORITIES, REFORM.

1417. Eitzen, D. Stanley and Dean A. Purdy. "The Academic Preparation and Achievement of Black and White Collegiate Athletes." Journal of Sport and Social Issues. 10, No.1 (Winter/Spring 1986), 15-27. BIG TIME COLLEGE SPORTS, FAILURE, EXPLOITATION.

1418. England, David A. "Athletics, Academics, and Ethics: An Interview with Bob Knight." Phi Delta Kappan. 64, No.3 (November 1982), 159-163. OLYMPICS, BASKETBALL, COACHING, ROLE OF THE COLLEGE PRESIDENT.

1419. Farrell, Charles S. "Athlete's Graduation Rates Eyed as 'Exploitation Index' For College Sports." The Chronicle of Higher Education. 33, No.44 (July 15, 1987), 35-36. MAKING GRADUATION RATES OF ATHLETES PUBLIC, NAACP, CORRUPTION.

1420. Farrell, Charles S. "College Officials Assail Decision Permitting Ineligible Athletes to Play Professional Football." The Chronicle of Higher Education. 34, No.1 (September 2, 1987), A98. NFL, ELIGIBILITY, ACCEPTING MONEY FROM AGENTS, PENALTIES.

1421. Farrell, Charles S. "Colleges 'Owe Those Kids an Education', Ex-Player Says." The Chronicle of Higher Education. 31, No.7 (October 16, 1985), 38. THOMAS SANDERS, OBLIGATION OF THE COLLEGE.

1422. Fiske, Edward B. "Athletes' Test Scores." The New York Times. 132 (January 14, 1983), A11. NCAA, ELIGIBILITY RULE, DEBATE OVER COLLEGE ENTRANCE EXAMS, ATTACK BY BLACK LEADERS, SAT SCORES, DISCRIMINATION.

1423. Freedman, Morris. "Let's Admit that Athletes Are An Integral Part of U.S. Education." The Chronicle of Higher Education. 31, No.18 (January 15, 1986), 43. WINNING, REFORM, VALUE AND BENEFIT OF SPORTS.

1424. Gerdy, John R. "No More 'Dumb Jocks'." The College Board Review. No.143 (Spring 1987), 2-3+. CHEATING, DRUGS, CHANGE IN THE PERCEPTION OF ATHLETES, REFORM AND CHANGE, ATHLETIC DIRECTORS, COACHES, PROPOSITION 48, BENEFIT AND HARM.

1425. Gladwell, Malcolm. "Dunk and Flunk." The New Republic. 194, No.20 (May 19, 1986), 13-15. COLLEGE SPORTS, SCANDALS, JAN KEMP, PREFERENTIAL TREATMENT TO ATHLETES, LAWSUITS, BIG TIME COLLEGE SPORTS, EXPLOITATION, PROPOSITION 48.

1426. Hochfield, George. "We're All Playing Games: The Incompatibility of Athletic and Academic Excellence." Academe: Bulletin of the American Association of University Professors. 73, No.4 (July/August 1987), 39-43. EXCELLENCE, BIG TIME COLLEGE SPORTS, ALUMNI, BENEFIT AND HARM, CORRUPTION.

1427. Hooks, Benjamin L. "Schools That Miseducate." The Crisis. 90, No.5 (May 1983), 4. NCAA, SAT SCORES, ACADEMICS, DISCRIMINATION.

1428. Horn, Stephen. "Toward Justice for the Student-Athlete." The Center Magazine. 15, No.1 (January/February 1982), 28-30. PHYSICAL EDUCATION, EXPLOITATION, BALANCED ATHLETIC PROGRAM, DUE PROCESS, BENEFIT AND HARM.

1429. Howe, LeRoy T. "Academics and Athletics at SMU: A View From a Swaying Bridge." Academe: Bulletin of the American Association of University Professors. 73 (July/August 1987), 18-24. RECRUITMENT, ACADEMIC INTEGRITY, SPORTSMANIA, PROFESSIONALISM, ALUMNI, METHODIST CHURCH, SOUTHERN METHODIST UNIVERSITY.

1430. Keihn, Dennis J. "Balancing Academics and Athletics: It's Not an Impossible Task." The Chronicle of Higher Education. 30, No.6 (April 10, 1985), 88. REFORM, STUDENT-ATHLETES, ROLE OF THE ATHLETIC DIRECTOR.

1431. Keith, Larry. "Sitting, Waiting and Hoping." Sports Illustrated. 52, No.14 (March 31, 1980), 30-33. GLENN FLETCHER, COLLEGE FOOTBALL, PURDUE UNIVERSITY, UTAH STATE UNIVERSITY.

1432. Kirshenbaum, Jerry. "An American Disgrace." Sports Illustrated. 70, No.9 (February 27, 1989), 16-26+. LAW, VIOLENCE, LAWLESSNESS AMONG COLLEGE ATHLETES.

1433. Kirshenbaum, Jerry. "As Bad As Anything That's Ever Come Along." Sports Illustrated. 52, No.8 (February 25, 1980), 11. UNIVERSITY OF NEW MEXICO, SCANDAL, BASKETBALL, NORM ELLENBERGER, PHONY TRANSFER CREDITS, BRIBERY, ACADEMIC INTEGRITY.

1434. Kirshenbaum, Jerry (ed.). "Majoring in Sports at Arizona." Sports Illustrated. 55, No.18 (October 26, 1981), 17-18. PAC 10 REGULATIONS, LOW GRADES, ELIGIBILITY, UNIVERSITY OF ARIZONA, REFORM.

1435. Kirshenbaum, Jerry (ed.). "Stung By A Swarm of B's." Sports Illustrated. 51, No.22 (November 26, 1979), 25. USE OF INELIGIBLE PLAYERS, ARIZONA STATE SUN DEVILS, TRANSFER CREDITS.

1436. Kruszewska, Eva. "Let's Produce Literates, Then Most Valuable Players!" Seventeen. 39 (August 1980), 182. DUMB JOCK STEREOTYPE, BIG BUSINESS.

1437. Lapchick, Richard Edward. "The High School Athlete as the Future College Student-Athlete." Journal of Sport and Social Issues. 11, Nos.1&2 (Fall/Winter 1987-1988), 104-118. RED-SHIRTING, ACADEMIC STANDARDS FOR HIGH SCHOOL ATHLETES, GRADUATION FROM COLLEGE PERCENTAGES, BLACK AND MINORITY ATHLETES, PROPOSITION 48, "NO PASS/NO PLAY".

1438. Laughlin, Neil T. "Athletic Participation and the Grade Point Average, Absences, Cuts, and Disciplinary Referrals of High School Athletes." International Journal of Sport Psychology. 9, No.2 (1978), 79-89. YOUTH, HIGH SCHOOL ATHLETICS.

1439. Leavy, Walter. "Athletes Give Up Big Bucks for Books." Ebony. 36, No.5 (March 1981), 74-76+. COLLEGE AND PRO BASKETBALL, HARDSHIP RULE.

1440. Leerhsen, Charles. "Texas: Benching the Dunces." Newsweek. 106, No.19 (November 4, 1985), 58. NO PASS/NO PLAY, LAWSUITS.

1441. Martin, Warren Bryan. "Why Won't Accreditors Investigate the Abuses in College Athletics?" The Chronicle of Higher Education. 21, No.20 (January 26, 1981), 64. RULE VIOLATIONS, REFORMS, RECRUITING, RACISM, ROLE OF ACCREDITING AGENCIES.

1442. Nack, William. "This Case Was One for the Books." Sports Illustrated. 64, No.8 (February 24, 1986), 34-36. UNIVERSITY OF GEORGIA ATHLETICS, ACADEMIC ABUSES, PROFESSOR JAN KEMP, WHISTLEBLOWING, $2.58 SUIT WON.

1443. Nelson, Eileen S. "How the Myth of the Dumb Jock Becomes Fact: A Developmental View for Counselors." Counseling and Values. 27, No.3 (April 1983), 176-185. AUTONOMY VS. SHAME AND DOUBT, INITIATIVE VS. GUILT, INDUSTRY VS. INFERIORITY, IDENTITY VS. ROLE DIFFUSION, TEACHING PHYSICAL EDUCATION.

1444. Nikou, Nick and Bob Dinardo. "Academics Versus Athletics: Are the Pressures Too Great?" Journal of Physical Education, Recreation and Dance. 56, No.8 (October 1985), 72-73. STUDENT-ATHLETES, RECRUITMENT, ATHLETES AS WHOLE PEOPLE.

1445. Norman, Geoffrey. "Smart Ball." Sports Illustrated. 73, No.10 (September 3, 1990), 114-125. NCAA DIVISION III FOOTBALL, ACADEMIC STANDARDS, VALUE PRIORITIES, MASSACHUSETTS INSTITUTE OF TECHNOLOGY, SWARTHMORE UNIVERSITY, UNIVERSITY OF CHICAGO, "THINKING MAN'S" FOOTBALL.

1446. Oberlander, Susan. "NCAA's Division III Bars Members From Considering Students' Athletic Ability in Giving Financial Aid." The Chronicle of Higher Education. 34, No.19 (January 20, 1988), A37+. UNIVERSITY ATHLETIC ASSOCIATION, BLINDNESS TO ATHLETIC PROWESS.

1447. Ofari, Earl. "Basketball's Biggest Losers." The Progressive. 43, No.4 (April 1979), 48-49. BLACK ATHLETES, DWIGHT SLAUGHTER, CALIFORNIA STATE UNIVERSITY AT LOS ANGELES, LAWSUITS.

1448. Ostro, Harry. "Quality Education and Athletic Integrity." Scholastic Coach. 56, No.8 (March 1987), 4+. SPORT AS A REFLECTION OF SOCIETY, SCANDALS, LEADERSHIP.

1449. Ostro, Harry. "Should Athletes Be Required to Maintain a Specific Academic Level?" Scholastic Coach. 52, No.7 (February 1983), 4-8. SPECIAL TREATMENT, RULES, DISCRIMINATION, SPORTS AS A RIGHT VS A PRIVILEGE, ROLE OF THE ATHLETIC DIRECTOR AND COACH.

1450. Ostro, Harry. "When Athletics Become More Important Than Academics." Scholastic Coach. 55, No.10 (May/June 1986), 4+. JAN KEMP, LAWSUITS, NO PASS-NO PLAY, NCAA, REFORM, RULES, WINNING.

1451. Park, Roberta J. "Three Major Issues: The Academy Takes a Stand." Journal of Physical Education, Recreation and Dance. 54, No.1 (January 1983), 52-53. CONSUMER EDUCATION MOVEMENT, EMPHASIS ON MORAL AND ETHICAL JUDGMENTS, TEACHING PHYSICAL EDUCATION.

1452. Phelps, Terry O. and Jay Miller. "A Team Study Hall Rx for Academic Ills." Scholastic Coach. 57, No.9 (April 1988), 44-45+. BIWEEKLY PROGRESS REPORT, RESPONSIBILITY OF COACHES, TEAM STUDY HALLS, RETREATS.

1453. Phillips, Patricia A. "The Sport Experience in Education." Quest. 23 (January 1975), 94-97. AESTHETICS, SKILL ACQUISITION, IDEAL AND MEANING, SYMBOLIC LANGUAGE.

1454. Purdy, Dean A., D. Stanley Eitzen and Rick Hufnagel. "Are Athletes Also Students? The Educational Attainment of College Athletes." Social Problems. 29, No.4 (April 1982), 439-448. RELATIONSHIP BETWEEN PARTICIPATION IN SPORTS AND EDUCATIONAL ATTAINMENT, BLACKS, SCHOLARSHIP ATHLETES.

1455. Raney, Joseph F. and Terry J. Knapp.   "Student-Athletes and Academic Departments: Allies and Adversaries." The College Student Journal. 21, No.1 (Spring 1987), 86-89. CREDITS EARNED IN VARIOUS DEPARTMENTS, GRADING OF DEPARTMENTS, CONCENTRATION OF CREDITS IN PHYSICAL EDUCATION COURSES, DEVIANT GRADING PRACTICES.

1456. Raney, Joseph F., Terry J. Knapp and Mark Small. "Pass One For the Gipper: Student-Athletes and University Coursework." Arena Review. 7, No.3 (November 1983), 53-60. TRANSCRIPTS OF STUDENT-ATHLETES, PASS-FAIL CLASSES, TRANSFER CREDITS, COURSEWORK BY DEPARTMENT.

1457. Rehberg, Richard A. "Behavioral and Attitudinal Consequences of High School Interscholastic Sports: A Speculative Consideration." Adolescence. 4, No.13 (Spring 1969), 69-88. BENEFIT AND HARM, RELATIONSHIP BETWEEN EDUCATIONAL PURSUITS AND ATHLETIC PARTICIPATION, HIGH SCHOOL SPORTS.

1458. Rogers, Phil. "To Earn or Learn." Sports Illustrated. 72, No.23 (June 4, 1990), 54-56+. TODD VAN POPPEL, TOP HIGH SCHOOL PITCHER, COLLEGE BOUND, ACADEMICS BEFORE FAME AND FORTUNE, HIGH SCHOOL BASEBALL.

1459. Ross, C. Thomas. "Is 'Student-Athlete' a Contradiction in Terms?" The Education Digest. 49, No.4 (December 1983), 32-35. LITIGATION, EXPLOITATION, NCAA, DEGREE IN ATHLETICS, REFORM.

1460. Ross, Kevin. "Late in the Game, A College Athlete Learns to Read." People Weekly. 19, No.7 (February 21, 1983), 47-48. KEVIN ROSS, ACADEMICS, CREIGHTON UNIVERSITY.

1461. Sack, Allen L. "College Sport and the Student-Athlete." Journal of Sport and Social Issues. 11, Nos.1&2 (December 1987), 31-48. COMMERCIALIZATION, PROFESSIONALISM, ROLE CONFLICT OF STUDENT-ATHLETES, COMPENSATION.

1462. "School Athletes Hit the Books--or Else." U. S. News and World Report. 99, No.19 (November 4, 1985), 10. NO PASS/NO PLAY, REFORM, TEXAS, LAWSUITS.

1463. Schott, Joseph L. "If You Flunk, Billy, It'll Cost Us the Game." The Chronicle of Higher Education. 22, No.5 (March 23, 1981), 25. JOCK DOCS, PASSING GRADES TO ATHLETES, FANATICISM.

1464. Shaara, Michael. "Colleges Short-Change Their Football Players." The Saturday Evening Post. 239, No.23 (November 5, 1966), 10+. BENEFIT AND HARM, COLLEGE ATHLETICS, ACADEMICS, INJURIES, PROFESSIONALISM, REFORM.

1465. Shecter, Leonard. "Coming Revolt of the Athletes." Look. 34, No.15 (July 28, 1970), 43-47. JOCK LIB, FREEDOM FOR ATHLETES, JACK SCOTT, AUTHORITARIANISM, COACHES, ATHLETES' BILL OF RIGHTS, REFORM.

1466. Sullivan, Robert. "Acquitted But Still on Trial at Virginia." Sports Illustrated. 61, No.28 (December 24-31, 1984), 100+. OLDEN POLYNICE, UNIVERSITY OF VIRGINIA, PLAGIARISM, HONOR CODE.

1467. "Thoughts on Scholarships: Should a Collegian Major in Football?" The New
       York Times. 124 (December 1, 1974), Section 5, Page 2. ACADEMICS, ROLE
       OF THE COLLEGE PRESIDENT, REFORM, VALUES.

1468. Uehling, Barbara S.   "Academics and Athletics: Creative Divorce or
       Reconciliation." Vital Speeches of the Day. 49, No.16 (June 1, 1983), 504-507.
       COMPETITION, PROPOSITION 48, NCAA, PROFESSIONALISM.

1469. Underwood, John. "Casting a Special Light." Sports Illustrated. 58, No.1
       (January 10, 1983), 58-60+. NOTRE DAME UNIVERSITY, COLLEGE FOOTBALL,
       ACADEMIC STANDARDS, THEODORE M. HESBURGH, STUDENT-ATHLETES.

1470. Underwood, John. "The Writing Is On the Wall." Sports Illustrated. 52, No.21
       (May 19, 1980), 36-72. STUDENT-ATHLETES, PHONY TRANSCRIPTS, EASY
       GRADES, ACADEMIC CHEATING, LOW GRADUATION RATES, NCAA STANDARDS.

1471. Watts, Emily Stipes. "Academics and Athletics: The Balance Point." Athletic
       Administration. 18, No.1 (Fall 1983), 10-12. RULE 48, SAT SCORES,
       SCHOLARSHIPS.

1472. Welling, Brenton. "Athletic Stars, Academic Flops: The NCAA Still Won't
       Tackle the Issue." Business Week. No.2931 (February 3, 1986), 71. RACISM,
       MONEY, ACADEMIC RESPONSIBILITY, ODDS OF BECOMING A STAR, ACADEMICS.

1473. Wheeler, Stanton. "Knowns and Unknowns in Intercollegiate Athletics: A
       Report to the President's Commission." Journal of Sport and Social Issues. 11,
       Nos.1&2 (December 1987), 1-14. FINANCING ATHLETIC PROGRAMS,
       RETIREMENT, ACADEMIC SUPPORT SYSTEMS, WOMEN, RECRUITMENT.

1474. Whitner, Phillip A. and Randall C. Myers. "Academics and an Athlete." The
       Journal of Higher Education. 57, No.6 (November/December 1986), 659-672.
       CASE STUDY, NCAA, ACADEMIC ADVISORS, POLICIES, REFORM.

1475. Williams, Dennis A. "Making Athletes Hit the Books." Newsweek. 100
       (November 29, 1982), 108. STUDENT-ATHLETES, STANDARDS, REFORM,
       CHANCES FOR STARDOM.

BENEFIT AND HARM OF SPORT

Books

1476. Clark, Steven. Fight Against Time: Five Athletes--A Legacy of Courage. New
       York: Atheneum, 1979. FREDDIE STEINMARK, DANNY THOMPSON, JOE ROTH,
       HARRY AGGANIS, ERNIE DAVIS.

1477. Elias, Norbert and Eric Dunning. Quest for Excitement: Sport and Leisure in
       The Civilizing Process. Oxford: Basil Blackwell Ltd., 1986. THEORY OF
       LEISURE, VIOLENCE, SOCIAL PSYCHOLOGY OF SPORTS, GROUP DYNAMICS, SPORTS
       AS A MALE PRESERVE.

1478. Hall, Elizabeth Ray. <u>Moral Development Levels of Athletes in Sport Specific and General Social Situations</u>. PhD Thesis, Texas Woman's University, 1981. MORAL REASONING, LAWRENCE KOHLBERG, COACHES, TEACHING PHYSICAL EDUCATION.

1479. Linehan, Don. <u>Soft Touch: A Sport That Lets You Touch Life</u>. Washington: Acropolis Books, 1976. BASKETBALL, AESTHETICS, POETRY OF MOVEMENT.

1480. Neal, Patsy. <u>Sport and Identity</u>. Philadelphia: Dorrance and Company, 1972. PLAY, COMPETITION, PHILOSOPHY OF PHYSICAL EDUCATION, PHILOSOPHY OF SPORT AND COMPETITION, VALUES, FREEDOM, IDEAL AND MEANING, MORALITY, MARTIN BUBER'S <u>I-THOU</u>.

Articles

1481. Alapack, Rich. "The Distortion of a Human Value." <u>The Journal of Physical Education</u>. 72, No.4 (March/April 1975), 118-119. SOCIALIZATION, DEFINITION OF COMPETITION, SPORTS AS A MIRROR OF SOCIETY, SUCCESS VS QUALITY OF PERFORMANCE.

1482. "Are Sports Good For The Soul?" <u>Newsweek</u>. 77, No.2 (January 11, 1971), 51-52. IDEAL AND MEANING, BENEFIT AND HARM OF SPORT, VALUES, CHARACTER.

1483. Bennett, William J. "In Defense of Sports." <u>Commentary</u>. 61, No.2 (February 1976), 68-70. EXCELLENCE, DEVELOPMENT OF CHARACTER, POSITIVE ASPECTS OF SPORTS.

1484. Bouet, Michel. "The Function of Sport in Human Relations." <u>International Review of Sport Sociology</u>. 1 (1966), 137-140. COMPETITION, FRIENDSHIP.

1485. Chandler, Timothy J. L. "Sports, Winning and Character Building: What Can We Learn From Goffman's Notion of Self Formulation?" <u>Physical Education Review</u>. 11, No.1 (Spring 1988), 3-10. ERVING GOFFMAN, MORAL GROWTH AND DEVELOPMENT, STRIVING TO WIN, DEFINITIONS OF WINNING, GOFFMAN'S CHARACTER TRAITS, JUSTICE AS FAIRNESS.

1486. "Character." <u>The New Yorker</u>. 60 (April 23, 1984), 38-39. SPORTS AND THE NATIONAL CHARACTER SYMPOSIUM, BENEFIT AND HARM, OLYMPICS, SCANDAL.

1487. Cheska, Alyce Taylor. "Sports Spectacular: The Social Ritual of Power." <u>Quest</u>. 30 (Summer 1978), 58-71. POWER, SYMBOLISM, DRAMA, EMOTIONALITY, REPETITION, RITUAL AS COMMUNITY, RITUAL AS POWER.

1488. Cooper, W. E. "Association: An Answer to Egoism." <u>Journal of the Philosophy of Sport</u>. 9 (1982), 66-68. PHILOSOPHY OF SPORT, ALTRUISM, ASSOCIATION WITH OTHERS.

1489. Cowell, Charles C. "The Contributions of Physical Activity to Social Development." <u>Research Quarterly</u>. 31, No.2 (May 1960, Part II), 286-306. SOCIALIZATION, COMMUNICATION, SOCIAL INTERACTION, GROWTH.

1490. Crepeau, Richard C. "Sport, Heroes and Myth." Journal of Sport and Social Issues. 5, No.1 (Spring/Summer 1981), 23-31. SPORT AS A CONVEYOR OF SOCIAL MYTH, HEROES.

1491. Duquin, M. E. "Power and Authority: Moral Consensus and Conformity in Sport." International Review for the Sociology of Sport. 19, Nos.3-4 (1984), 295-304. EFFECT OF SPORT ON CHARACTER, PERSONALITY.

1492. Fairchild, David L. "Creative Sports: Antidote to Alienation?" Journal of the Philosophy of Sport. 5 (Fall 1978), 57-62. INTEGRATION, SPORT AS AN ANTIDOTE TO ALIENATION, MARXISM.

1493. Feigley, David A. "Psychological Burnout in High-Level Athletes." The Physician and Sportsmedicine. 12, No.10 (October 1984), 109-119. PERFECTIONISTS, FEEDBACK, AUTONOMY, DEFINING BURNOUT, MOTIVATION, EXCELLENCE, STRESS.

1494. Ferran, Jacques. "Sport: Its Values and Its Hazards." Olympic Message. 6 (December 1983), 55-58. CORRUPTION, NATURE OF SPORTS, IDEOLOGY, POLICY, COMPETENCE AND AUTHORITY OF SPORTS.

1495. Figley, Grace E. "Moral Education Through Physical Education." Quest. 36, No.1 (1984), 89-101. TEACHING PHYSICAL EDUCATION, LAWRENCE KOHLBERG.

1496. Fimrite, Ron. "These Guys Are Leaders?" Sports Illustrated. 68, No.21 (May 23, 1988), 102. CHARACTER BUILDING, LEADERSHIP CRISIS, AGGRESSIVENESS.

1497. Fraleigh, Warren P. "An Examination of Relationships of Inherent, Intrinsic, Instrumental, and Contributive Values of the Good Sports Contest." Journal of the Philosophy of Sport. 10 (1983), 52-60. VALUES, DEFINITION OF SPORT, NORMATIVE VIEW OF THE GOOD, INHERENT VALUE OF SPORT, GOOD CONTESTS, BAD CONTESTS.

1498. Gallmeier, Charles P. "Traded, Waived, or Gassed: Failure in the Occupational World of Ice Hockey." Journal of Sport and Social Issues. 13, No.1 (Spring 1989), 25-45. DIGNITY, PRO HOCKEY, FAILURE.

1499. "Good Clean Fun." The New Republic. 187, No.5 (August 2, 1982), 10. IDEALISM, MEDIA, HEROES, SCANDALS.

1500. Green, J. H. "Competitive Sport, Morality and Education." Research Papers in Physical Education. 3, No.3 (December 1977), 24-26. CHARACTER, VALUES, TEAMWORK, FAIRNESS.

1501. Haerle, Rudolf K. Jr. "The Athlete as 'Moral' Leader: Heroes, Success Themes and Basic Cultural Values in Selected Baseball Autobiographies, 1900-1970." Journal of Popular Culture. 8, No.2 (Fall 1974), 392-401. SPORT AS A MAJOR FOCUS OF VALUE, INSTITUTIONALIZATION OF SPORT, PRO BASEBALL, PLAYER BIOGRAPHIES, VALUES, CHANGES, SPORT AS A MIRROR OF SOCIETY.

1502. Harris, Donald S. and D. Stanley Eitzen. "The Consequences of Failure in Sport." Urban Life: A Journal of Ethnographic Research. 7, No.2 (July 1978), 177-188. TYPES OF FAILURE, MOBILITY THROUGH SPORTS MYTH, EFFECTS OF THE REMOVAL PROCESS.

1503. Hathaway, Bruce. "Running To Ruin." Psychology Today. 18, No.7 (July 1984), 14-15. MENTAL WELL-BEING, FITNESS FANATICS, COMPULSIVITY, RUNNING.

1504. Hill, Grant Michael and Jeffrey Simons. "A Study of the Sport Specialization on High School Athletics." Journal of Sport and Social Issues. 13, No.1 (Spring 1989), 1-13. HIGH SCHOOL SPORTS, SPECIALIZATION.

1505. Hoberman, John M. "The Body As an Ideological Variable: Sportive Imagery of Leadership and the State." Man and World. 14, No.3 (1981), 309-330. MARXIST ATTITUDE TOWARD THE BODY, NARCISSISM, IDEOLOGY.

1506. Horn, Jack C. "Last Guys Finish Nice." Psychology Today. 13, No.6 (November 1979), 43+. FAVORITISM, GYMNASTICS, POSITION ASSIGNMENTS.

1507. Hyland, Drew A. "Competition and Friendship." Journal of the Philosophy of Sport. 5 (Fall 1978), 27-37. ALIENATION, PLAY AS RESPONSIVE OPENNESS.

1508. Johnson, William Oscar. "What's Happened to Our Heroes?" Sports Illustrated. 59, No.7 (August 15, 1983), 32-42. ATHLETE'S MISDEEDS, ALCOHOL, DRUGS, GAMBLING, SEXUAL ASSAULTS, BRAWLS, FRAUD, DEMISE OF SPORTS, ROLE OF MEDIA.

1509. Kantzer, Kenneth S. "In Search of Heroes." Christianity Today. 29, No.16 (November 8, 1985), 16-17. DRUGS, MEDIA, VALUES, ROLE MODELS.

1510. Keating, James W. "Athletics and the Pursuit of Excellence." Education. 85, No.7 (March 1965), 428-431. HISTORY, MEANING, VALUES, REFORM.

1511. Kelly, Barbara J. "Getting It All Together: The Integrated Learning Semester." Journal of Health, Physical Education, and Recreation. 45, No.8 (October 1974), 32-35. SPORT AND HUMAN VALUES, TEACHING ETHICS, TEACHING PHYSICAL EDUCATION, COMPETITIVE ETHIC, SPORTS IN LITERATURE.

1512. Kiester, Edwin. "The Uses of Anger." Psychology Today. 18, No.7 (July 1984), 26. MOTIVATION, CONCENTRATION, ANGER, OPPONENT, DISTRACTION.

1513. Kleiber, Douglas A. "The Meaning of Power in Sport." International Journal of Sport Psychology. 11, No.1 (1980), 34-41. POWER, MOTIVATION.

1514. Kleiber, Douglas A. and Patricia B. Malik. "Educational Involvement of College Athletes and Subsequent Well-Being in Early Adulthood." Journal of Sport Behavior. 12, No.4 (December 1989), 203-211. ACADEMICS, ACADEMIC EXPERIENCE HAS SIGNIFICANT IMPACT, NCAA DIVISION I, GRADUATION RATES.

1515. Kniker, Charles R. "The Values of Athletics in Schools: A Continuing Debate." Phi Delta Kappan. 56, No.2 (October 1974), 116-120. SELF DISCIPLINE, COACHES AND PLAYERS, COMPETITION, PHYSICAL WELL BEING.

1516. Kucharsky, David. "It's Time to Think Seriously About Sports." Christianity Today. 20 (November 7, 1975), 18-20. SATURATION IN SPORTS, STEWARDSHIP, ORAL ROBERTS UNIVERSITY, RECRUITMENT, BALANCE.

1517. Kuntz, Paul Grimley. "Serious Play: An Absurdity or a Paradox That Integrates Life?" Listening: Journal of Religion and Culture. 16, No.1 (Winter 1981), 68-85. SERIOUS PLAY, MORALITY, AESTHETICS, NATURE OF SPORT.

1518. Lowrey, Burling. "The Dehumanization of Sports." The Virginia Quarterly Review. 52, No.4 (Autumn 1976) 545-559. ROLE IN SOCIETY, HEROES, AMERICAN CHARACTER, GREED, VIOLENCE, BREAKDOWN OF VALUES, PRO SPORTS, ECONOMICS, WINNING AT ALL COSTS, SPECIALIZATION, FAIR PLAY, DARK SIDE, DIRTY TACTICS, OVERSIZED PLAYERS, SADISM.

1519. Lueschen, Guenther. "Cooperation, Association and Contest." The Journal of Conflict Resolution. 14, No.1 (March 1970), 21-34. DEFINITION, COOPERATION BETWEEN GROUP MEMBERS, INTERGROUP ASSOCIATION, ASSOCIATION OF OPPONENTS, RITUAL, REWARDS.

1520. Melnick, Merrill J. "Values of Social Conflict for Sport." The Physical Educator. 31, No.2 (May 1974), 82-86. GROUP COHESIVENESS, FUNCTIONALISM.

1521. Morford, W. R. "Is Sport the Struggle or the Triumph?" Quest. 19 (January 1973), 83-87. DEFINITION OF SPORT, AGON IDEAL IN SPORT.

1522. Morris, Willie. "Football Has 'Helped Moderate Southern Racism'." U. S. News and World Report. 95, No.22 (November 28, 1983), 78. SPORTS AS A MICROCOSM OF SOCIETY, VIOLENCE, PURPOSE, CHANGES.

1523. O'Hanlon, Timothy P. "School Sports As Social Training: The Case of Athletics and the Crisis of World War I." Journal of Sport History. 9, No.1 (Spring 1982), 5-29. BENEFIT OF SPORTS, TRAINING FOR JOBS, TRAINING FOR MILITARY, TRAINING FOR DEMOCRACY AND CAPITALISM, WINNING, YOUTH, ARMED FORCES AND ATHLETES.

1524. Park, Roberta J. "Critics and Criticisms of American College Athletics, 1890-1910." Abstracts of Research Papers. (1980), 115. INTERCOLLEGIATE ATHLETICS, COMPETITION, NCAA, RISE OF SPORTS, COLLEGE PRESIDENT ATTITUDES, HISTORICAL.

1525. Park, Roberta J. "Play and Sport As Moral Education: The Problem of Is and Ought." The Academy Papers. 14 (December 1980), 34-42. VALUES, MORALITY, PLAY, MORAL EDUCATION, PLAY AND SPORT.

1526. Pearson, K. "Some Comments on Philosophic Inquiry Into Sport as a Meaningful Human Experience." Journal of the Philosophy of Sport. (1974), 132-136. EPISTEMOLOGY, ACADEMIC STUDY OF SPORT, PHENOMENOLOGY.

1527. Polednak, Anthony P. and Albert Damon. "College Athletics, Longevity, and Cause of Death." Human Biology. 42, No.1 (February 1970), 28-46. CAUSE OF DEATH, LENGTH OF LIFE, MAJOR AND MINOR ATHLETICS, PHYSIQUE.

1528. Sadler, William A. Jr. "Creative Existence: Play as a Pathway to Personal Freedom and Community." Humanitas: Journal of the Institute of Man. 5, No.1 (Spring 1969), 57-79. PLAY AS A FORM OF CREATIVITY, PLAY IN THE EVERYDAY WORLD, PLAY AS BEHAVIOR.

1529. Schindler, Toni Marie and Marie Waters. "Athletic Involvement and Aspects of Self Actualization." Journal of Sport Behavior. 9, No.2 (June 1986), 59-69. COMPARATIVE STUDY: ATHLETES AND NON-ATHLETES, MEN AND WOMEN, BLACKS AND WHITES, SELF ACTUALIZATION, COUNSELING ATHLETES.

1530. Scruton, Joan. "Sir Ludwig Guttmann: Creator of a World Sports Movement for the Paralysed and Other Disabled." Paraplegia. 17, No.1 (May 1979), 52-55. ARCHERY, WHEEL CHAIR BASKETBALL, OLYMPICS FOR THE DISABLED, "FRIENDSHIP, UNITY, AND SPORTSMANSHIP" MOTTO, SPORTS AND MEDICINE.

1531. Segal, Erich. "It is Not Strength, But Art, Obtains the Prize." The Yale Review. 56, No.4 (Summer 1967), 605-609. GREEK ATHLETICS, SPORTS LITERATURE, OLYMPICS.

1532. "Self-Esteem and Sport." Women's Sports and Fitness. 6, No.8 (August 1984), 71. TEACHING PHYSICAL EDUCATION, LEARNING DISABLED CHILDREN, PARENTS.

1533. Sheehan, George. "The Moral Minority." The Physician and Sportsmedicine. 9, No.7 (July 1981), 33. JOGGERS, ATTITUDES, OBSESSION.

1534. Sisk, John P. "Hot Sporting Blood." Commonweal. 97, No.21 (March 2, 1973), 495-498. COACHES, JOHAN HUIZINGA.

1535. Smith, Garry J. "The Sport Hero: An Endangered Species." Quest. 19 (January 1973), 59-70. WHY PEOPLE WORSHIP HEROES, HOW HERO-WORSHIP DEVELOPS, MANIFESTATIONS OF HERO-WORSHIP, CHANGE AND DEMISE.

1536. Spreitzer, Elmer M. and Eldon E. Snyder. "Sports Involvement and Quality of Life Dimensions." Journal of Sport Behavior. 12, No.1 (March 1989), 3-11. GENDER DIFFERENCES, SPORTS AS ESCAPISM, COMPENSATION FOR LIFE DEFICITS.

1537. Stuck, M. F. "Beliefs and Behaviors--Sport and Clean Living." Arena Review. 12, No.1 (May 1988), 13-24. RELATIONSHIP OF SPORTS AND CLEAN LIVING, DRINKING AND DRUG USE, MYTHS, YOUTH.

1538. Weinberg, S. Kirson and Henry Arond.   "The Occupational Culture of the Boxer." The American Journal of Sociology. 57, No.5 (March 1952), 460-469. SOCIO-ECONOMIC LEVELS, RECRUITMENT, ETHNICS, ROLE MODELS, CULTURE, SOCIAL MOBILITY.

1539. Wohl, Andrzej. "Competitive Sport and Its Social Function." International Review of Sport Sociology. 5 (1970) 117-124. COMPETITION, SOCIAL FUNCTIONS OF SPORTS, EDUCATIONAL FUNCTION, INTEGRATIONAL FUNCTION, MASS SPORT.

1540. Wohl, Andrzej and Halina Szwarc. "The Humanistic Content and Values of Sport for Elderly People." International Review of Sport Sociology. 16, No.4 (1981), 5-13. SPORT AS AN INSTRUMENT OF SOCIAL PROGRESS.

1541. Wynne, Edward A. "Competitive Sports--Inevitably Controversial." Journal of Physical Education, Recreation and Dance. 58, No.3 (March 1987), 80-86. BONDING AMONG FANS AND PLAYERS, OLYMPICS, COMPETITION, YOUTH, CHARACTER.

BIG BUSINESS OF SPORT

Books

1542. Ballinger, Lee. In Your Face: Sports for Love and Money. Chicago: Vanguard Books, 1981. OWNERS, PLAYERS, FANS, OLYMPICS, MINORITIES, MUHAMMAD ALI, WOMEN, ECONOMICS, COLLEGE SPORTS, HIGH SCHOOL SPORTS, RULES.

1543. Berry, Robert C., William B. Gould IV, and Paul D. Staudohar. Labor Relations in Professional Sports. Dover, MA: Auburn House Publishing Company, Inc., 1986. RIGHTS, BASEBALL, FOOTBALL, HOCKEY, BASKETBALL, HISTORICAL PERSPECTIVES, LEGAL CONTEXT, RACE RELATIONS.

1544. Cole, Lewis. A Loose Game: The Sport and Business of Basketball. Indianapolis: The Bobbs Merrill Company, Inc., 1978. SCANDALS, MERGERS.

1545. Davidson, Gary with Bill Libby. Breaking the Game Wide Open. New York: Atheneum, 1974. WORLD FOOTBALL LEAGUE, AMERICAN BASKETBALL ASSOCIATION, WORLD HOCKEY ASSOCIATION, OWNERS, PLAYERS.

1546. Demmert, Henry G. The Economics of Professional Team Sports. Lexington, MA: Lexington Books, 1973. SPORTS INDUSTRY, EQUITY, PUBLIC POLICY.

1547. Denlinger, Kenneth and Leonard Shapiro. Athletes for Sale. New York: Thomas Y. Crowell Company, 1975. RECRUITING, PLAYER PAYOFFS, ALTERED TRANSCRIPTS, ALUMNI SLUSH FUNDS, NCAA, BIG TIME COLLEGE SPORTS, REFORM.

1548. Durso, Joseph. The All-American Dollar: The Big Business of Sports. Boston: Houghton Mifflin Company, 1971. PRO SPORTS, CORRUPTION, FANS, COMMERCIALIZATION.

1549. Dworkin, James B. Owners Versus Players: Baseball and Collective Bargaining. Boston: Auburn House Publishing Company, 1981. UNIONS, MAJOR LEAGUE, BASEBALL PLAYERS ASSOCIATION, RESERVE CLAUSE, FREE AGENCY, SALARIES, LABOR RELATIONS.

1550. Freedman, Warren. Professional Sports and Antitrust. New York: Quorum Books, 1987. ANTITRUST, MONOPOLY, ELIGIBILITY, DISCRIMINATION, CONTRACTS, FIRST AMENDMENT.

1551. Gallner, Sheldon M. Pro Sports: The Contract Game. New York: Charles Scribner's Sons, 1974. CONTRACTS, OPTIONS, SALARIES, NEGOTIATIONS, LITIGATION, EXPLOITATION.

1552. Halberstam, David. The Breaks of the Game. New York: Alfred A. Knopf, Inc., 1981. PORTLAND TRAILBLAZERS, BASKETBALL.

1553. Hofmann, Dale and Martin J. Greenberg. Sport$biz: An Irreverent Look at Big Business in Pro Sports. Champaign, IL: Leisure Press, 1989. CONTRACTS, SPORTS LAW, UNIONS, AGENTS, CORPORATE SPONSORS, GAMBLING, BIG BUSINESS.

1554. King, Peter. The Season After: Are Sports Dynasties Dead? New York: Warner Books, Inc., 1989. FOOTBALL, DRAFT, MONEY, CORPORATE SPONSORS, WINNING AT ALL COSTS, CONTRACTS, AGENTS.

1555. Klatell, David A. and Norman Marcus. Sports for Sale: Television, Money and the Fans. New York: Oxford University Press, Inc., 1988. HISTORY, ECONOMICS, SOCIOLOGY OF TELEVISION, FUTURE, COMMERCIALIZATION, OLYMPICS.

1556. Klein, Gene and David Fisher. First Down and a Billion: The Funny Business of Pro Football. New York: William Morrow and Company, 1987. SAN DIEGO CHARGERS, COACHES, AGENTS, PLAYERS, LITIGATION, DRAFT, DRUGS, AL DAVIS.

1557. Lawrence, Paul R. Unsportsmanlike Conduct: The National Collegiate Athletic Association and the Business of College Football. New York: Praeger Publishers, 1987. NCAA, COMPETITION, TELEVISION, CARTELS, FUTURE.

1558. Lineberry, William P. The Business of Sports. New York: H. W. Wilson Company, 1973. MONEY, COMMERCIALISM, CORRUPTION, TELEVISION, OLYMPICS, COLLEGE SPORTS, PRO SPORTS, GAMBLING, REFORM.

1559. Lowenfish, Lee Elihu and Tony Lupien. The Imperfect Diamond: The Story of Baseball's Reserve System and the Men Who Fought to Change It. New York: Stein and Day, 1980. LABOR RELATIONS, BASEBALL'S RESERVE SYSTEM, CASE STUDIES, SALARIES, PENSIONS, JUSTICE, FREEDOM, RIGHTS.

1560. Markham, Jesse William and Paul V. Teplitz. Baseball Economics and Public Policy. Lexington, MA: Lexington Books, 1981. ROLE OF SPORT IN SOCIETY, ECONOMICS, PUBLIC POLICY, MONEY.

1561. Scully, Gerald W. The Business of Major League Baseball. Chicago: The University of Chicago Press, 1989. RULES, FANS, EMPHASIS ON WINNING, BUSINESS, SALARIES, DISCRIMINATION.

1562. Sloane, Peter J. Sport in the Market? The Economic Causes and Consequences of the 'Packer Revolution'. London: The Institute of Economic Affairs, 1980. DEFINITION, COMPETITION, BIG BUSINESS, CARTELS, EXPLOITATION.

1563. Staudohar, Paul D. The Sports Industry and Collective Bargaining. Ithaca, NY: Cornell University Press, 1986. LABOR RELATIONS, PRO BASEBALL, BASKETBALL, FOOTBALL, HOCKEY, SALARIES, PLAYER MOBILITY, DRUG TESTING, ANTITRUST LAWS.

1564. Stedman, Randy M.   Professional Baseball and the Antitrust Laws: An Arbitrated Impasse? M.S. Thesis, California State University at Hayward, 1984. RESERVE CLAUSE, FREEDOM, MONOPOLIES, ANTITRUST LAWS, BASEBALL, UNIONS.

1565. Voigt, David Quentin.   Cash and Glory: The Commercialization of Major League Baseball as a Sports Spectacular, 1865-1892. Ph.D. Thesis, Syracuse University, 1963. PRO BASEBALL, MONEY, SPORT AND SOCIETY.

Articles

1566. Beamish, Rob.   "Understanding Labor as a Concept for the Study of Sport." Sociology of Sport Journal. 2, No.4 (December 1985), 357-364. WILLIAM J. MORGAN, MARX, HEGEL, CREATIVE DIMENSION OF LABOR, ALIENATION, DEHUMANIZATION, USE-VALUE.

1567. Boyle, Robert H.   "And Then the Clock Showed 00:00." Sports Illustrated. 57, No.14 (September 27, 1982), 14-17. PRO FOOTBALL, PLAYER STRIKE, NFLPA, NFL MANAGEMENT COUNCIL, GENE UPSHAW, JACK DONLON, MONEY, DRUG TESTING.

1568. Carlson, Robert S.   "The Business of Professional Sports: A Reexamination in Progress."   New York Law Forum.   18, No.4 (Spring 1973), 915-933. FORMATION OF THE AMERICAN BASKETBALL ASSOCIATION, RESERVE CLAUSE, PLAYER DRAFT, FOUR YEAR RULE, EXCLUSIVE TERRITORY AGREEMENTS.

1569. Chass, Murray.   "Commissioner of Baseball Ends Steinbrenner's Control of Yanks." The New York Times. 134 (July 31, 1990), A1+. PRO BASEBALL, GEORGE STEINBRENNER, INCOMPLETE BAN FOR $40,000 PAYOFF, HOWARD SPIRA, FAY VINCENT, COMMISSIONER OF BASEBALL, NEW YORK YANKEES, END OF STEINBRENNER ERA.

1570. Collins, Patrick J.   "Athletes For Hire." America. 140, No.1 (January 6-13, 1979), 9-11. FANS, PLAYERS, OWNERS, INVESTORS, SPECTATOR SPORTS.

1571. Crowl, John A.   "NCAA Rejects Bid for Autonomy by Big-Time Football Colleges."   The Chronicle of Higher Education.   27, No.19 (January 18, 1984), 33. DIVISION 1-A, AUTONOMY, RULES.

1572. Dworkin, James B. and Jay Park.   "Collective Bargaining in Professional Basketball: An Empirical Investigation."   Journal of Sport Behavior.   9, No.4 (September 1986), 131-140. OSCAR ROBERTSON CASE, FREE AGENCY.

1573. Ellenberger, Norman.   "Tell It Like It Is: We Have To Make Money."   The Center Magazine.   15, No.1 (January/February 1982), 21-22. FOOTBALL, BASKETBALL, PRO ATHLETICS, HEROES, ACADEMICS, NCAA RULES.

1574. Goodman, Cary.   "Corporate Colonization of Sport."   Arena Review.   5, No.3 (November 1981), 1-2. CORPORATE SPONSORSHIPS, FREEDOM.

1575. Hardy, Stephan H.   "Entrepreneurs, Organizations and the Sport Marketplace: Subjects in Search of Historians."   Journal of Sport History.   13, No.1 (Spring 1986), 14-33.   OBLIGATIONS OF SPORT ACADEMICS, HISTORICAL STUDIES, ECONOMICS, SPORT MARKETPLACE, SPORT INDUSTRY, IMPACT OF SPORTS.

1576. Hughes, Robert H. and Jay J. Coakley.   "Mass Society and the Commercialization of Sport."   Sociology of Sport Journal.   1, No.1 (1984), 57-63. MASS MEDIA, CASE STUDY, MASS APPEAL OF SPORTS.

1577. Jacobs, Michael S. and Ralph K. Winter, Jr. "Antitrust Principles and Collective Bargaining by Athletes: Of Superstars in Peonage." The Yale Law Journal. 81, No.1 (November 1971), 1-29. LABOR LAW, RESERVE CLAUSE, FREEDOM OF CONTRACT, DUTY OF FAIR REPRESENTATION.

1578. Johnson, Arthur T.   "Municipal Administration and the Sports Franchise Relocation   Issue."   Public   Administration   Review.   43,   No.6 (November/December 1983), 519-528. COSTS AND BENEFITS OF A SPORT FRANCHISE TO A CITY, POLICY OPTION TO RESTRICT THE FRANCHISE MOMENTUM.

1579. Johnson, William Oscar.   "Sports and Suds."   Sports Illustrated.   69, No.6 (August 8, 1988), 68-82. BEER BUSINESS, NUMBER ONE SPORT TEAM SPONSOR, PROFITS, COMPETITION, FAN BEHAVIOR, BEER COMMERCIALS, NEGATIVE EFFECTS.

1580. Kahn, Roger.   "Can Sports Survive Money?"   Esquire.   84, No.4 (October 1975), 105-109. MATERIALISM, HIGH SALARIES, CORRUPTION, TELEVISION.

1581. Kanfer, Stefan.   "Football: Show Business With a Kick."   Time.   102, No.15 (October 8, 1973), 54+. MEDIA, TELEVISION, FANS.

1582. Kennedy, Ray and Nancy P. Williamson.   "Money in Sports: For the Athlete, How Much is Too Much?" Sports Illustrated. 49, No.4 (July 24, 1978), 34-49. SALARIES, PLAYERS, MILLIONAIRES, JOCK ELITES, SPORTS AS SHOW BIZ, MONEY AS PLAYER MOTIVATION, COMPARATIVE SPORT SALARIES.

1583. Kennedy, Ray and Nancy P. Williamson. "Money in Sports: The Monster Threatening Sports." Sports Illustrated. 49, No.3 (July 17, 1978), 29+. MONEY, SPORTS INDUSTRY, SELF REGULATING MONOPOLY, UNFAIR FRANCHISE DISTRIBUTION, TELEVISION INCOME, OWNER-PLAYER IMBALANCE, FREE AGENTS, TAX HAVEN.

1584. Kilpatrick, James J. "Of Greenbacks and Quarterbacks." Nation's Business. 70, No.11 (November 1982), 14. FOOTBALL STRIKE, HIGH PLAYER SALARIES.

1585. King, Larry W. "What the Pros Need Now." Women's Sports and Fitness. 7, No.7 (August 1985), 56. MONEY, SPONSORS, FANS.

1586. Koppett, Leonard. "Antitrust in the Ball Park: What the Rhubarb is All About." The Nation. 222, No.19 (May 15, 1976), 587-592. CHANGE, RESERVE SYSTEM, PLAYER FREEDOM, BASEBALL, FOOTBALL, BASKETBALL, ANTITRUST LAWS.

1587. Large, Arlen J. "Blowing the Whistle on Pro Sports." Wall Street Journal. 178, No.78 (October 20, 1971), 20. MONEY, WHISTLEBLOWING, RESERVE CLAUSE, TELEVISION RECEIPTS.

1588. Lichtenstein, Grace. "Playing for Money." Rolling Stone. No.379 (September 30, 1982), 44-45+. BIG TIME COLLEGE SPORTS, STUDENT-ATHLETES, SCANDALS, PLAYERS FIGHT BACK.

1589. Lowell, Cym H.   "Collective Bargaining and the Professional Team Sport Industry." Law and Contemporary Problems. 38, No.1 (Winter/Spring 1973), 3-41. NATIONAL LABOR RELATIONS ACT, ANTITRUST LAWS, SALARY, STRIKES, PLAYERS' RIGHTS.

1590. Lublin, Joann S. "Sports as Political Football." Wall Street Journal. 195, No.9 (January 14, 1980), 18. FEDERAL RULES, SEX-BIAS RULES, TITLE IX, COMPLIANCE REVIEWS.

1591. Lynch, Mitchell C. "Tackling the Pros: Antitrust Forces Study Possible Big Changes in Professional Sports." Wall Street Journal. 186, No.117 (December 15, 1975), 1+. TEAM HOLD ON PLAYERS, GOVERNMENT INTERVENTION, MONOPOLIES, MERGERS, LABOR RELATIONS.

1592. Nocera, Joseph. "The Screwing of the Average Fan: Edward Bennett Williams and the Washington Redskins." The Washington Monthly. 10, No.4 (June 1978), 34-41. PRO FOOTBALL, EDWARD BENNETT WILLIAMS, WASHINGTON REDSKINS.

1593. Odenkirk, James E.   "Intercollegiate Athletics: Big Business or Sport?" Academe: Bulletin of the American Association of University Professors. 67, No.2 (April 1981), 62-66. EXCESSIVE ECONOMIC NEEDS OF COLLEGE ATHLETIC PROGRAMS, RECRUITMENT ABUSES, FINANCIAL SUBSIDIES, RESPONSIBILITY OF COLLEGE PRESIDENTS.

1594. Poe, Randall. "Moneyball." Across the Board. 18, No.8 (September 1981), 12-21. PRO BASEBALL, SALARIES, BIG BUSINESS, FREE AGENCY, ANTITRUST, PLAYER CONTRACTS.

1595. Roberts, Michael. "Ball and Chains." The New Republic. 172, No.5 (February 1, 1975), 9-10. RESERVE CLAUSE, PLAYER RIGHTS, CONTRACTS, CHANGE.

1596. Rosen, Sherwin. "The Economics of Superstars." The American Scholar. 52 (Autumn 1983), 449-460. SALARIES, PROBABILITY OF SUCCESS, TECHNOLOGY.

1597. Sage, George H. "The Intercollegiate Sport Cartel and Its Consequences for Athletes." Arena Review. 3, No.3 (October 1979), 2-8. NCAA, RULES, BUREAUCRACY, MONOPOLY POWER, BENEFIT AND HARM.

1598. Sanoff, Alvin P. "Even Bigger Bucks Ahead for Pro Sports." U. S. News and World Report. 93, No.15 (October 11, 1982), 74-75. MEDIA, HOCKEY, BASEBALL, BASKETBALL, FOOTBALL, CABLE TELEVISION.

1599. Scully, Gerald W. "Economic Discrimination in Professional Sports." Law and Contemporary Problems. 38, No.1 (Winter/Spring 1973), 67-84. BLACK ATHLETES, PLAYING POSITIONS, ENTRY BARRIERS, SALARY DISCRIMINATION.

1600. Seiden, Melvin. "The Business of Tennis." Dissent. 31, No.4 (Fall 1984), 487-491. COMPETITION, TECHNOLOGY, TENNIS AS A SOCIAL PHENOMENON, WIMBLEDON, CHANGE, TEAM TENNIS.

1601. Smith, Paul. "Saturday Afternoon Fever." The Times Literary Supplement. No.4019 (April 4, 1980), 379. REVIEW OF ASSOCIATION FOOTBALL AND ENGLISH SOCIETY 1863-1915 BY TONY MASON, HISTORY, WORKING CLASS, CHARACTER BUILDING.

1602. "Sports: How Dirty a Game?" Harper's. 271, No.1624 (September 1985), 45-56. MONEY, CHANGE, SPORTS AS A REFLECTION OF SOCIETY, CORRUPTION, NO PASS/NO PLAY.

1603. Staudohar, Paul D. "Professional Football and the Great Salary Dispute." Personnel Journal. 61, No.9 (September 1982), 673-679. BIG BUSINESS, LABOR RELATIONS, PLAYER MOBILITY, TELEVISION REVENUES, FRANCHISE TAX STRUCTURES, FREE AGENTS.

1604. Stewart, Robert M. (Reviewed by Wray Vamplew). "Sport as Big Business." Journal of Sport History. 13, No.3 (Winter 1986), 279-280. CORPORATE SPONSORSHIP OF AUSTRALIAN SPORT, COMMERCIALIZATION OF SPORT.

1605. Stone, Marvin. "Megabucks for Athletes." U. S. News and World Report. 94, No.12 (March 28, 1983), 80. HERSCHEL WALKER, ESCAPE CLAUSE.

1606. Symington, James W. "The Art of Special Pleading." Harper's. 271, No.1623 (August 1985), 20-21. NHL, DEDUCTIONS FOR SPORTS TICKETS, PUBLIC GOOD.

1607. Telander, Rick. "Senseless." Sports Illustrated. 72, No.20 (May 14, 1990), 36-49. NIKE SNEAKERS, ADVERTISING, MINORITIES.

1608. "Upheaval in Pro Sports." U. S. News and World Report. 77, No.7 (August 12, 1974), 51-54. GOVERNMENT INVOLVEMENT, CHANGE AND DEMISE, RESERVE RULE, SALARIES.

1609. Wheeler, Robert F. "Organized Sport and Organized Labour: The Workers' Sports Movement." Journal of Contemporary History. 13, No.2 (April 1978), 191-210. WORKING CLASS ATTRACTION TO SPORTS, CAPITALISM, CULTURE.

BIG TIME NCAA COLLEGE SPORT

Books

1610. Atwell, Robert H., Bruce Grimes and Donna A. Lopiano. The Money Game: Financing Collegiate Athletics. Washington, D.C: American Council on Education, 1980. MINORITIES, TELEVISION, ALUMNI GIVING, RECRUITING, WINNING.

1611. Chu, Donald B. The Character of American Higher Education and Intercollegiate Sport. Albany, NY: State University of New York Press, 1989. ACADEMICS, CHANGE AND REFORM, MONEY.

1612. Chu, Donald B., Jeffrey O. Segrave and Beverly J. Becker (eds.). Sport and Higher Education. Champaign, IL: Human Kinetics Publishers, 1985. COMMERCIALIZATION, STUDENT-ATHLETES, BOOSTERISM, CHARACTER BUILDING, VALUES, ECONOMICS, WOMEN, MINORITIES, REFORM, PROPOSITION 48.

1613. DeVenzio, Dick. Rip-off U: The Annual Theft and Exploitation of Major College Revenue Producing Student-Athletes. Charlotte, NC: The Fool Court Press, 1986. BASKETBALL, FOOTBALL, CHEATING, CORRUPTION, SCANDALS, NCAA, ACADEMICS, REFORM.

1614. Durso, Joseph. The Sports Factory: An Investigation into College Sports. New York: Quadrangle/New York Times Book Company, 1975. RECRUITING VIOLATIONS, PLAYER PAYOFFS, WINNING AT ALL COSTS, NCAA RULES.

1615. Evans, J. Robert. Blowing the Whistle on Intercollegiate Sports. Chicago: Nelson-Hall Company, 1974. FINANCING COLLEGE ATHLETICS, RECRUITING, SCHOLARSHIPS, COACHES AND PLAYERS, REFORM.

1616. Flath, Arnold William. A History of Relations Between the National Collegiate Athletic Association and the Amateur Athletic Union of the United States (1905-1963). Champaign, IL: Stipes Publishing Company, 1964. SEMI PROFESSIONALISM, FORWARD BY EARLE F. ZEIGLER, AMATEURISM, PROFESSIONALISM, ELIGIBILITY.

1617. Locke, Tates. Caught in the Net. West Point, NY: Leisure Press, 1982. CLEMSON UNIVERSITY, COLLEGE BASKETBALL, CHEATING, TAYLOR O. LOCKE, PLAYER PAYOFFS, ACADEMICS, NCAA PROBE.

1618. Smith, Ronald A. Sports and Freedom: The Rise of Big-Time College Athletics. New York: Oxford University Press, Inc., 1988. DEFINITION OF SPORT, AMATEURISM, PROFESSIONALISM, LEISURE, PRIVILEGED CLASS, HISTORY, COLLEGE ATHLETICS.

1619. Whitford, David. A Payroll to Meet: A Story of Greed, Corruption and Football at SMU. New York: Macmillan Publishing Company, 1989. RECRUITING VIOLATIONS, NCAA, COLLEGE FOOTBALL.

Articles

1620. "24 Institutions Under NCAA Sanctions." The Chronicle of Higher Education. 35, No.14 (November 30, 1988), A38. RECRUITING VIOLATIONS, IMPROPER BENEFITS TO PLAYERS, DRUGS, PENALTIES.

1621. Applebome, Peter. "Is There Life After Football?" The New York Times Magazine. (October 4, 1987), 73-76+. SOUTHERN METHODIST UNIVERSITY, COLLEGE FOOTBALL.

1622. Atwood, John. "Winning One for the Giver is a Loser." Psychology Today. 13, No.12 (May 1980), 18-19. RELATIONSHIP BETWEEN ATHLETIC SUCCESS AND ALUMNI GIVING, WOMEN, REDISTRIBUTION OF FUNDS.

1623. Axthelm, Pete. "The Pac-10 Tackles the Empty Helmets." Newsweek. 96 (August 25, 1980), 56. SCANDALS, TRANSCRIPT TAMPERING, PENALTIES.

1624. Axthelm, Pete. "The Shame of College Sports." Newsweek. 96 (September 22, 1980), 54-55+. ACADEMICS, EXPLOITATION OF STUDENT-ATHLETES, RECRUITING, SPORTSMANIA.

1625. Beezley, William H. "The 1961 Scandal at North Carolina State and the End of the Dixie Classic." Arena Review. 7, No.3 (November 1983), 33-52. SPORTS AND GAMBLING, PUNISHMENT, PUBLIC DISCUSSION, ECONOMIC RESULTS, GAMBLERS AND THE COURTS.

1626. Berryman, Jack W. "Historical Roots of the Collegiate Dilemma." Proceedings, 79th Annual Meeting of National Collegiate Physical Education Association for Men. (1976), 141-154. ROLE OF SPORT IN COLLEGES, BIG BUSINESS, EDUCATIONAL, RECREATIVE DEBATE, HISTORY.

1627. Blumenthal, Karen. "Spirited Giving: Overzealous Boosters Threaten the Integrity of College Sports." Wall Street Journal. 206, No.126 (December 27, 1985), 1+. NCAA CRACK DOWN, BOOSTERS, PENALTIES FOR ABUSE, PAYMENTS TO ATHLETES BY FANS.

1628. Boyle, Robert H. "Scandal That Just Gets Worse and Worse (University of New Mexico Basketball Probe)." Sports Illustrated. 52, No.24 (June 9, 1980), 22-25. GAMBLING, FORGED TRANSCRIPTS, MANIPULATION OF ATHLETIC GRADES, INDICTMENTS, FRAUD, UNIVERSITY OF NEW MEXICO.

1629. Brooker, George and T. D. Klastorin. "To the Victors Belong the Spoils? College Athletics and Alumni Giving." Social Science Quarterly. 62, No.4 (December 1981), 744-750. RELATIONSHIP BETWEEN ATHLETIC SUCCESS AND ALUMNI CONTRIBUTIONS, BENEFIT AND HARM.

1630. Coughlin, Cletus C. and O. Homer Erekson. "An Examination of Contributions to Support Intercollegiate Athletics." Southern Economic Journal. 51, No.1 (July 1984), 180-195. MODEL OF ATHLETIC CONTRIBUTIONS, DONORS, RECIPIENTS, DETERMINANTS OF CONTRIBUTIONS.

1631. Coughlin, Cletus C. and O. Homer Erekson. "Contributions to Intercollegiate Athletic Programs: Further Evidence." Social Science Quarterly. 66, No.1 (March 1985), 194-202. RELATIONSHIP BETWEEN ATHLETIC CONTRIBUTIONS AND SUCCESS, WINNING.

1632. Creamer, Robert W. (ed.). "Furor in San Diego: A Testing Problem for the NCAA." Sports Illustrated. 58, No.3 (January 24, 1983), 9. PROPOSITION 48, SAT SCORES, GRADE POINT AVERAGES, REACTION OF BLACK COLLEGE PRESIDENTS.

1633. "Curing the Ills of Big-Time College Athletics: 22 Sports Figures Give Their Prescriptions." The Chronicle of Higher Education. 31, No.1 (September 4, 1985), 75-76. ACADEMICS, ATHLETIC DIRECTORS, WOMEN.

1634. "'Death' to S.M.U. Football." Time. 129 (March 9, 1987), 72. SOUTHERN METHODIST UNIVERSITY, COLLEGE FOOTBALL, RECRUITING.

1635. Deford, Frank. "An Honorable Pursuit." Sports Illustrated. 69, No.17 (October 17, 1988), 102. ROLE OF THE COLLEGE PRESIDENT, CHASE PETERSON, UNIVERSITY OF UTAH.

1636. Desruisseaux, Paul. "Colleges Accused of Exploiting Student Athletes." The Chronicle of Higher Education. 24, No.7 (April 14, 1982), 6. EXPLOITATION, MARK NAISON, CORRUPTION, LOW GRADUATION RATES, SALARIES FOR ATHLETES, REFORM.

1637. Donnelly, Harrison. "College Sports Under Fire." Editorial Research Reports. 2, No.6 (August 15, 1986), 591-608. ACADEMICS, BIG TIME COLLEGE SPORTS, RESPONSIBILITY OF COLLEGE PRESIDENTS, GRADUATION RATES, RECRUITMENT SCANDALS, REFORM.

1638. Dunkle, Margaret. "College Athletics: Tug of War for the Purse Strings." Ms. 3, No.3 (September 1974), 114-117. COLLEGE SPENDING FOR WOMEN'S SPORTS, FINANCIAL AID FOR FEMALE ATHLETES, TITLE IX.

1639. Eitzen, D. Stanley. "How We Can Clean Up Big-Time College Sports." The Chronicle of Higher Education. 31, No.22 (February 12, 1986), 96. QUEST FOR BIG MONEY, WIN AT ANY COST ATTITUDE, ROLE OF THE COLLEGE PRESIDENT, MONITORING COACHES, ELIGIBILITY, FAIR COMPENSATION.

1640. Farrell, Charles S. "26 Former Players at University of Kentucky Report Under-the-Table Payments." The Chronicle of Higher Education. 31, No.10 (November 6, 1985), 37. UNIVERSITY OF KENTUCKY, PAYMENTS TO ATHLETES, JOE HALL, COACH.

1641. Farrell, Charles S. "Governor Assails Virginia Tech Board for Backing Big-Time Athletics and Risking Scandal." The Chronicle of Higher Education. 33, No.41 (June 24, 1987), 31-32. GERALD L. BALILES, SCANDALS, ILLEGAL RECRUITING, VIRGINIA POLYTECHNIC INSTITUTE AND STATE UNIVERSITY.

1642. Farrell, Charles S. "Memphis State University Forfeits Nearly $1-Million in Basketball Earnings for NCAA Violations." The Chronicle of Higher Education. 32, No.14 (June 4, 1986), 27-28. MEN'S BASKETBALL, PENALTIES, LOSS OF SCHOLARSHIPS, PAYMENTS TO ATHLETES.

1643. Farrell, Charles S. "NCAA Drops Its Suspension of 60 Football Players at University of Nebraska for Misusing Their Free Tickets." The Chronicle of Higher Education. 33, No.3 (September 17, 1986), 40. UNIVERSITY OF NEBRASKA, GAME-PASS RULE, UNIVERSITY OF TENNESSEE.

1644. Farrell, Charles S. "NCAA Penalizes Southern Methodist University for Violations, Cuts 45 Scholarships." The Chronicle of Higher Education. 31, No.1 (September 4, 1985), 71+. SOUTHERN METHODIST UNIVERSITY, RECRUITING VIOLATIONS, PROBATION, PAYMENTS TO ATHLETES, BOOSTERS.

1645. Farrell, Charles S. "Six in Ten Americans Think College Sports Are Overemphasized, Survey Finds." The Chronicle of Higher Education. 30, No.16 (June 19, 1985), 1+. REFORM, NCAA CONVENTION, NCAA RULE CHANGES.

1646. Farrell, Charles S. "SMU Campus is Stunned by Charge Board Knew of Payments to Players." The Chronicle of Higher Education. 33, No.26 (March 11, 1987), 1+. GOVERNOR WILLIAM CLEMENTS, BOOSTER PAYMENTS TO PLAYERS, SOUTHERN METHODIST UNIVERSITY, NCAA, PENALTIES.

1647. Farrell, Charles S. and Douglas Lederman. "NCAA's Tough Stance on SMU's Violations Shocks Many on Campus, Surprises Others." The Chronicle of Higher Education. 33, No.25 (March 4, 1987), 32-33. BOOSTERS, BAN ON COLLEGE FOOTBALL, PENALTIES, SOUTHERN METHODIST UNIVERSITY.

1648. Frey, James H. "Institutional Control of Athletics: An Analysis of the Role Played by Presidents, Faculty, Trustees, Alumni and the NCAA." Journal of Sport and Social Issues. 11, Nos.1&2 (December 1987), 49-60. ROLE OF PRESIDENT, FACULTY, TRUSTEE, ALUMNI, NCAA.

1649. Garrity, John. "Bad Business." Sports Illustrated. 73, No.2 (July 9, 1990), 46-49. GOLF, MARKETING GOLF EQUIPMENT, RIP-OFF, COPYING CLUBS, BUSINESS, CORRUPTION.

1650. Gup, Ted. "Foul!" Time. 133, No.14 (April 3, 1989), 54-60. OBSESSION WITH WINNING AND MONEY MAKING.

1651. Guttmann, Allen. "We Should Accept Professionalism in Big-Time Sports and Pay the Athletes Accordingly." The Chronicle of Higher Education. 35, No.3 (September 14, 1988), B2. PROFITS FROM SALE OF TICKETS, IMPROPER BENEFITS, REFORM, AMATEURISM.

1652. Hearn, Thomas K. Jr. "Sports and Ethics: The University Response." Vital Speeches of the Day. 55, No.1 (October 15, 1988), 20-22. RESPONSIBILITY OF COACHES, COLLEGE FOOTBALL, DRUGS, FAME, POWER, TERRORIZING PLAYERS, RULES.

1653. Heyman, Ira Michael. "Trapped in an 'Athletics Arms Race'." U. S. News and World Report. 103, No.3 (July 20, 1987), 7. REFORM, COLLEGE SPORTS, FINANCIAL AID, MINOR LEAGUES.

1654. "An Honest Buck for Athletes." The Progressive. 46, No.9 (September 1982), 13. STUDENT-ATHLETES, CRISIS IN BIG TIME SPORTS.

1655. "In Sports, The Big-Time is Getting Even Bigger." U. S. News and World Report. 85, No.15 (October 16, 1978), 61-62. FINANCIAL PROBLEMS, FANS, TELEVISION, WEAK FRANCHISES.

1656. Keating, James W. "The Heart of the Problem of Amateur Athletics." The Journal of General Education. 16, No.4 (January 1965), 261-272. DEFINITION OF AN AMATEUR, ADVANTAGES OF PRESERVING THE DISTINCTION BETWEEN AMATEURS AND PROFESSIONALS, DISTINCTION BETWEEN SPORTS AND ATHLETICS, VALUES.

1657. Keteyian, Armen. "The Tulane Scandal: A Time for Harsh Measures." Sports Illustrated. 62, No.15 (April 15, 1985), 17. ROLE OF THE UNIVERSITY PRESIDENT, POINT SHAVING, TULANE UNIVERSITY, BASKETBALL, PAYMENTS TO PLAYERS.

1658. Kirshenbaum, Jerry. "More Football Madness." Sports Illustrated. 67, No.24 (November 30, 1987), 110. OHIO STATE UNIVERSITY, COLUMBIA UNIVERSITY, RECRUITING VIOLATIONS, WINNING AT ALL COSTS, MONEY.

1659. Kirshenbaum, Jerry. "USC: The University of Special Cases." Sports Illustrated. 53, No.18 (October 27, 1980), 19. ACADEMIC CREDIT FOR NO WORK, RECRUITING VIOLATIONS, UNIVERSITY OF SOUTHERN CALIFORNIA.

1660. Kirshenbaum, Jerry (ed.). "On Tackling (the Morality Problem) and Holding That (Economic) Line." Sports Illustrated. 55, No.10 (August 31, 1981), 13-14. TELEVISED FOOTBALL GAMES, NCAA, COLLEGE FOOTBALL ASSOCIATION, FUNDING.

1661. Klein, Frederick C. "Money Plays: Sports Boosters Help and Sometimes Hurt, Major College Teams." Wall Street Journal. 200, No.85 (October 29, 1982), 1+. FAN GIFTS, RULES, ACADEMICS.

1662. Koch, James V. "Intercollegiate Athletics: An Economic Explanation." Social Science Quarterly. 64, No.2 (June 1983), 360-374. NCAA, TELEVISION, WOMEN, CARTELIZATION, INTERCOLLEGIATE ATHLETICS, BARRIERS TO ENTRY, PRICE FIXING, REVENUE SHARING, PROPERTY RIGHTS.

1663. Koch, James V. "The Economics of 'Big-Time' Intercollegiate Athletics." Social Science Quarterly. 52, No.2 (September 1971), 248-260. FUTURE, CARTEL, RULES, COSTS AND REVENUES.

1664. Lamme, Ary J. III. "How Big-Time Athletics Corrupt Universities." The Christian Science Monitor. 77, No.84 (February 25, 1985), 12. CORRUPTION, REPRESENTATIVE PLAYER MYTHS, CHARACTER BUILDING, AMATEUR VS PROFESSIONAL STATUS.

1665. Lawson, Hal A. and Alan G. Ingham. "Conflicting Ideologies Concerning the University and Intercollegaite Athletics: Harper and Hutchins at Chicago, 1892-1940." Journal of Sport History. 7, No.3 (Winter 1980), 37-67. ROLE OF SPORT IN UNIVERSITIES, UNIVERSITY OF CHICAGO PRESIDENTS--HARPER AND HUTCHINS, ALONZO STAGG, WINNING, BUREAUCRATIZATION OF SPORT, MIND AND BODY.

1666. Lederman, Douglas. "Athlete Who Lost Aid When Cut From Team Challenges One-Year Limit on Scholarships." The Chronicle of Higher Education. 33, No.15 (December 10, 1986), 34. NCAA RULES, LIMIT OF ATHLETIC SCHOLARSHIPS TO ONE YEAR, LAWSUITS, MARK VANELLI, NORTHERN MICHIGAN UNIVERSITY, HOCKEY.

1667. Lederman, Douglas. "Bishops Blame Governor in Scheme to Pay Football Players at Southern Methodist." The Chronicle of Higher Education. 33, No.42 (July 1, 1987), 23-24. ILLEGAL PAYMENTS TO ATHLETES, GOVERNOR WILLIAM CLEMENTS, POLITICALLY MOTIVATED INVESTIGATION.

1668. Lederman, Douglas. "Documents Suggest Football Players at Houston Were Paid: Governor Apologizes for Role in Southern Methodist Payoffs." The Chronicle of Higher Education. 33, No.27 (March 18, 1987), 47-49. PAYMENTS TO PLAYERS, COACH BILL YEOMAN.

1669. Lederman, Douglas. "Failure to Prove Wrongdoing at Kentucky Raises Questions About NCAA Inquiries." The Chronicle of Higher Education. 34, No.27 (March 16, 1988), A37-38. UNIVERSITY OF KENTUCKY, MEN'S BASKETBALL, ILLEGAL GIFTS TO PLAYERS, ROLE OF MEDIA.

1670. Lederman, Douglas. "Football Troubles at Southern Methodist Boil Down To: Who Runs the University?" The Chronicle of Higher Education. 33, No.17 (January 7, 1987), 34-37. PENALTIES, BANNING OF FOOTBALL PROGRAMS, CORRUPTION, HISTORY.

1671. Lederman, Douglas. "NCAA Bars Football at Southern Methodist For Year: Penalties Are The Toughest Ever." The Chronicle of Higher Education. 33, No.25 (March 4, 1987), 1+. BAN ON FOOTBALL, NCAA PENALTIES, PAYMENTS TO ATHLETES, BOOSTERS.

1672. Lederman, Douglas. "NCAA Forms Foundation To Give Scholarship Aid to Athletes Whose Eligibility Has Expired." The Chronicle of Higher Education. 34, No.5 (September 30, 1987), A35+. NATIONAL COLLEGIATE FOUNDATION, COLLEGE BASKETBALL, GRADUATION RATES.

1673. Lederman, Douglas. "Nearly Half the Members in Top Division of NCAA Cited for Violations This Decade." The Chronicle of Higher Education. 35, No.24 (February 22, 1989), A35. PENALTIES, PROBATION, SANCTIONS, RULE VIOLATIONS.

1674. Lederman, Douglas. "Oklahoma College Accused of Filing False Claims for Athletes." The Chronicle of Higher Education. 34, No.22 (February 10, 1988), A37. FRAUDULENT PAYROLL CLAIMS, USE OF STATE EDUCATION FUNDS TO FINANCE SCHOLARSHIPS FOR BASKETBALL PLAYERS, NORTHERN OKLAHOMA COLLEGE.

1675. Lederman, Douglas. "Proposal to Reduce Sports Scholarships Assailed As Unfair." The Chronicle of Higher Education. 33, No.40 (June 17, 1987), 1+. EFFECT ON WOMEN AND BLACKS, REFORM, REACTIONS TO PROPOSAL.

1676. Lederman, Douglas. "Review at Virginia Tech Uncovers Sports Violations; Governor Who Chided Board Picks 4 New Trustees." The Chronicle of Higher Education. 33, No.44 (July 15, 1987), 35-36. EXTORTION, GRAND JURY INVESTIGATION, GOVERNOR GERALD BALILES, RULE VIOLATIONS, VIRGINIA POLYTECHNIC INSTITUTE AND STATE UNIVERSITY.

1677. Lederman, Douglas. "Sports Charges Rock Southern Methodist University: Ill President Quits, Football Ban Threatened." The Chronicle of Higher Education. 33, No.14 (December 3, 1986), 34. SOUTHERN METHODIST UNIVERSITY, RECRUITING, PAYMENTS TO PLAYERS, REFORM.

1678. Lederman, Douglas. "Stanford's Mix of Big-Time Sports and Top Academics is Costly and Lonely." The Chronicle of Higher Education. 33, No.29 (April 1, 1987), 31-32. STANFORD AS A ROLE MODEL INSTITUTION, MESHING OF ATHLETICS AND ACADEMICS, AIRTIGHT ADMISSIONS.

1679. Lederman, Douglas. "University of North Carolina Faculty Council Pushes for Sports Reforms; Effort Could Set National Standard for Involvement of Professors." The Chronicle of Higher Education. 36, No.20 (January 31, 1990), A37-38. UNIVERSITY OF NORTH CAROLINA, REFORMS, REDUCTION OF LENGTH OF SPORT SEASONS, LIMIT OF ATHLETE ELIGIBILITY TIME, RECRUITMENT.

1680. Leo, John and Joseph J. Kane. "Pre-Emptive Purge in the Pac-10." Time. 116, No.8 (August 25, 1980), 51. ARIZONA STATE UNIVERSITY, BOGUS CREDITS, FORGED TRANSCRIPTS, PENALTIES.

1681. Leonard, Wilbert Marcellus II. "Exploitation in Collegiate Sport: The Views of Basketball Players in NCAA Divisions I, II, and III." Journal of Sport Behavior. 9, No.1 (March 1986), 11-30. COLLEGIATE SPORT, COLLEGE BASKETBALL, NCAA, EXPLOITATION OF DIVISION I STUDENT-ATHLETES, EMPIRICAL STUDY, CASE STUDY, SCANDALS, ACADEMICS, COACHES AND PLAYERS.

1682. Lipsyte, Robert. "Varsity Syndrome: The Unkindest Cut." The Annals of the American Academy of Political and Social Science. 445 (September 1979), 15-23. PARTICIPATION OPPORTUNITIES, ELITISM, EXPLOITATION, MEDIA, COMMERCIALISM, SEXISM.

1683. Looney, Douglas S. "Big Ten's Big Mess." Sports Illustrated. 54, No.22 (May 25, 1981), 79-86. PENALTIES, UNIVERSITY OF ILLINOIS, THREE YEAR PROBATION, DAVE WILSON, ACADEMIC INELIGIBILITY.

1684. Looney, Douglas S. "The Minefield." Sports Illustrated. 73, No.10 (September 3, 1990), 48-54+. UNIVERSITY OF SOUTHERN CALIFORNIA FOOTBALL, QUARTERBACK MACHINE, CALLED ROBO-QUARTERBACK, EXCELLENCE, DEDICATION, VALUES.

1685. Luken, Thomas A. "Big-Time College Athletics: Commercialization and Corruption." USA Today. 116, No.2506 (July 1987), 64-67. NCAA, DECAY OF STANDARDS, STUDENT-ATHLETES, REFORMS.

1686. Magnuson, Ed. "Payoff Hike! A Fumble for Clements." Time. 129, No.11 (March 16, 1987), 34. GOV. WILLIAM CLEMENTS, SOUTHERN METHODIST UNIVERSITY, PAYMENTS, COLLEGE FOOTBALL, POLITICS.

1687. McPherson, Barry D. "Sport in the Educational Milieu: Unanswered Questions and Untested Assumptions." Phi Delta Kappan. 61, No.9 (May 1980), 605-606. BENEFIT AND HARM, SOCIALIZATION, ACADEMICS, TITLE IX.

1688. Middleton, Lorenzo. "Colleges Check Athletes' Academic Records as Scandal Over Unearned Credit Spreads." The Chronicle of Higher Education. 19, No.16 (January 7, 1980), 1+. CREDIT FOR COURSES NOT ATTENDED, UNIVERSITY OF NEW MEXICO, FALSIFICATION OF TRANSCRIPTS, NORM ELLENBERGER, REFORM.

1689. Middleton, Lorenzo. "Excessive Boosterism Plagues Sports Program at Wichita State." The Chronicle of Higher Education. 23, No.20 (January 27, 1982), 5-6. WICHITA STATE UNIVERSITY, RECRUITING ABUSES, EXCESSIVE BOOSTERISM.

1690. Middleton, Lorenzo. "NCAA Rebuts Charge of Large Payments to Athletes." The Chronicle of Higher Education. 24, No.6 (April 7, 1982), 10. PAYMENTS TO ATHLETES, BOOSTERISM, NCAA PENALTIES.

1691. Miller, J. David and David Whitford. "Trouble in Tennessee." Sport. 78, No.11 (November 1987), 68-79. COLLEGE FOOTBALL, CHEATING, CASH PAYMENTS TO ATHLETES, FANS, UNIVERSITY OF TENNESSEE.

1692. Miller, Richard L. and Gary L. Carson. "Playboy Stuff and Other Variables: Scholarship, Athletics and Girl Friends." The Journal of Social Psychology. 95 (February 1975), 143-144. RELATIONSHIP OF PIN-UPS ON MALE DORMS, ACADEMIC PERFORMANCE, PARTICIPATION IN ATHLETICS.

1693. Mitchell, Maurice. "Big-Time Sports Should Be Banished From Campus." The Center Magazine. 15, No.1 (January/February 1982), 22-24. INTERCOLLEGIATE ATHLETICS, TELEVISION, ROLE OF COLLEGE PRESIDENTS, ALUMNI, BIG TIME COLLEGE SPORTS, GAMBLING, NCAA.

1694. Monaghan, Peter. "Ex-Trustee at Texas Christian Admits to a 'Stupid Mistake'." The Chronicle of Higher Education. 31, No.5 (October 2, 1985), 44. DICK LOWE, FORMER PLAYER, SLUSH FUND, PAYMENT TO ATHLETES.

1695. Monaghan, Peter. "Scandals and Allegations of Rules Violations Beset Members of the Southwest Conference." The Chronicle of Higher Education. 31, No.7 (October 16, 1985), 37+. SOUTHWEST ATLANTIC CONFERENCE, UNIVERSITY OF HOUSTON, RULE VIOLATIONS, SOUTHERN METHODIST UNIVERSITY, TEXAS CHRISTIAN UNIVERSITY, TEXAS TECH, TEXAS A&M, BAYLOR UNIVERSITY, PAYMENTS TO ATHLETES.

1696. Monaghan, Peter. "Seven Athletes Suspended in Slush-Fund Case at Texas Christian University." The Chronicle of Higher Education. 31, No.5 (October 2, 1985), 1+. BOOSTERS, PAYMENTS TO ATHLETES.

1697. Monaghan, Peter. "Texas A&M Says Newspaper Erred in Charging that Coaches and Boosters Paid Football Players." The Chronicle of Higher Education. 31, No.16 (December 18, 1985), 35-36. PAYMENTS TO ATHLETES, DALLAS TIMES HERALD, COACHES, SLUSH FUNDS, SALE OF COMPLIMENTARY TICKETS.

1698. Monaghan, Peter. "Two-Year Probe at Texas El Paso Campus Brings Stiff Sanctions on Track Teams." The Chronicle of Higher Education. 32, No.20 (July 16, 1986), 35-36. UNIVERSITY OF TEXAS AT EL PASO, RULE VIOLATIONS, PAYMENTS TO ATHLETES, COACH LARRY HEIDEBRECHT.

1699. Moriarty, Francis J. "Pros in Academic Drag." Women's Sports and Fitness. 6, No.9 (September 1984), 60+. ACADEMICS, CORRUPTION, REFORM.

1700. Nightingale, Dave. "USF: Where Boosterism Ran Rampant." The Sporting News. 194, No.15 (October 11, 1982), 16. NCAA, UNIVERSITY OF SAN FRANCISCO, BASKETBALL, FANS, SCANDAL.

1701. Oberlander, Susan. "Arizona State Penalized for Track Violations." The Chronicle of Higher Education. 34, No.43 (July 6, 1988), A31. ARIZONA STATE UNIVERSITY, PROBATION, TRACK AND FIELD, EXTRA BENEFITS TO ATHLETES, SUBMISSION OF FALSE QUALIFYING ENTRY TIMES.

1702. Oberlander, Susan. "Chapel Hill Professors Fear That Abuses in Big-Time Sports Upset University's Traditional Athletics-Academics Balance." The Chronicle of Higher Education. 34, No.26 (March 9, 1988), A37-38. INVESTIGATION OF THE ROLE OF INTERCOLLEGIATE ATHLETICS AT THE UNIVERSITY OF NORTH CAROLINA AT CHAPEL HILL, PRIORITIES, BUILDING OF A NEW ATHLETIC CENTER.

1703. Odenkirk, James E. "Intercollegiate Athletics - A Malignancy on Campus." Proceedings: National Association for Physical Education in Higher Education. 2 (1980), 27-34. RECRUITING, SCANDALS, EXCESSIVE ECONOMIC NEEDS.

1704. Olson, John R. "Who Is Your Booster Club Accountable To?" Athletic Purchasing and Facilities. 6, No.11 (November 1982), 11-12+. DEFINING AREAS OF RESPONSIBILITY, FUNDRAISING VS. POLICY FUNCTIONS, CONSTITUTION.

1705. Ostro, Harry. "Bonus Pay for Coaches Who Graduate Their Athletes." Scholastic Coach. 56, No.5 (December 1986), 7-9. OVEREMPHASIS ON WINNING, COACH CONTRACTS.

1706. Padwe, Sandy. "Big-Time College Football Is on the Skids." Look. 43, No.19 (September 22, 1970), 66-69. FINANCIAL PRESSURES, RECRUITING, DESPOTIC COACHES, DISSATISFIED PLAYERS, DRUGS.

1707. Papanek, John. "New Mexico: More Tremors." Sports Illustrated. 51, No.25 (December 17, 1979), 75-76. UNIVERSITY OF NEW MEXICO, SCANDAL, COLLEGE BASKETBALL, FORGED TRANSCRIPTS.

1708. Papanek, John. "Now New Mexico Feels the Heat." Sports Illustrated. 51, No.24 (December 10, 1979), 32-41. PHONY TRANSCRIPTS, BRIBERY, ARIZONA STATE UNIVERSITY, UNIVERSITY OF NEW MEXICO, RECRUITING.

1709. Pearlman, Michael. "To Make the University Safe for Morality: Higher Education, Football, and Military Training From the 1890's to the 1920's." The Canadian Review of American Studies. 12, No.1 (Spring 1981), 37-56. MORAL EDUCATION, HUMANISM, RELIGIOUS REVIVALS, FOOTBALL AND MILITARY AS SCHOOLS OF MORALITY.

1710. Petrie, Neil H. "Colleges Give Their Student Athletes an Especially Reprehensible Form of Hypocrisy." The Chronicle of Higher Education. 34, No.24 (February 24, 1988), B2-3. ABSENCES, DIVIDED LOYALTIES, PREFERENTIAL TREATMENT OF ATHLETES BY PROFESSORS, SPECIAL ATTENDANCE POLICIES.

1711. Reid, Ron. "There's the Devil to Pay." Sports Illustrated. 51, No.18 (October 29, 1979), 26-29. ARIZONA STATE UNIVERSITY, FRANK KUSH, RECRUITING VIOLATIONS, KEVIN RUTLEDGE, COACH BRUTALITY TO PLAYERS.

1712. Renick, Jobyann. "The Use and Misuse of College Athletics." The Journal of Higher Education. 45, No.7 (October 1974), 545-552. POLICY DECISIONS, STUDENT-ATHLETES, CONTROL.

1713. Rhatigan, James J. "Serving Two Masters: The Plight of the College Student-Athlete." New Directions for Student Services. No.28 (1984), 5-11. RULES, REFORM, EXPLOITATION, MONEY.

1714. Roberts, Gary R. "Big-Time College Athletics: Academic Eligibility Rules Are Elitist." USA Today. 116, No.2506 (July 1987), 68-70. INTERCOLLEGIATE ATHLETES, PROPOSITION 48, NCAA, ACADEMIC ELIGIBILITY.

1715. Sack, Allen L. "Are 'Improper Benefits' Really Improper? A Study of College Athletes' Views Concerning Amateurism." The Journal of Sport and Social Issues. 12, No.1 (Spring 1988), 1-16. NCAA AMATEUR CODE, FINANCIAL COMPENSATION OF ATHLETES, FEMALE AND BLACK VIEWS, POLICY IMPLICATIONS.

1716. Sack, Allen L. "Big Time College Football: Whose Free Ride?" Quest. 27 (Winter 1977), 87-96. REFORM, CORRUPTION, COMMERCIALIZATION, EXPLOITATION.

1717. Sanoff, Alvin P. "Behind Scandals in Big-Time College Sports." U. S. News and World Report. 88, No.5 (February 11, 1980), 61-63. PRESTIGE OF WINNING, COLLEGE TRANSCRIPTS, SCANDALS, RECRUITING.

1718. Sanoff, Alvin P. "Big-Time College Sports: Behind Scandals." U. S. News and World Report. 92, No.13 (April 5, 1982), 60-61. RECRUITING ABUSES, EMPHASIS ON WINNING, SALARIES, ACADEMICS, SCANDAL.

1719. Sanoff, Alvin P. "Classroom Crackdown on College Athletes." U. S. News and World Report. 94, No.3 (January 24, 1983), 75-76. BLACK ATHLETES, STANDARDS, SAT SCORES, GRADUATION RATES, ALUMNI.

1720. Sanoff, Alvin P. "College Sports' Real Scandal." U. S. News and World Report. 101, No.11 (September 15, 1986), 62-63. ACADEMICS, STANDARDS, GRADUATION RATES.

1721. Santomier, James P., William G. Howard, Wendy L. Piltz, and Thomas J. Romance. "White Sock Crime: Organizational Deviance in Intercollegiate Athletics." Journal of Sport and Social Issues. 4, No.2 (Fall/Winter 1980), 26-32. SCANDALS, SYSTEMATIC CORRUPTION, DEVIANCE.

1722. Shapiro, Beth J. "John Hannah and the Growth of Big-Time Intercollegiate Athletics at Michigan State University." Journal of Sport History. 10, No.3 (Winter 1983), 26-40. JOHN HANNAH, ACADEMICS, HISTORY, REFORM, ABUSES, POSITIVE USE OF INTERCOLLEGIATE SPORTS, INTEGRATION, RULE VIOLATIONS, BOOSTER CLUBS.

1723. Sheehan, George. "Athletic Scholarships Yes, Academic Scholarships No." The New York Times. 124 (November 10, 1974), Section 5, Page 2. ATHLETICS AS A FORCE FOR GOOD, BENEFIT AND HARM, STUDENT-ATHLETES.

1724. Sigelman, Lee and Robert Carter. "Win One for the Giver? Alumni Giving and Big-Time College Sports." Social Science Quarterly. 60, No.2 (September 1979), 284-294. LINK BETWEEN ATHLETICS AND ALUMNI GIVING, BENEFIT AND HARM, IDEOLOGY.

1725. Sigelman, Lee and Samuel Bookheimer. "Is It Whether You Win or Lose? Monetary Contributions to Big-Time College Athletic Programs." Social Science Quarterly. 64, No.2 (June 1983), 347-359. RELATIONSHIP BETWEEN SUCCESS AND VOLUNTARY ALUMNI CONTRIBUTIONS, PRIVATE GIVING AND BIG TIME INTERCOLLEGIATE ATHLETICS.

1726. Smith, Bruce and Joseph Murphy. "A Study of the Effects of a Stricter Eligibility Rule on High School Student-Athletes' Academic Programs." The High School Journal. 70, No.3 (February/March 1987), 160-165. ELIGIBILITY RULES, NCAA, DISCRIMINATION.

1727. "Status of Sports Investigations on College Campuses." The Chronicle of Higher Education. 35, No.11 (November 9, 1988), A41. RECRUITING VIOLATIONS, IMPROPER BENEFITS TO PLAYERS, DRUGS, PENALTIES.

1728. Stevens, William J. "Proposition 48 and the Inner-School Athlete." Scholastic Coach. 57, No.2 (September 1987), 86-87. NCAA, STANDARDS, PARENTS, SAT SCORES, WEEKLY REPORT CARDS.

1729. Telander, Rick. "Their Moment Has Come: Letting College Juniors Into the NFL Draft Was Long Overdue." Sports Illustrated. 72, No.17 (April 23, 1990), 96. CONSTITUTIONAL RIGHTS, RIGHT TO WORK, NCAA FOOTBALL COACHES, COLLEGE FOOTBALL, PRO FOOTBALL.

1730. Underwood, John. "Partly Cloudy Week in the Sunshine State." Sports Illustrated. 61, No.13 (September 10, 1984), 22-28. UNIVERSITY OF FLORIDA, CHEATING, RECRUITING VIOLATIONS, TICKET SCALPING.

1731. "University of Miami Tries to Repair Damage to Its Reputation Inflicted by Football Players' Scrapes With the Law." The Chronicle of Higher Education. 34, No.5 (September 30, 1987), A35-36. UNIVERSITY OF MIAMI, CODE OF CONDUCT, STRESS OF ATHLETES.

1732. Wall, James M. "Institutional Greed Taints College Sports." The Christian Century. 102, No.15 (May 1, 1985), 435-436. POINT SHAVING, COLLEGE BASKETBALL, COCAINE, GAMBLING, COACHES, CORRUPTION, GREED, ACADEMICS.

1733. Warford, Terry. "Get Schools Out of the Athletic Business." Thrust. 11, No.2 (November 1981), 36. PRIVATE SPORTS CLUBS, RECRUITMENT, ACADEMICS.

1734. Weiss, Paul. "Pro Sports in College." U. S. News and World Report. 100, No.9 (March 10, 1986), 75. JAN KEMP, PREFERENTIAL TREATMENT, LAWSUIT, PAYING ATHLETES.

1735. Westby, David L. and Allen L. Sack. "The Commercialization and Functional Rationalization of College Football: Its Origins." The Journal of Higher Education. 47, No.6 (November/December 1976), 625-647. YALE, HARVARD, SPORT AND THE NEW RICH, PATRICIAN VALUES, MONEY, COMMERCIALISM, HISTORICAL PERSPECTIVE.

1736. Williams, Roger M. "Away With Big-Time Athletics." Saturday Review. 3 (March 6, 1976), 10+. TITLE IX, NCAA, REFORM, INTERCOLLEGIATE ATHLETICS, RECRUITMENT, SCHOLARSHIPS, ALUMNI.

1737. Winkler, Karen J. "Trustees Urged to Join Fight Against Abuses in College Sports, Avoid 'Athletic Fanaticism'." The Chronicle of Higher Education. 28, No.7 (April 11, 1984), 33-34. ROLE OF THE TRUSTEES, SCANDALS, FANATICISM, RECRUITING ABUSES.

1738. Zeigler, Earle F. "The Illinois Slush-Fund Scandal of the 1960's: A Preliminary Analysis." The Physical Educator. 42, No.2 (Spring 1985), 82-88. BIG TEN INVESTIGATION, ATHLETIC DIRECTORS, COACHES, NCAA, SCANDALS.

CHILDREN, YOUTH, AND SPORT

Books

1739. Bissinger, H. G. Friday Night Lights: A Town, A Team, and a Dream. Reading, MA: Addison-Wesley Publishing Company, 1990. HIGH SCHOOL FOOTBALL, ODESSA, TEXAS, SPORTSMANIA, ROLE OF SPORT IN SOCIETY, RACE RELATIONS, COACHES AND PLAYERS, WINNING, RELIGION, MYTHOLOGY, FAN BEHAVIOR.

1740. Brown, Eugene W. and Crystal F. Branta (eds.). Competitive Sports for Children and Youth: An Overview of Research and Issues. Champaign, IL: Human Kinetics Publishers, 1988. COMPETITION, BENEFIT AND HARM.

1741. Emmett, Isabel. Youth and Leisure in an Urban Sprawl. Manchester: Manchester University Press, 1971. SOCIAL CLASSES, WOMEN.

1742. Fine, Gary Alan. With the Boys: Little League Baseball and Preadolescent Culture. Chicago: The University of Chicago Press, 1987. SPORTS AND PLAY, SOCIALIZATION, AGGRESSION.

1743. Horrocks, Robert Norman. The Relationship of Selected Prosocial Play Behaviors in Children to: Moral Reasoning, Youth Sports Participation, and Perception of Sportsmanship. Ed.D. Thesis, The University of North Carolina at Greensboro, 1979. FAIR PLAY, CHARACTER, VIRTUE, BENEFIT OF SPORT, COOPERATION.

1744. Jacko, Diane Newell. Jock Momma: A Guide to Success on the Kid Sidelines. Boston: Faber and Faber, Inc., 1985. PRIORITIES, PLAY, FUN, OVEREMPHASIS ON WINNING, HARM TO CHILDREN.

1745. Magill, Richard A., Michael J. Ash and Frank L. Smoll (eds.). Children in Sport. Champaign, IL: Human Kinetics Publishers, Inc., 1982. HISTORY, FUTURE, CHANGE, COMPETITION, GIRLS, INJURIES, PSYCHOLOGICAL ISSUES, BENEFIT AND HARM, SOCIALIZATION, VIOLENCE.

1746. Martens, Rainer. Joy and Sadness in Children's Sports. Champaign, IL: Human Kinetics Publishers, 1978. BENEFIT AND HARM, LITTLE LEAGUE, COACHES, WINNING IS EVERYTHING, COMPETITION, GIRLS, SPORTSMANSHIP, VIOLENCE, CHARACTER BUILDING, PARENTS.

1747. McInally, Pat. Moms and Dads, Kids and Sports. New York: Charles Scribner's Sons, 1988. INJURIES, COACHING, FOOTBALL, BASKETBALL, BASEBALL, SPECIALIZATION.

1748. Morris, G. S. Don. How To Change the Games Children Play. Minneapolis, MN: Burgess Publishing Company, 1976. GAMES ANALYSIS, ROLE MODELS.

1749. Ralbovsky, Martin. Destiny's Darlings: A World Championship Little League Team Twenty Years Later. New York: Hawthorn Books, 1974. LITTLE LEAGUE BASEBALL, CHARACTER, VALUES.

1750. Schock, Bernie. Parents, Kids and Sports. Chicago: Moody Press, 1987. BENEFIT AND HARM, CHARACTER, VALUES.

1751. Smoll, Frank L. and Ronald E. Smith (eds.). Psychological Perspectives in Youth Sports. Washington, D.C: Hemisphere Publishing Corporation, 1978. VIOLENCE, ANXIETY, COMPETITION, SOCIALIZATION, MOTIVATION, WINNING AND LOSING, COACHES, HOCKEY, LITTLE LEAGUE BASEBALL, COOPERATION, DISABLED, SPECIAL OLYMPICS.

1752. Yablonsky, Lewis and Jonathan J. Brower. The Little League Game: How Kids, Coaches and Parents Really Play It. New York: Times Books, 1979. WINNING, PARENTS, COACHES.

1753. Zimet, Lloyd. Children's Sport Trait Anxiety and Professionalized Sport Attitude in Three Racially Different Communities. PhD Thesis, University of Maryland, 1984. GENDER DIFFERENCES, ATTITUDES TOWARD SPORTS, RACISM, ACHIEVEMENT ORIENTATION.

Articles

1754. Alves, Rubem Azevedo. "Play, or How to Subvert the Dominant Values." Union Seminary Quarterly Review. 26, No.1 (Fall 1970), 43-57. DEFINITION OF PLAY, PLAY AS A PLEASURE PRODUCER, PRODUCTION AND CONSUMPTION.

1755. Berlage, Gai Ingham. "Are Children's Competitive Team Sports Teaching Corporate Values?" Arena Review. 6, No.1 (May 1982), 15-21. SOCIALIZATION, SOCCER, BENEFIT AND HARM, VALUES, ICE HOCKEY.

1756. Berryman, Jack W. "From the Cradle to the Playing Field: America's Emphasis On Highly Organized Competitive Sport for PreAdolescent Boys." Journal of Sport History. 2, No.2 (Fall 1975), 112-31. HISTORY, COMPETITIVE SPORTS, INCLUSION OF SPORTS IN SCHOOL SYSTEM, LITTLE LEAGUE, PARENTS, SPORTSMANIA.

1757. Bissinger, H. G. "Friday Night Lights." Sports Illustrated. 73, No.12 (September 17, 1990), 82-86+. HIGH SCHOOL FOOTBALL, ODESSA, TEXAS, SPORTSMANIA, RACE RELATIONS, FAN BEHAVIOR, COACHES AND PLAYERS, WINNING.

1758. Brower, Jonathan J. "The Professionalization of Organized Youth Sport: Social-Psychological Impacts and Outcomes." The Annals of the American Academy of Political and Social Science. 445 (September 1979), 39-46. PROFESSIONALIZATION, YOUTH SPORTS, WINNING, LITTLE LEAGUE BASEBALL, EXTERNAL AUTHORITY, PARENTS AND COACHES.

1759. Brown, Ron. "Coming of Age: Sports Fiction for Young Adults." School Library Journal. 29, No.4 (December 1982), 28-29. WOMEN, CHANGES IN SPORT LITERATURE, BIBLIOGRAPHY OF YOUNG ADULT SPORTS NOVELS.

1760. Bryn, Katherine. "Does Kids' Competition Really Make Better Adults?" Science Digest. 76, No.5 (November 1974), 38-44. PARENTS, PLAYING TO WIN VS PLAYING FOR FUN, HOSTILITY, COMPETITION, CHARACTER BUILDING, LEADERSHIP.

1761. Buchholz, Butch. "Talent and Temper: Kids in the Pros." World Tennis. 29, No.11 (April 1982), 68. WORLD CLASS JUNIOR TENNIS, ROLE MODELS, CODE OF CONDUCT.

1762. Bula, Michael R. "Competition for Children: The Real Issue." Journal of Health, Physical Education and Recreation. 42 (September 1971), 40. BENEFIT AND HARM, SUPERVISION, PARENTAL EDUCATION, COACHES, COMPETITION.

1763. Burhmann, Hans G. "Athletics and Deviancy: An Examination of the Relationship Between Athletic Participation and Deviant Behavior of High School Girls." Review of Sport and Leisure. 2 (June 1977), 17-35. CHARACTER BUILDING, RELATIONSHIP BETWEEN SPORT PARTICIPATION AND DEVIANT BEHAVIOR.

1764. Coleman, Mick and Patsy Skeen. "Play, Games and Sport: Their Use And Misuse." Childhood Education. 61, No.3 (January/February 1985), 192-198. DEVELOPMENTAL PERSPECTIVE, DEFINITION OF PLAY, GAMES, SPORT, DEVELOPMENT OF MOTOR SKILLS, GENDER DIFFERENCES, TEACHING PHYSICAL EDUCATION.

1765. Dellinger, Bill. "Kids Should Play, Not Train." Track & Field News. 32, No.2 (March 1979), 39. PLAY VS DISCIPLINE, PUSHING TOO EARLY.

1766. Dubois, Paul E. "Competition in Youth Sports: Process or Product?" The Physical Educator. 37, No.3 (October 1980), 151-154. COMPETITION AS PROCESS, COMPETITION AS PRODUCT.

1767. Duda, Joan L. "Consider the Children: Meeting Participants' Goals in Youth Sport." Journal of Physical Education, Recreation and Dance. 56, No.6 (August 1985), 55-56. COMPETITION, MOTIVATION, ANXIETY, CONTROL.

1768. Ebihara, Osamo, Mosaru Ikeda, and Mitsumasa Myiashita. "Birth Order and Children's Socialization into Sport." International Review of Sport Sociology. 18, No.3 (1983), 69-90. GENDER, PARENTS, BENEFIT AND HARM, EXCELLENCE.

1769. "Fair Play Codes for Children in Sport." Sports Coach. 4, No.4 (1980), 37-39. VALUES, CHARACTER.

1770. Fallon, Dennis J. "Child's Play: A Run for the Trophy." Quest. 24 (Summer 1975), 59-62. DEFINITION OF PLAY AND WORK, CHILDREN'S PLAY, FORCES IN SOCIETY WHICH DETERMINE THE CONDITION OF PLAY.

1771. Feltz, Deborah L. "Athletics in the Status System of Female Adolescents." Review of Sport and Leisure. 3, No.1 (Fall 1978), 98-108. LEADERSHIP, INTEREST IN ATHLETICS, ENTHUSIASM, TITLE IX.

1772. Goodman, H. N. Nick. "The Schoolboys of Summer: Juvenile Literature and the Sports Metaphor in America." North American Society for Sport History Proceedings and Newsletter. (1980), 37-38. MERRIWELL EPISODES, BARBOUR NOVELS.

1773. Hardy, Rex. "Son 'Pushers'." The Physical Educator. 35, No.3 (October 1978), 127-128. STATUS SEEKERS, REFORM, TEN COMMANDMENTS FOR FATHERS.

1774. Hicks, Donald. "Teaching Children Values Through Sports Participation." Arizona Journal, HPER. 25 (Spring 1982), 8-11. ETHICS, MORAL DEVELOPMENT, CHARACTER, TEAMWORK, COOPERATION.

1775. Hutslar, Jack. "For Whom Does Youth Sport Exist." Arena Review. 6, No.1 (May 1982), 1-2. IDEAL AND MEANING, BUSINESS.

1776. "Is the Boom in 'Kid Sports' Good for the Kids?" U. S. News and World Report. 76, No.5 (February 4, 1974), 60-62. ADULT RUN SPORTS, ADULT PRESSURES, INJURIES, EMOTIONAL DAMAGE, MYTHS, EGOS.

1777. Jantz, Richard K. "Moral Thinking in Male Elementary Pupils as Reflected by Perception of Basketball Rules." Research Quarterly. 46, No.4 (December 1975), 414-421. PIAGET'S "RULES OF THE GAME," MORALITY OF CONSTRAINT, MORALITY OF COOPERATION, MORAL DEVELOPMENT, LAWRENCE KOHLBERG.

1778. Kalyn, Wayne. "What Price Success?" World Tennis. 29, No.11 (April 1982), 62-64. BIG BUSINESS, SPONSORS, JUNIOR TENNIS, AGENTS.

1779. Kantrowitz, Barbara. "Heroes With Feet of Clay." Newsweek. 112 (October 31, 1988), 65. HEROES, PINE TAR BATS, STEROIDS, COCAINE, ALCOHOLISM, ROLE MODELS.

1780. Keller, Richard D. "Kids and Sports Books." North American Society for Sport History Proceedings and Newsletter. (1980), 36. MORALITY PLAYS, LESSONS OF LIFE, GREAT AMERICAN DREAM.

1781. Lee, Martin J. "Values and Responsibilities In Children's Sports." Physical Education Review. 11, No.1 (Spring 1988), 19-27. BENEFIT AND HARM, RULES, REFERENCES, COMPETITION, EDUCATIONAL ROLE OF SPORT, SPORTSMANSHIP, MORAL DEVELOPMENT, RESPONSIBILITY.

1782. Lee, Robert E. III and Harold M. Schroder. "Effects of Outward Bound Training on Urban Youth." The Journal of Special Education. 3, No.2 (Summer 1969), 187-205. OUTWARD BOUND, BENEFIT AND HARM, URBAN YOUTH, DISADVANTAGED INNER CITY YOUTH, ATTITUDES, MOTIVATION, OTHER-REGARDINGNESS, SELF IDENTITY.

1783. Lever, Janet. "Sex Differences in the Complexity of Children's Play and Games." American Sociological Review. 43, No.4 (August 1978), 471-483. SOCIAL SKILLS ACQUIRED THROUGH PLAY, GENDER DIFFERENCES, COMPLEXITY OF PLAY, ROLE DIFFERENTIATION, PLAY INTERDEPENDENCE, RULES, TEAMWORK.

1784. Lewis, Guy. "Sport, Youth Culture and Conventionality, 1920-1970." Journal of Sport History. 4, No.2 (Summer 1977), 129-150. HISTORY, RISE OF SPORT, YOUTH CULTURE, CONVENTIONAL MORALITY.

1785. Maddocks, Melvin. "New Awakening in Orr Land: Little League Mania." Sports Illustrated. 35, No.15 (October 11, 1971), 32-37. YOUTH HOCKEY, PARENTS.

1786. Maxwell, Theresa. "Kidsport: How To Finally Achieve What We Say Are the Benefits of the Program." CAHPER ACSEPL Journal. 51, No.6 (July/August 1985), 4-8. BENEFIT AND HARM, REFORM, PHYSICAL BENEFITS, SOCIALIZING ASPECTS, PSYCHOLOGICAL AND MORAL DEVELOPMENT.

1787. McCalep, George O. "Child's Play: It Isn't Fun Anymore." Women's Sports. 5, No.2 (February 1983), 60. COMPETITION, WINNING AT ALL COSTS, DRAFT SYSTEM, POSITION ROTATION, COACHES.

1788. Messner, Michael A. "Boyhood, Organized Sports and the Construction of Masculinities." Journal of Contemporary Ethnography. 18, No.4 (January 1990), 416-444. GENDER IDENTITY, PARENTS, SELF WORTH, COMPETITION, STATUS, SOCIALIZATION.

1789. Ogilvie, Bruce C. "The Child Athlete: Psychological Implications of Participation in Sport." The Annals of the American Academy of Political and Social Science. 445 (September 1979), 47-58. PARENTS, CHILD CENTERED VS PROFESSIONAL MODEL, REFORM, MOTIVATION, COMPETITION, SELF CONCEPT.

1790. Ogilvie, Bruce C. "The Ties That Bind." Women's Sports. 6, No.2 (February 1984), 12. ROLE OF SPORTS IN THE FAMILY, LIMITS OF PARENTAL INVOLVEMENT.

1791. Ostro, Harry. "What Confuses Our Young People." Scholastic Coach. 57, No.1 (August 1987), 4+. COACHES, ROLE MODELS, RULES, MORALITY, CHEATING, DRUGS, CODE OF CONDUCT.

1792. Pease, Dale G. and Dean F. Anderson. "Longitudinal Analysis of Children's Attitudes Toward Sport Team Involvement." Journal of Sport Behavior. 9, No.1 (March 1986), 3-10. ATTITUDE TOWARD SPORT TEAM INVOLVEMENT, GENDER DIFFERENCES, EXTRINSIC FACTORS.

1793. Peterson, Robert W. "You Really Hit That One, Man!" The New York Times Magazine. (May 19, 1974), 36. GIRLS ON LITTLE LEAGUE TEAMS, TEANECK, NEW JERSEY, LAWSUITS, LITTLE LEAGUE BASEBALL.

1794. Phillips, B. J. "Fattening Them Up For Football." Time. 117, No.10 (March 9, 1981), 41. VOLUNTARY GRADE REPETITION, ACADEMICS.

1795. Sadler, William A. Jr. "Alienated Youth and Creative Sports Experience." Journal of the Philosophy of Sport. 4 (Fall 1977), 83-95. PERSONALITY DEVELOPMENT, CHARACTER BUILDING, SOCIOLOGICAL ANALYSIS, ALIENATED YOUTH, SPORT AS CREATIVE ENDEAVOR.

1796. Sage, George H. "Parental Influence and Socialization into Sport for Male and Female Intercollegiate Athletes." Journal of Sport and Social Issues. 4, No.2 (Fall/Winter 1980), 1-13. WOMEN, PARENTS.

1797. Seefeldt, Vern. "Why Are Children's Sports Programs Controversial?" Journal of Physical Education, Recreation and Dance. 56, No.3 (March 1985), 16. CHILDREN'S SPORT PROGRAMS, BENEFIT AND HARM, COMPETITION, COACHES.

1798. Segrave, J. and D. Chu. "Athletics and Juvenile Delinquency." Review of Sport and Leisure. 3 (1978), 1-24. VALUES, JUSTICE, MORAL DEVELOPMENT, ROLE OF SPORT IN SOCIETY.

1799. Segrave, Jeffrey O. "Athletic Delinquency: A Preliminary Analysis." Abstracts of Research Papers. (1979), 35. RELATIONSHIP OF JUVENILE DELINQUENCY AND PARTICIPATION IN ATHLETICS, ANTI-SOCIAL BEHAVIOR.

1800. Segrave, Jeffrey O. "Delinquency and Athletics: Review and Reformulation." Journal of Sport Psychology. 2, No.2, (1980), 82-89. JUVENILE DELINQUENCY, INTERCOLLEGIATE ATHLETICS, ATHLETICS AS A PREVENTION FOR DELINQUENCY, EPIDEMIOLOGY, SOCIOLOGY, SOCIAL PSYCHOLOGY.

1801. Segrave, Jeffrey O. and Douglas N. Hastad. "Future Directions in Sport and Juvenile Delinquency Research." Quest. 36, No.1 (1984), 37-47. FUTURE, JUVENILE DELINQUENCY, OUTWARD BOUND.

1802. Seurin, Pierre. "The Manipulation of the Child for Sporting Exploits." The FIEP Bulletin. 49, No.3 (July/September 1979), 6-7. COMPETITION, BENEFIT AND HARM, SPECIALIZATION.

1803. Spring, Joel H. "Mass Culture and School Sports." History of Education Quarterly. 14, No.4 (Winter 1974), 483-499. MORAL DEVELOPMENT, ATHLETICS: AN INSTRUMENT OF CONTROL, JUVENILE DELINQUENCY PREVENTION.

1804. Stratton, Richard K. "Aggression in Children's Sports: A Social-Learning Perspective." Motor Skills: Theory into Practice. 3, No.2 (Spring 1979), 123-128. YOUTH SPORTS PROGRAMS, OUTLETS FOR AGGRESSIVE BEHAVIOR, SOCIAL LEARNING THEORY.

1805. Sugden, John P. and Andrew Yiannakis. "Sport and Juvenile Delinquency: A Theoretical Base." Journal of Sport and Social Issues. 6, No.1 (Spring/Summer 1982), 22-30. OUTWARD BOUND, SPORTS AS A PANACEA FOR JUVENILE DELINQUENCY.

1806. Thomas, Jerry R. "Is Winning Essential In Youth Sports Contests?" The Education Digest. 43, No.9 (May 1978), 53-55. SELF PERCEPTION, ADULT DESIRES, EFFECTS OF COMPETITION ON CHILDREN, MOTIVATION, REWARDS.

1807. Underwood, John. "Taking the Fun Out of a Game." Sports Illustrated. 43, No.20 (November 17, 1975), 86-98. FOOTBALL, LITTLE LEAGUE FOOTBALL, TEXAS YOUTH FOOTBALL, PARENTS INTERFERING, OVER-ZEALOUS COACHES, EXAGGERATED IMPORTANCE OF WINNING.

1808. Warner, Gary. "Little-League Sports Can Be Immoral." U. S. Catholic. 46, No.5 (May 1981), 13-15. SCOREBOARD MENTALITY, COACHING, INJURIES, COMPETITION VS. PLAY, PRESSURE, BURN OUT, MONSTER ATHLETES.

1809. Watson, G. G. and R. Collis. "Adolescent Values in Sport: A Case of Conflicting Interests." International Review of Sport Sociology. 17, No.3 (1982), 73-90. PSYCHOLOGY, PARENTS, CLASSES.

1810. Watson, Geoffrey G. "Games, Socialization, and Parental Values: Social Class Differences in Parental Evaluation of Little League Baseball." International Review of Sport Sociology. 12, No.1 (1977), 17-48. BENEFIT AND HARM, ROLE OF SPORT IN SOCIETY, COMPETITION, MORAL DEVELOPMENT.

1811. Watson, Geoffrey G. "Social Conflict and Parental Involvement in Little League Baseball." Quest. 27 (Winter 1977), 71-86. SOCIAL CONFLICT, INSTITUTIONALIZATION, ACHIEVEMENT TRAINING.

1812. Westlake, Helen Gum. "When Child's Play is Serious Business." Forecast for Home Economics. 30, No.1 (September 1984),62-65. ROLE OF PLAY, BENEFIT AND HARM, READINESS FOR TEAM SPORTS.

1813. Wiggins, David K. "The Play of Slave Children in the Plantation Communities of the Old South, 1820-1860." Journal of Sport History. 7, No.2 (Summer 1980), 21-39. BASEBALL, DESEGREGATION, SOCIALIZATION, FUN.

1814. Yiannakis, Andrew. "Delinquent Tendencies and Participation in an Organized Sports Program." Research Quarterly. 47, No.4 (December 1976), 845-849. JUVENILE DELINQUENCY, SOCIAL DEVELOPMENT OF ECONOMICALLY UNDERPRIVILEGED CHILDREN, NATIONAL SUMMER YOUTH SPORTS PROGRAM.

1815. Zeigler, Earle F. "Providing Every Child With Play Competencies: The Basic Responsibility of Sport and Physical Education." International Journal of Physical Education. 19, No.3 (1982), 13-18. TEACHING PHYSICAL EDUCATION, DEFINITION OF PLAY, ART AND WORK, REFORM.

EXPOSÉS AND CRITIQUES

Books

1816. Allen, Maury. Where Have You Gone, Joe DiMaggio? The Story of America's Last Hero. New York: E. P. Dutton and Company, 1975. HEROES, PRO BASEBALL.

1817. Angell, Roger. The Summer Game. New York: The Viking Press, 1972. FUTURE, PRO BASEBALL, FANS, AESTHETICS.

1818. Bavasi, Buzzie with John Strege. Off the Record. Chicago: Contemporary Books, Inc., 1987. MANAGERS, PRO BASEBALL, BROOKLYN DODGERS, LOS ANGELES DODGERS, SAN DIEGO PADRES, CALIFORNIA ANGELS, RACISM, FREE AGENCY, AGENTS.

1819. Beer, Tom with George Kimball. Sunday's Fools: Stomped, Tromped, Kicked, and Chewed in the NFL. Boston: Houghton, Mifflin, 1974. PRO FOOTBALL, LOSING, NEW YORK STARS.

1820. Berkow, Ira. Five Part Series on the State of Intercollegiate Football. New York: Newspaper Enterprise Association, 1970. BIG BUSINESS, NCAA DIVISION I FOOTBALL, RECRUITING VIOLATIONS, ACADEMICS, DRUGS, COACH-PLAYER RELATIONS, VALUES, CHANGE.

1821. Bouton, Jim. I'm Glad You Didn't Take It Personally. New York: William Morrow and Company, Inc., 1971. TELEVISION, MEDIA, PRO BASEBALL.

1822. Brosnan, Jim. The Long Season. New York: Harper, 1960. BASEBALL, PLAYERS, SOCIOLOGY.

1823. Bryant, Paul W. and John Underwood. Bear: The Hard Life and Good Times of Alabama's Coach Bryant. Boston: Little, Brown and Company, 1974. COACHES, COLLEGE FOOTBALL, UNIVERSITY OF ALABAMA.

1824. Deford, Frank. Big Bill Tilden: The Triumphs and the Tragedy. London:
       Victor Gollancz Ltd., 1977. HEROES, FAIR PLAY, TENNIS.

1825. DeLillo, Don. End Zone. Boston: Houghton Mifflin Company, 1972.
       NUCLEAR WAR, FOOTBALL, FICTION, LITERATURE, NOVEL, LANGUAGE, FEAR OF
       COMMITMENT.

1826. Dryden, Ken and Roy MacGregor. Home Game: Hockey and Life in Canada.
       Toronto: McClelland and Stewart, 1989. VIOLENCE, MONEY, SPORTSMANIA.

1827. Feinstein, John. A Season on the Brink: A Year with Bob Knight and the
       Indiana Hoosiers. New York: Macmillan Publishing Company, 1986. COLLEGE
       BASKETBALL, BOB KNIGHT, WINNING AND LOSING, INDIANA UNIVERSITY.

1828. Flood, Curt with Richard Carter. The Way It Is. New York: Trident Press,
       1971. WINNING, PRO BASEBALL.

1829. Garvey, Cynthia and Andy Meisler. The Secret Life of Cyndy Garvey. New
       York: Doubleday and Company, Inc., 1989. PRO BASEBALL, CYNDY GARVEY,
       LOS ANGELES DODGERS, STEVE GARVEY.

1830. Gent, Peter. North Dallas Forty. New York: William Morrow and Company,
       Inc., 1973. FICTION, NOVEL, PRO FOOTBALL, DALLAS COWBOYS, DRUGS,
       INJURIES, VIOLENCE.

1831. Gibson, Althea. I Always Wanted To Be Somebody. New York: Harper and
       Brothers, 1958. BLACK ATHLETES, WOMEN, TENNIS, PREJUDICE, RACISM,
       DISCRIMINATION.

1832. Gibson, Bob. From Ghetto to Glory; The Story of Bob Gibson. Englewood
       Cliffs, NJ: Prentice Hall, Inc., 1968. BASEBALL, BLACK ATHLETES, RACISM.

1833. Harris, Sydney J. The Best of Sydney J. Harris. Boston: Houghton Mifflen,
       1975. VIOLENCE, COMPETITION, PRO SPORTS.

1834. Jenkins, Dan. 'You Call it Sports, But I Say It's a Jungle Out There'. New
       York: Simon and Schuster, Inc., 1989. SPORTS WRITING, COLLEGE FOOTBALL,
       GOLF, COMPETITION.

1835. Johnson, Blaine. What's Happenin'?: A Revealing Journey Through the World
       of Professional Basketball. Engelwood Cliffs, NJ: Prentice-Hall, Inc., 1978.
       PRO BASKETBALL, FUN, SEATTLE SUPERSONICS, SPORTS JOURNALISM, INSIDE
       SRORY.

1836. Johnson, Jack. Jack Johnson is a Dandy: An Autobiography. New York:
       Chelsea House Publishers, 1969. RACISM, BOXING, PREJUDICE, DISCRIMINATION.

1837. Kahn, Roger. The Boys of Summer. New York: Harper and Row Publishers,
       Inc., 1972. BROOKLYN DODGERS, AMERICAN CULTURE, PRO BASEBALL, ROLE OF
       SPORT IN SOCIETY.

1838. Karras, Alex with Herb Gluck. Even Big Guys Cry. New York: Holt, Rinehart, and Winston, Inc., 1977. BENEFIT AND HARM, VIOLENCE, VALUES.

1839. Keteyian, Armen. Big Red Confidential: Inside Nebraska Football. Chicago: Contemporary Books, 1989. PLAYER PAYOFFS, GAME-FIXING, STEROIDS, CORRUPTION, UNIVERSITY OF NEBRASKA, COLLEGE FOOTBALL.

1840. King, Billie Jean and Kim Chapin. Billie Jean. New York: Harper and Row Publishers, Inc., 1974. WOMEN, BILLIE JEAN KING, LESBIANISM, PRO TENNIS.

1841. Libby, Bill. Goliath: The Wilt Chamberlain Story. New York: Dodd, Mead and Company, 1977. WILT CHAMBERLAIN, PRO BASKETBALL.

1842. Lomax, Neil with J. David Miller. Third and Long. Old Tappan, NJ: Fleming H. Revell Company, 1986. PORTLAND STATE UNIVERSITY, ST. LOUIS CARDINALS, COLLEGE FOOTBALL, PRO FOOTBALL.

1843. Louis, Joe with Edna Rust and Art Rust Jr. Joe Louis: My Life. New York: Harcourt Brace Jovanovich, 1978. PRO BOXING, RACISM, DISCRIMINATION.

1844. Love, Stan and Ron Rapoport. Love in the NBA: A Player's Uninhibited Diary. New York: Saturday Review Press, 1975. NBA, PRO BASKETBALL, INJURIES.

1845. Luciano, Ron and David Fisher. The Umpire Strikes Back. Toronto: Bantam Books, Inc., 1982. UMPIRES, BASEBALL, MANAGERS, MEDIA.

1846. Lynn, Elizabeth A. Babe Didrikson Zaharias. New York: Chelsea House Publishers, 1989. GOLF, TRACK AND FIELD, OLYMPICS, LADIES PROFESSIONAL GOLF ASSOCIATION, CANCER.

1847. Mann, Arthur William. The Jackie Robinson Story. New York: F. J. Low Company, 1950. DESEGREGATION, INTEGRATION, JUSTICE.

1848. Martin, Billy with Phil Pepe. Billyball. Garden City, NY: Doubleday and Company, 1987. PRO BASEBALL, OWNERS, NEW YORK YANKEES.

1849. Meggyesy, Dave. Out of Their League. Berkeley: Ramparts Press, 1970. ST. LOUIS CARDINALS, COACHES, RECRUITING, PLAYER PAYOFFS, DRUGS.

1850. Nash, Bruce and Allan Zullo. The Baseball Hall of Shame. New York: Pocket Books, Inc., 1986. CHEATING, FANS, VIOLENCE, SPORTSMANSHIP, BASEBALL.

1851. Oliver, Chip. High for the Game. New York: William Morrow and Company, Inc., 1971. BLACK ATHLETES, WOMEN, COACHES, PRO FOOTBALL.

1852. Oriard, Michael V. The End of Autumn: Reflections on My Life in Football. Garden City, NY: Doubleday and Company, Inc., 1982. INJURIES, VIOLENCE, RELIGION, NOTRE DAME UNIVERSITY, KANSAS CITY CHIEFS, PRO FOOTBALL, COLLEGE FOOTBALL.

1853. Parrish, Bernie. They Call It a Game. New York: Dial Press, 1971. EXPLOITATION OF COLLEGE ATHLETES, PRO FOOTBALL, COLLEGE FOOTBALL, BENEFIT AND HARM, SPORTSMANIA.

1854. Roberts, Randy. Papa Jack: Jack Johnson and the Era of White Hopes. New York: The Free Press, 1983. BLACK ATHLETES, CHANGE, WHITE WOMEN, BOXING.

1855. Robinson, Jackie. I Never Had it Made. New York: Putnam, 1972. RACISM, PRO BASEBALL, BROOKLYN DODGERS, DISCRIMINATION.

1856. Rust, Art Jr. Get That Nigger Off the Field! New York: Delacorte Press, 1976. RACISM, BLACK BASEBALL PLAYERS, PRO BASEBALL, DISCRIMINATION, INFORMAL HISTORY, BIOGRAPHY, MINORITIES.

1857. Sample, Johnny. Confessions of a Dirty Ballplayer. New York: Dial Press, 1970. VIOLENCE, DIRTY PLAY, NEW YORK JETS, PRO FOOTBALL, COMPETITION, RULES.

1858. Scott, Jack. Athletics for Athletes. Oakland, CA: Other Ways Book Dept., 1969. COACHES, REFORM, IDEAL AND MEANING, AMATEURISM, OLYMPICS, BLACK ATHLETES.

1859. Shaw, Gary. Meat on the Hoof: The Hidden World of Texas Football. New York: St. Martin's Press, Inc., 1972. CHILDREN, YOUTH, COLLEGE FOOTBALL, VALUES, FANS, SPORTSMANIA, AMERICAN CULTURE.

1860. Switzer, Barry with Bud Shrake. Bootlegger's Boy. New York: Morrow, 1990. OKLAHOMA UNIVERSITY FOOTBALL COACH, BARRY SWITZER, PERSONAL STORY, SPORTSMANIA, NCAA INFRACTIONS, ACADEMICS, RECRUITING.

1861. Taylor, Lawrence with David Falkner. Living on the Edge. New York: Times Books, 1987. PRO FOOTBALL, NEW YORK GIANTS, DRUGS, VIOLENCE.

1862. Thomas, Duane L. and Paul Zimmerman. Duane Thomas and the Fall of America's Team. New York: Warner Books, Inc., 1988. PRO FOOTBALL, DALLAS COWBOYS, COACH AND PLAYERS.

1863. Thompson, Charles and Allan Sonnenschein. Down and Dirty: The Life and Crimes of Oklahoma Football. New York: Carroll and Graf Publishers, 1990. EX-OKLAHOMA UNIVERSITY FOOTBALL PLAYERS REVELATIONS, SEX, BRIBERY, MONEY, DRUGS, VIOLENCE.

1864. Tygiel, Jules. Baseball's Great Experiment: Jackie Robinson and His Legacy. New York: Oxford University Press, Inc., 1983. PRO BASEBALL, BLACK ATHLETES, JUSTICE, ROY CAMPANELLA, BRANCH RICKEY, DON NEWCOMBE.

1865. Vare, Robert. Buckeye: A Study of Coach Woody Hayes and the Ohio State Football Machine. New York: Harper's Magazine Press, 1974. COLLEGE FOOTBALL, WINNING.

1866. Wolf, David. Foul! The Connie Hawkins Story. New York: Holt, Rinehart, and Winston, Inc., 1972. RECRUITING, SCANDALS, COACHES, GAMBLING, LAW, PRO BASKETBALL, CORRUPTION, RACISM, EXPLOITATION.

Articles

1867. Boyle, Robert H. and Roger Jackson. "Bringing Down the Curtain." Sports Illustrated. 57, No.6 (August 9, 1982), 62-66+. UNIVERSITY OF SAN FRANCISCO, BASKETBALL SCANDAL, ASSAULT OF COED, RECRUITING VIOLATIONS, PLAYER PAYOFFS, ABOLISHED BASKETBALL PROGRAM, QUINTIN DAILEY.

1868. Brubaker, Bill. "Bittersweet." Sports Illustrated. 62, No.5 (February 4, 1985), 58-64+. MICHAEL RAY RICHARDSON, PRO BASKETBALL, COCAINE, NEW JERSEY NETS, TRAGEDY.

1869. Carlson, Margaret B. "Charlie Hustle's Final Play." Time. 134, No.10 (September 4, 1989), 64. GAMBLING AND POINT SHAVING, PRO BASEBALL, PETE ROSE.

1870. Chass, Murray. "Owner's Varying Explanations Are At Issue." The New York Times. 134 (July 19, 1990), B9. GEORGE STEINBRENNER, OWNER, NEW YORK YANKEES, HOWARD SPIRA, PAYOFF: $40,000, PRO BASEBALL.

1871. Church, George J. "Why Pick on Pete?" Time. 134, No.2 (July 10, 1989), 16-21. GAMBLING AND POINT SHAVING, PRO BASEBALL, PETE ROSE.

1872. Diaz, Jaime. "Racism Issue Shakes World of Golf." The New York Times. 134 (July 29, 1990), Section 8, Pages 1-2. PGA CHAMPIONSHIP, SHOAL CREEK COUNTRY CLUB, RACISM, SEGREGATION, PRO GOLF.

1873. Dolphin, Ric. "A Game of Chance." Maclean's. 102, No.16 (April 17, 1989), 52-53. GAMBLING, MANAGERS, PRO BASEBALL, PETE ROSE.

1874. Gair, Chris and William J. Baker. "The Manhood Game: American Football in Critical Perspective." The South Atlantic Quarterly. 82, No.2 (Spring 1983), 145-153. VALUES, AUTHORITARIAN COACHES, PLAYERS AS CHATTEL, COACH-PLAYER RELATIONS, FOOTBALL, CHARACTER DEVELOPMENT.

1875. Jordan, P. "War of the Roses." Gentlemen's Quarterly. 59 (April 1989), 274-279+. GAMBLING AND POINT SHAVING, PRO BASEBALL, PETE ROSE.

1876. Kirkpatrick, Curry. "Isn't This Unbelievable?" Sports Illustrated. 63, No.22 (November 18, 1985), 22-27. LOUISIANA STATE UNIVERSITY, ATHLETIC DIRECTOR, BOB BROADHEAD, BUGGING OFFICES, FBI PROBE, RECRUITING VIOLATIONS.

1877. Koufax, Sandy. "Koufax on Koufax." Sports Illustrated. 23, No.25 (December 20, 1965), 34-42. PHYSICAL DISABILITIES, SPORTSMAN OF THE YEAR, SENSE OF RESPONSIBILITY, MANAGMENT OF EXCELLENCE.

1878. Koufax, Sandy with Ed Linn. "The Sandy Koufax Story: My Salary Fights."
      Look. 30, No.12 (June 14, 1966), 90-92+. PRO BASEBALL, BARGAINING,
      BUSINESS.

1879. Leerhsen, Charles. "All the Odds Against Him." Newsweek. 114, No.2 (July
      10, 1989), 74-75. GAMBLING, PRO BASEBALL, PETE ROSE.

1880. Leerhsen, Charles. "The End of the Affair." Newsweek. 114, No.10
      (September 4, 1989), 58-59. GAMBLING AND POINT SHAVING, PRO BASEBALL,
      PETE ROSE.

1881. Leerhsen, Charles with Jeanne Gordon. "Basketball Was His Life." Newsweek.
      115, No.12 (March 19, 1990), 52. WINNING, HANK GATHERS, SPORTS MEDICINE,
      COLLEGE BASKETBALL.

1882. Lieber, Jill. "No Bones About It." Sports Illustrated. 71, No.9 (August 28,
      1989), 54-62. PRO FOOTBALL, SAN FRANCISCO FORTY-NINERS, VIOLENCE,
      BENEFIT AND HARM, JOHN FRANK, BRUTALITY OF FOOTBALL.

1883. Lieber, Jill and Craig Neff. "An Idol Banned." Sports Illustrated. 71, No.10
      (September 4, 1989), 29-30. GAMBLING AND POINT SHAVING, PRO BASEBALL,
      PETE ROSE.

1884. Lieber, Jill and Craig Neff. "Deeper and Deeper." Sports Illustrated. 72, No.6
      (February 12, 1990), 50+. GAMBLING, PRO BASEBALL, PETE ROSE.

1885. Lieber, Jill and Craig Neff. "The Case Against Pete Rose." Sports Illustrated.
      71, No.1 (July 3, 1989), 10-20+. GAMBLING AND POINT SHAVING, PRO
      BASEBALL, PETE ROSE.

1886. Lieber, Jill and Jerry Kirshenbaum. "Stormy Weather at South Carolina."
      Sports Illustrated. 56, No.5 (February 8, 1982), 30-37. WOMEN'S BASKETBALL,
      UNIVERSITY OF SOUTH CAROLINA, PAM PARSONS, COACH AND PLAYERS,
      LESBIANISM, RECRUITING VIOLATIONS, DRUGS, ACADEMICS.

1887. Lumley, Albert E. "The Intercollegiate Athletic Scandals." The American
      Scholar. 21, No.2 (Spring 1952), 193-198. GAMBLING, POINT SHAVING,
      COMMERCIALIZATION, CHEATING, CORRUPTION, DISHONESTY, SCANDALS,
      INTERCOLLEGIATE ATHLETICS, COACHES, PLAYERS, PAYMENTS TO ATHLETES,
      ADMISSION COLLABORATION, ROLE OF THE COLLEGE PRESIDENT, REFORM.

1888. McLaughlin, Lee. "How My 'Quick Fix' Turned Into a Bad Dream." Women's
      Sports and Fitness. 8, No.11 (November 1986), 70. DRUG USE, HIGH SCHOOL
      ATHLETES.

1889. Meggyesy, Dave. "Sex and Racism in the NFL." Look. 34, No.24 (December
      1, 1970), 65-74. RACISM, ST. LOUIS CARDINALS, COACHES, REFORM.

1890. Meggyesy, Dave. "The Football Racket." Look. 34, No.23 (November 17,
      1970), 66-77. FOOTBALL, VIOLENCE, DRUGS, PAYOFFS.

1891. Murdock, Eugene C. "The Tragedy of Ban Johnson." Journal of Sport History. 1, No.1 (Spring 1974), 26-40. BYRON JOHNSON, PRO BASEBALL, ACADEMICS, CORRUPTION, GAME-THROWING.

1892. Neff, Craig. "The Rose Probe." Sports Illustrated. 70, No.13 (March 27, 1989), 13. GAMBLING, MANAGERS, PRO BASEBALL, PETE ROSE.

1893. Neff, Craig (ed.). "Guilty." Sports Illustrated. 72, No.18 (April 30, 1990), 13-14. GAMBLING, PRO BASEBALL, PETE ROSE.

1894. Neff, Craig (ed.). "The Rose Probe (continued)." Sports Illustrated. 70, No.20 (May 8, 1989), 11-12. GAMBLING AND POINT SHAVING, PRO BASEBALL, PETE ROSE.

1895. Neff, Craig (ed.). "The Rose Probe (continued)." Sports Illustrated. 70, No.17 (April 17, 1989), 13+. GAMBLING AND POINT SHAVING, PRO BASEBALL, PETE ROSE.

1896. Neff, Craig and Jill Lieber. "Rose's Grim Vigil." Sports Illustrated. 70, No.14 (April 3, 1989), 52-54+. GAMBLING AND POINT SHAVING, PRO BASEBALL, PETE ROSE.

1897. Neugeboren, Jay. "My Life and Death in the Negro American Baseball League: A Slave Narrative." The Massachusetts Review. 14, No.3 (Summer 1973), 545-566. MINORITIES, DISCRIMINATION, BASEBALL.

1898. Nichols, Mark. "Troubled Times." Maclean's. 102, No.28 (July 10, 1989), 42. GAMBLING AND POINT SHAVING, PRO BASEBALL, PETE ROSE.

1899. Otto, Solomon with John Solomon Otto. "I Played Against 'Satchel' for Three Seasons: Blacks and Whites in the 'Twilight Leagues'." Journal of Popular Culture. 7, No.4 (Spring 1974), 797-803. SATCHEL PAIGE, BASEBALL, MINORITIES.

1900. Rashad, Ahmad as told to Frank Deford. "Journal of a Plagued Year." Sports Illustrated. 57, No.17 (October 18, 1982), 42-46+. PRO FOOTBALL, AHMAD RASHAD, WIDE RECEIVER, PLAYERS STRIKE, DRUGS, MINNESOTA VIKINGS, BLACK PLAYERS, SEGREGATION.

1901. Reese, Don (ed. by John Underwood). "I'm Not Worth A Damn." Sports Illustrated. 56, No.24 (June 14, 1982), 66-82. PRO FOOTBALL, DON REESE, COCAINE, DRUGS, MIAMI POLICE, MIAMI DOLPHINS, REHABILITATION.

1902. Remnick, David. "Still on the Outside." Sports Illustrated. 67, No.15 (October 5, 1987), 44-47+. DAVE MEGGYESY, NFL FOOTBALL PLAYER, SCATHING INDICTMENT OF THE NFL, UNION/PLAYER GRIEVANCES, JACK SCOTT.

1903. Simpson, George. "College Football's B.M.O.C. Crisis: Battered and Maimed on Campus." Sport. 63, No.5 (November 1976), 19-30. VIOLENCE, INJURIES, FOOTBALL.

1904. Smith, Claire. "Arbitrator Finds Third Case of Baseball Collusion." The New York Times. 134 (July 19, 1990), B9. PLAYERS UNION, COLLUSION, BASEBALL OWNERS, PLAYER SALARIES.

1905. Smith, Gary. "Hello, Trouble, I'm Dale Brown." Sports Illustrated. 63, No.22 (November 18, 1985), 28-32+. LOUISIANA STATE UNIVERSITY, COLLEGE BASKETBALL, COACH, DALE BROWN, BATTLES NCAA, CRITICISM OF NCAA RULES, FLAMBOYANT BEHAVIOR, RECRUITING, CHEATING CHARGE.

1906. Smith, Ronald A. "The Paul Robeson--Jackie Robinson Saga and a Political Collision." Journal of Sport History. 6, No.2 (Summer 1979), 5-27. POLITICS, MINORITIES, BASEBALL.

1907. Telander, Rick. "The Descent of a Man." Sports Illustrated. 56, No.10 (March 8, 1982), 62-69. CLEMSON BASKETBALL, TAYLOR O. LOCKE, COACH, CHEATING, PLAYER PAYOFFS, NCAA RULE VIOLATIONS, ACADEMICS, ACADEMIC TRICKS, RECRUITING VIOLATIONS.

1908. Trakhtenberg, Leonid. "A Man of Character." Soviet Literature. No.1 (1981), 79-84. SPORTSMANSHIP, DISCIPLINE.

1909. Underwood, John. "The NCAA Goes on the Defense." Sports Illustrated. 48, No.10 (February 27, 1978), 20-29. CONGRESSIONAL HEARING, NCAA, ABUSE OF POWER, JERRY TARKANIAN, WALTER BEYERS, OKLAHOMA STATE UNIVERSITY, RULE INFRACTIONS.

1910. Vecsey, George. "Golf Can Be Rescued From Shoal Creek." The New York Times. 134 (July 29, 1990), Section 8, Page 2. RACISM, SEGREGATION, PRO GOLF, PGA CHAMPIONSHIP, SOUTHERN CHRISTIAN LEADERSHIP CONFERENCE.

1911. Vecsey, George. "The Owner Who Paid A Gambler." The New York Times. 134 (July 19, 1990), B9. GEORGE STEINBRENNER, OWNER, FAY VINCENT, COMMISSIONER OF BASEBALL, PAY OFF: $40,000, NEW YORK YANKEES, PRO BASEBALL.

1912. Weaver, Harold D. Jr. "Paul Robeson: Beleaguered Leader." The Black Scholar. 5, No.4 (December 1973-January 1974), 25-32. PAUL ROBESON, PRO BASEBALL, MINORITIES. HEROES.

1913. Wright, Robert. "Up to Speed." The New Republic. 201, No.5 (July 31, 1989), 42. GAMBLING AND POINT SHAVING, PRO BASEBALL, PETE ROSE.

INTERNATIONAL SPORT

Books

1914. Archer, Robert and Antoine Bouillon. The South African Game: Sport and Racism. London: Zed Press, 1982. APARTHEID, BOYCOTTS, RACISM, OPPRESSION, SOCIAL CLASSES, SOCIOLOGY.

1915. Baker, William J. and James Anthony Mangan (eds.). Sport in Africa: Essays in Social History. New York: Africana Publishing Company, 1987. WRESTLING, GAMBLING, HUNTING, BOXING, WOMEN, POLITICS, SOUTH AFRICA, USSR.

1916. Brickhill, Joan. Race Against Race: South Africa's 'Multi-national' Sport Fraud. London: International Defense and Aid Fund for Southern Africa, 1976. APARTHEID, POLICY, RACISM, DISCRIMINATION.

1917. Brokhin, Yuri. The Big Red Machine: The Rise and Fall of Soviet Olympic Champions. New York: Random House, Inc., 1978. USSR, EXPLOITATION, OLYMPICS, OLGA KORBUT.

1918. Chavoor, Sherman and Bill Davidson. The 50-Meter Jungle. New York: Coward, McCann Geoghegan, Inc., 1973. POWER, SWIMMING, MUNICH OLYMPICS.

1919. de Garay, Alfonso L., Louis Levine and J. E. Lindsay Carter (eds.). Genetic and Anthropological Studies of Olympic Athletes. New York: Academic Press, 1974. RACIAL DIFFERENCES, BIOLOGY.

1920. Espy, Richard. The Politics of the Olympic Games: With An Epilogue, 1976-1980. Berkeley: University of California Press, 1981. ROLE OF OLYMPICS IN INTERNATIONAL POLITICS, NATIONALISM, TRANSNATIONALISM, AMATEURISM, PROFESSIONALISM, TELEVISION.

1921. Faria, Norman. Sports and Apartheid, Caribbean Sports People and the Boycott of South Africa. St. Michael, Barbados: Southern Africa Liberation Committee, 1983. DISCRIMINATION, RACISM, SOUTH AFRICA, POLITICS.

1922. Finley, M. I. and H. W. Pleket. The Olympic Games: The First Thousand Years. New York: The Viking Press, 1976. ANCIENT GAMES, OLYMPICS, FANS, RULES, OFFICIALS, PLAYERS, POLITICS.

1923. Fraser, Dawn and Harry Gordon. Below the Surface: Confessions of an Olympic Champion. New York: William Morrow and Company, Inc., 1965. WOMEN, OLYMPICS, DRUGS, SCANDAL, SWIMMING, DAWN FRASER.

1924. Groussard, Serge. The Blood of Israel: The Massacre of the Israeli Athletes. New York: William Morrow and Company, Inc., 1975. INTERNATIONAL OLYMPIC COMMITTEE, ISRAEL, TERRORISM, MUNICH OLYMPICS, VIOLENCE.

1925. Guttmann, Allen. The Games Must Go On: Avery Brundage and the Olympic Movement. New York: Columbia University Press, 1984. MONEY, NAZI OLYMPICS, OLYMPIC IDEAL, AMATEURISM, COLD WAR, POLITICS, DEVELOPING COUNTRIES.

1926. Hain, Peter. Don't Play With Apartheid: The Background to the Stop the Seventy Tour Campaign. London: Allen and Unwin, 1971. CRICKET, SOUTH AFRICA, BRITAIN, RACE RELATIONS, HISTORY, APARTHEID, REFORM.

1927. Hazan, Baruch. Olympic Sports and Propaganda Games: Moscow 1980. New Brunswick, NJ: Transaction Inc., 1982. USSR, HISTORY, FUNCTION OF SPORTS, MOSCOW OLYMPICS, BOYCOTTS.

1928. Henry, William Mellors. An Approved History of the Olympic Games. New York: G. P. Putnam's Sons, 1976. PHILOSOPHY, ORIGINS OF OLYMPICS.

1929. Hoberman, John M. The Olympic Crisis: Sport, Politics and the Moral Order. New Rochelle, NY: Aristide D. Caratzas, Publisher, 1986. OLYMPICS, POLITICS, PROPAGANDA, SYMBOLIC NATURE OF OLYMPICS, NATIONALISM, AMATEURISM, RACISM.

1930. Irwin, Wallace Jr. The Politics of International Sport: Games of Power. New York: Foreign Policy Association, 1988. OLYMPICS, DEVELOPING COUNTRIES, UNITED STATES.

1931. Jarvie, Grant. Class, Race and Sport in South Africa's Political Economy. London: Routledge and Kegan Paul, 1985. SOUTH AFRICA, APARTHEID, RACISM, PREJUDICE, DISCRIMINATION.

1932. Kanin, David B. A Political History of the Olympic Games. Boulder, CO: Westview Press, 1981. COLD WAR, MOSCOW OLYMPICS, LOS ANGELES OLYMPICS.

1933. Killanin, Lord. My Olympic Years. New York: William Morrow and Company, Inc., 1983. MONTREAL OLYMPICS, MOSCOW OLYMPICS, MUNICH OLYMPICS, LOS ANGELES OLYMPICS, SOUTH AFRICA, VIOLENCE, DEVELOPING COUNTRIES, WOMEN, PROFESSIONALISM VS AMATEURISM, MONEY, DRUGS.

1934. Killanin, Lord, Michael Morris and John Rodda (eds.). The Olympic Games: 80 Years of People, Events and Records. New York: Macmillan Publishing Company, 1976. MODERN OLYMPICS, ANCIENT GAMES, RULES, HISTORY.

1935. Kleinman, Seymour. Mind and Body: East Meets West. Champaign, IL: Human Kinetics Publishers, 1986. EPISTEMOLOGY, BODY-MIND PROBLEM, CULTURAL NARCISSISM, FITNESS CRAZE, YOGA, MARTIAL ARTS.

1936. Kolatch, Jonathan. Sports, Politics and Ideology in China. New York: Jonathan David Publishers Inc., 1972. COMMUNISM, POLITICS, VALUES, YMCA, FOREIGN POLICY, IDEOLOGY, COMPETITION.

1937. La Guma, Alex. Apartheid: A Collection of Writings on South African Racism by South Africans. New York: International Publishers, 1978. PREJUDICE, JUSTICE, DISCRIMINATION, RACISM.

1938. Lapchick, Richard Edward. The Politics of Race and International Sport: The Case of South Africa. Westport, CT: Greenwood Press, Inc., 1975. APARTHEID, OLYMPICS, BOYCOTTS, HISTORY, RACISM.

1939. Louw, Johan. Sport and Race Relations in South Africa. Ph.D. Thesis: University of Alberta, 1977. JUSTICE, ROLE OF SPORT IN SOCIETY, POLITICS.

1940. Lowe, Benjamin, David B. Kanin, and Andrew Strenk (eds.). Sport and International Relations. Champaign, IL: Stipes Publishing Company, 1978. SPORT AND CULTURE, OLYMPICS, SPORTSMANSHIP, POLITICS, IDEOLOGY, INTERNATIONAL SPORTS.

1941. MacAloon, John J. This Great Symbol: Pierre de Coubertin and the Origins of the Modern Olympic Games. Chicago: The University of Chicago Press, 1981. OLYMPICS, HISTORICAL, PIERRE DE COUBERTIN.

1942. Mandell, Richard D. The Nazi Olympics. New York: The Macmillan Publishing Company, 1971. GERMANY, SPORTSMANSHIP, HEROES.

1943. Miller, Geoffrey. Behind the Olympic Rings. Lynn, MA: H. O. Zimman, 1979. HISTORY, AMATEURISM, AFRICAN BOYCOTT, DRUGS, TELEVISION.

1944. Morton, Henry W. Soviet Sport: Mirror of Soviet Society. New York: Collier Books, 1963. WINNING AT ALL COSTS, OLYMPICS, POLITICS, SOCIOLOGY OF SPORT, PROFESSIONALISM, HOOLIGANISM, HISTORY.

1945. Newnham, Thomas Oliver. A Cry of Treason. Palmerston North, NZ: Dunmore Press, 1978. SOUTH AFRICA, APARTHEID, DISCRIMINATION, RACISM.

1946. Newnham, Thomas Oliver. By Batons and Barbed Wire. Auckland, NZ: Real Pictures, 1981. RACISM, SOUTH AFRICA, POLITICS, DISCRIMINATION, APARTHEID.

1947. Ramsamy, Sam. Apartheid, The Real Hurdle: Sport in South Africa and the International Boycott. London: International Defence and Aid Fund for Southern Africa, 1982. SOUTH AFRICAN SPORTS ASSOCIATION, SOUTH AFRICAN NON-RACIAL OLYMPIC COMMITTEE (SAN-ROC), SOUTH AFRICAN COUNCIL ON SPORT, LAW, BOYCOTTS.

1948. Ramsamy, Sam. Racial Discrimination in South African Sport. New York: United Nations, 1980. APARTHEID, RACISM, AFRIKANER CULTURE, ROLE OF SPORT IN SOCIETY, JUSTICE, INEQUALITIES.

1949. Reich, Kenneth. Making It Happen: Peter Ueberroth and the 1984 Olympics. Santa Barbara, CA: Capra Press, 1986. SOCIAL ASPECTS, POLITICS, ETHICS, ECONOMICS, SOVIET BOYCOTT, PETER UEBERROTH, LOS ANGELES OLYMPICS.

1950. Riordan, James (ed.). Sport Under Communism: The U.S.S.R., Czechoslovakia, the G.D.R., China, Cuba. Montreal: McGill-Queens University Press, 1978. DRUGS, POLITICS, HISTORY.

1951. Segrave, Jeffrey O. and Donald B. Chu (eds.).   The Olympic Games in
      Transition. Champaign, IL: Human Kinetics Books, 1988. ANCIENT GAMES,
      MODERN OLYMPICS, NAZI OLYMPICS, CAPITALIST OLYMPICS, MUNICH,
      AMATEURISM, POLITICS, NATIONALISM, COMMERCIALISM, WOMEN, STEROIDS,
      FUTURE.

1952. Thompson, Richard. Retreat From Apartheid: New Zealand's Sporting Contacts
      with South Africa. Wellington: Oxford University Press, 1975. APARTHEID,
      SOUTH AFRICA, NEW ZEALAND.

Articles

1953. Adedeji, John A.   "Social and Cultural Conflict in Sport and Games in
      Developing Countries."   International Review of Sport Sociology.   14, No.1
      (1979), 81-88. TECHNOLOGY, CHRISTIAN VALUES.

1954. Adedeji, John A. "The Acceptance of Nigerian Women in Sport." International
      Review of Sport Sociology. 13, No.1 (1978), 39-47. EQUALITY, DEVELOPING
      COUNTRIES.

1955. Allen, Caroline.   "A Boycott That Works."   Africa Report.   33, No.2
      (March/April 1988), 56-58.   OLYMPICS, NEW ZEALAND, SOUTH AFRICA,
      APARTHEID, TENNIS, INTERNATIONAL BOYCOTTS, RUGBY.

1956. "Apartheid in South Africa: Special Committee Discusses Sports Boycott of
      South Africa." UN Monthly Chronicle. 8 (August-September 1971), 45-49.
      APARTHEID, AUSTRALIA, RUGBY, ARMS EMBARGO, DISCRIMINATION.

1957. "Apartheid in Sports." UN Chronicle. 19, No.7 (July 1982), 37-39. SOUTH
      AFRICAN SPENDING ON SPORTS, RACISM, CONVENTION AGAINST APARTHEID,
      DISCRIMINATION.

1958. Ashe, Arthur. "Playing Tennis in South Africa." Africa Report. 20, No.5
      (September/October 1975), 51-55. APARTHEID, DISCRIMINATION, SANCTIONS.

1959. "Athlete Power Over South Africa." Senior Scholastic. 110, No.2 (September
      22, 1977), 8. APARTHEID, RACISM, OLYMPICS, BOYCOTTS.

1960. Axthelm, Pete. "Cheating As An Olympic Event." Newsweek. 96 (August 11,
      1980), 51. MOSCOW OLYMPICS, USSR, CHEATING, AMATEURISM.

1961. Axthelm, Pete. "Money and Hypocrisy." Newsweek. 104, No.5 (July 30,
      1984), 68-69. CORPORATE SPONSORSHIP, AMATEUR STATUS, FAIRNESS.

1962. Axthelm, Pete. "The Olympics: Boycotts Can Work." Newsweek. 102, No.15
      (October 10, 1983), 63. MOSCOW OLYMPICS, AFGHANISTAN, USSR.

1963. Baker, Robert D. "An International Convention Against Apartheid in Sports: Its Legal Significance." Journal of Sport and Social Issues. 2, No.2 (Fall/Winter 1978), 11-23. LEGAL ACTION, NATIONAL FORUMS, UN INTERNATIONAL CONVENTION AGAINST APARTHEID IN SPORTS, DISCRIMINATION.

1964. Bazunov, Boris. "Why We Are Not Going to Los Angeles." New Times. No.21 (May 1984), 14-15. COMMERCIALISM IN SPORTS, OLYMPIC SPIRIT, SAFETY, HATE-MONGERING ATMOSPHERE, USSR.

1965. "Bearing the Boycott Torch." Far Eastern Economic Review. 108, No.18 (April 25-May 1, 1980), 23. AFGHANISTAN OLYMPIC TEAM, ADHAM WARSAC, USSR, BOYCOTT, MOSCOW OLYMPICS.

1966. Beck, Peter J. "Politics and the Olympics: The Lesson of 1924." History Today. 30 (July 1980), 7-9. AFGHANISTAN, GAMES AS A MICROCOSM OF THE LARGER POLITICAL ARENA, COOPERATION VS. FRICTION.

1967. Behrens, Gerd. "South Africa's Sports Isolation." World Press Review. 34, No.4 (April 1987), 57. RUGBY, SPRINGBOKS, CRICKET, SPORTS BOYCOTT, WORLD BOXING ASSOCIATION, DISCRIMINATION.

1968. Benjamin, Daniel. "Shame of the Games." Time. 132, No.15 (October 10, 1988), 74-77. SEOUL OLYMPICS, BEN JOHNSON, DRUGS, BANNED SUBSTANCES.

1969. Bose, Mihir. "Sport and South Africa." Marxism Today. 26, No.9 (September 1982), 14-17. APARTHEID, DISCRIMINATION, RACISM.

1970. Boyarsky, Bill. "Olympic Boycott as Political Weapon." The Center Magazine. 13, No.3 (May/June 1980), 7-13. MOSCOW OLYMPICS, BOYCOTT, SPORTS AND POLITICS, SPORTS AND BUSINESS, COMMERCIALIZATION, TELEVISION.

1971. "Boycott Blues." Time. 117, No.13 (March 30, 1981), 52. SOUTH AFRICA, BOYCOTT AGAINST ATHLETES ASSOCIATING WITH SOUTH AFRICA, SUPREME COUNCIL FOR SPORTS IN AFRICA, BLACKLIST.

1972. "Boycotts and Barbed Wire." The Economist. 260 (July, 10, 1976), 53. OLYMPICS, TAIWAN, CANADA.

1973. Buckley, William F. Jr. "Get Out." National Review. 32, No.4 (February 22, 1980), 244-245. BOYCOTT, MOSCOW OLYMPICS, DEPRIVING ATHLETES OF THE OPPORTUNITY TO COMPETE.

1974. Caldwell, Geoffrey. "International Sport and National Identity." International Social Science Journal. 34, No.2 (1982), 173-183. AUSTRALIA, HISTORY, CANADA, OLYMPICS, COMMONWEALTH GAMES, USSR, SPORTS AS A WAY TO ESTABLISH CULTURE.

1975. Carter, Jimmy. "Summer Olympics in Moscow." Department of State Bulletin. 80, No.2036 (March 1980), 50-52. MOSCOW OLYMPICS, USSR, AFGHANISTAN, PERMANENT SITE FOR THE OLYMPICS.

1976. Charters, David A. "Terrorism and the 1984 Olympics." Conflict Quarterly. 3, No.4 (Summer 1983), 37-47. VIOLENCE, POLITICS.

1977. Chataway, Chris. "Let's End This Hypocrisy Now." Sports Illustrated. 13, No.7 (August 15, 1960), 83. OLYMPIC CODE, AMATEURISM, PRETENSE.

1978. Cheffers, J. "The Foolishness of Boycott and Exclusion in the Olympic Movement." Olympic Review. (September 1979), 512-513. POLITICS, UNITED STATES AND THE SOVIET UNION.

1979. Christie, Irene. "Politics in the Modern Olympic Games Up to 1980." The Physical Educator. 43, No.1 (Late Winter 1986), 44-55. IDEALISM, NATIONALISM, MOSCOW BOYCOTT.

1980. Christie, James. "The Olympics Controversy: The Politics of Sport." World Press Review. 31, No.7 (July 1984), 39-44. EAST/WEST STRUGGLE, COMMERCIALISM IN OLYMPICS, RED OLYMPICS, PROFESSIONALISM.

1981. Clumpner, R. A. "Sport and American Foreign Policy." International Journal of Physical Education. 23, No.3 (1986), 37-43. U.S. PRESIDENTIAL ATTITUDES, CULTURAL EXCHANGE PROGRAMS, "SPORT FOR UNDERSTANDING," SPORT AS A TOOL OF FOREIGN POLICY, OLYMPICS.

1982. "Conference Calls for Continued Olympic Ban Against South Africa." UN Chronicle. 22, No.5 (1985), 61-63. APARTHEID, BOYCOTT, RUGBY, WOMEN, STUDENT ACTION, AUSTRALIA, USSR.

1983. Cousins, Norman. "The Statesmen and the Athletes." Saturday Review. 7 (April 12, 1980), 10. 1936 OLYMPICS, HARM OF BOYCOTTS, BOYCOTT OF MOSCOW OLYMPICS.

1984. "Cricket: I'm All White, Jack." The Economist. 234, No.6600 (February 21, 1970), 25. CRICKET, SOUTH AFRICA, DISCRIMINATION.

1985. Czula, Roman. "Sport as an Agent of Social Change." Quest. 31, No.1 (1979), 45-49. FUTURE, INTERNATIONAL SPORTS, OLYMPICS, INTRA-NATIONAL SPORTS, PREJUDICE, CONTACT THEORY.

1986. Czula, Roman. "The Munich Olympics Assassinations: A Second Look." Journal of Sport and Social Issues. 2, No.1 (Spring/Summer 1978), 19-23. MUNICH, OLYMPICS, VIOLENCE, ISRAEL.

1987. Davidson, Spencer. "Horror and Death at the Olympics." Time. 100, No.12 (September 18, 1972), 22-24+. MUNICH OLYMPICS, GERMANY, BLACK SEPTEMBER, ISRAELIS, TERRORISM, HOSTAGES.

1988. Deford, Frank. "Lull Beneath the Jacaranda Tree." Sports Illustrated. 39, No.24 (December 10, 1973), 30-35. SOUTH AFRICA, DISCRIMINATION, ARTHUR ASHE, TENNIS, BOB FOSTER, BOXING, APARTHEID.

1989. Delloff, Linda Marie. "Olympics and Politics." The Christian Century. 97, No.7 (February 27, 1980), 221. MOSCOW OLYMPICS, POLITICS, NATIONALISM, PERMANENT SITE FOR THE GAMES.

1990. Derwinski, Edward J. and Robert J. Kane. "Should U. S. Boycott Olympics?" U. S. News and World Report. 88, No.2 (January 21, 1980), 27-28. MOSCOW OLYMPICS, SOVIET AGGRESSION, OLYMPIC PRINCIPLES, POLITICS, BOYCOTT.

1991. "The Dirty Dozen." Africa. No.128 (April 1982), 57-58. SOUTH AFRICA, GLENEAGLES AGREEMENT, SANCTIONS, CRICKET, RACISM.

1992. "Does International Sport Competition Promote or Reduce Goodwill and Understanding?" Journal of Physical Education, Recreation and Dance. 59, No.8 (October 1988), 6. POLITICS, BENEFIT AND HARM, GOODWILL.

1993. Dommisse, John. "The Psychology of Apartheid Sport." Journal of Sport and Social Issues. 1, No.2 (Summer/Fall 1977), 32-53. HISTORY, MEANING OF SPORT, SOUTH AFRICA, RACISM.

1994. Eisen, George. "The Hungarian Sport Culture." Quest. 22 (June 1974), 100-103. IDEOLOGY, YOUTH.

1995. Evans, Richard. "South Africa and Tennis: Shades of Gray." World Tennis. 25, No.11 (April 1978), 35-37. SOUTH AFRICA, APARTHEID, CRICKET, TENNIS, DISCRIMINATION.

1996. Evfarestov, Alexander. "The Most Secretive Business." New Times. No.3 (January 1981), 28-30. FINANCIAL AFFAIRS OF TEAMS, SECRECY, TWO SETS OF BOOKS, BUSINESS, CORPORATE SPONSORSHIP, VIOLENCE, FUTURE.

1997. Faria, Norman. "Storm Over Wicked Wickets." Africa. No.168 (August 1985), 60-61. SPORTS LINKS WITH SOUTH AFRICA, CRICKET, GLENEAGLES AGREEMENT, COMMONWEALTH NATIONS.

1998. Farrell, Charles S. "Anti-Apartheid Conference Votes to Blacklist Coaches Who Recruit South African Athletes." The Chronicle of Higher Education. 30, No.13 (May 29, 1985), 27-28. UNITED NATIONS SPECIAL COMMITTEE AGAINST APARTHEID, COACHES, POLITICS.

1999. Farrell, Charles S. "Apartheid Foe Urges Blacklist of U. S. Coaches Who Recruit South Africans for College Teams." The Chronicle of Higher Education. 30, No.12 (May 22, 1985), 31-32. BLACKLISTING OF COLLEGE COACHES WHO RECRUIT SOUTH AFRICAN ATHLETES, SPORTS BOYCOTTS AGAINST SOUTH AFRICA, NCAA.

2000. Galliher, John F. and Richard M. Hesslet. "Sports Competition and International Capitalism." Journal of Sport and Social Issues. 3, No.1 (Spring/Summer 1979), 10-21. INDIVIDUAL EXCELLENCE, COMPETITIVENESS, VIOLENCE, DEHUMANIZATION.

2001. Gammon, Clive. "Swirling Shades of Gray." Sports Illustrated. 58, No.20 (May 16, 1983), 78-94. SOUTH AFRICAN SPORTS, INTEGRATION, ILLUSION OF PROGRESS, MULTIRACIAL SPORT, APARTHEID, AFRIKANERS, REFORM, JUSTICE, POLITICS, RACISM, TRACK AND FIELD, RUGBY, GOLF, SWIMMING.

2002. "The Gleneagles Declaration (Concerning Apartheid in Sport)." Journal of Sport and Social Issues. 2, No.2 (Fall/Winter 1978), 55-56. SOUTH AFRICA, PREJUDICE, DISCRIMINATION, RACISM.

2003. "Go and Show." The Economist. 268, No.7045 (September 9, 1978), 17. MOSCOW OLYMPICS, POLITICS, BOYCOTT.

2004. Good, Paul. "The Selling of Our Olympic Teams." Sport. 69, No.1 (July 1979), 30-32+. BIG BUSINESS, AMATEUR ATHLETES, SPONSORS, COMMERCIALIZATION.

2005. Gottlieb, Moshe. "The American Controversy Over the Olympic Games." American Jewish Historical Quarterly. 61, No.3 (March 1972), 181-213. 1938 OLYMPIC BOYCOTT, NAZISM, GERMANY, COMMITTEE ON FAIR PLAY IN SPORTS.

2006. Griffiths, Alison. "Muscles for Money: The Brawn Drain to the U.S." Maclean's. 92, No.27 (July 2, 1979), 13. CANADIAN ATHLETES ATTENDING U.S. COLLEGES, ATHLETIC BUDGETS.

2007. Hain, Peter. "The Politics of Sport in South Africa." New Society. 50, No.890 (October 25, 1979), 183-185. MULTINATIONAL SPORTS POLICY, SOUTH AMERICAN GAMES, COMMITTEE FOR FAIRNESS IN SPORT, ISOLATION, DISCRIMINATION, RACISM.

2008. Heinila, Kalevi. "Sport and International Understanding--A Contradiction in Terms?" Sociology of Sport Journal. 2, No.3 (September 1985), 240-248. NATIONAL INTEREST VS THE COMMON GOOD, OLYMPICS, LEGITIMATION CRISIS, INCOMPATIBLE VALUE.

2009. Herr, Robert. "A Stillborn Olympics." The New Republic. 182, No.7 (February 16, 1980), 12-14. MOSCOW OLYMPICS, AFGHANISTAN, SOVIET UNION, BOYCOTT.

2010. Hunter, Maxine Grace. "The United Nations and the Anti-Apartheid in Sport Movement." Canadian Journal of History of Sport and Physical Education. 11, No.1 (May 1980), 19-35. OLYMPICS, INTERNATIONAL DECLARATION AGAINST APARTHEID IN SPORTS.

2011. "If the West Won't Play." The Economist. 274, No.7117 (January 26, 1980), 53-54. MOSCOW OLYMPICS, BOYCOTT, AFGHANISTAN.

2012. "International Declaration Against Apartheid In Sports." Journal of Sport and Social Issues. 2, No.2 (Fall/Winter 1978), 50-54. DISCRIMINATION, SOUTH AFRICA, RACISM, APARTHEID.

2013. "International Sports: Like It or Not, They're Tied to Politics."   Athletic Business.   8, No.10 (October 1984), 20-24.   DEVELOPING COUNTRIES, INTERNATIONAL IDENTITY, OLYMPICS.

2014. Jaakko, Ahokas.   "The Land of Competition: Observations on the Sociology of Games in Finland."   Diogenes.   No.26 (Summer 1959), 97-106.   COMPETITION, EQUITY, CAILLOIS' CONCEPTS OF ALEA AND AGON.

2015. Jarvie, Grant.   "Apartheid and Sport: A Response to Professor Krotee." Physical Education Review.   11, No.1 (Spring 1988), 61-62.   SOUTH AFRICA, MARXIST ANALYSIS OF SOUTH AFRICA, CLASS ISSUES.

2016. Jefferies, Stephen C.   "Sport and Education: Theory and Practice in the USSR." Quest.   36, No.2 (1984), 164-176.   USSR, ACADEMICS, SPECIALIZATION, SCHOOL SPORT.

2017. Kanfer, Stefan.   "The Great Sports Swindle."   The New Republic.   190, No.7 (February 20, 1984), 27-32.   OLYMPICS, POLITICS, EXPLOITATION, CHEATING.

2018. Kass, D. A.   "The Issue of Racism at the 1936 Olympics."   Journal of Sport History.   3, No.3 (Winter 1976), 223-235.   MINORITIES, OLYMPICS, HISTORICAL, JESSE OWENS.

2019. Kidd, B.   "Boycotts That Worked: The Campaign Against Apartheid in the Commonwealth."   CAHPER Journal.   49, No.6 (July/August 1983), 8-11.   CODE OF CONDUCT, COMMONWEALTH GAMES FEDERATION, APARTHEID, BOYCOTT.

2020. Kiester, Edwin.   "The Playing Fields of the Mind."   Psychology Today.   18, No.7 (July 1984), 18-24.   MENTAL PREPARATION, ATTENTION CONTROL, ANXIETY, VISUALIZATION, POSITIVE REINFORCEMENT.

2021. Kirshenbaum, Jerry.   "Sanctuary Violated."   Sports Illustrated.   37, No.12 (September 18, 1972), 24-31.   MUNICH OLYMPICS, DEATH OF ISRAELI ATHLETES.

2022. Kirshenbaum, Jerry (ed.).   "Moscow '80: An Olympics Under Seige."   Sports Illustrated.   52, No.3 (January 21, 1980), 7.   MOSCOW OLYMPICS, USSR, AFGHANISTAN, BOYCOTT, PRESIDENT CARTER, POLITICS.

2023. Kiviaho, Pekka.   "Sport and Intracultural Social Change: A Longitudinal Analysis."   Acta Sociologica.   21, No.1 (1978), 3-22.   SPORTS AND SOCIETY, POLITICS, FINLAND, SOCIAL CLASSES, ETHNIC GROUPS, SPORTS ORGANIZATIONS, LABOR UNIONS.

2024. Kropke, Robert.   "International Sports and the Social Sciences."   Quest.   22 (June 1974), 25-32.   DEVELOPING NATIONS, INTERNATIONAL SPORTS AS A WORTHY TOPIC OF RESEARCH.

2025. Krotee, March L.   "Apartheid and Sport: South Africa Revisited."   Sociology of Sport Journal.   5, No.2 (June 1988), 125-135.   OLYMPICS, EXTERNAL PRESSURES, CONSTRUCTIVE ENGAGEMENT, DISCRIMINATION.

2026. Krotee, March L. "The Rise and Demise of Sport: A Reflection of Uruguayan Society." The Annals of the American Academy of Political and Social Science. 445 (September 1979), 141-154. URUGUAY, DEMISE, INTERRELATIONSHIP OF SPORT AND SOCIETY IN LATIN AMERICA, TECHNOLOGY, SOCCER.

2027. Krotee, March L. and Luther C. Schwick. "The Impact of Sporting Forces on South African Apartheid." Journal of Sport and Social Issues. 3, No.1 (Spring/Summer 1979), 33-42. OLYMPICS, RACISM, DISCRIMINATION.

2028. Lapchick, Richard Edward. "Apartheid and the Politics of Sport." Africa Report. 21, No.5 (September/October 1976), 37-40. SPORT ISOLATION, POLICIES, SOUTH AFRICA, APARTHEID, RACISM, NEW ZEALAND, RUGBY, OLYMPICS.

2029. Lapchick, Richard Edward. "Don't Play With South Africa." Women's Sports. 4, No.2 (February 1982), 8-9. SPRINGBOKS, SOUTH AFRICA, RUGBY, GLENEAGLES AGREEMENT, SPORTS AS A REFLECTION OF APARTHEID, DISCRIMINATION.

2030. Lapchick, Richard Edward. "South Africa: Sport and Apartheid Politics." The Annals of the American Academy of Political and Social Science. 445 (September 1979), 155-165. OLYMPICS, CHANGE, PROTEST, DISCRIMINATION.

2031. Lapchick, Richard Edward and Franklin H. Williams. "We Say 'No' To Apartheid Sport." The Crisis. 90, No.1 (January 1983), 42-45. RUGBY, VIOLENCE, SOUTH AFRICA, DISCRIMINATION.

2032. Lucas, John A. "Coubertin's Overarching Views of Ten Olympic Games 1896-1936." Olympic Message. 15 (September 1986), 61-67. SPIRIT OF THE OLYMPIC MOVEMENT, INTERNATIONAL BROTHERHOOD-SISTERHOOD, FAIR PLAY AND SPORTSMANSHIP, RESTORATION OF DIGNITY AND NOBILITY, BARON PIERRE DE COUBERTIN.

2033. Lucas, John A. "The Modern Olympic Games: Fanfare and Philosophy, 1896-1972." Quest. 22 (June 1974), 6-18. SELF UNDERSTANDING, CLEAN LIVING, CHAUVINISM, COMMERCIALISM.

2034. Martin, Paul. "South African Sport: Apartheid's Achilles Heel?" The World Today. 40, No.6 (June 1984), 234-243. DEVELOPMENT OF SPORT POLICIES, ATTITUDE REGARDING MIXED SPORT, BOYCOTT, REFORM.

2035. Martin, Robert P. "Olympic Boycott: What it Proved, What it Didn't." U. S. News and World Report. 89, No.6 (August 11, 1980), 43-44. MOSCOW OLYMPICS, USSR, AFGHANISTAN.

2036. Martin, Robert P. "Sputtering Flame of Moscow Olympics." U. S. News and World Report. 89, No.5 (August 4, 1980), 20-21. MOSCOW OLYMPICS, AFGHANISTAN, BOYCOTT, POLITICS.

2037. Maslow, Jonathan Evan. "Tough Questions on Olympic Boycott." Saturday Review. 7 (May 1980), 24-25. RELATIONSHIP OF ATHLETES TO THE GOVERNMENT, SOVIET SPORTS POLICY, PRECEDENTS FOR THE OLYMPIC BOYCOTT, HARM TO ATHLETES.

2038. Meyer, Evelyn S. "The Olympic Games: A Select Bibliography of Bibliographies." Reference Services Review. 12, No.2 (Summer 1984), 95-101. BIBLIOGRAPHY, OLYMPICS, POLITICS, REFERENCE.

2039. Moore, Kenny. "Decision: No Go on Moscow." Sports Illustrated. 52, No.17 (April 21, 1980), 30-33. AMERICAN BOYCOTT, MOSCOW OLYMPICS, FAIRNESS TO ATHLETES, POLITICS.

2040. Moore, Kenny. "Stating 'Iron Realities'." Sports Illustrated. 52, No.14 (March 31, 1980), 16-17. MOSCOW OLYMPICS, BOYCOTTS, USSR, AFGHANISTAN.

2041. Moore, Kenny. "The 'Pawns' Make a Move." Sports Illustrated. 52, No.5 (February 4, 1980), 22-25. MOSCOW OLYMPICS, BOYCOTT, SPORTS AND POLITICS, REACTION OF ATHLETES.

2042. "The Munich Killings: The Blackest September." The Economist. 244, No.6733 (September 9, 1972), 31-32. BLACK SEPTEMBER, VIOLENCE.

2043. Neier, Aryeh. "The Wrong Reason." The Nation. 230, No.5 (February 9, 1980), 131-132. OLYMPIC BOYCOTT, AFGHANISTAN, OPPRESSION, HUMAN RIGHTS.

2044. Nightingale, Dave. "Olympic Terrorism." The Sporting News. 197, No.21 (May 21, 1984), 12-13. MUNICH OLYMPICS, SECURITY, LOS ANGELES OLYMPICS, TERRORISM.

2045. "Not Cricket." The Economist. 291, No.7348 (June 30, 1984), 35-36. CRICKET, BOYCOTT, INCENTIVES.

2046. Ogouki, Stephane A. "Stigma on South African Sport." UNESCO Courier. 30, No.10 (November 1977), 26-27. RACISM, APARTHEID, SOUTH AFRICA, MULTI-RACIAL GAMES, DISCRIMINATION.

2047. "The Olympics: 'Political Blackmail'." Newsweek. 80, No.10 (September 4, 1972), 41-42. MUNICH OLYMPICS, DIPLOMACY THROUGH SPORTS, GERMANY.

2048. "Olympics: To Go or Not To Go." Time. 115, No.4 (January 28, 1980), 15-16. MOSCOW OLYMPICS, USSR, EFFECT ON ATHLETES.

2049. Osterhoudt, Robert G. "The Philosophical Ground of Modern Socialist Sport." Quest. 37, No.1 (1985), 16-26. ONTOLOGY, POLITICS, HEGEL, MARXISM.

2050. Paisner, Richard D. "The Olympic Games: Why Are They Controversial? What Can Be Done About It?" Vital Issues. 21, No.9 (May 1972), 1-4. PROFESSIONALISM, PARALLELS BETWEEN ANCIENT AND MODERN GAMES, POLITICS, GERMANY, SOUTH AFRICA, REFORMS, OLYMPICS.

2051. "Pariah Protest." Africa. No.156 (August 1984), 58. LOS ANGELES OLYMPICS, BOYCOTTS, SOUTH AFRICA, POLITICS, APARTHEID.

2052. Player, Gary A. "A Movement Toward Equality For All People is Painful." U. S. News and World Report. 90, No.18 (May 11, 1981), 68. GOVERNMENT INVOLVEMENT IN SPORTS, SOUTH AFRICA, APARTHEID, GOLF.

2053. "Political Olympics." National Review. 24, No.38 (September 29, 1972), 1047-1048. MUNICH OLYMPICS, PAN AM GAMES, GERMANY, POLITICS.

2054. "Pressure on Apartheid Sporting Friends." Africa. No.117 (May 1981), 56-58. AUSTRALIA, CRICKET, NEW ZEALAND, RUGBY, IRELAND, TENNIS, SOUTH AFRICA.

2055. Schwick, Luther C. and March L. Krotee. "Changes in South African Sport Apartheid." Florida Journal of Health, Physical Education and Recreation. 17, No.4 (November 1979), 10-12. POLITICS, JUSTICE, ROLE OF SPORT IN SOCIETY.

2056. Seymour, Gerald. "Massacre at Munich." Contemporary Review. 221, No.1282 (November 1972), 259-265. MUNICH OLYMPICS, GERMANY, NAZISM.

2057. "Shadow of Death at Munich." Life. 73, No.11 (September 15, 1972), 4-11. VIOLENCE, MUNICH OLYMPICS, GERMANY.

2058. Shaw, Susan M. "Sport and Political Ideology in South Africa." Arena Review. 1, No.2 (1977). APARTHEID, POLITICS, JUSTICE.

2059. Shaw, Susan M. "Sport and Politics: The Case of South Africa." Journal of the Canadian Association for Health, Physical Education and Recreation. 43, No.1 (September/October 1976), 30-38. RELATIONSHIP BETWEEN SPORTS AND POLITICS, SOUTH AFRICA, APARTHEID, SPORTS BOYCOTT, MULTINATIONALISM POLICY.

2060. Shaw, Timothy M. and Susan M. Shaw. "Sport as Transnational Politics: A Preliminary Analysis of Africa." Journal of Sport and Social Issues. 1, No.2 (Summer/Fall 1977), 54-79. POLITICS, APARTHEID, SOUTH AFRICA, RACISM.

2061. Shinnick, Phillip K. "Progressive Resistance to Nationalism and the 1980 Boycott of the Moscow Olympics." Journal of Sport and Social Issues. 6, No.2 (Fall/Winter 1982), 13-21. REFORMS, DEFINITION OF AMATEURISM.

2062. "Should the Torch Be Passed?" Time. 115, No.3 (January 21, 1980), 21. MOSCOW OLYMPICS, USSR, AFGHANISTAN, BOYCOTT, RELOCATION OF GAMES.

2063. Singer, Robert N. "Sport and International Relations." Quest. 22 (June 1974), 45-51. INTERNATIONAL UNDERSTANDING, MEDIA, BUSINESS.

2064. Smith, Terence and Jane Gross. "President Proposes Deadline of Month for Olympics Move." The New York Times. 79 (January 21, 1980), A1+. MOSCOW OLYMPICS, MOVING THE OLYMPICS TO ANOTHER LOCATION, ATHLETE REACTIONS, USSR, AFGHANISTAN.

2065. Soubhi, Akram M. "Physical Education and Sport in the Life of Iraqi Women." International Review of Sport Sociology. 12, No.2 (1977), 107-109. RELIGION, GENDER.

2066. "South Africa: A Losing Game." Newsweek. 75, No.21 (May 25, 1970), 52. SOUTH AFRICA, APARTHEID, RACISM, OLYMPIC BOYCOTT, DISCRIMINATION.

2067. Strenk, Andrew. "The Thrill of Victory and the Agony of Defeat: Sport and International Politics." Orbis. 22, No.2 (Summer 1978), 453-469. SPORTS AS SOCIAL HISTORY, SPORTS AND THE CONDUCT OF INTERNATIONAL RELATIONS, DIPLOMATIC RECOGNITION, PROTEST, PROPAGANDA, PRESTIGE, COOPERATION, CONFLICT.

2068. Strenk, Andrew. "What Price Victory? The World of International Sports and Politics." The Annals of the American Academy of Political and Social Science. 445 (September 1979), 128-140. OLYMPICS, HISTORY, WAR WITHOUT WEAPONS, AGGRESSION.

2069. Tatz, Colin. "Sport in South Africa: The Myth of Integration." The Australian Quarterly. 55, No.4 (Summer 1983), 405-420. UNEQUAL OPPORTUNITY, GOVERNMENT POLICY, APARTHEID, VALUES, BOYCOTTS, TRADE, DISCRIMINATION.

2070. "Terror at the Olympics." Newsweek. 80, No.12 (September 18, 1972), 24-32. MUNICH OLYMPICS, ISRAELIS, HOSTAGES, POLITICS.

2071. "A Time of Mourning." The Christian Century. 89, No.33 (September 20, 1972), 911. MUNICH OLYMPICS, WEST GERMANY, DISCONTINUATION OF GAMES.

2072. "Track's Longest-Running Win Streak." Sports Illustrated. 67, No.4 (July 27, 1987), 16. JOHAN FOURIE, TRACK, SOUTH AFRICA, APARTHEID.

2073. Tyler, Ronald. "Clearing the Boycott Hurdle." Far Eastern Economic Review. 109, No.28 (July 4-10, 1980), 24-25. U.S. BOYCOTT, MOSCOW OLYMPICS, TOURISM DECLINE, SECURITY.

2074. "A U. S. Boycott of Moscow Olympics?" U. S. News and World Report. 85, No.8 (August 28, 1978), 33-34. MOSCOW OLYMPICS, USSR, POLITICS, HUMAN RIGHTS.

2075. Umedum, Simon O. "Sport and Culture in Nigeria." Quest. 22 (June 1974), 97-99. MODERN INDUSTRIAL SOCIETY, EFFECTS OF URBANIZATION ON SPORTS AND CULTURE, WOMEN, SPORTS AND EDUCATION.

2076. "UN Cracks Down on Apartheid Sports Links." Africa. No.119 (July 1981), 127. UN SPECIAL COMMITTEE AGAINST APARTHEID, BOYCOTT, SOUTH AFRICA.

2077. "USSR Pulls Out of Los Angeles Olympics." The Current Digest of the Soviet Press. 36, No.19 (June 6, 1984), 1-6+. HATRED, FEAR, OLYMPIC IDEALS, WORLD RESPONSE, OLGA KORBUT.

2078. "USSR Slams Bid for Olympics Boycott." The Current Digest of the Soviet Press. 32, No.5 (March 5, 1980), 6-7. MOSCOW OLYMPICS, POLITICS AND SPORTS, MUHAMMAD ALI.

2079. Ustimenko, Y. "Trampling on Olympic Principles." New Times. No.17 (April 1984), 28-30. LOS ANGELES OLYMPICS, BUSINESS, COMMERCIALIZATION, ANTI-SOVIET.

2080. Uys, Stanley. "'No' to Arthur Ashe: Sporting News From South Africa." The New Republic. 162 (February 14, 1970), 17-18. DISCRIMINATION, DIPLOMATIC REPERCUSSIONS.

2081. Vayrynen, Raimo. "Nationalism and Internationalism in Sports." Current Research on Peace and Violence. 5, Nos.2-3 (1982), 122-132. SOCIAL ROLE OF SPORTS, SPORTS AND NATION BUILDING, OLYMPICS, CONFLICT PERSPECTIVE, INTEGRATIVE PERSPECTIVE.

2082. Walker, LeRoy T. "Ethics in the Modern Olympic Games." The Journal of Physical Education. 76, No.4 (March/April 1979), 76-77. MATERIALISM, INDIVIDUALISM, HISTORY.

2083. Weisman, Steven B. "As Deadline Passes, White House Says Its Olympic Decision is Final." The New York Times. 79 (February 21, 1980), A1+. MOSCOW OLYMPICS, USSR, AFGHANISTAN, BOYCOTT.

2084. Williams, Roger M. "Troubled Olympics: Moscow '80: Playing for Political Points." Saturday Review. 6 (September 1, 1979), 12-16. MOSCOW GAMES, NATIONAL EGOTISM, POLITICAL STRIFE, COMMERCIALISM, TELEVISION, HISTORY.

2085. "World Religious Leaders Condemn Olympic Slayings." The Christian Century. 89, No.33 (September 20, 1972), 915. AMERICAN JEWISH CONGRESS, WORLD COUNCIL OF CHURCHES, POPE PAUL VI.

2086. Wright, Stephen. "Are the Olympics Games? The Relationship of Politics and Sport." Millenniuum: Journal of International Studies. 6, No.1 (Spring 1977), 30-44. POLITICS IN OLYMPICS, AFRICAN BOYCOTT, NATIONALISM, RELATIONSHIP OF POLITICS AND SPORTS.

2087. "XXII: The Sad Olympiad." America. 142, No.4 (February 2, 1980), 73-74. PLUSES AND MINUSES OF GOING TO MOSCOW, BOYCOTTS, POLITICS, MOSCOW OLYMPICS.

2088. Yamashita, Kazuhiko. "Feudality of College Sports in Japan." Journal of the Philosophy of Sport. 13 (1986), 35-44. DISTINCTION BETWEEN JAPANESE AND AMERICAN SPORT, SPECTATORS, OLYMPICS, SHIGOKI (SQUEEZING THROUGH), PLAYER-COACH RELATIONS, PATERNALISM, CONFUCIAN ETHIC.

MINORITIES AND SPORT

Books

2089. Allen, Maury. Jackie Robinson: A Life Remembered. New York: Franklin Watts, 1987. PRO BASEBALL, RACISM, DISCRIMINATION.

2090. Ashe, Arthur with Frank Deford. Arthur Ashe: Portrait in Motion. Boston: Houghton Mifflin Company, 1975. AUSTRALIA, SOUTH AFRICA, RACISM, TENNIS.

2091. Baker, William J. Jesse Owens: An American Life. New York: Free Press, 1986. BERLIN OLYMPICS, TAX EVASION, POLITICS, SEX, HISTORY.

2092. Behee, John Richard. Hail to the Victors! Ann Arbor, MI: Ulrich's Books Inc., 1974. UNIVERSITY OF MICHIGAN, BLACK ATHLETES, RACISM, DISCRIMINATION.

2093. Brashler, William. Josh W. Gibson: A Life in the Negro Leagues. New York: Harper and Row Publishers, Inc., 1978. BLACK BASEBALL PLAYER, AMERICAN CULTURE, DISCRIMINATION, NEGRO LEAGUES, PRO BASEBALL.

2094. Campanella, Roy. It's Good to be Alive. Boston: Little, Brown and Company, 1959. BASEBALL, BLACK ATHLETES, BRANCH RICKEY.

2095. Cashmore, Ernest. Black Sportsmen. London: Routledge and Kegan Paul, 1982. HISTORY, FAMILIES OF BLACK ATHLETES, RELATIONSHIP WITH TEACHERS, PRIORITIES, FUTURE, FAILURE.

2096. Chalk, Ocania. Black College Sport. New York: Dodd, Mead and Company, 1976. INTERCOLLEGIATE ATHLETICS, HISTORY, BLACK ATHLETES, OLYMPICS, RACISM.

2097. Chalk, Ocania. Pioneers of Black Sport: The Early Days of the Black Professional Athlete in Baseball, Basketball, Boxing, and Football. New York: Dodd, Mead and Company, 1975. BLACK ATHLETES, RACISM, JACK JOHNSON, HEROES.

2098. Davis, Lenwood G. and Belinda S. Daniels (comps.). Black Athletes in the United States: A Bibliography of Books, Articles, Autobiographies and Biographies on Black Professional Athletes in the United States, 1800-1981. Westport, CT: Greenwood Press, Inc., 1981. BASEBALL, BASKETBALL, BOXING, FOOTBALL, GOLF, TENNIS, REFERENCES.

2099. Edwards, Harry. The Revolt of the Black Athlete. New York: Free Press, 1969. OLYMPIC BOYCOTT, BLACK ATHLETES, ATHLETICS AS A ROAD TO RACIAL EQUALITY, PREJUDICE, HISTORY.

2100. Edwards, Harry. The Struggle That Must Be: An Autobiography. New York: Macmillan Publishing Company, 1980. BLACK ATHLETES, RACISM, FUTURE, MYTH OF EQUALITY THROUGH ATHLETICS.

2101. Farr, Finis. Black Champion: The Life and Times of Jack Johnson. New York: Charles Scribner's Sons, 1964. PRO BOXING, BLACK ATHLETES, DISCRIMINATION, RACISM.

2102. Foreman, Thomas Elton. Discrimination Against the Negro in American Athletics. San Francisco: R and E Research Associates, 1975. BOXING, BASEBALL, TENNIS, BOWLING, GOLF, COLLEGE FOOTBALL, LAW, POLICY.

2103. Frommer, Harvey. Rickey and Robinson: The Men Who Broke Baseball's Color Barrier. New York: MacMillan Publishing Company, 1982. BRANCH RICKEY, JACKIE ROBINSON, BROOKLYN DODGERS, PRO BASEBALL, DISCRIMINATION, HISTORY.

2104. Gilmore, Al-Tony. Bad Nigger! The National Impact of Jack Johnson. Port Washington, NY: Kennikat Press, 1975. JACK JOHNSON, BOXING, RACISM.

2105. Henderson, Edwin. The Black Athlete: Emergence and Arrival. Cornwells Heights, PA: The Publishers Agency, Inc., 1976. BOXING, JACKIE ROBINSON, BASEBALL, BASKETBALL, FOOTBALL, TRACK, TENNIS, GOLF.

2106. Holway, John B. Blackball Stars: Negro League Pioneers. Westport, CT: Meckler Books, 1988. BASEBALL, BLACK ATHLETES, HISTORY.

2107. Holway, John B. Voices From the Great Black Baseball Leagues. New York: Dodd, Mead and Company, 1975. NEGRO LEAGUES, BASEBALL, BUCK LEONARD, COOL PAPA BELL, WILLIE WELLS, HISTORY.

2108. Jones, Wally and Jim Washington. Black Champions Challenge American Sports. New York: David McKay Company, Inc., 1972. BLACK ATHLETES, REVOLT, MEXICO CITY OLYMPICS, EQUALITY, HISTORY.

2109. Lapchick, Richard Edward. Broken Promises: Racism in American Sports. New York: St. Martin's/Marek, 1984. DISCRIMINATION, PREJUDICE, COACHES.

2110. Lucas, Robert. Black Gladiator: A Biography of Jack Johnson. New York: Dell Publishing Company, Inc., 1970. PRO BOXING, BLACK ATHLETES, RACISM, DISCRIMINATION.

2111. Mays, Willie. Willie Mays: My Life In and Out of Baseball. New York: E. P. Dutton and Company, Inc., 1966. WILLIE MAYS, PRO BASEBALL, BLACK ATHLETES, RACISM.

2112. Mead, Chris. Champion--Joe Louis: Black Hero in White America. New York: Charles Scribner's Sons, 1985. BOXING, SEGREGATION, RACISM, CIVIL RIGHTS MOVEMENT, BLACK POWER.

2113. Moore, Joseph Thomas. Pride Against Prejudice: The Biography of Larry Doby. New York: Praeger Publishers, 1988. PRO BASEBALL, CLEVELAND INDIANS, RACISM, DISCRIMINATION, LARRY DOBY, BREAKING COLOR BARRIER IN AMERICAN LEAGUE.

2114. Newcombe, Jack. The Best of the Athletic Boys: The White Man's Impact on Jim Thorpe. Garden City, NY: Doubleday and Company 1975. TRACK AND FIELD, FOOTBALL, NATIVE AMERICANS, RACISM.

2115. Olsen, Jack. The Black Athlete: A Shameful Story: The Myth of Integration in American Sports. New York: Time-Life Books, 1968. INTEGRATION, RACISM, PREJUDICE, DISCRIMINATION.

2116. Orr, Jack. The Black Athlete: His Story in American History. New York: Lion Press, 1969. BOXING, FOOTBALL, BASEBALL, TENNIS, TRACK AND FIELD, BASKETBALL.

2117. Owens, Jesse with Paul G. Neimark. Blackthink: My Life as Black Man and White Man. New York: William Morrow and Company, Inc., 1970. BLACK ATHLETES, EQUALITY, TRACK AND FIELD.

2118. Oxendine, Joseph B. American Indian Sports Heritage. Champaign, IL: Human Kinetics Publishers, 1988. CHILDREN, JIM THORPE, FUTURE, HISTORY.

2119. Pascal, Anthony H. and Leonard A. Rapping (eds.). Racial Discrimination in Organized Baseball. Santa Monica, CA: The Rand Corporation, 1970. DISCRIMINATION, INTEGRATION, DESEGREGATION.

2120. Pennington, Richard. Breaking the Ice: The Racial Integration of Southwest Conference Football. Jefferson, NC: McFarland and Company, Inc., Publishers, 1987. WARREN MCVEA, JOHN WESTBROOK, JERRY LEVIAS, SOUTHERN METHODIST UNIVERSITY, UNIVERSITY OF TEXAS, BAYLOR UNIVERSITY, UNIVERSITY OF HOUSTON.

2121. Peterson, Robert. Only the Ball Was White. Englewood Cliffs, NJ: Prentice-Hall, Inc., 1970. BLACK ATHLETES, NEGRO LEAGUES, PRO BASEBALL, RACISM.

2122. Reid, Clifford E. Racial Salary Discrimination in Major League Baseball: Some Recent Evidence. Princeton, NJ: Industrial Relations Section, Princeton University, 1983. MONEY, PRO BASEBALL, OWNERS, SALARY DISCRIMINATION.

2123. Ribalow, Harold U. and Meir Z. Ribalow. Jewish Baseball Stars. New York: Hippocrene Books, Inc., 1984. JEWISH ATHLETES, PREJUDICE, DISCRIMINATION.

2124. Ribalow, Harold U. and Meir Z. Ribalow. The Jew in American Sports. New York, Hippocrene Books, 1966. JEWISH ATHLETES, PREJUDICE, DISCRIMINATION.

2125. Robinson, Jackie. Baseball Has Done It. Philadelphia: J. B. Lippincott Company, 1964. DISCRIMINATION, RACISM, PRO BASEBALL.

2126. Robinson, Louie. Arthur Ashe, Tennis Champion. Garden City, NY: Doubleday and Company, 1967. AMATEUR TENNIS, RACISM, COACHES, U.S. OPEN, DAVIS CUP.

2127. Robinson, Sugar Ray with Dave Anderson. Sugar Ray. New York: Viking Press, 1969. RACISM, DISCRIMINATION, PRO BOXING.

2128. Rogosin, Donn. Invisible Men: Life in Baseball's Negro Leagues. New York: Atheneum, 1985. BLACK PROFESSIONAL BASEBALL, RUBE FOSTER, ROLE PLAYED BY THE NEGRO LEAGUES IN THE BLACK COMMUNITY, INTEGRATION OF PROFESSIONAL BASEBALL, DISCRIMINATION.

2129. Ruck, Robert Lewis. Sandlot Seasons: Sport in Black Pittsburgh. Urbana, IL: University of Illinois Press, 1987. COMMUNITY PRIDE, BLACK CONSCIOUSNESS, HISTORY, NUMBERS RACKET.

2130. Telander, Rick. Heaven is a Playground. New York: St. Martin's Press, 1976. BLACK YOUTH, INNER CITY, BLACK BASKETBALL PLAYERS, CASE STUDIES.

2131. Thompson, Richard. Race and Sport. London: Oxford University Press, 1964. RACE RELATIONS, APARTHEID, SOUTH AFRICA, CRICKET.

2132. Wheeler, Robert W. Jim Thorpe, World's Greatest Athlete. Norman, OK: University of Oklahoma Press, 1979. NATIVE AMERICANS, TRACK AND FIELD, FOOTBALL.

2133. Williams, Doug with Bruce Hunter. Quarterblack: Shattering the NFL Myth. Chicago: Bonner Books, 1990. PROFESSIONAL FOOTBALL, WASHINGTON REDSKINS BLACK QUARTERBACK, DOUG WILLIAMS, RACISM IN THE NFL, DRUG TESTING.

2134. Woods, Donald.   Black and White.   Dublin: Ward River, 1981. DISCRIMINATION, RACISM, SOUTH AFRICA, APARTHEID, JUSTICE.

Articles

2135. Aikens, Charles. "The Struggle of Curt Flood." The Black Scholar. 3, No.3 (November 1971), 10-15.   CURT FLOOD, MINORITIES, SUITS, CHATTEL, INEQUALITIES, RESERVE CLAUSE, PRO BASEBALL, RACISM.

2136. Allison, Maria T. "On the Ethnicity of Ethnic Minorities in Sport." Quest. 31, No.1 (1979), 50-56. ASSIMILATION, ACCULTURATION, IDEOLOGY, UTOPIA, HETEROGENEITY.

2137. Axthelm, Pete. "The Angry Black Athlete." Newsweek. 72, No.3 (July 15, 1968), 56-60. OLYMPICS, BOYCOTT, BLACK REVOLT, RACISM.

2138. Axthelm, Pete. "The Case of Billie Jean King." Newsweek. 97 (May 18, 1981), 133. TENNIS, STEREOTYPES, LESBIANISM.

2139. Bannister, Frank T. Jr. "Search For 'White Hopes' Threatens Black Athletes." Ebony. 35, No.4 (February 1980), 130-132+. WHITE FANS, SYMBOLS OF POWER, RACISM, HEROES.

2140. Becker, Ken. "Just One Room at the Top." Maclean's. 94, No.26 (June 29, 1981), 38-39. WILLIE WOOD, BLACK HEAD COACH, GREEN BAY PACKERS.

2141. Behee, John Richard. "Race Militancy and Affirmative Action in the Big Ten Conference."   The Physical Educator.   32, No.1 (March 1975), 3-8. ACADEMICS, ACADEMIC COUNSELORS, RACISM.

2142. Bennett, Bruce L. "Critical Incidents and Courageous People in the Integration of Sports." Journal of Health, Physical Education and Recreation. 42, No.4 (April 1971), 83-85. BLACK ATHLETES, HISTORY, RACISM.

2143. Berghorn, Forrest J. and Norman R. Yetman with William E. Hanna. "Racial Participation and Integration in Men's and Women's Intercollegiate Basketball: Continuity and Change, 1958-1985." Sociology of Sport Journal. 5, No.2 (June 1988), 107-124.   INTERRACIAL PARTICIPATION, RACIAL INTEGRATION, INTERCOLLEGIATE BASKETBALL, NCAA, EQUAL OPPORTUNITIES FOR BLACKS, STACKING.

2144. "Black Boycott?" Time. 100, No.9 (August 28, 1972), 42-47. ZIMBABWE, AFRICAN BOYCOTT, MUNICH OLYMPICS, RACISM.

2145. "The Black Dominance." Time. 109, No.19 (May 9, 1977), 57-60. PHYSICAL DIFFERENCES OF RACES, LACK OF BLACKS IN MANGEMENT, SPORT AS AN AVENUE FOR MOBILITY, BLACK ATHLETE REVOLT, EXCELLENCE.

2146. Braddock, Jomills Henry II. "Race and Leadership in Professional Sports: A Study of Institutional Discrimination in the National Football League." Arena Review. 5, No.2 (September 1981), 16-25. RECRUITMENT, PRO FOOTBALL.

2147. Braddock, Jomills Henry II. "Race, Athletics, and Educational Attainment: Dispelling the Myths." Youth and Society. 12, No.3 (March 1981), 335-350. ACADEMICS, MYTHS, MINORITIES, DISCRIMINATION, YOUTH, INTERSCHOLASTIC ATHLETICS, SELF ESTEEM.

2148. Braddock, Jomills Henry II. "The Sports Pages: In Black and White." Arena Review. 2, No.2 (Spring 1978), 17-25. MEDIA, RACISM, DISCRIMINATION, BIASED SPORTS REPORTING.

2149. Brown, Ronald H. "Educational Plans of Black and White Athletes and Non-Athletes." Sport Sociology Bulletin. 5, No.1 (Spring 1976), 57-65. MINORITIES, ACADEMICS, ATHLETIC PARTICIPATION, EDUCATIONAL ATTAINMENT.

2150. Brown, Roscoe C. Jr. "Is Sport Really Colorblind." Quest. 19 (January 1973), 91-92. MINORITY ATHLETES, EXCELLENCE, EXPLOITATION, SELF-FULFILLMENT.

2151. Brutus, Dennis. "New Zealand Protest Against Racism in Sport." Africa Today. 17, No.6 (November/December 1970), 8. SOUTH AFRICA, APARTHEID, RUGBY, PROTESTS.

2152. Brutus, Dennis. "The Blacks and Whites in Sport." Africa Today. 17, No.6 (November/December 1970), 2-5. SOUTH AFRICA, APARTHEID, PUBLICITY, REACTIONS IN SOUTH AFRICA, RUGBY, DISCRIMINATION, PROTESTS.

2153. "Calling Them As They See Them: Racism in Sportscasting." Interracial Books for Children Bulletin. 9, No.1 (1978), 11. BIAS, SPECULATION, LUCK VS. SKILL, HOWARD COSELL, PREJUDICE.

2154. Capeci, Dominic J. Jr. and Martha Wilkerson. "Multifarious Hero: Joe Louis, American Society and Race Relations During World Crisis, 1935-1945." Journal of Sport History. 10, No.3 (Winter 1983), 5-25. RACISM, PRO BOXING, HEROES.

2155. Carlston, Donal E. "An Environmental Explanation for Race Difference in Basketball Performance." Journal of Sport and Social Issues. 7, No.2 (Summer/Autumn 1983), 30-51. BASKETBALL, INNER CITY, RULES.

2156. Cashmore, Ernest. "The Champions of Failure: Black Sportsmen." Ethnic and Racial Studies. 6, No.1 (January 1983), 90-102. FAILURE, STRUCTURAL INEQUALITY, EXPLOITATION, HISTORY.

2157. Castine, Sandra C. and Glyn C. Roberts. "Modeling in the Socialization Process of the Black Athlete." International Review of Sport Sociology. 9, Nos.3-4 (1974), 59-74. RACISM, MEDIA.

2158. Chass, Murray. "Campanis Is Out; Racial Remarks Cited by Dodgers." The New York Times. 136 (April 9, 1987), B13+. AL CAMPANIS, RACISM, LOS ANGELES DODGERS, BLACKS IN MANAGEMENT.

2159. Christiano, Kevin J. "Salaries and Race in Professional Baseball: Discrimination 10 Years Later." Sociology of Sport Journal. 5, No.2 (June 1988), 136-149. PRO BASEBALL, RACIAL DISCRIMINATION, FREE AGENCY VS MONOPSONY.

2160. Clark, Vernon L., Floyd Horton and Robert L. Alford. "NCAA Rule 48: Racism or Reform?" The Journal of Negro Education. 55, No.2 (Spring 1986), 162-170. ACADEMIC ELIGIBILITY OF ATHLETES, GRADE POINT AVERAGES, CORE CURRICULUM, SAT SCORES, DISCRIMINATION.

2161. Crase, Darrell. "The Negro in Sport and Physical Education: Some Considerations." The Physical Educator. 27, No.4 (December 1970), 158-160. COMMUNICATION, SOCIAL ACCEPTANCE, REPRESENTATION.

2162. Dandridge, Bob. "'Athletics Softens the Bigotry' of Many American Sports Fans." U. S. News and World Report. 86, No.23 (June 11, 1979), 64-65. RACE RELATIONS, BUSINESS, SALARIES, ROLE MODELS, SPECTATORS.

2163. David, Peter. "Blacks Lose Their Sporting Chance." The Times Higher Education Supplement. No. 533 (January 21, 1983), 6. REFORM, INTERCOLLEGIATE ATHLETICS, NCAA, DISCRIMINATION, RULES, ACADEMICS.

2164. Dillard, Sherman. "A Speck in the Crowd: Black Athletes on White Campuses." Journal of Physical Education and Recreation. 48, No.4 (April 1977), 66-68. MINORITY ATHLETES, RECRUITING, ACADEMICS, DEHUMANIZATION.

2165. Dougherty, Joseph. "Race and Sport: A Follow-Up Study." Sport Sociology Bulletin. 5, No.1 (Spring 1976), 1-12. SPORT AS A VEHICLE FOR UPWARD MOBILITY, RACIAL EQUALITY, DISCRIMINATION, BASEBALL, FOOTBALL.

2166. Edwards, Harry. "Beyond Symptoms: Unethical Behavior In American Collegiate Sport and The Problem of the Color Line." Journal of Sport and Social Issues. 9, No.2 (Summer/Fall 1985), 3-13. INSTITUTIONALIZED RACISM, POLITICS, ACADEMICS, BLACK COACHES.

2167. Edwards, Harry. "Black Athletes and Sports in America." The Western Journal of Black Studies. 6, No.3 (Fall 1982), 138-144. SPORT AS A REFLECTION OF CHARACTER AND HUMAN RELATIONS, LACK OF BLACK REPRESENTATION AT MANAGEMENT LEVELS, RACISM.

2168. Edwards, Harry. "Sport Within the Veil: The Triumphs, Tragedies, and Challenges of Afro-American Involvement." The Annals of the American Academy of Political and Social Science. 445 (September 1979), 116-127. RACISM, DISCRIMINATION, JUSTICE, IDEOLOGY, HIGH SCHOOL SPORT, COLLEGE SPORT, PRO SPORTS, FUTURE.

2169. Edwards, Harry. "The Black 'Dumb Jock': An American Sports Tragedy." The College Board Review. No. 131 (Spring 1984), 8-13. SYSTEMATIC DISCRIMINATION, INTERCOLLEGIATE ATHLETICS, ACADEMICS, RULE 48, REFORMS, BLACKS.

2170. Edwards, Harry. "The Black Athletes: Twentieth Century Gladiators for White America." Psychology Today. 7, No.6 (November 1973), 43-52. BLACK ATHLETES, EXPLOITATION, YOUTH, BLACK FANS, SPORTS AS AN OPIATE, VALUES, WOMEN, ACADEMICS, RACISM.

2171. Edwards, Harry. "The Exploitation of Black Athletes." AGB Reports. 25, No.6 (November/December 1983), 37-46. REFORM, ACADEMICS, RULE 48, RACISM.

2172. Edwards, Harry. "The Sources of The Black Athlete's Superiority." The Black Scholar. 3, No.3 (November 1971), 32-41. SPORT AS A REFLECTION OF SOCIETY, DISCRIMINATION, REVOLT OF BLACK ATHLETES, RACIALLY LINKED PHYSICAL AND PHYSIOLOGICAL CHARACTERISTICS, RACE-RELATED PSYCHOLOGICAL FACTORS, HISTORY.

2173. Eitzen, D. Stanley and David Furst. "Racial Bias in Women's Collegiate Volleyball." Journal of Sport and Social Issues. 13, No.1 (Spring 1989), 46-51. JUSTICE, RACISM, COLLEGE VOLLEYBALL, WOMEN.

2174. Eitzen, D. Stanley and David C. Sanford. "The Segregation of Blacks By Playing Position in Football: Accident or Design?" Social Science Quarterly. 55, No.4 (March 1975), 948-959. EXPLANATIONS FOR RACIAL STACKING, DISCRIMINATION, STEREOTYPES HELD BY COACHES.

2175. Eitzen, D. Stanley and Irl Tessendorf. "Racial Segregation by Position in Sports: The Special Case of Basketball." Review of Sport and Leisure. 3, No.1 (Fall 1978), 109-128. PLAYING POSITIONS, STEREOTYPES, STACKING.

2176. Eitzen, D. Stanley and Norman R. Yetman. "Immune From Racism? Blacks Still Suffer From Discrimination in Sports." Civil Rights Digest. 9, No.2 (Winter 1977), 3-13. STACKING, STEREOTYPES, SALARY DISCRIMINATION, LACK OF BLACK COACHES AND OFFICIALS.

2177. Elliot, Jeffrey. "Quincy Trouppe: Portrait of a 'Super-Star'." Negro History Bulletin. 41, No.2 (March/April 1978), 804-807. BASEBALL, BLACK ATHLETES, DISCRIMINATION.

2178. Evans, Arthur. "Joe Louis As A Key Functionary: White Reactions Toward a Black Champion." Journal of Black Studies. 16, No.1 (September 1985), 95-111. SOCIAL-RACIAL STRATIFICATION, ANALYSIS OF LOUIS-SCHMELING FIGHT, RACISM.

2179. Fabianic, David. "Minority Managers in Professional Baseball." Sociology of Sport Journal. 1, No.2 (1984), 163-171. MINORITIES IN MANAGEMENT, CAREER MOBILITY, MAJOR LEAGUE BASEBALL, PLAYING POSITIONS.

2180. Farrell, Charles S. "650 Athletes Who Failed to Meet New Standards Are in College: Most Are Black." The Chronicle of Higher Education. 33, No.35 (May 13, 1987), 44. PROPOSITION 48, ELIGIBILITY, BLACKS, SAT SCORES, RACISM.

2181. Farrell, Charles S. "A Critic Sees His Protest Against Racism in Sports Vindicated After 20 Years." The Chronicle of Higher Education. 25, No.20 (January 26, 1983), 17-19. HARRY EDWARDS, RACISM, BLACK POWER SALUTE, TIGHTENING OF STANDARDS.

2182. Farrell, Charles S. "Black Educators Call for Repeal of NCAA's Academic Requirement." The Chronicle of Higher Education. 26, No.4 (March 23, 1983), 1+. JESSE JACKSON, REPEAL OF ACADEMIC STANDARDS RULE, SAT SCORES, GRADE POINT AVERAGES, DISCRIMINATION.

2183. Farrell, Charles S. "Black Hockey Player Faces 'Rednecks', Racial Stereotypes." The Chronicle of Higher Education. 31, No.13 (November 27, 1985), 27-28. RITCHIE HERBERT, ROCHESTER INSTITUTE OF TECHNOLOGY, RACISM.

2184. Farrell, Charles S. "NCAA Division II Votes Academic Rules Over Objections of Black Colleges." The Chronicle of Higher Education. 33, No.18 (January 14, 1987), 41-42. ACADEMIC STANDARDS, MINIMUM GRADE POINT AVERAGE, SAT SCORES, REFORM.

2185. Farrell, Charles S. "Racial Problems in Intramural Sports Concern Campus Recreation Officials." The Chronicle of Higher Education. 32, No.5 (April 2, 1986), 33-34. UNIVERSITY OF OKLAHOMA, INTRAMURAL SPORTS, RACISM, ROLE OF THE ATHLETIC DIRECTOR.

2186. Farrell, Charles S. "Scarcity of Blacks in Top Jobs in College Sports Prompts Founding of Group to Monitor Hiring." The Chronicle of Higher Education. 33, No.34 (May 6, 1987), 40+. BLACK ATHLETIC DIRECTORS, LACK OF BLACK COMMISSIONERS, BLACK HEAD COACHES, HARRY EDWARDS, NATIONAL ORGANIZATION ON THE STATUS OF MINORITIES IN SPORTS.

2187. Farrell, Charles S. "Sport Rule Will Bar Able Blacks, NCAA Study Says." The Chronicle of Higher Education. 29, No.2 (September 5, 1984), 1+. RECRUITING VIOLATIONS, FINANCIAL AID, BIG TIME COLLEGE SPORTS, NCAA, PENALTIES, PROBATION.

2188. Farrell, Charles S. "Tough Challenge For A Basketball Recruiter: Finding Blacks to Play at Brigham Young University." The Chronicle of Higher Education. 30, No.3 (March 20, 1985), 33-34. LIFESTYLE, EFFECTS OF MORMON TEACHING, SELF INTEREST.

2189. Farrell, Charles S. and N. Scott Vance. "Black Leaders Weigh Proposals to Revise Rules For Athletes." The Chronicle of Higher Education. 26, No.3 (March 16, 1983), 1+. FIVE YEAR SCHOLARSHIPS, SAT SCORES, GRADE POINT AVERAGES, DISCRIMINATION.

2190. Farrell, Charles S. and N. Scott Vance. "Two Civil-Rights Leaders Denounce NCAA's New Academic Standards." The Chronicle of Higher Education. 25, No.20 (January 26, 1983), 1+. TOUGHER ACADEMIC STANDARDS, JESSE JACKSON, JOSEPH LOWERY, SOUTHERN CHRISTIAN LEADERSHIP CONFERENCE, OPERATION PUSH, DISCRIMINATION, SAT SCORES, GRADE POINT AVERAGES.

2191. Fisher, Anthony LeRoy. "The Best Way Out of the Ghetto." Phi Delta Kappan. 60, No.3 (November 1978), 240. ACADEMICS, YOUTH, BLACK ATHLETES.

2192. Gaston, John C. "The Destruction of the Young Black Male: The Impact of Popular Culture and Organized Sports." The Journal of Black Studies. 16, No.4 (June 1986), 369-384. CULTURAL, MEDIA INFLUENCE ON BLACKS, ACADEMICS, DIGNITY, RACISM.

2193. George, Nelson. "The New Bidding Game in Sports." Black Enterprise. 13, No.6 (January 1983), 28-32. BLACK AGENT, BIG BUSINESS, MONEY, FUTURE.

2194. Gilmore, Al-Tony. "The Myth, Legend and Folklore of Joe Louis: The Impression of Sport on Society." The South Atlantic Quarterly. 82, No.3 (Summer 1983), 256-268. RELATIONSHIP BETWEEN THE IMAGE AND ACTIVITIES OF SPORTSMEN, IMPACT ON GROUP RELATIONS, RACE RELATIONS, INTERNATIONAL ATHLETICS.

2195. Glamser, Francis D. "Contest Location, Player Misconduct and Race: A Case From English Soccer." Journal of Sport Behavior. 13, No.1 (March 1990), 41-49. BLACK AND WHITE PLAYERS' CONDUCT, HOME AND AWAY-FROM-HOME CONDUCT, RACISM, ROWDYISM, HOSTILITY, SOCCER.

2196. Govan, Michael. "The Emergence of the Black Athlete in America." The Black Scholar. 3, No.3 (November 1971), 16-28. SPORTS REPORTERS, PRO ATHLETES, MYTHS.

2197. Graves, Earl G. "Scandal in the Sports Business." Black Enterprise. 13, No.6 (January 1983), 7. DISCRIMINATION, AGENTS, PARENTS.

2198. Green, Robert L., Joseph R. McMillan, and Thomas S. Gunnings. "Blacks in the Big Ten." Integrated Education: A Report on Race and Schools. 10, No.3 (May-June 1972), 32-39. ACADEMICS, LACK OF BLACK REPRESENTATION IN THE BIG TEN COACHING AND OFFICIAL LEVELS, ACADEMIC COUNSELING, EXPLOITATION, FINANCIAL AID DISCRIMINATION.

2199. Grundman, Adolph. "The Image of Intercollegiate Sports and the Civil Rights Movement: An Historian's View." Arena Review. 3, No.3 (October 1979), 17-24. FAILURE OF RACIAL INTEGRATION IN SPORT, MIDDLE CLASS EXPECTATIONS AND ATTITUDES, BLACK ATHLETES, TOKENISM IN SPORTS, RACISM.

2200. Hare, Nathan. "A Study of The Black Fighter." The Black Scholar. 3, No.3 (November 1971), 2-8. OPPRESSION, PROBABILITY OF SUCCESS.

2201. Harrison, Walter L. "Six-Pointed Diamond: Baseball and American Jews." Journal of Popular Culture. 15, No.3 (Winter 1981), 112-118. BASEBALL AS A CEREBRAL GAME, APPEAL OF BASEBALL TO JEWS, BASEBALL--THE AMERICAN GAME, ROLE OF SPORT IN SOCIETY, JEWISH IDENTITY.

2202. Haskins, Jim. "Racial Quotas in Pro Basketball? A Commentary." The Western Journal of Black Studies. 6, No.3 (Fall 1982), 145-147. NBA, PROPORTION OF BLACK PLAYERS, RACISM.

2203. Haslam, Gerald. "Oil Town Rumble: The Young Men of Taft." The Nation. 221, No.7 (September 13, 1975), 208-211. TAFT, CALIFORNIA, RACIAL VIOLENCE, SPORTS IN SOCIETY.

2204. Hawthorne, Peter. "A Few Cracks in the Racial Barrier." Sports Illustrated. 45, No.21 (November 22, 1976), 36-43. BLACKS PLAYING IN SOUTH AFRICA, DISCRIMINATION, REFORM.

2205. "A Heavyweight Bout That Hits Below the Belt." Christianity Today. 26, No.12 (July 16, 1982), 14. PRO BOXING, HOLMES-COONEY FIGHT, RACISM.

2206. Hoferek, Mary J. "Going Forth: Equal Employment Opportunity in a Deregulatory Climate." Quest. 37, No.2 (1985), 203-212. DEREGULATION, EQUAL OPPORTUNITY, WOMEN, MINORITIES, DISABLED, TITLE IX.

2207. Holway, John B. "Before You Could Say Jackie Robinson." Look. 35, No.14 (July 13, 1971), 46-50. RACISM, BLACK LEAGUES, HISTORY.

2208. Holway, John B. "Sam Streeter, Smartest Pitcher in Negro Leagues." Baseball Research Journal. 13 (1984), 71-72. SEGREGATION, RACISM, INVISIBLE ERA OF BASEBALL HISTORY, SAM STREETER.

2209. Houzer, Shirley. "Black Women in Athletics." The Physical Educator. 31, No.4 (December 1974), 208-209. HISTORY, PARTICIPATION, CHANGE AND REFORM.

2210. Ivey, Saundra. "Dilemma at Vanderbilt: Civil-Rights Threaten Protests if University Lets South African Tennis Team Play On Campus in Davis Cup Matches." The Chronicle of Higher Education. 16, No.1 (February 27, 1978), 1+. VANDERBILT UNIVERSITY, SOUTH AFRICA, DAVIS CUP, TENNIS, APARTHEID.

2211. Izenberg, Jerry. "Pro Football's Lily White Position." True. 50, No.381 (February 1969), 32-34+. PREJUDICE, PLAYING POSITIONS.

2212. Jackson, Reggie (ed. by Peter Gammons). "We Have a Serious Problem That Isn't Going Away." Sports Illustrated. 66, No.19 (May 11, 1987), 40-48. BLACKS IN BASEBALL, LACK OF BLACKS IN MANAGMENT, PREJUDICE, REFORM.

2213. Jares, Joe. "Violent Return to a Troubled Past." Sports Illustrated. 42, No.25 (June 23, 1975), 32-38+. BLACK ATHLETES, TAFT, CALIFORNIA, BIGOTRY, KU KLUX KLAN, RACISM.

2214. "Jocks." People Weekly. 11, No.1 (February 19, 1979), 52. ACADEMICS, LAWSUIT BY ATHLETES, CALIFORNIA STATE AT LOS ANGELES, FRAUD, T. P. MOORE.

2215. Jones, J. C. H. and William D. Walsh. "Salary Determination in the National Hockey League: The Effects of Skills, Franchise Characteristics, and Discrimination." Industrial and Labor Relations Review. 41, No.4 (July 1988), 592-604. SALARIES, HOCKEY, DISCRIMINATION, SKILL, FRENCH CANADIANS.

2216. Jones, Terry. "Racial Practices in Baseball Management." The Black Scholar. 18, No.3 (May/June 1987), 16-24. LEGISLATIVE CENSURE, STEREOTYPES, PUBLIC QUESTIONING, AL CAMPANIS, LOS ANGELES DODGERS, RACISM, PETER UEBERROTH, OLD BOY NETWORK.

2217. Kahn, Lawrence M. "Racial Differences in Professional Basketball Players' Compensation." Journal of Labor Economics. 6, No.1 (January 1988), 40-61. CUSTOMER DISCRIMINATION, LABOR RELATIONS, NBA.

2218. Kantzer, Kenneth S. "Varsity Racism?" Christianity Today. 29, No.16 (November 8, 1985), 17-18. RULE 48, SAT SCORES, REFORM, ACADEMICS.

2219. Kirshenbaum, Jerry (ed.). "Facing Up to Billie Jean's Revelations." Sports Illustrated. 54, No.20 (May 11, 1981), 13-16. BIOLOGICAL VS. CULTURAL CAUSES, EXTENT OF HOMOSEXUALITY IN SPORTS.

2220. Kleinknecht, Merl F. (Reviewed by David Q. Voigt). "Blacks in 19th Century Organized BasebalL." Journal of Sport History. 8, No.1 (Spring 1981), 74-75. MEDIA, DISCRIMINATION, HISTORY.

2221. Koch, James V. and C. Warren Vander Hill. "Is There Discrimination in the 'Black Man's Game'?" Social Science Quarterly. 69, No.1 (March 1988), 83-94. NBA, SALARY DISCRIMINATION, PERFORMANCE, FAN RACISM, NEGOTIATIONS BY BLACK PLAYERS.

2222. Kort, Michele. "Sexual Politics of Sports." Ms. 11, No.12 (June 1983), 22. STEREOTYPES OF FEMALE ATHLETES AS MASCULINE AND HOMOSEXUAL, HOMOPHOBIA.

2223. Kramer, William M. and Norton B. Stern. "San Francisco's Fighting Jew." California Historical Quarterly. 53, No.4 (Winter 1974), 333-346. JOE CHOYNSKI, HEAVYWEIGHT BOXING, HISTORY, BIOGRAPHY, STEREOTYPES.

2224. Kruger, Arnd. "'Fair Play for American Athletes': A Study in Anti-Semitism." Canadian Journal of History of Sport and Physical Education. 9, No.1 (May 1978), 43-57. ANTISEMITISM, BOYCOTT, AVERY BRUNDAGE.

2225. Lapchick, Richard Edward. "Discovering Fools Gold on the Golden Horizon: Race and Sport Revisited." The World and I. 3, No.10 (October 1988), 603-611. RACISM IN SPORT, BLACKS IN MANAGMENT POSITIONS, STACKING, COLLEGE SPORT, FUTURE, ACADEMICS, SPORT AS AN AVENUE FOR MOBILITY.

2226. Lapchick, Richard Edward. "The Olympic Movement and Racism: An Analysis in Historical Perspective." Africa Today. 17, No.6 (November/December 1970), 14-16. SOUTH AFRICA, GERMANY, RACISM, INTERNATIONAL OLYMPIC COMMITTEE.

2227. Lawson, Hal A. "Physical Education and Sport in the Black Community: The Hidden Perspective." The Journal of Negro Education. 48, No.2 (Spring 1979), 187-195. MEDIA, ACADEMICS, SOCIALIZATION, BLACK ATHLETES, WOMEN, YOUTH, HARRY EDWARDS.

2228. Leach, Bob and Bob Conners. "Pygmalion on the Gridiron: The Black Student-Athlete at a White University." New Directions for Student Services. No.28 (1984), 31-49. NEEDS OF BLACK STUDENT-ATHLETES, ROLE OF THE STUDENT AFFAIRS ADMINISTRATION, DEGRADATION, SELF CONCEPT, CONTRACTS, FACULTY INDIFFERENCE, POLICY.

2229. Leaman, O. and B. Carrington. "Athleticism and the Reproduction of Gender and Ethnic Marginality." Journal of Leisure Studies. 4 (1985), 205-217. WOMEN, GENDER, ETHNICS, MARGINAL ATHLETES.

2230. Leavy, Walter. "The Billion Dollar Ripoff of Black Athletes." Ebony. 39, No.11 (September 1984), 153-158. AGENTS, CORRUPTION, BRIBES, BLACK ATHLETES.

2231. Lederman, Douglas. "Tactics Vary in Drive to Persuade Colleges to Hire Blacks for Top Sports Jobs." The Chronicle of Higher Education. 34, No.19 (January 20, 1988), A37+. LACK OF BLACKS IN MANAGEMENT, BOYCOTTS, ENCOURAGEMENT FROM NCAA TO HIRE MINORITIES AND FEMALES.

2232. Leonard, Wilbert M. II. "Salaries and Race in Professional Baseball: The Hispanic Component." Sociology of Sport Journal. 5, No.3 (September 1988), 278-284. REPLICATION OF CHRISTIANO'S STUDY, PRO BASEBALL, HISPANICS, BLACKS.

2233. Leonard, Wilbert M. II. "Stacking and Performance Differentials of Whites, Blacks and Latins in Professional Baseball." Review of Sport and Leisure. 2 (June 1977), 77-106. STACKING, PLAYER POSITIONS, ETHNIC MINORITIES, PERFORMANCE DIFFERENCES.

2234. Lewis, Ida. "Tennis: Ashe vs. Racism." Africa Report. 15, No.5 (May/June 1970), 31. ARTHUR ASHE, SOUTH AFRICA, DAVIS CUP, APARTHEID, RACISM.

2235. Lombardo, Ben. "The Harlem Globetrotters and the Perpetuation of the Black Stereotype." The Physical Educator. 35, No.2 (May 1978), 60-63. RACISM, SPORTS AS A MICROCOSM OF SOCIETY, ABE SAPERSTEIN.

2236. Looney, Douglas S. "Sacked by the Pros." Sports Illustrated. 72, No.20 (May 14, 1990), 78-83. BLACK QUARTERBACKS, TONY RICE, MAJOR HARRIS, RECRUITING.

2237. Lowenfish, Lee Elihu. "Sport, Race and the Baseball Business: The Jackie Robinson Story Revisited." Arena Review. 2, No.2 (Spring 1978), 2-16. RACISM, DISCRIMINATION, PREJUDICE.

2238. Loy, John W. and Joseph F. Elvogue. "Racial Segregation in American Sport." International Review of Sport Sociology. 5 (1970), 5-24. PRO BASEBALL, PRO FOOTBALL, SOCIAL MECHANISMS OF SEGREGATION, SOCIAL CONSEQUENCES OF SEGREGATION.

2239. Mackler, Bernard. "Black Superstar: The Athlete in White America." The Journal of Intergroup Relations. 4, No.4 (November 1975), 39-53. BLACK ATHLETES, INJUSTICE, PREJUDICE, ACADEMICS, DRIVE FOR RESPECT, INTERNATIONAL POLITICS.

2240. Maloney, Lawrence D. "Sports-Crazy Americans." U. S. News and World Report. 97, No.7 (August 13, 1984), 23-24. MEDIA, REPLACEMENT OF RELIGION, WOMEN, ELDERLY.

2241. Marable, Manning. "Black Olympians?" The Nation. 230, No.11 (March 22, 1980), 326. OLYMPIC BOYCOTT, LINK OF POLITICS AND SPORTS, BLACKS.

2242. Martin, Paul. "White 'n Black Split on Games." New Statesman. 109, No.2830 (June 14, 1985), 20-21. COMMONWEALTH GAMES, SOUTH AFRICA, RUGBY, NEW ZEALAND, DISCRIMINATION.

2243. McClendon, McKee J. and D. Stanley Eitzen. "Interracial Contact on Collegiate Basketball Teams: A Test of Sherif's Theory of Superordinate Goals." Social Science Quarterly. 55, No.4 (March 1975), 926-938. RACISM, INTERDEPENDENCE, ATTITUDE CHANGES, MUZAFER SHERIF.

2244. McPherson, Barry D. "The Segregation by Playing Position Hypothesis in Sport: An Alternative Explanation." Social Science Quarterly. 55, No.4 (March 1975), 960-966. SOCIALIZATION, VALUES, ROLE MODELS, SELF SEGREGATION.

2245. Medoff, Marshall H. "A Reappraisal of Racial Discrimination Against Blacks in Professional Baseball." The Review of Black Political Economy. 5, No.3 (Spring 1975), 259-268. SALARY DISCRIMINATION, SALARY BARGAINING, BARRIERS TO ENTRY.

2246. Mogull, Robert G. "Racial Discrimination in Professional Sports." Arena Review. 5, No.2 (September 1981), 12-15. UNEQUAL SALARIES, POSITION SEGREGATION, JUSTICE.

2247. Mogull, Robert G. "Salary Discrimination in Major League Baseball." The Review of Black Political Economy. 5, No.3 (Spring 1975), 269-279. SALARY AND BONUS PAYMENTS.

2248. Naison, Mark. "A Failed Game Plan; Shooting for Lasting Goals." Commonweal. 114, No.7 (April 10, 1987), 199-200. SPORTS AS AN AVENUE FOR MOBILITY, LOWER CLASSES, REFORM, SPORTS AND SOCIETY.

2249. Naison, Mark and Claude Mangum. "Protecting the Educational Opportunities of Black College Athletes: A Case Study Based on Experiences at Fordham University." The Journal of Ethnic Studies. 11, No.3 (Fall 1983), 119-125. COMMERCIALIZATION OF COLLEGE SPORTS, BENEFIT AND HARM, BIG TIME COLLEGE ATHLETICS, REFORM.

2250. Newcomb, John Timberman. "'Say It Ain't Snow, Joe': On the White Mythology of American Baseball." The South Atlantic Quarterly. 85, No.3 (Summer 1986), 297-300. OWNERS, FANS, PLAYERS, IDOLIZATION.

2251. Newman, Bruce. "Black, White--And Gray." Sports Illustrated. 68, No.18 (May 2, 1988), 62+. DENNIS RODMAN, DETROIT PISTONS, INFLAMMATORY WORDS ABOUT LARRY BIRD, CHARGES OF PREFERENTIAL TREATMENT FOR WHITES, RACISM.

2252. Newnham, Tom. "No Side for Apartheid--A Diary of Protest." Africa Today. 17, No.6 (November/December 1970), 9-11. NEW ZEALAND, CRICKET, DEMONSTRATIONS, SOUTH AFRICA, APARTHEID, RACISM.

2253. "No-Pass/No-Play Hurts Minorities More Than Whites." Phi Delta Kappan. 68, No.7 (March 1987), 561. BLACKS, HISPANICS, WOMEN, ACADEMICS.

2254. "Olympics Boycott Commended: No Compromise on Racism in Sports." UN Monthly Chronicle. 13, No.8 (August-September 1976), 28-30. APARTHEID, SOUTH AFRICA, NEW ZEALAND, RUGBY.

2255. Perkins, Huel D. "Higher Academic Standards For Athletes Do Not Discriminate Against Blacks." The Chronicle of Higher Education. 27, No.2 (September 7, 1983), 88. RACISM, STEREOTYPES, PROPOSITION 48, SAT SCORES, GRADE POINT AVERAGES, STUDENT-ATHLETES.

2256. Phillips, John C. "Blacks and Baseball." Harper's. 268, No.1608 (May 1984), 35. FAIR PLAY, RACISM, MARGINALITY, POSITION DISCRIMINATION.

2257. Phillips, John C. "Race and Career Opportunities in Major League Baseball: 1960-1980." Journal of Sport and Social Issues. 7, No.2 (Summer/Fall 1983), 1-17. RACISM, DISCRIMINATION, MARGINALITY.

2258. Picou, J. Steven. "Race, Athletic Achievement, and Educational Aspiration." The Sociological Quarterly. 19, No.3 (Summer 1978), 429-438. RELATIONSHIP BETWEEN ATHLETIC ACHIEVEMENT AND EDUCATIONAL ASPIRATION, BLACK AND WHITE ATHLETES, REFORM, PEERS, INTERSCHOLASTIC ATHLETICS.

2259. "Players Go To Bat Against Baseball." Business Week. No.2113 (February 28, 1970), 74. LAWSUITS, CURT FLOOD, ANTITRUST, DEHUMANIZATION, RACISM, OPTION CLAUSE.

2260. Pudelkiewicz, Eugeniusz. "The Socio-Historic Background of the Ideology of Racism in Sport." International Review of Sport Sociology. 8, Nos.3-4 (1973), 89-114. SOUTH AFRICA, NEW ZEALAND, ZIMBABWE, UNITED STATES.

2261. "Racism and International Sports." Objective: Justice. 2, No.3 (July 1970), 4-7+. SOUTH AFRICA, APARTHEID, ARTHUR ASHE, OLYMPICS.

2262. Reynolds, James E. "The Batboy Who Swung for Equality." Sports Illustrated. 73, No.1 (July 2, 1990), 74. COLOR BARRIER BROKEN, CLASS D GEORGIA LEAGUE, YOUTH--12 YEAR OLD, BASEBALL, RACE RELATIONS, DESEGREGATION.

2263. Rhoden, Bill. "Are Black Athletes Naturally Superior?" Ebony. 30, No.2 (December 1974), 136-138+. INNATE ABILITY, PSYCHOLOGICAL, POLITICAL AND RACIAL HURDLES.

2264. Rhoden, Bill. "Black Quarterbacks: One Foot in the Door." Ebony. 30, No.1 (November 1974), 166-170+. JOE GILLIAM, PLAYING POSITIONS.

2265. Rhoden, Bill. "Howard Cosell Tells It Like It Is." Ebony. 32, No.2 (December 1976), 76-77+. RACISM, MEDIA, LIBERALISM.

2266. Rhoden, Bill. "What's In A (Nick) Name?" Ebony. 31, No.7 (May 1976), 70-72+. SPORTS WRITING, NICKNAMES, HUMOR.

2267. Rhoden, Bill. "Who Are the Highest Paid Athletes?" Ebony. 30, No.7 (May 1975), 33-36+. DISCRIMINATION, SALARIES.

2268. Rhodes, Lodis and Johnny S. Butler. "Sport and Racism: A Contribution to Theory Building in Race Relations?" Social Science Quarterly. 55, No.4 (March 1975), 919-925. RACISM, STACKING, LACK OF BLACK MANAGERS, SALARY DISCRIMINATION.

2269. Riley, Norman. "Is Sports the Great Career It's Cracked Up to Be For Blacks?" The Crisis. 93, No.8 (October 1986), 30-35. PLAYING POSITIONS, SALARY DISCRIMINATION, RETIREMENT.

2270. Robinson, Frank and Berry Stainback. "Fighting the Baseball Blackout." Sport. 79, No.7 (July 1988), 66-67. BLACKS IN BASEBALL, DISCRIMINATION.

2271. Robinson, Louie. "Black Athletes--Are There Any Winners?" The Crisis. 90, No.5 (May 1983), 6-7. BENEFIT AND HARM, DRUGS, INJURIES, YOUTH ASPIRATIONS, ACADEMICS.

2272. Rosenblatt, Aaron. "Negroes in Baseball: The Failure of Success." Trans-action. 4, No.9 (September 1967), 51-53. RACIAL DISCRIMINATION, TOKENISM, PLAYER POSITION, MANAGEMENT JOBS.

2273. Ruck, Robert Lewis. "Sandlot Seasons: Sport in Black Pittsburgh." Journal of Sport History. 13, No.2 (Summer 1986), 182. RISE AND DECLINE OF COMMUNITY BASED SPORTS.

2274. Sailes, Gary A. "The Exploitation of the Black Athlete: Some Alternative Solutions." The Journal of Negro Education. 55, No.4 (Fall 1986), 439-442. WINNING IS EVERYTHING, EXPLOITATION, COACHES, ACADEMICS, ROLE MODELS.

2275. Sammons, Jeffrey T. "Boxing As a Reflection of Society: The Southern Reaction to Joe Louis." Journal of Popular Culture. 16, No.4 (Spring 1983), 23-33. BLACK ATHLETES, ROLE OF SPORT IN SOCIETY, SPORT HEROES, RACE.

2276. Sanoff, Alvin P. "The Foul Ball That Shook Baseball's Front Office." U. S. News and World Report. 102, No.15 (April 20, 1987), 12-13. BLACKS IN BASEBALL MANAGEMENT, PREJUDICE, RACISM.

2277. Segal, Erich. "Black, White and Very Blue." The New Republic. 175, No.5 (July 31, 1976), 7. MONTREAL OLYMPICS, NEW ZEALAND, RUGBY, SOUTH AFRICA, AFRICAN BOYCOTT.

2278. Semyonov, Moshe. "Sport and Beyond: Ethnic Inequalities In Attainment." Sociology of Sport Journal. 1, No.4 (December 1984), 358-365. SPORTS AS A CHANNEL FOR UPWARD MOBILITY, SOCCER PLAYERS, ISRAEL, ETHNICS, EDUCATION LEVEL.

2279. Shapiro, Richard. "Interview with Arthur Ashe." Africa Today. 17, No.6 (November/December 1970), 6-7. TENNIS, RACISM, SOUTH AFRICA, APARTHEID, ROLE MODELS.

2280. Sheed, Wilfred. "And Playing Second Base for Brooklyn...Jackie Robinson." Esquire. 100, No.6 (December 1983), 82-86. BRANCH RICKEY, RACISM, SPORTS AND SOCIETY.

2281. Simons, William. "Jackie Robinson and the American Mind: Journalistic Perceptions of the Reintegration of Baseball." Journal of Sport History. 12, No.1 (Spring 1985), 39-64. IDEOLOGY, VALUES, INTEGRATION, PRESS COVERAGE, BASEBALL AS A MIRROR OF AMERICAN VALUES.

2282. Smith, Earl and Monica A. Seff. "Race, Position, Segregation and Salary Equity in Professional Baseball." Journal of Sport and Social Issues. 13, No.2 (Fall 1989), 92-110. PLAYING POSITIONS, JUSTICE, RACISM, PRO BASEBALL, DISCRIMINATION.

2283. Smith, Thomas G. "Civil Rights on the Gridiron: The Kennedy Administration and the Desegregation of the Washington Redskins." Journal of Sport History. 14, No.2 (Summer 1987), 189-208. GEORGE P. MARSHALL'S SEGREGATED REDSKINS, FEDERAL GOVERNMENT'S ROLE IN DESEGREGATING THE REDSKINS, STEWART L. UDALL, JOHN F. KENNEDY, PRO FOOTBALL, RACISM, POLITICS.

2284. Smith, Thomas G. "Outside the Pale: The Exclusion of Blacks from the National Football League, 1934-1946." Journal of Sport History. 15, No.3 (Winter 1988), 255-281. DISCRIMINATION, DEMOCRATIC IDEALISM, PROTEST OF WRITERS AND FANS.

2285. Solomon, Eric. "Jews, Baseball, and the American Novel." Arete: The Journal of Sport Literature. 1, No.2 (Spring 1984), 43-66. JEWISH BASEBALL PLAYERS, RELIGION, POLITICS.

2286. Spivey, Donald. "'End Jim Crow in Sports': The Protest at New York University, 1940-1941." Journal of Sport History. 15, No.3 (Winter 1988), 282-303. RACISM, DISCRIMINATION, BIG TIME COLLEGE SPORTS, INTERCOLLEGIATE ATHLETICS.

2287. Spivey, Donald. "The Black Athlete in Big-Time Intercollegiate Sports, 1941-1968." Phylon: The Atlanta University Review of Race and Culture. 44, No.2 (June 1983), 116-125. BIG TIME COLLEGE SPORTS, HISTORY, BLACK ATHLETES, JESSE OWENS, JOE LOUIS, ACADEMICS, WORLD WAR II, RECRUITING SCANDALS, RACISM.

2288. Spivey, Donald and Thomas A. Jones. "Intercollegiate Athletic Servitude: A Case Study of the Black Illini Student-Athletes, 1931-1967." Social Science Quarterly. 55, No.4 (March 1975), 939-947. PREJUDICE, SCHOLARSHIPS, UNIVERSITY OF ILLINOIS, ACADEMICS, BIG TIME ATHLETICS.

2289. "A Sporting Chance?" The Economist. 286, No.7273 (January 22, 1983), 25-26. NCAA RULES, BLACKS, CORE CURRICULUM, SAT SCORES, EXPLOITATION, RECRUITING, ACADEMICS.

2290. Stockard, Bessie. "The Black Female Athlete--Past and Present." The Crisis. 90, No.5 (May 1983), 16-18. HISTORY, BLACK ATHLETES, EXPOSES.

2291. Thomas, Ron. "The Dollar Games." Black Enterprise. 10, No.10 (May 1980), 20. STUDENT-ATHLETES, BLACKS, LAWSUITS, KICKBACKS.

2292. Thompson, Richard. "New Zealand: The Issue of Apartheid and Sport." Africa Today. 17, No.6 (November/December 1970), 12-13. DISCRIMINATION, SOUTH AFRICA, UNITED NATIONS COMMITTEE ON APARTHEID.

2293. Tygiel, Jules. "Beyond the Point of No Return." Sports Illustrated. 58, No.25 (June 20, 1983), 62-76. BRANCH RICKEY, JACKIE ROBINSON, PROFESSIONAL BASEBALL, MINORITIES, HISTORY, INTEGRATION, BROOKLYN DODGERS, NEGRO LEAGUES, JUSTICE.

2294. Tygiel, Jules. "Those Who Came After." Sports Illustrated. 58, No.26 (June 27, 1983), 40-42+. PROFESSIONAL BASEBALL, JACKIE ROBINSON, ROY CAMPANELLA, DON NEWCOMBE, JUSTICE, REFORM.

2295. Unger, Norman O. "Forty Years After Jackie Robinson, Baseball Still Has No Black Managers." Jet. 72, No.6 (May 4, 1987), 48-51. RACISM, DISCRIMINATION.

2296. Vance, N. Scott. "Academic Rules Would Affect Blacks Far More Than Whites, Study Finds." The Chronicle of Higher Education. 25, No.23 (February 16, 1983), 17-18. DISCRIMINATION, SAT SCORES, GRADE POINT AVERAGES, UNFAIR TO BLACKS.

2297. Washington, Michael. "From Jack Johnson to Muhammad Ali: The Story Continues." Arena Review. 2, No.2 (Spring 1978), 26-31. RACISM, BOXING, DISCRIMINATION, WHITE HOPES, ROLE OF BLACK ATHLETES IN SOCIETY.

2298. Welch, Harvey Jr. "The Exploitation of the Black Athlete: A Proposal for Change." National Association of Student Personnel Administrators Journal. 19, No.3 (Winter 1982), 10-14. REFORM, INTERCOLLEGIATE ATHLETICS, EXPLOITATION, BLACK ATHLETES, ROLE OF COLLEGE PRESIDENTS, ACADEMICS.

2299. Wiggins, David K. "'The Future of College Athletics Is At Stake': Black Athletes and Racial Turmoil on Three Predominantly White University Campuses, 1968-1972." Journal of Sport History. 15, No.3 (Winter 1988), 304-333. RACISM, BLACK REVOLTS, UNIVERSITY OF CALIFORNIA AT BERKELEY, SYRACUSE UNIVERSITY, OREGON STATE UNIVERSITY, FRED MILTON.

2300. Wiggins, David K. "Clio and the Black Athlete in America." Quest. 32, No.2 (1980), 217-225. BLACKS ARE NOT A HOMOGENOUS GROUP, BLACK CULTURE.

2301. Wiggins, David K. "From Plantation to Playing Field: Historical Writings on the Black Athlete in American Sport." Research Quarterly for Exercise and Sport. 57, No.2 (June 1986), 101-116. BLACK SPORT HISTORY, HISTORICAL SURVEYS.

2302. Wiggins, David K. "Great Speed But Little Stamina: The Historical Debate Over Black Athletic Superiority." Journal of Sport History. 16, No.3 (Summer 1989), 158-185. BLACK SPORT PARTICIPATION AND ECONOMICS, BASKETBALL AND TRACK POSSIBLE FOR BLACKS, STEREOTYPES, MYTHS, RACISM, DISCRIMINATION, JIMMY THE GREEK, BOXING, EMPIRICAL STUDIES.

2303. Wiggins, David K. "Isaac Murphy: Black Hero in Nineteenth Century American Sport, 1861-1896." Canadian Journal of History of Sport and Physical Education. 10, No.1 (May 1979), 15-32. HORSE RACING, BLACK ATHLETES, HONESTY, HISTORY, RACISM.

2304. Wiggins, David K. "Peter Jackson and the Elusive Heavyweight Championship: A Black Athlete's Struggle Against the Late Nineteenth Century Color-Line." Journal of Sport History. 12, No.2 (Summer 1985), 143-168. HISTORY, AUSTRALIA, RACISM, DISCRIMINATION, PRO BOXING.

2305. Wiggins, William H. Jr. "Boxing's Sambo Twins: Racial Stereotypes in Jack Johnson and Joe Louis Newspapaer Cartoons, 1908-1938." Journal of Sport History. 15, No.3 (Winter 1988), 242-254. RACISM, GREAT WHITE HOPE, JACK JOHNSON EATING WATERMELON, STEREOTYPES.

2306. Williams, Alexander Jr. "The Impact of Rule 48 Upon the Black Student Athlete: A Comment." The Journal of Negro Education. 52, No.3 (Summer 1983), 362-373. NCAA, ACADEMIC STANDARDS, EQUAL PROTECTION, SAT SCORES, DISCRIMINATION.

2307. Williams, Roger L. and Zakhour I. Youssef. "Division of Labor in College Football Along Racial Lines." International Journal of Sport Psychology. 6, No.1 (1975), 3-13. PLAYER POSITIONS, DISCRIMINATION, COLLEGE FOOTBALL.

2308. Williams, Roger L. and Zakhour I. Youssef. "Race and Position Assignment in High School, College and Professional Football." International Journal of Sport Psychology. 10, No.4 (1979), 252-258. RACISM, FOOTBALL, PLAYING POSITIONS.

2309. Wilson, V. Jean. "Sport Discrimination." CAHPER ACSEPL Journal. 51, No.3 (January/February 1985), 56-57. SCHOOL SPORTS, ELITISM, COOPERATIVE GAMES, REFORM, OPPORTUNITY FOR ALL TO PARTICIPATE.

2310. Winbush, Raymond A. "The Furious Passage of the African-American Intercollegiate Athlete." Journal of Sport and Social Issues. 11, Nos.1&2 (December 1987), 97-103. BLACK ATHLETES, BLACK INSTITUTIONS, WOMEN.

2311. Wood, E. R. and L. B. Carrington. "School, Sport and the Black Athlete." Physical Education Review. 5, No.2 (Autumn 1982), 131-137. WEST INDIAN STUDENTS, CHANNELING BLACKS INTO SPORTS, STEREOTYPES, ACADEMICS, TEACHING PHYSICAL EDUCATION.

2312. Wright, George Vandergriff Jr. "Racism in Sport: An Update." Africa Today. 21, No.2 (Spring 1974), 9-14. APARTHEID, SOUTH AFRICA, OLYMPICS, NEW ZEALAND, ARTHUR ASHE.

2313. Wulf, Steve (ed.). "Baseball Takes Steps." Sports Illustrated. 66, No.25 (June 22, 1987), 11. EQUAL OPPORTUNITY, JESSE JACKSON, HARRY EDWARDS, FAIRNESS IN SPORTS COMMITTEE.

2314. Yetman, Norman R. and D. Stanley Eitzen. "Black Americans in Sports: Unequal Opportunity for Equal Ability." Civil Rights Digest. 5, No.2 (August 1972), 20-34. EXPLOITATION, SALARY DISCRIMINATION, RACISM, PLAYING POSITIONS, LACK OF BLACK OFFICIALS, COACHES AND ADMINISTRATORS, UNEQUAL OPPORTUNITY FOR EQUAL ABILITY, RACIAL BARRIERS.

2315. Young, A. S. "Basketball's Black Entrepreneur." Ebony. 26, No.5 (March 1971), 96-98+. MARQUES HAYNES, FABULOUS MAGICIANS.

2316. Young, A. S. "The Trading Game." Ebony. 26, No.6 (April 1971), 139-142+. CONTRACTS, TRADES, DEMORALIZATION, EXPLOITATION.

2317. Zuckerman, Jerome, G. Alan Stull, and Marvin H. Eyler. "The Black Athlete in Post-Bellum 19th Century." The Physical Educator. 29, No.3 (October 1972), 142-146. BOXING, HORSE RACING, CYCLING, BASEBALL, FOOTBALL, EXCELLENCE, DISCRIMINATION.

ROLE OF SPORT IN SOCIETY

Books

2318. Adelman, Melvin L. A Sporting Time: New York City and the Rise of Modern Athletics, 1820-1870. Urbana, IL: University of Illinois Press, 1986. RACING, BASEBALL, TRACK AND FIELD, BOXING, MODERNIZATION THEORY, COMMERCIALIZATION, PROFESSIONALISM.

2319. Amdur, Neil. The Fifth Down: Democracy and the Football Revolution. New York: Coward, McCann and Geoghegan, Inc., 1971. COACHES, MINORITIES, ALUMNI, OWNERS, MEDIA, GAMBLING, PLAYERS.

2320. Applin, Albert Gammon II. From Muscular Christianity to the Market Place: The History of Men's and Boy's Basketball in the United States, 1891-1957. PhD Thesis, University of Massachusetts, 1982. YMCA, ALTRUISM, HISTORY, CHILDREN.

2321. Baker, William J. and John M. Carroll. Sports in Modern America. St. Louis: River City Publishers, Ltd., 1981. INDUSTRIALIZATION, RISE OF ORGANIZED SPORT, REFORM, COLLEGE SPORTS, HEROES, BLACK ATHLETES, BIG BUSINESS, WOMEN, VIOLENCE, POLITICS, OLYMPICS.

2322. Ball, Donald W. and John W. Loy (eds.). Sport and Social Order: Contributions to the Sociology of Sport. Reading, MA: Addison-Wesley Publishing Company, Inc., 1975. INEQUALITY, POLITICS, CONSUMERISM, VIOLENCE, OCCUPATIONAL SUBCULTURES, COACHES.

2323. Betts, John Rickards. America's Sporting Heritage, 1850-1950. Reading, MA: Addison-Wesley Publishing Company, Inc., 1974. CLASS SPORTS, MASS SPORTS, RURAL AND URBAN SPORTS, SOCIAL CLASSES, URBANIZATION, TECHNOLOGY, RELIGION.

2324. Blanchard, Kendall. The Mississippi Choctaws at Play: The Serious Side of Leisure. Urbana, IL: University of Illinois Press, 1981. WORK AND PLAY, HISTORY, ECONOMICS, MYTHS, RITUAL, CHANGE.

2325. Blanchard, Kendall and Alyce Taylor Cheska. The Anthropology of Sport: An Introduction. South Hadley, MA: Bergin and Garvey Publishers, Inc., 1985. IDEAL AND MEANING, HISTORY, WOMEN, VIOLENCE, INTERNATIONAL SPORTS.

2326. Boyle, Robert H. Sport: Mirror of American Life. Boston: Little, Brown and Company, 1963. IMPACT OF SPORTS ON AMERICAN LIFE, IDEAL AND MEANING, COMPETITION.

2327. Brailsford, Dennis. Sport and Society: Elizabeth to Anne. London: Routledge and Kegan Paul, 1969. HISTORY, EDUCATION, POLITICS, PURITANS, PHILOSOPHY.

2328. Cady, Edwin H. The Big Game: College Sports and American Life. Knoxville: The University of Tennessee Press, 1978. BIG TIME COLLEGE SPORTS, AESTHETICS, COACHES, STUDENT-ATHLETES, RECRUITING, WOMEN, MINORITIES, MEDIA.

2329. Calhoun, Donald W. Sports, Culture and Personality. Champaign, IL: Human Kinetics Publishers, Inc., 1987. FANS, FREEDOM, BUSINESS, FUN, COACHES, MEDIA, WOMEN, JOCK LIBERATION, BLACK ATHLETES, DEVELOPING COUNTRIES, CHILDREN, PLAY, GAMES, PURITANISM, USSR, CHINA, POWER, SOCIAL PSYCHOLOGY, SOCIALIZATION, VIOLENCE.

2330. Cantelon, Hart and Richard S. Gruneau. Sport, Culture and the Modern State. Toronto: University of Toronto Press, 1982. SOCIAL ASPECTS, CAPITALISM, SOCIAL ETHICS.

2331. Carson, Jane. Colonial Virginians at Play. Charlottesville, VA: The University Press of Virginia, 1965. HOME ENTERTAINMENT, GAMES, SPORTS, PUBLIC OCCASIONS, WILLIAMSBURG, HISTORY.

2332. Cashman, Richard and Michael McKernan (eds.). Sport in History: The Making of Modern Sporting History. St. Lucia, Australia: University of Queensland Press, 1979. WAR, TECHNOLOGY, AUSTRALIA, UNITED STATES, WOMEN, GERMANY, POLITICS, HORSE RACING, CYCLING, CRICKET, ENGLAND, INDIA, BASEBALL, FOOTBALL, SOUTH AFRICA, NEW ZEALAND, RUGBY, COMMERCIALIZATION.

2333. Cavallo, Dominick. Muscles and Morals: Organized Playgrounds and Urban Reform, 1880-1920. Philadelphia: University of Pennsylvania Press, 1981. CHILDREN, SOCIALIZATION, SEX ROLES, MORAL CHANGES.

2334. Coakley, Jay J. Sport in Society: Issues and Controversies. St Louis, MO: C. V. Mosby Company, 1981. VIOLENCE, WOMEN, DRUGS.

2335. Cozens, Frederick Warren and Florence Scovil Stumpf. Sports in American Life. New York: Arno Press, Inc., 1976. SOCIOLOGY, GROWTH OF SPORTS, ROLE OF THE CHURCH, ATTITUDE OF LABOR, MEDIA, GOVERNMENT, RACISM, INTERNATIONAL SPORTS, DEMOCRACY.

2336. Crepeau, Richard C. Baseball, America's Diamond Mind, 1919-1941. Orlando: University Presses of Florida, 1980. AMERICAN CULTURE, MYTHOLOGY, SOCIAL ASPECTS, IMPACT OF BASEBALL ON THE AMERICAN CHARACTER, HISTORY.

2337. Culin, Stewart. Games of the North American Indians. New York: Dover Publications, Inc., 1975. GAMES OF CHANCE, GAMES OF DEXTERITY, GAMES DERIVED FROM EUROPEANS, MYTHS, RITUAL, RELIGION.

2338. Dunleavy, Aidan O., Andrew W. Miracle, and C. Roger Rees (eds.). Studies in the Sociology of Sport. Fort Worth, TX: Texas Christian University Press, 1981. EFFECTS OF PARTICIPATION IN SPORT, BENEFIT AND HARM, YOUTH AND SPORT.

2339. Dunning, Eric (ed.). Sport: Readings from a Sociological Perspective. Toronto: University of Toronto Press, 1972. DEVELOPMENT OF SPORTS AND GAMES, SOCIALIZATION, SOCIAL CLASSES, RACISM, CONFLICT, SOCIAL CONTROL, SOCIOLOGY OF SPORT.

2340. Dunning, Eric (ed.). The Sociology of Sport: A Selection of Readings. London: Frank Cass and Company Ltd., 1971. PLAY, FOOTBALL, BASEBALL, INTERSCHOLASTIC ATHLETICS, RACISM, MINORITIES, BOXING, WRESTLING, CONFLICT, HOOLIGANISM.

2341. Edwards, Harry. Sociology of Sport. Homewood, IL: The Dorsey Press, 1973. DEFINITION OF SPORTS, IDEOLOGY, RACISM, FUTURE, SOCIAL CHANGE, MYTHS.

2342. Eitzen, D. Stanley. Sport in Contemporary Society: An Anthology. New York: St. Martin's Press, Inc., 1984. MEDIA, WOMEN, MINORITIES, YOUTH.

2343. Eitzen, D. Stanley and George H. Sage. Sociology of North American Sport. Dubuque, IA: William C. Brown Publishers, 1978. SPORTS AS A MICROCOSM OF SOCIETY, TECHNOLOGY, INDUSTRIALIZATION, URBANIZATION, CULTURE, VALUES, CHILDREN, EDUCATION, RELIGION, POLITICS, ECONOMICS, MEDIA, SOCIAL MOBILITY, RACISM, WOMEN, FUTURE.

2344. Flath, Arnold William (ed.). Athletics in America. Corvallis, OR: Oregon State University Press, 1972. SPORT AND SOCIETY, WOMEN, EXCELLENCE, STUDENT-ATHLETES, AMATEURISM, GREEK ATHLETES.

2345. Gardner, Paul. Nice Guys Finish Last: Sport and American Life. London: Allen Lane, 1974. SOCIOLOGY OF SPORTS, BLACK ATHLETES, GAMBLING, SCANDALS, COLLEGE SPORTS, HISTORY.

2346. Glassford, Robert Gerald. Application of a Theory of Games to the Transitional Eskimo Culture. New York: Arno Press, Inc., 1976. CONCEPT OF PLAY AND GAMES, CANADIAN ESKIMO, PLAY TYPOLOGY.

2347. Greendorfer, Susan Louise and Andrew Yiannakis. Sociology of Sport: Diverse Perspectives. West Point, NY: Leisure Press, 1981. SOCIALIZATION, SOCIAL ROLES, POLICY, WINNING, WOMEN, ROLE CONFLICT, COACHES.

2348. Gruneau, Richard S. Class, Sports, and Social Development. Amherst, MA: University of Massachusetts Press, 1983. MARXIST CRITIQUE, BUREAUCRATIZATION OF SPORT, MAX WEBER, KARL MARX, FREEDOM, ALIENATION, SOCIAL INTERACTION.

2349. Guttmann, Allen. A Whole New Ball Game: An Interpretation of American Sports. Chapel Hill, NC: University of North Carolina Press, 1988. HISTORY, SPORTS AS A REFLECTION OF SOCIETY, BASEBALL, BASKETBALL, WOMEN, DRUGS, INTERCOLLEGIATE ATHLETICS, REJECTION OF MODERN SPORTS, FUTURE, CORRUPTION, EXPLOITATION OF MINORITIES.

2350. Hart, Marie (ed.). Sport in the Socio-Cultural Process. Dubuque, IA: William C. Brown Publishers, 1972. PLAY, CULTURE, NATURE OF SPORTS, SEXUAL IDENTITY, ETHNICS, MEDIA, EDUCATION, POLITICS.

2351. Heiman, Lee, David Weiner, and Bill Gutman. When the Cheering Stops: Ex-Major Leaguers Talk About Their Game and Their Lives. New York: Macmillan Publishing, 1990. HISTORY, MYTHOLOGY, HEROES, BASEBALL AS A REFLECTION OF SOCIETY.

2352. Ibrahim, Hilmi. Sport and Society: An Introduction to Sociology of Sport. Long Beach, CA: Hwong Publishing Company, Inc., 1975. NATURE OF SPORTS, RELIGION, POLITICS, ECONOMICS, TECHNOLOGY, CULTURE.

2353. Inglis, Fred. The Name of the Game: Sport and Society. London: Heinemann Educational Books Ltd., 1977. HEROES, MYTHS, MEDIA, TECHNOLOGY, BUSINESS.

2354. Isaacs, Neil David. Jock Culture U.S.A. New York: W. W. Norton and Company, Inc., 1978. INFLUENCE OF SPORTS ON LANGUAGE, EDUCATION, SOCIETY, IDEALS, SPORTSMANIA, MYTHS, MASS MEDIA.

2355. Izenberg, Jerry. How Many Miles to Camelot: The All-American Sport Myth. New York: Holt, Rinehart and Winston, Inc., 1972. GREED, COMMERCIALIZATION, SPORT AS A REFLECTION OF SOCIETY.

2356. Jenkins, Dan. Saturday's America. Boston: Little, Brown and Company, 1970. FOOTBALL, SPORTS REPORTING.

2357. Kenyon, Gerald S. (ed.). Aspects of Contemporary Sport Sociology. Chicago: The Athletic Institute, 1969. IDEAL AND MEANING, INTERSCHOLASTIC ATHLETICS, SOCIAL MOBILITY, CHILDREN.

2358. Kenyon, Gerald S. (ed.). Contemporary Psychology of Sport. Chicago: The Athletic Institute, 1970. AGGRESSION, COACHES, CONFLICT, MOTIVATION, PSYCHOLOGY, CHARACTER BUILDING, FANS, SPORT AND PLAY, CHILDREN.

2359. Krotee, March L. (ed.). The Dimensions of Sport Sociology. West Point, NY: Leisure Press, 1979. HISTORY, SOCIOLOGY OF SPORTS, WOMEN, SOCIALIZATION, ROLE MODELS, LITTLE LEAGUE BASEBALL, SOCIAL CLASSES, MASS SPORTS, AGGRESSION, OLYMPICS, MINORITIES.

2360. Lapchick, Richard Edward (ed.). Fractured Focus: Sport As A Reflection of Society. Lexington, MA: Lexington Books, 1986. INTERCOLLEGIATE ATHLETICS, RULE 48, CARTELS, ACADEMICS, DEMISE OF SPORTS, RACISM, WOMEN, CHILDREN, VIOLENCE, GAMBLING, DRUGS, MEDIA, INTERNATIONAL SPORT.

2361. Lenk, Hans. Social Philosophy of Athletics: A Pluralistic and Practice-Oriented Philosophical Analysis of Top Level Amateur Sport. Champaign, IL: Stipes Publishing Company, 1979. PHILOSOPHY, MOTIVATION, ALIENATION, FREEDOM, OLYMPICS, VALUES.

2362. Leonard, Wilbert Marcellus II. A Sociological Perspective of Sport. Minneapolis: Burgess Publishing Company, 1980. SOCIALIZATION, DEVIANCE, DISCRIMINATION, CULTURE, COLLECTIVE BEHAVIOR.

2363. Levine, Peter. A. G. Spaulding and the Rise of Baseball: The Promise of American Sport. New York: Oxford University Press, Inc., 1985. NATIONAL BASEBALL LEAGUE, HISTORY, UNIONS.

2364. Lipsky, Richard. How We Play the Game: Why Sports Dominate American Life. Boston: Beacon Press, Inc., 1981. POLITICS, SOCIALIZATION, HEROES, SPORTS LANGUAGE.

2365. Lipsyte, Robert. SportsWorld: An American Dreamland. New York: Quadrangle/New York Times Book Company, 1975. SPORTS TRENDS, BASEBALL, FOOTBALL, BASKETBALL, FRAUD, BIG BUSINESS, MUHAMMAD ALI.

2366. Loy, John W., Barry D. McPherson and Gerald S. Kenyon. Sport and Social Systems: A Guide to the Analysis, Problems and Literature. Reading, MA: Addison-Wesley Publishing Company, Inc., 1978. SPORT AS A SOCIAL PHENOMENON, SOCIOLOGY, SPORTS ORGANIZATIONS, SPORT SUBCULTURES, SOCIALIZATION, REGULATIVE INSTITUTIONS, RELIGION, MEDIA, ARTS, MINORITIES, WOMEN, DEMOCRATIZATION.

2367. Lueschen, Guenther (ed.). The Cross-Cultural Analysis of Sport and Games. Champaign, IL: Stipes Publishing Company, 1970. SOCIOLOGY OF SPORT, CANADIAN ESKIMO, INTERDEPENDENCE OF SPORTS AND CULTURE, PSYCHOLOGICAL STUDY OF GAMES, CHILDREN, INTER-GROUP CONFLICT.

2368. Lueschen, Guenther and George H. Sage (eds.). Handbook of Social Science of Sport: With an International Classified Bibliography. Champaign, IL: Stipes Publishing Company, 1981. SOCIOLOGY OF SPORT, SOCIAL INSTITUTIONS AND SPORTS, SOCIAL STRUCTURES, SOCIAL PROCESSES AND SPORTS, SPORT ORGANIZATIONS, FANS, DEVIANCE, PLAY.

2369. Mandell, Richard D. Sport: A Cultural History. New York: Columbia University Press, 1984. HISTORY, MYTHS, CULTURE.

2370. McIntosh, Peter C. Sport in Society. London: C. A. Watts and Company Ltd., 1971. HISTORY, AMATEURISM, PROFESSIONALISM, POLITICS, INTERNATIONAL SPORTS.

2371. Mrozek, Donald J. Sport and American Mentality 1880-1910. Knoxville: University of Tennessee Press, 1983. SOCIAL DYNAMICS OF SPORTS, SOCIAL CLASSES, VALUES, EMPHASIS ON WINNING, SPORTS AS PREPARATION FOR THE MILITARY, NATIONALISM, SECULARISM, IDEALISM, IDEAL AND MEANING.

2372. Natan, Alex. Sport and Society. London: Bowes and Bowes Publishers, 1958. BRITAIN, FRANCE, ITALY, POLAND, MEDIA, EDUCATION, LITERATURE, OLYMPICS, AMATEURISM, FAIR PLAY.

2373. Nixon, Howard L. II. Sport and the American Dream. New York: Leisure Press, 1984. CHILDREN, ACADEMICS, COLLEGE SPORTS, PROFESSIONAL SPORTS ORGANIZATIONS, OLYMPICS.

2374. Pankin, Robert M. (ed.). Social Approaches to Sport. London: Associated University Presses, 1982. SOCIOLOGY OF SPORT, SPORT AND SOCIAL DIFFERENTIATION, SPORT AS ADAPTIVE BEHAVIOR, PLAY.

2375. Rader, Benjamin G. American Sports: From the Age of Folk Games to the Age of Spectators. Englewood Cliffs, NJ: Prentice-Hall, Inc., 1983. EVOLUTION OF SPORTS, RULE CHANGES, HISTORY, SOCIOLOGY, CULTURAL, ECONOMIC ASPECTS.

2376. Riess, Steven A. Touching Base: Professional Baseball and American Culture in the Progressive Era. Westport, CT: Greenwood Press, Inc., 1980. HISTORY, CULTURE, PRO BASEBALL, SOCIAL REFORM, SOCIAL MOBILITY, SOCIAL FUNCTION OF BASEBALL.

2377. Sage, George H. (ed.). Sport and American Society: Selected Readings. Reading, MA: Addison-Wesley Publishing Company, Inc., 1970. SOCIOLOGY, COACHES, PLAYERS, VALUES, IDEOLOGY, COMPETITION.

2378. Sammons, Jeffrey T. Beyond the Ring: The Role of Boxing in American Society. Urbana, IL: University of Illinois Press, 1988. CRIME, BOXING, RACISM, REFORM, HEROES, JOE LOUIS, TELEVISION, CIVIL RIGHTS, MUHAMMAD ALI, MYTHS.

2379. Sansone, David. Greek Athletics and The Genesis of Sport. Berkeley: University of California Press, 1988. DEFINITION OF SPORTS, RITUAL, RELATIONSHIP OF SPORTS IN CONTEMPORARY SOCIETY AND EARLIER CIVILIZATION, RELIGION, GREEK ATHLETICS.

2380. Schafer, Walter E. Sport, Socialization and the School: Toward Maturity or Enculturation? Eugene, OR: Oregon School Study Council, University of Oregon, 1974. ENCULTURATION, ACADEMICS, SOCIOLOGY OF SPORTS.

2381. Seymour, Harold. Baseball: The People's Game. New York: Oxford University Press, 1990. BASEBALL, HISTORY, WOMEN'S BASEBALL, BLACK BASEBALL, AMERICAN VALUES, IDEOLOGY.

2382. Smith, Leverett T. Jr. The American Dream and the National Game. Bowling Green, OH: Bowling Green University Popular Press, 1975. CHANGES, BASEBALL, FOOTBALL, ROLE OF PLAY IN CULTURE, PRO SPORTS.

2383. Snyder, Eldon E. and Elmer M. Spreitzer. Social Aspects of Sport. Englewood Cliffs, NJ: Prentice Hall, 1978. BENEFIT AND HARM, VALUES, CHARACTER, COMMUNITY, AMERICAN CULTURE, SOCIOLOGY.

2384. Somers, Dale A. The Rise of Sports in New Orleans 1850-1900. Baton Rouge: Louisiana State University Press, 1972. DEMOCRATIZING INFLUENCE OF SPORTS, HEROES, SOCIOLOGY, HISTORY.

2385. Spears, Betty and Richard A. Swanson. History of Sport and Physical Activity in the United States. Dubuque, IA: William C. Brown Publishers, 1978. HISTORY, TECHNOLOGY, COLLEGE SPORTS, OLYMPICS.

2386. Spivey, Donald (ed.). Sport in America: New Historical Perspectives. Westport, CT: Greenwood Press, Inc., 1985. HISTORY, ELITISM, MINORITIES, URBAN AND RURAL SPORT, VIOLENCE.

2387. Talamini, John T. and Charles H. Page (eds.). Sport and Society: An Anthology. Boston: Little, Brown and Company, 1973. EMERGENCE OF SPORTS AS A MAJOR SOCIAL INSTITUTION, RELATIONSHIP OF SPORTS TO EDUCATION, WOMEN, MEDIA, CULTURE, SOCIOLOGY OF SPORTS.

2388. Ueberroth, Peter. Made in America: His Own Story. New York: William Morrow and Company, Inc., 1985. LOS ANGELES OLYMPICS, BOYCOTTS, TERRORISM, FREE ENTERPRISE, CORPORATE SPONSORSHIP.

2389. Umphlett, Wiley Lee. The Sporting Myth and the American Experience: Studies in Contemporary Fiction. Lewisburg, PA: Bucknell University Press, 1975. MYTH, COMPETITION, WINNING, DESTINY, AMERICAN CULTURE.

2390. Umphlett, Wiley Lee (ed.). American Sport Culture: The Humanistic Dimensions. Cranbury, NJ: Associated University Presses, 1985. SOCIOLOGY, CORRUPTION, POLITICS, HEROES, TELEVISION, GAMBLING, RIGHTS, ACADEMICS, DRAFT, WOMEN, SPECTATORS, RELIGION.

2391. Voigt, David Quentin. America Through Baseball. Chicago: Nelson-Hall, Inc., 1976. AMERICAN CULTURE, SOCIOLOGY, SOCIALIZATION, CUSTOMS, BASEBALL.

2392. Weaver, Robert B. Amusements and Sports in American Life. Westport, CT: Greenwood Press Inc., 1968. HISTORY, BENEFIT AND HARM, MONEY.

2393. Welch, Paula D. and Harold A. Lerch. History of American Physical Education and Sport. Springfield, IL: Charles C. Thomas, Publisher, 1981. HISTORY, URBANIZATION, INDUSTRIALIZATION, WOMEN, WAR, OLYMPICS.

2394. Yiannakis, Andrew, Thomas D. McIntyre, Merrill J. Melnick and Dale P. Hart (eds.). Sport Sociology: Contemporary Themes. Dubuque, IA: Kendall/Hunt Publishing Company, 1976. SOCIOLOGY, SPORT AND SOCIETY, POLITICS, HEROES, VALUES, COMPETITION, CHILDREN, INTERSCHOLASTIC SPORTS, RACISM, SEX DISCRIMINATION, VIOLENCE, FUTURE.

Articles

2395. Arens, William. "The Great American Football Ritual." Natural History. 84, No.8 (1975), 72-81. RITUAL, SYMBOL, ROLE OF FOOTBALL IN AMERICA.

2396. Arnold, Peter J. "Democracy, Education and Sport (Presidential Address: Philosophic Society for the Study of Sport)." Journal of the Philosophy of Sport. 16 (1989), 100-110. MEANING OF DEMOCRACY, KANT, CATEGORICAL IMPERATIVE, JOHN DEWEY, MORAL EDUCATION, JUSTICE, FAIRNESS, EQUALITY, FREEDOM, GOVERNMENT.

2397. Booth, Bernard F. "Games, Sport and Societal Autonomy." International Social Science Journal. 34, No.2 (1982), 219-232. SPORTS AS A BAROMETER OF SOCIAL CHANGE, SPORT ENCOMPASSING ELEMENTS OF AUTONOMY, INUIT AND MOTU SOCIETIES, GAMES AND SOCIAL ORGANIZATION, SPORT IN COMPLEX SOCIETIES.

2398. Brickman, Philip. "Crime and Punishment in Sports and Society." The Journal of Social Issues. 33, No.1 (1977), 140-164. CRIME, DEVIANCE, EQUITY, JUSTICE.

2399. Burke, William. "Football, Literature, Culture." Southwest Review. 60, No.4 (Autumn 1975), 391-398. SEMI TOUGH, A FAN'S NOTES, END ZONE, SYMBOLISM, LITERATURE.

2400. Cheska, Alyce Taylor. "Sport Spectacular: A Ritual Model of Power." International Review of Sport Sociology. 14, No.2 (1979), 51-72. RITUAL, RELIGION, POWER.

2401. Cooper, W. E. "Do Sports Have an Aesthetic Aspect?" Journal of the Philosophy of Sport. 5 (Fall 1978), 51-55. AESTHETICS, CRITIQUE OF PAUL ZIFF.

2402. Creekmore, C. R. "Games Athletes Play." Psychology Today. 18, No.7 (July 1984), 40-44. MENTAL MANIPULATION, PSYCHOLOGICAL AROUSAL, INTIMIDATION, DISTRACTION OF OPPONENTS.

2403. Davidson, Judith A. "Sport and Modern Technology: The Rise of Skateboarding, 1963-1978." Journal of Popular Culture. 18, No.4 (Spring 1985), 145-157. ROLE OF TECHNOLOGY IN SPORT, MARKETING, SKATEBOARD PARKS.

2404. Edwards, Harry. "Common Myths Hide Flaws in the Athletic System." The Center Magazine. 15, No.1 (January/February 1982), 17-21. SPORTS AND SOCIETY, IDEOLOGY, MYTH OF THE DUMB JOCK, MYTH OF SPORTS AS WHOLESOME, MYTH OF IMMANENT ACHIEVABILITY.

2405. Epstein, Joseph. "Obsessed with Sport." Harper's. 253, No.1514 (July 1976), 67-72. SPECTATORS, SPORTS AS A REFLECTION OF SOCIETY, OUTLET FOR VIOLENCE, CULTURE.

2406. Fielding, Lawrence W. "War and Trifles: Sport in the Shadows of Civil War Army Life." Journal of Sport History. 4, No.2 (Summer 1977), 151-168. CIVIL WAR, ROLE OF SPORT FOR SOLDIER'S ATTITUDES, SOCIAL COHESION, SELF WORTH.

2407. Fleisher, Mark S. "More on Athletes, Values, and United States Culture." Current Anthropology. 20, No.1 (March 1979), 244. NONHOMOGENEITY OF CULTURE, REPLY TO MUNROE AND CONROY.

2408. Goodger, John M. and Brian C. Goodger. "Excitement and Representation: Toward a Sociological Explanation of the Significance of Sport in Modern Society." Quest. 41, No.3 (December 1989), 257-272. SOCIOLOGY, COLLECTIVE REPRESENTATION, EMILE DURKHEIM.

2409. Greendorfer, Susan Louise. "Sociology of Sport: Knowledge of What." Quest. 28 (Summer 1977), 58-65. SOCIALIZATION, SOCIAL STRATIFICATION.

2410. Halberstam, David. "Baseball and the National Mythology." Harper's Magazine. 241, No.1444 (September 1970), 22-25. IMAGE OF BASEBALL, ILLUSION AND REALITY, SPORTS WRITERS.

2411. Hoberman, John M. "Sport and Social Change: The Transformation of Maoist Sport." Sociology of Sport Journal. 4, No.2 (June 1987), 156-170. CHINA, COMMUNISM, INTERNATIONAL SPORTS.

2412. Ingham, Alan G. "Methodology in the Sociology of Sport: From Symptoms of Malaise to Weber for a Cure." Quest. 31, No.2 (1979), 187-215. VERSTEHEN THESIS, IDEAL TYPE.

2413. Kennedy, Ray. "Oh, What An Era!" Sports Illustrated. 51, No.7 (August 13, 1979), 52-57. AMERICAN SOCIETY, JOCKOCRACY, TELEVISION, BLACK ATHLETES, WOMEN, BIG BUSINESS.

2414. Kirshenbaum, Jerry and Robert Sullivan. "Hold On There, America." Sports Illustrated. 58, No.5 (February 7, 1983), 60+. FITNESS BOOM, SPORTSMANIA, BENEFIT AND HARM.

2415. Lueschen, Guenther. "The Interdependence of Sport and Culture." International Review of Sport Sociology. 2 (1967), 127-142. ACTION, SPORT AS PART OF CULTURE AND SOCIETY, CULTURAL VALUES AND SPORT, INDUSTRIALIZATION AND TECHNOLOGY, SPORT AS A PROTESTANT SUBCULTURE, BENEFIT AND HARM.

2416. MacAloon, John J. "An Observer's View of Sport Sociology." Sociology of Sport Journal. 4, No.2 (June 1987), 103-115. SPORT AND SOCIAL LIFE, SPORT HISTORY, SPORT SOCIOLOGY, SOCIOLOGY OF CULTURE, FUTURE.

2417. MacAloon, John J. "Double Visions: Olympic Games and American Culture." The Kenyon Review. 4, No.1 (Winter 1982), 98-112. RITUALS, UNITED STATES, SYMBOLS, POLITICS.

2418. Maheu, Rene. "Sport and Culture." Journal of Health, Physical Education and Recreation. 34, No.8 (October 1963), 30-32+. SPORT IN A VARIETY OF CULTURES, LEISURE, AESTHETICS.

2419. Mark, Melvin M. and Jerald Greenberg. "Evening the Score." Psychology Today. 21, No.1 (January 1987), 44-50. JUSTICE, PENALTIES, RULES, SALARIES, FAIRNESS.

2420. McCaffrey, Patrick. "Sports Mania." American Demographics. 3, No.5 (May 1981) 14-17+. SPORTS DEMOGRAPHICS, FANS, MARKETING SPORTS, TELEVISION, WOMEN, FUTURE OF SPORTS.

2421. McKay, Jim and Kent Pearson. "Objectives, Strategies and Ethics in Teaching Introductory Courses in Sociology of Sport." Quest. 36, No.2 (1984), 134-146. SOCIOLOGY, TEACHING PHYSICAL EDUCATION.

2422. McMurtry, John. "Smash Thy Neighbor." The Atlantic Monthly. 229, No.1 (January 1972), 77-80. SPORT AS A SOCIAL PARADIGM. RESEMBLANCE BETWEEN FOOTBALL AND WAR, INJURIES.

2423. Munroe, Robert L. and Mary Conroy. "Games and the Values of Athletes in United States Culture." Current Anthropology. 19, No.1 (March 1978), 152. GAMES AS A REFLECTION OF CULTURAL VALUES, CONSERVATIVISM OF GAMESMEN.

2424. Niwa, Takaaki. "The Function of Sport in Society Today." International Review of Sport Sociology. 8, No.1 (1973), 53-68. JAPANESE BUSINESS, COMPETITION, ALIENATION, FUTURE.

2425. Nixon, Howard L. II. "Acceptance of the 'Dominant American Sports Creed' Among College Students." Review of Sport and Leisure. 4, No.2 (Winter 1979), 141-159. CHARACTER BUILDING, SELF DISCIPLINE, FITNESS, TOLERANCE TOWARD OTHERS, STEREOTYPES, CONSERVATIVISM, BENEFIT AND HARM.

2426. O'Hanlon, Timothy P. "Interscholastic Athletics, 1900-1940: Shaping Citizens for Unequal Roles in the Modern Industrial State." Educational Theory. 30, No.2 (Spring 1980), 89-103. HISTORY, INDUSTRIAL STATE, INEQUALITY.

2427. Robinson, David. "An Attributional Analysis of Student Demoralization in Physical Education Settings." Quest. 42, No.1 (April 1990), 27-39. FAILURE, DEMORALIZATION, COMPETITION, EQUITY, ATTRIBUTION THEORY, TEACHING PHYSICAL EDUCATION.

2428. Rominger, Donald W. Jr. "From Playing Field to Battleground: The United States Navy V-5 Preflight Program in World War II." Journal of Sport History. 12, No.3 (Winter 1985), 252-264. SPORT AS ANALOGOUS TO WAR, ATHLETICS AS MILITARY TRAINING, CHARACTER DEVELOPMENT.

2429. Sage, George H. "Sport and the Social Sciences." The Annals of the American Academy of Political and Social Science. 445 (September 1979), 1-14. FUNCTIONS OF PLAY, GAMES AND SPORTS, SPORTS AND SOCIAL INSTITUTIONS, SOCIALIZATION.

2430. Santomier, James P. "Myth, Legitimation, and Stress in Formal Sports Organizations." Journal of Sport and Social Issues. 3, No.2 (Fall/Winter 1979), 11-16. MYTHS, STRESS, LEGITIMATION, CONSTRAINTS.

2431. Sheard, Kenneth G. and E. G. Dunning. "The Rugby Football Club as a Type of 'Male Preserve': Some Sociological Notes." International Review of Sport Sociology. 8, Nos.3-4 (1973), 5-24. GENDER, COMPETITION, AGGRESSION.

2432. Stott, Jon C. "Biographies of Sports Heroes and the American Dream." Children's Literature in Education. 10, No.4 (Winter 1979), 174-185. AMERICAN DREAM, BIOGRAPHY OF SPORT HEROES, LITERATURE, REALITY VS. FAIRY TALES.

2433. Struna, Nancy L. "Sport and Societal Values: Massachusetts Bay." Quest. 27 (Winter 1977), 38-46. HISTORY, RELIGION, PURITANS, CALLINGS, SPORT AS A REFLECTION OF SOCIETY.

2434. Underwood, John. "American Renewal." Sports Illustrated. 54, No.9 (Febrary 23, 1981), 66-80. COMPETITION, TEAMWORK, AMERICAN SOCIETY, ROLE OF SPORT IN VALUE CHANGE, BENEFIT AND HARM, CALL FOR CHANGE, WINNING, EXAGGERATED EMPHASIS, INTEGRITY.

2435. VanderZwaag, Harold J. "Ball Games: The Heart of American Sport." Quest. 27 (Winter 1977), 61-70. HISTORY, COMPETITION, IDEAL AND MEANING OF SPORT, SOCIAL BENEFIT OF SPORT.

2436. Voigt, David Quentin. "Reflection on Diamonds: American Baseball and American Culture." Journal of Sport History. 1, No.1 (Spring 1974), 3-25. NATIONAL CHARACTER, INTERNATIONALISM, HERO WORSHIP, INSTITUTIONALIZED INDIVIDUALISM, CULTURAL PLURALISM.

2437. Wagner, Eric A. and Lawrence G. Hlad. "Sport as Reflector of Change: Football, Wilderness Sport and Dominant American Values." Arena Review. 10 (July 1986), 43-54. SPORT AS A REFLECTION OF SOCIETY, DOMINANT AMERICAN SPORTS CREED, ORIENTEERING, FOOTBALL, CHANGES.

2438. Young, T. R. "The Sociology of Sport: A Critical Overview." Arena Review. 8, No.3 (November 1984), 1-14. SOCIOLOGY, ALIENATION, VIOLENCE, BIG BUSINESS, METAPHYSICS, ADVERTISING.

SPORT AND LAW

Books

2439. Appenzeller, Herb. Athletics and the Law. Charlottesville, VA: The Michie Company, 1975. INJURIES, ATHLETES' RIGHTS.

2440. Appenzeller, Herb and Thomas Appenzeller. Sports and the Courts. Charlottesville, VA: The Michie Company, 1980. INJURIES, DISABLED, DISCRIMINATION, COACHES, OFFICIALS, FANS, PHYSICIANS, TRAINERS.

2441. Arnold, Don E. Legal Considerations in the Administration of Public School Physical Education and Athletic Programs. Springfield, IL: Charles C. Thomas Publishers, 1983. LIABILITY, INJURIES, INTERSCHOLASTIC ATHLETICS, DUE PROCESS, EQUAL PROTECTION, SEX DISCRIMINATION, DISABLED.

2442. Baley, James A. and David L. Matthews. Law and Liability in Athletics, Physical Education and Recreation. Dubuque, IA: William C. Brown Publishers, 1988. LITIGATION, RIGHTS, INJURIES, FUTURE.

2443. Berry, Robert C. Law and Business of the Sports Industries. Dover, MA: Auburn House Publishing Company, Inc., 1986. CONTRACTS, ANTITRUST, LABOR, COLLECTIVE BARGAINING, UNIONS.

2444. Clement, Annie. Law in Sport and Physical Activity. Indianapolis, IN: Benchmark Press, Inc., 1988. NEGLIGENCE, CASE STUDIES, TORTS, LIABILITIES, CONTRACTS, FREEDOM ISSUES, TITLE IX.

2445. Decof, Leonard and Richard Godosky. Sports Injury Litigation. New York: Practicing Law Institute, 1979. INJURIES, FOOTBALL, GYMNASTICS, RACKET SPORTS, SKIING.

2446. Diamond, Barbara M. Athletic Sex Discrimination Cases in the Courts. St. Paul: State of Minnesota, House of Representatives Research Department, 1980. EQUAL PROTECTION CLAUSE, SEGREGATED TEAMS, DUE PROCESS, TITLE IX, CASE STUDIES.

2447. Grieve, Andrew. The Legal Aspects of Athletics. South Brunswick, NJ: A. S. Barnes and Company, 1969. NEGLIGENCE, MEDICAL ASPECTS, INJURIES, INSURANCE, ELIGIBILITY STANDARDS, COMPETITION, FUTURE.

2448. Koehler, Robert W. Law, Sport Activity, and Risk Management. Champaign, IL: Stipes Publishing Company, 1987. NEGLIGENCE, PHILOSOPHY, INJURIES, VIOLENCE.

2449. Nafziger, James A. R. International Sports Law. Dobbs Ferry, NY: Transnational Publishers, Inc., 1988. HISTORY, OLYMPICS, POLITICS, POLICY, RULES, BOYCOTTS, AMATEURISM, DRUGS, COMMERCIALIZATION, DISCRIMINATION.

2450. Nygaard, Gary and Thomas H. Boone. <u>Coaches Guide to Sport Law</u>. Champaign, IL: Human Kinetics Publishers, Inc., 1985. NEGLIGENCE, SUPERVISION, INJURIES, RIGHTS, FANS.

2451. Riffer, Jeffrey K. <u>Sports and Recreational Injuries</u>. New York: McGraw-Hill Book Company, 1985. GOVERNMENT, SCHOOLS, FANS.

2452. Sloan, Philip Samuel. <u>The Athlete and the Law</u>. New York: Oceana Publications Inc., 1983. AMATEURISM, PRO ATHLETICS, CONTRACTS, DRUGS, RACISM, SEX DISCRIMINATION, ELIGIBILITY, ANTITRUST, DRAFT, COLLECTIVE BARGAINING, VIOLENCE.

2453. Sobel, Lionel S. <u>Professional Sports and the Law</u>. New York: Law-Arts Publishers, 1977. LEGAL ISSUES AND SPORT, NEW TRENDS, ANTITRUST, RELEVANT STATUTES, LABOR LAW, COLLEGE ATHLETICS, PROFESSIONAL SPORT.

2454. Tokarz, Karen. <u>Women, Sports and the Law: A Comprehensive Research Guide to Sex Discrimination in Sports</u>. Buffalo, NY: William S. Hein and Company, Inc., 1986. CASE STUDIES, EQUAL OPPORTUNITY, TITLE IX, NCAA, EQUAL FUNDING, SEGREGATION.

2455. Uberstine, Gary A. (ed.). <u>Law of Professional and Amateur Sports</u>. New York: Clark Boardman Company, Ltd., 1988. AGENTS, CONTRACTS, ELIGIBILITY, RULES, VIOLENCE, INJURIES, TAXATION.

2456. Waicukauski, Ronald J. <u>Law and Amateur Sports</u>. Bloomington, IN: Indiana University Press, 1982. DUE PROCESS, INJURIES, SEX DISCRIMINATION, AMATEUR SPORTS ACT, ACADEMIC STANDARDS, UNSPORTSMANLIKE CONDUCT, RULES.

2457. Weistart, John C. and Cym H. Lowell. <u>The Law of Sports</u>. Indianapolis: The Bobbs-Merrill Company, Inc., 1979. REGULATIONS, CONTRACTS, ANTITRUST, COLLECTIVE BARGAINING, INJURIES.

2458. Williams, Melvin H. <u>Beyond Training: How Athletes Enhance Performance Legally and Illegally</u>. Champaign, IL: Leisure Press, 1989. ERGOGENIC AIDS, STEROIDS, DRUGS, BLOOD DOPING.

2459. Wong, Glenn M. <u>Essentials of Amateur Sports Law</u>. Dover, MA: Auburn House Publishing Company, 1988. CONTRACTS, AMATEUR ATHLETIC ASSOCIATION, SEX DISCRIMINATION, TITLE IX, MEDIA, AGENTS, DRUG TESTING.

2460. Yasser, Raymond L. <u>Torts and Sports: Legal Liability in Professional and Amateur Athletics</u>. Westport, CT: Quorum Books, 1985. CASE STUDIES, SPECTATORS, MEDICAL MALPRACTICE, DEFECTIVE ATHLETIC EQUIPMENT, INVASION OF PRIVACY, WORKER'S COMPENSATION, CONTRACTS.

Articles

2461. Appenzeller, Herb. "Is the Law Ruining Sports?" <u>Update on Law-Related Education</u>. 7, No.2 (Fall 1983) 43-44. LAWSUITS, SAFETY, HISTORY.

2462. Ayers, Deanne L. "Random Urinalysis: Violating the Athlete's Individual Rights?" Howard Law Journal. 30, No.1 (1987), 93-142. DRUG TESTING AGREEMENTS, VOLUNTARY TESTING, REASONABLE CAUSE, CONSTITUTIONAL ANALYSIS, RIGHT TO PRIVACY, DUE PROCESS.

2463. Blucker, Judy A. and Sarah W. J. Pell. "Legal and Ethical Issues: Essential for Professional Preparation Curricula." Journal of Physical Education, Recreation and Dance. 57, No.1 (January 1986), 19-22+. LAWSUITS, KNOWLEDGE OF LAW, ROLE OF ETHICS, TEACHING PHYSICAL EDUCATION.

2464. Bodnar, Leslie M. "Women, Sports and the Law." The American Journal of Sports Medicine. 8, No.4 (July/August 1980), 291-293. STEREOTYPES, TITLE IX, LITIGATION, NCAA VS AIAW.

2465. Carlsen, Chris J. and Matthew Shane Walker. "The Sports Court: A Private System to Deter Violence in Professional Sports." Southern California Law Review. 55, No.2 (January 1982), 399-440. WHY VIOLENCE EXISTS, SYSTEMS OF VIOLENCE CONTROL, SPORTS COURT AS AN ARBITRATOR OF GRIEVANCES.

2466. Carpenter, Linda Jean. "Drug Testing." Journal of Physical Education, Recreation, and Dance. 58, No.4 (April 1987), 8-9. CONSTITUTIONALITY OF DRUG TESTING, LAW, DISCRIMINATION, PROBABLE CAUSE, COMPELLING REASON.

2467. Christmas, Faith. "Scrimmage in the Courtroom." Black Enterprise. 10, No.2 (September 1979), 22. LAWSUITS, MEDIA, NBC, SPORTSWORLD.

2468. "Courts and Sports: A Changing Picture." U. S. News and World Report. 80, No.3 (January 19, 1976), 32-34. CHANGES, RESERVE CLAUSE, ROZELLE RULE, DRAFT, OPTION CLAUSE.

2469. Frazier, Charles S. "Sports Litigation! The New Attitude." Coach and Athlete. 41, No.7 (May/June 1979), 11+. INSURANCE, AUTHORITY.

2470. Grayson, Edward. "Sport in Court." Sport and Leisure. 28, No.6 (January/February 1988), 40. PUBLIC AND PRIVATE PARTNERSHIP, PRIVATIZATION, SPONSORSHIP, COMMERCIALIZATION.

2471. Hechter, William. "The Criminal Law and Violence in Sports." The Criminal Law Quarterly. 19 (1976-77), 425-453. VIOLENCE IN HOCKEY, FOOTBALL, BASEBALL, CONSENT OF OPPONENT, SELF DEFENSE, PROVOCATION.

2472. Hoch, David. "What is Sports Law? Some Introductory Remarks and Suggested Parameters for a Growing Phenomenon." Quest. 37, No.1 (1985), 60-70. NEGLIGENCE LIABILITY CLAIMS, CONTRACTS, VIOLENCE.

2473. Hogan, John C. "Sports in the Courts." Phi Delta Kappan. 56, No.2 (October 1974), 132-135. INTERSCHOLASTIC ATHLETICS, RACISM, ALCOHOL, WOMEN.

2474. Johnson, Derek Quinn. "Educating Misguided Student Athletes: An Application of Contract Theory." Columbia Law Review. 85, No.1 (January 1985), 96-124. ACCOUNTABILITY, STUDENT-ATHLETES, CONFLICT OF INTEREST, CONTRACT DOCTRINE.

2475. Johnson, William Oscar. "A Walk On the Sordid Side." Sports Illustrated. 47, No.5 (August 1, 1977), 10-15. SLANDER, SUITS, LOS ANGELES RAIDERS, GEORGE ATKINSON, PITTSBURGH STEELERS, CHUCK NOLL, COACHES, PRO FOOTBALL.

2476. Kirshenbaum, Jerry (ed.). "Coping Fitfully With the Sports World's Growing Case Load." Sports Illustrated. 59, No.4 (July 25, 1983), 9-12. SELF REGULATION, PUNISHMENT MENTALITY, STEVE HOWE, COCAINE USE, NFL.

2477. Kirshenbaum, Jerry (ed.). "Judge Burciaga Gets Down To Business With College Football." Sports Illustrated. 57, No.14 (September 27, 1982), 9-12. SHERMAN ANTITRUST ACT, NCAA CONTROL OF COLLEGE FOOTBALL TELECASTS, LITIGATION.

2478. Knipe, Michael. "Courting A Relay of Drug Suits." The Times Higher Education Supplement. 723 (September 12, 1986), 9. DRUG TESTING, LAWSUITS, NCAA.

2479. Krakora, Joseph E. "The Application of Title IX to School Athletic Programs." Cornell Law Review. 68, No.2 (January 1983), 222-235. TITLE IX, SEX DISCRIMINATION, HEW REGULATIONS, CASE LAW, LITIGATION.

2480. Kutner, Joan Ruth. "Sex Discrimination in Athletics." Villanova Law Review. 21, Nos.5&6 (October 1976), 876-903. TITLE IX, SEX DISCRIMINATION IN ATHLETICS, LITTLE LEAGUE, WOMEN.

2481. Lederman, Douglas. "Civil Libertarians Forcing NCAA Into Court to Defend Mandatory Drug Tests." The Chronicle of Higher Education. 33, No.47 (August 5, 1987), 1+. VIOLATION OF PRIVACY RIGHTS, MANDATORY DRUG TESTING, CONSENT FORMS.

2482. Monaghan, Peter. "Colleges That Examine Athletes for Recreational Drugs are on Shaky Legal Ground, Guideline Draft Suggests." The Chronicle of Higher Education. 32, No.10 (May 7, 1986), 31-32. DRUG TESTING GUIDELINES, AMERICAN COUNCIL ON EDUCATION, LEGALITY OF TESTING.

2483. Monaghan, Peter. "Mandatory Drug Tests for College Athletes May Face Court Challenges, Lawyers Warn." The Chronicle of Higher Education. 29, No.11 (November 7, 1984), 31-32. COURT CHALLENGES, MANDATORY DRUG TESTS, WAIVER FORMS.

2484. Monaghan, Peter. "Opponents of Drug Tests for College Players Have Trouble Getting Arguments into Courts." The Chronicle of Higher Education. 33, No.6 (October 8, 1986), 45-46. DISQUALIFICATION OF ENTIRE TEAMS, MANDATORY DRUG TESTING, LAWSUITS, ACLU, LEGAL PRECEDENT.

2485. Mottl, Ronald and Rick Horrow. "The Legislative Perspective: The Sports Violence Act of 1980 and 1981." Arena Review. 5, No.1 (February 1981), 19-21. SPORTS VIOLENCE ACT, AMBIGUITY OF THE LAW, SELF REGULATION, PROFESSIONAL SPORT VIOLENCE, YOUTH AND AMATEUR SPORTS.

2486. Porto, Brian L. "Athletic Scholarships as Contracts of Employment: The Rensing Decisions and the Future of College Sports." Journal of Sport and Social Issues. 9, No.1 (Winter/Spring 1985), 20-37. EMPLOYMENT CONTRACTS, WORKER'S COMPENSATION, PROFESSIONALISM, LAWSUITS.

2487. Porto, Brian L. "College Athletics on Trial: The Mark Hall Decision and Its Implication for the Future." Journal of Sport and Social Issues. 8, No.1 (Winter/Spring 1984), 23-34. LAWSUITS, ACADEMICS.

2488. Quinn, Hal. "Law, Order and the NHL." Maclean's. 96, No.46 (November 14, 1983), 60. TOM LYSIAK, SUSPENSION RESTRAINED BY COURT, VIOLENCE, RULES.

2489. "Semi-Tough Justice." Time. 105, No.3 (January 20, 1975), 61. UNIVERSITY OF OKLAHOMA, ALTERED HIGH SCHOOL TRANSCRIPTS, BIG TIME COLLEGE FOOTBALL, JOE WOOLLEY.

2490. Steinbach, Sheldon Elliot. "Workmen's Compensation and the Scholarship Athlete." Cleveland State Law Review. 19, No.3 (1970), 521-527. CONTRACTS, FINANCIAL AID, ACADEMICS, BIG BUSINESS.

SPORT AND MEDIA

Books

2491. Cashman, Richard and Michael McKernan, (eds.). Sport: Money, Morality and the Media. Kensington, New South Wales: New South Wales University Press Ltd., 1981. AUSTRALIA, GAMBLING, PROFESSIONALIZATION, BASEBALL, UNITED STATES, ENGLAND, MEDIA, CRICKET, POLITICS, SOCCER, SCOTLAND, FOOTBALL, METHODISM.

2492. Chandler, Joan M. Television and National Sport: The United States and Britain. Urbana, IL: University of Illinois Press, 1988. BASEBALL, FOOTBALL, CRICKET, SOCCER, TENNIS.

2493. Cosell, Howard. Cosell. Chicago: Playboy Press, 1973. BOXING, FOOTBALL, OLYMPICS, MEDIA, SPORTS JOURNALISM.

2494. Cosell, Howard. Like It Is. Chicago: Playboy Press, 1974. INVESTIGATIVE SPORTS JOURNALISM, FANS.

2495. Cosell, Howard with Peter Bonventre. I Never Played the Game. New York: William Morrow and Company, 1985. MEDIA, BOXING, FOOTBALL.

2496. Fisher, Art and Neal Marshall with Charles Einstein. Garden of Innocents. New York: E. P. Dutton, 1972. JOE FRAZIER, MUHAMMAD ALI, PRO BOXING, TELEVISION.

2497. Izenberg, Jerry. The Jerry Izenberg Collection (The Sportswriter's Eye Series). Dallas: Taylor Publishing Company, 1989. SPORTS WRITING, BOXING, HORSE RACING, DEATH.

2498. Kaplan, Jim. Pine-Tarred and Feathered: A Year on the Baseball Beat. Chapel Hill, NC: Algonquin Books of Chapel Hill, 1985. BASEBALL, SPORTS WRITING.

2499. Koppett, Leonard. Sports Illusion, Sports Reality: A Reporter's View of Sports, Journalism, and Society. Boston: Houghton Mifflin Company, 1981. EFFECTS OF MASS SPECTATOR SPORTS ON U.S. AND CANADIAN CULTURE, RELATIONSHIP OF JOURNALISM AND SPORTS, SPORTS LEAGUES, MINORITIES, WOMEN, CHILDREN, BENEFIT AND HARM.

2500. Lieb, Fred. Baseball as I Have Known It. New York: Coward, McCann and Geoghegan, 1977. TY COBB, HEROES, SCANDALS, HAL CHASE, CARL MAYO, LOU GEHRIG, FUTURE.

2501. Powers, Ron. Supertube: The Rise of Television Sports. New York: Coward-McCann, 1984. HISTORICAL PERSPECTIVES, DELETERIOUS IMPACT, CORRUPTING SPORT.

2502. Rader, Benjamin G. In Its Own Image: How Television Has Transformed Sports. New York: Free Press, 1984. IMPACT OF TELEVISION ON SPORTS, BOXING, BASEBALL, FOOTBALL, SPORTS AS ENTERTAINMENT, TECHNOLOGY, FAIR PLAY, WINNING AT ALL COSTS, COMMERCIALIZATION, GREED, HISTORY.

2503. Spence, Jim with Dave Diles. Up Close and Personal: The Inside Story of Network Television Sports. New York: Atheneum, 1988. EGOTISM, HOWARD COSELL, INFLUENCE OF TELEVISION ON SPORTS, BUSINESS, AL MICHAELS, ROONE ARLEDGE.

2504. Wenner, Lawrence A. (ed.). Media, Sports, and Society. Newbury Park, CA: Sage Publications, Inc., 1989.   HISTORY, PRO SPORTS ORGANIZATIONS, TELEVISION, SUPER BOWL, WORLD CUP SOCCER, WINNING AND LOSING, DRUGS, LEN BIAS, SEX TYPING.

Articles

2505. Altheide, David L. and Robert P. Snow. "Sports Versus the Mass Media." Urban Life: A Journal of Ethnographic Research. 7, No.2 (July 1978), 189-204. TELEVISION COVERAGE, TELEVISION ALTERS THE CHARACTER OF PRO SPORTS, RULES, SPORTSCASTERS, PLAYER SALARIES.

2506. Amdur, Neil. "The Changing Face of Sports: The Television Dollars Foster New Perceptions." The New York Times. 132 (October 30, 1982), Section 1, Page 9. SEOUL OLYMPICS, DEADLOCK BETWEEN OWNERS AND PLAYERS, FUTURE OF SPORTS, TECHNOLOGY.

2507. Barendse, Michael A. "Individualism, Technology and Sport: The Speedway Nexus." Journal of Sport and Social Issues. 7, No.1 (Winter/Spring 1983), 15-23. AUTO RACING, IDENTITY, VICARIOUS EXPERIENCE.

2508. Betts, John Rickards. "The Impact of Technology on Sport in the Nineteenth Century." Journal of Health, Physical Education and Recreation. 40, No.9 (November/December 1969), 87-90. CONTRIBUTION OF SPORT TO THE TECHNOLOGICAL REVOLUTION.

2509. Betts, John Rickards. "The Technological Revolution and the Rise of Sport, 1850-1900." The Mississippi Valley Historical Review. 40, No.2 (September 1953), 231-256. INDUSTRIAL REVOLUTION, RISE OF SPORTS.

2510. Birrell, Susan and John W. Loy, Jr. "Media Sport: Hot and Cool." International Review of Sport Sociology. 1, No.14 (1979), 5-19. MARSHALL MCLUHAN, SPORT AS A REFLECTION OF CULTURE, FUTURE OF MEDIA SPORT.

2511. Crepeau, Richard C. "The Jake Powell Incident and the Press: A Study in Black and White." North American Society for Sport History Proceedings and Newsletter. (1980), 33. NEW YORK YANKEES, RACISM, PRO BASEBALL.

2512. Eskenazi, Gerald. "Harassment Charge Draws NFL's Attention." New York Times. (September 27, 1990), B11+. SEXUAL HARASSMENT, BOSTON HERALD REPORTER, LISA OLSON, NEW ENGLAND PATRIOTS, WOMEN IN LOCKER ROOMS, VICTOR KIAM, OWNER, ZEKE MOWATT, MIND RAPE.

2513. Farrell, Charles S. "Is There Too Much College Sport on TV? Conflicting Views Make the Picture Fuzzy." The Chronicle of Higher Education. 32, No.4 (March 26, 1986), 34-35. FUTURE, TELEVISION REVENUES, OVEREXPOSURE.

2514. Floerke, Jill Drum. "Woman in the Press Box." The Christian Century. 91, No.40 (November 20, 1974), 1086-1087. WOMEN'S RIGHTS, SPORTS EDITORS, CAREER OPPORTUNITIES.

2515. Frizzi, Ginny. "An Open Door For Women Sports Reporters." Scholastic Editor. 56, No.6 (March 1977), 28-29. WOMEN SPORTS REPORTERS, PREPARING FOR CAREERS IN SPORTS.

2516. Gantz, Walter. "An Exploration of Viewing Motives and Behaviors Associated with Television Sports." Journal of Broadcasting. 25, No.3 (Summer 1981), 263-275. MOTIVATION, GENDER, BEHAVIORAL AND AFFECTIVE CORRELATES OF SPORTS VIEWING.

2517. Garrison, Bruce. "Ethics, Sports, and College Journalists." College Media Review. 28 (Spring 1989), 28-30. ETHICS, COLLEGE SPORTS, HONESTY.

2518. Garrison, Bruce and Michael Salwen. "Newspaper Sports Journalists: A Profile of the 'Profession'." Journal of Sport and Social Issues. 13, No.2 (Fall 1989), 57-68. ETHICS, AUTONOMY, CODES OF ETHICS.

2519. Hilliard, Dan C. "Media Images of Male and Female Professional Athletes: An Interpretative Analysis of Magazine Articles." Sociology of Sport Journal. 1, No.3 (1984), 251-262. TENNIS PLAYERS, STEREOTYPES, GENDER ROLES, SPORTS AS A MALE PRESERVE, COMMERCIAL SPONSORSHIP.

2520. Hochberg, Philip R. "Second and Goal to Go: The Legislative Attack in the 92nd Congress on Sports Broadcasting Practices." New York Law Forum. 18, No.4 (Spring 1973), 841-896. CONGRESS, BLACKOUTS, COLLEGE SPORTS, SUPER BOWL.

2521. Holder, Dennis. "Dallas Station Refuses to Flinch as It Topples A Gridiron Power." Channels: The Business of Communications. 7, No.5 (May 1987), 13. SOUTHERN METHODIST UNIVERSITY, SCANDAL, AIRING OF STORY DESPITE LOYALTIES, NCAA RULE VIOLATIONS.

2522. Izenberg, Jerry. "Back to the Future Again?" Newark Star Ledger. (September 27, 1990), 55+. FEMALE REPORTER FOR BOSTON HERALD, SEXUAL HARASSMENT, EQUALITY, WOMEN IN LOCKER ROOMS, VICTOR KIAM, ZEKE MOWATT, DECENCY, LISA OLSON.

2523. Johnson, Roy S. "Take the V Out of TV, Please." Sports Illustrated. 72, No.25 (June 18, 1990), 90. JIMMY VALVANO, NORTH CAROLINA STATE UNIVERSITY, COLLEGE BASKETBALL, ABC TELEVISION, SCANDAL, POINT SHAVING, VALVANO HIRED BY ABC.

2524. Kelley, William G. "Jackie Robinson and the Press." Journalism Quarterly. 53, No.1 (Spring 1976), 137-139. MEDIA COVERAGE OF THE SIGNING OF JACKIE ROBINSON, "NEGRO" PUBLICATIONS, METROPOL NEWSPAPERS, MAGAZINES, RACISM.

2525. Lupica, Mike. "Newk's Interview with Vitas: Smoking Out the Truth." World Tennis. 25, No.9 (February 1978), 32-35. JOHN NEWCOMBE, TENNIS, VITAS GERULAITIS, SPORTSWRITING.

2526. Lupica, Mike. "Pat's Kiam Embarrasses Himself as an Owner, a Man, and a Father." The National Sports Daily. 1, No.204 (September 24, 1990), 2. BOSTON HERALD REPORTER, LISA OLSON, SEXUAL HARASSMENT, NEW ENGLAND PATRIOTS, WOMEN IN THE LOCKER ROOM, VICTOR KIAM, ZEKE MOWATT.

2527. McIntosh, Peter C. "Mass Media: Friends or Foes in Sport." Quest. 22 (June 1974), 33-44. SOCIAL RESPONSIBILITY, MASS SPORT, RITUAL, CEREMONIES, FUTURE.

2528. Morrison, Stan. "Media Money Threatens the Integrity of Education." The Center Magazine. 15, No.1 (January/February 1982), 24-26. PRESSURE TO WIN, HEROISM, ALLIANCE BETWEEN MEDIA MONEY AND INTERCOLLEGIATE ATHLETICS, REFORM.

2529. Neff, Craig. "Protrait of the Sportswriter as a Young Man." Gannett Center Journal. 1, No.2 (Fall 1987), 47-55. DILEMMAS IN SPORTSWRITING, PUBLISHING OF ODDS.

2530. Perelman, Richard B. "Television and Sport." Olympic Message. 18 (August 1987), 57-61. INFLUENCE OF THE TELEVISION ENVIRONMENT ON ATHLETES, ROLE MODELS, SALARIES, MARKETING OF SPORTS, COMPETITION.

2531. Phillips, David P. "The Impact of Mass Media Violence on U. S. Homocides." American Sociological Review. 48, No.4 (August 1983), 560-568. HEAVYWEIGHT CHAMPIONSHIP FIGHTS AS A FACTOR IN HOMOCIDE INCREASES, MODELING, GAMBLING.

2532. Phillips, David P. and John E. Hensley. "When Violence is Rewarded or Punished: The Impact of Mass Media Stories on Homicide." Journal of Communication. 34, No.3 (Summer 1984), 101-116. BOXING, REWARD AND PUNISHMENT OF VIOLENCE ON TELEVISION.

2533. Pilson, Neal H. "Television and Sports: A Cautionary Note." USA Today. 113, No.2474 (November 1984), 84-85. RIGHTS, FEES, CHANGES, FUTURE.

2534. Preising, Wulf W. "Mass Media, Sport and International Understanding." The FIEP Bulletin. 55, No.2 (April/June 1985), 9-20. SPORTS AS A WAY TO PROMOTE UNDERSTANDING, OLYMPICS, ROLE OF SPORTS JOURNALISTS, SPECTATORS.

2535. Rainville, Raymond E., Al Roberts and Andrew Sweet. "Recognition of Covert Racial Prejudice." Journalism Quarterly. 55, No.2 (Summer 1978), 256-259. RACISM, SPORTS ANNOUNCERS, MEDIA, FANS.

2536. Reid, Leonard N. and Lawrence C. Soley. "Sports Illustrated's Coverage of Women in Sports." Journalism Quarterly. 56, No.4 (Winter 1979), 861-863. STEREOTYPES, SOCIAL CHANGE, WINTER OLYMPICS, SEXISM.

2537. Smith, Garry J. and Terry A. Valeriote. "Ethics in Sports Journalism." Arena Review. 7, No.2 (July 1983), 7-14. SPORTS WRITERS, ACADEMIC STANDARDS, CODE OF ETHICS.

2538. Straw, Phil. "Pointspreads and Journalistic Ethics." Arena Review. 7, No.1 (February 1983), 43-48. MEDIA, ETHICAL ASPECTS, GAMBLING.

2539. Surface, Bill. "The Shame of the Sports Beat." Columbia Journalism Review. 10, No.5 (January/February 1972), 48-55. INGRATIATING SPORTS WRITERS, REFORM, ROTATION OF STAFF.

2540. Taaffe, William. "TV to Sports: The Bucks Stop Here." Sports Illustrated. 64, No.8 (February 24, 1986), 20-22+. HIGH RIGHTS FEES, ADVERTISING FEES, MONDAY NIGHT FOOTBALL, PETE ROZELLE, PETER UEBERROTH.

2541. Taaffe, William. "Unfounded Findings." Sports Illustrated. 58, No.4 (January 31, 1983), 54-57. PBS EXPOSE ON THE NFL, "AN UNAUTHORIZED HISTORY OF NFL", FRONTLINE.

2542. Torrens, Thomas M.   "Professional Football Telecasts and the Blackout Privilege." Cornell Law Review. 57, No.2 (January 1972), 297-312. HISTORY OF THE BLACKOUT PRIVILEGE, REFORM OF THE BLACKOUT EXEMPTION, REPEAL OF BLACKOUT PRIVILEGES.

SPORT AND POLITICS

Books

2543. Allison, Lincoln (ed.).   The Politics of Sport.   Manchester: Manchester University Press, 1986. INTERNATIONAL SPORTS, LAW, AUTONOMY, SOUTH AFRICA, OLYMPICS.

2544. Booker, Christopher. The Games of War: A Moscow Journal. London: Faber and Faber Ltd., 1981. MOSCOW OLYMPICS, USSR, AFGHANISTAN, BOYCOTT, INTERNATIONAL SPORTS.

2545. Brohm, Jean-Marie. Sport: A Prison of Measured Time. London: Ink Links, 1978. SPORTS AS A TOOL TO ADVANCE POLITICAL POWER AND CONTROL, CAPITALISM, SOCIALISM, INDUSTRIALIZATION, INSTITUTIONALIZATION OF SPORTS, IDEOLOGY.

2546. Hargreaves, Jennifer (ed.). Sport, Culture and Ideology. London: Routledge and Kegan Paul, 1982. CULTURE, IDEOLOGY, MEDIA, WOMEN, CHILDREN, VIOLENCE, HOOLIGANISM, DRUGS, COMMUNISM, APARTHEID.

2547. Hart-Nibbrig, Nand and Clement Cottingham. The Political Economy of College Sports. Lexington, MA: Lexington Books, 1986. CORPORATE ATHLETICISM, COMMERCIALISM, MEDIA, ECONOMICS, POLITICS, REFORM.

2548. Hoberman, John M. Sport and Political Ideology. Austin: University of Texas Press, 1984. MARXISM, NAZISM, IDEAL AND MEANING, CONSERVATIVISM.

2549. Johnson, Arthur T. and James H. Frey (eds.). Government and Sport: The Public Policy Issues. Totowa, NJ: Rowman and Allanheld, 1985. RIGHTS OF ATHLETES, TITLE IX AND FRANCHISE RELOCATION, REGULATION, AGENTS, RECRUITING, TEAM OWNERS, PUBLIC POLICY, SOCIAL-POLITICAL PHILOSOPHY, GOVERNMENT.

2550. MacFarlane, Neil with Michael Herd. Sport and Politics: A World Divided. London: Willow Books, 1986. FOOTBALL, GLENEAGLES DECLARATION, RUGBY, MONEY, DRUGS, CORPORATE SPONSORSHIP, CRICKET, OLYMPICS.

2551. Mangan, James Anthony. The Games Ethic and Imperialism: Aspects of the Diffusion of an Ideal. New York: Viking, 1986. VALUES, BRITISH ETHNOCENTRISM, DEVELOPING COUNTRIES, ROLE OF SPORT IN SOCIETY, IDEOLOGY, IMPERIALISM.

2552. Noll, Roger G. (ed.). Government and the Sports Business. Washington, D.C: The Brookings Institution, 1974. DISCRIMINATION, BASEBALL, BIG BUSINESS OF SPORT, MINORITIES, GOVERNMENT, MONEY.

2553. Redmond, Gerald (ed.). Sport and Politics. Champaign, IL: Human Kinetics Publishers, 1986. ROLE OF GOVERNMENT, ELITE AND MASS SPORTS, OLYMPICS, FUTURE.

2554. Shaikin, Bill. Sport and Politics: The Olympics and the Los Angeles Games. New York: Praeger Publishers, 1988. OLYMPICS, LOS ANGELES GAMES, POLITICS.

2555. Vinokur, Martin Barry. More Than a Game: Sports and Politics. New York: Greenwood Press, 1988. ROMANIA, GERMANY, EAST-WEST IDEOLOGIES, OLYMPIC BOYCOTTS.

2556. Whannel, Garry. Blowing the Whistle: The Politics of Sport. London: Pluto Press, 1983. OLYMPICS, GOVERNMENT, BUSINESS, RULE CHANGES, CAPITALISM, SOCIALISM, CULTURE.

Articles

2557. Ashe, Arthur (ed. by Elizabeth Dowling).   "Arthur Ashe: On Politics and Sports." Senior Scholastic. 110, No.2 (September 22, 1977), 4-6+. TENNIS, SOUTH AFRICA, BOYCOTTS, RACISM.

2558. Collins, Robert M. "Richard M. Nixon: The Psychic, Political, and Moral Uses of Sport." Journal of Sport History. 10, No.2 (Summer 1983), 77-84. SPORTS METAPHORS, FAN, COMPETITION, SPORT AS AN EMOTIONAL OUTLET, WINNING.

2559. Grigoryev, Alexei. "Sport, Business and Politics." New Times. No.28 (July 15, 1970), 28-31. BUSINESS AND SPORTS, COMMERCIALIZATION OF SPORTS, WEST GERMANY, UNITED STATES, CAPITALISM.

2560. Hoberman, John M. "Communist Sport Theory Today: The Case of Andrzej Wohl." Arena Review. 4, No.1 (February 1980), 13-16. STRUGGLE BETWEEN EAST AND WEST, IDEOLOGY OF COMMUNIST SPORT, POLISH SPORT SOCIOLOGIST ANDRZEJ WOHL, MODERNISM.

2561. Hoberman, John M. "Sport and Political Ideology." Journal of Sport and Social Issues. 1, No.2 (Summer/Fall 1977), 80-114. CULTURE, CONSERVATISM, MARXISM.

2562. Johnson, Arthur T. "Congress and Professional Sports: 1951-1978." The Annals of the American Academy of Political and Social Science. 445 (September 1979), 102-115. RELATIONSHIP BETWEEN GOVERNMENT AND PRO SPORTS, SPORT LEGISLATION, BIG BUSINESS.

2563. Johnson, Arthur T. "Government, Opposition and Sport: The Role of Domestic Sports Policy in Generating Political Support." Journal of Sport and Social Issues. 6, No.2 (Fall/Winter 1982), 22-34. USE OF SPORTS TO GENERATE POLITICAL SUPPORT, VALUES, EXPLOITATION OF SPORTS.

2564. Johnson, Arthur T. "Public Sports Policy." American Behavioral Scientist. 21, No.3 (January/February 1978), 319-344. ROLE OF SPORTS, SPORTS AS A PUBLIC POLICY CONCERN, ECONOMIC BENEFITS, SPORTS AS AN AGENT OF SOCIALIZATION, MONOPOLIES, ATHLETE RIGHTS.

2565. Leppanen, Aulis. "Politics and Sport." World Marxist Review. 23, No.10 (October 1980), 16-19. BOYCOTTS, MOSCOW OLYMPICS, AFGHANISTAN.

2566. Lipsky, Richard. "The Athleticization of Politics: The Political Implication of Sports Symbolism." Journal of Sport and Social Issues. 3, No.2 (Fall/Winter 1979), 28-37. AESTHETICS, SOCIAL AND POLITICAL CONTEXT, SYMBOLIC FORM OF SPORT, SPORT AND PERSONALIZATION.

2567. Lunn, Sir Arnold. "Sports and Politics." Quest. 1 (December 1963), 33-36. SKIING, OLYMPICS, GERMANY, NAZISM.

2568. McKay, Jim. "Marxism as a Way of Seeing: Beyond the Limits of Current 'Critical' Approaches to Sport." Sociology of Sport Journal. 3, No.3 (September 1986), 261-272. NEO-MARXISM, FEMINIST CRITIQUE, DOMINATION.

2569. Nafziger, James A. R. and Andrew Strenk. "The Political Uses and Abuses of Sports." Connecticut Law Review. 10, No.2 (1978), 259-289. SPORTS AS AN EXPRESSION OF DIPLOMATIC RECOGNITION AND NONRECOGNITION, GERMANY, CHINA, SPORTS AS A CATALYST OF CONFLICT, SPORTS AS A MEANS OF PROTEST, SPORTS AS A VEHICLE OF PROPAGANDA, SPORTS AS A MEANS TO GAIN PRESTIGE, SPORTS AS A VEHICLE FOR INTERNATIONAL COOPERATION.

2570. Naison, Mark. "Sports and the American Empire." Radical America. 6, No.4 (July-August 1972), 95-120. SPORT AS A MEANS OF POLITICAL CONTROL, SPORT AND REBELLION, NEW FORMS OF SOCIALIZATION, ROLE OF SPORT IN SOCIETY.

2571. Parry, S. J. "Hegemony and Sport." Journal of the Philosophy of Sport. 10 (1983), 71-83. SOCIOLOGY OF SPORT, ANALYTICAL MODEL, MARXISM, GRAMSCI, THEORY OF SPORT, CULTURE.

2572. Petrie, Brian M. "Examination of a Stereotype: Athletes as Conservatives." International Review of Sport Sociology. 12, No.3 (1977), 51-62. COACHES, IDEOLOGY, VALUES.

2573. "Politics and Sports: The Deadly Games Nations Play." Senior Scholastic. 102, No.4 (February 26, 1973), 14-15. DIPLOMACY, OLYMPICS, COMMUNIST ATHLETES.

2574. Pooley, John C. and Arthur V. Webster. "Sport and Politics: Power Play." Journal of the Canadian Association for Health, Physical Education, and Recreation. 41, No.3 (January/February 1975), 13. DEFINITION OF SPORT, CATEGORIES OF SPORT, SPORT AS AN OPIATE OF THE MASSES, POWER, MUNICIPAL, NATIONAL AND INTERNATIONAL SPORT.

2575. Spring, Joel H. "Athletics and the Modern Industrial State." Phi Delta Kappan. 56, No.2 (October 1974), 114-115. PROFESSIONALISM, COMMERCIALISM, SPORTS AS A CONSERVATIVE SOCIAL FORCE.

2576. Walsh, Chris. "Sports and Politics." Rowing U.S.A. 15, No.2 (April/May 1983), 39. MOSCOW OLYMPICS, BOYCOTTS, USSR, AFGHANISTAN.

2577. "World Athletes: Victims of Political Games." U. S. News and World Report. 81, No.4 (July 26, 1976), 52. MONTREAL OLYMPICS, TAIWAN, BOYCOTTS, CANADA.

SPORT AND RELIGION

Books

2578. Arndt, Richard. Safe at Home: Ten Major League Baseball Players Discuss Their Careers and Their Christian Commitment. St. Louis: Concordia Publishing House, 1979. RELATIONSHIP OF CHRISTIANITY TO CAREERS.

2579. Baum, Gregory and John Coleman (eds.). Sport (Concilium: Religion in the Eighties). Edinburgh: T. and T. Clark, 1989. SPORT AND SOCIETY, SPORT AND VIOLENCE, ETHICS OF SPORT, CHRISTIANITY, ZEN BUDDHISM, POLITICS AND RELIGION.

2580. Carse, James P. Finite and Infinite Games: A Vision of Life as Play and Possibility. New York: Free Press, 1986. SPORTS METAPHORS, SEX, SOCIAL ROLES, POLITICS, RELIGION, MYTHS.

2581. Cox, Harvey Gallagher. Feast of Fools: A Theological Essay on Festivity and Fantasy. Cambridge, MA: Harvard University Press, 1969. PLAY, FUN, RITUAL, MYTHOLOGY, TRANSCENDENCE.

2582. DeSensi, Joy Theresa. A Study of Martin Buber's I-Thou and I-It Relationships in Sport. Ed.D. Thesis: The University of North Carolina at Greensboro, 1980. PRO SPORTS, OTHERREGARDINGNESS, MUTUALITY, DIRECTNESS, PRESENTNESS, INTENSITY, INEFFABILITY.

2583. The Goal and the Glory. Old Tappan, NJ: Fleming H. Revell Company, 1986. OVERCOMING FAMILY TRAGEDY, INJURIES, DRUGS, CHRISTIANITY.

2584. Hayes, Elvin and Bill Gilbert. They Call Me 'The Big E'. Englewood Cliffs, NJ: Prentice-Hall, Inc., 1978. PREJUDICE, VIOLENCE, COLLEGE BASKETBALL, HISTORY, NBA, PRO BASKETBALL, VALUES.

2585. Heinrich, Donald H. A Critical Study of the Place of Sports in the Lives of American Christians: With Implications for Church and Society. D. Min. Thesis: San Francisco Theological Seminary, 1984. SPORT AND SOCIETY, RITUAL, BENEFIT AND HARM.

2586. Jackson, Madeline Manning. Running for Jesus. Waco, TX: Word Books, 1977. MUNICH OLYMPICS, CHRISTIANITY, BLACK FEMALE ATHLETES.

2587. Janssen, Al. Fast Break: Heroes of the NBA. San Bernadino, CA: Here's Life Publishers, Inc., 1987. NBA, EVANGELISM, CHRISTIANITY, ROLE MODELS.

2588. John, Tommy and Sally John with Joe Musser. The Tommy John Story. Old Tappan, NJ: Fleming H. Revell Company, 1978. PRO BASEBALL, LOS ANGELES DODGERS, DISABLED, FAITH, EVANGELISM.

2589. King, LeRoy (ed.). Courage to Conquer: America's Athletes Speak Their Faith. Westwood, NJ: Fleming H. Revell Company, 1966. IDEAL AND MEANING, POWER, SIN, WINNING, TEAMWORK, STANDARDS, ROLE MODELS.

2590. Landry, Fernand and William A. R. Orban (eds.). Philosophy, Theology, and History of Sport and of Physical Activity. Miami: Symposia Specialists, Inc., 1978. VALUES, OLYMPICS, POLITICS, PHILOSOPHY, AMATEURISM, RELIGION, ALIENATION, HISTORY.

2591. Miller, David. Gods and Games: Toward a Theology of Play. New York: Harper and Row, 1970. MYTHS, CHEATING, ACADEMICS.

2592. Morton, Craig and Robert Burger. The Courage to Believe. Englewood Cliffs, NJ: Prentice-Hall, Inc., 1981. RELIGION, IDEAL AND MEANING, CHRISTIANITY, EVANGELISM.

2593. Neale, Robert Edward. In Praise of Play: Toward a Psychology of Religion. New York: Harper and Row Publishers Inc., 1969. PLAY AND WORK, CULTURE, BENEFIT AND HARM, MYTHS, RITUAL.

2594. Neale, Robert Edward. Play and the Sacred: Toward a Theory of Religion As Play. Unpublished Th.D. Dissertation, Union Theological Seminary, 1964. PHENOMENOLOGY, PLAY, FREUD, JOHAN HUIZINGA, CULTURE, RITUAL.

2595. Novak, Michael. The Joy of Sports: End Zones, Bases, Baskets, Balls and the Consecration of the American Spirit. New York: Basic Books, Inc., 1976. SPORT AS A CREATION OF THE HUMAN SPIRIT, CULTURE, SPECTATOR BEHAVIOR, AMERICAN CIVIL RELIGION, RELIGION, VIOLENCE, RATIONALISM, SECULARISM, POLITICS, MYTHS.

2596. Ryan, Thomas. <u>Wellness, Spirituality and Sports</u>. New York: Paulist Press, 1986. SPORTS FOR WELLNESS, LEISURE, HOLISTIC APPROACH TO SPORTS, RUNNING, SWIMMING, SKIING, DANCING.

2597. Sandul, Duane G.   <u>When Faith Steals Home</u>.   Plainfield, NJ: Logos International, 1980. PRO BASEBALL, RELIGION, CHRISTIANITY, RELIGIOUS LIFE, BASEBALL LIFE.

2598. Schindler, Claude E. Jr. with Pacheco Pyle and Steve Karnehm. <u>The Role of Athletics in the Christian School</u>. Whittier, CA: Association of Christian School International, 1981.   PHILOSOPHY, RULES, INJURIES, EXAMS, ELIGIBILITY, ACADEMICS.

2599. Sloan, Steve. <u>A Whole New Ballgame</u>. Nashville: Broadman Press, 1975. COACHING, FOOTBALL, CHRISTIANITY, LIFESTYLE.

2600. Slusher, Howard S.   <u>Man, Sport and Existence: A Critical Analysis</u>. Philadelphia: Lea and Febiger, 1967. EXISTENTIALISM, PHENOMENOLOGY, IDEAL AND MEANING, WORK AND PLAY.

2601. Stogsdill, Skip. <u>Three Cheers for Discipline: And Other Priority Reading for Athletes and Coaches</u>. Dubuque, IA: Kendall/Hunt Publishing Company, 1985. COACHES AND PLAYERS, EXCELLENCE.

2602. Wagner, Hans-Peter. <u>Puritan Attitudes Towards Recreation in Early Seventeenth-Century New England: With Particular Consideration of Physical Recreation</u>. Frankfurt: Peter Lang Publishing, Inc., 1982. DIFFERENCES BETWEEN PURITAN THEORY AND NEW ENGLAND REALITY, MYTHS, WORK VS PLAY ETHIC, HISTORY.

2603. Whittingham, Richard. <u>Sunday Mayhem: A Celebration of Pro Football in America</u>. Dallas: Taylor Publishing Company, 1987. ROLE OF SPORT IN SOCIETY, PRO FOOTBALL.

Articles

2604. Ardolino, Frank R.   "Christian Symbolism in Serling's <u>Requiem for a Heavyweight</u>." <u>Arete: The Journal of Sport Literature</u>. 2, No.1 (Fall 1984), 159-168. EXPLOITATION, TRUTH, REALITY, DECEPTION, REDEMPTION, PRO BOXING.

2605. Bennett, Bruce L.   "The Curious Relationship of Religion and Physical Education." <u>Journal of Health, Physical Education and Recreation</u>. 41, No.7 (September 1970), 69-71. HISTORICAL PERSPECTIVES, EARLY CHURCH, MIDDLE AGES, REFORMATION, MODERN PERIOD, CHURCH LEADERS, THEOLOGY.

2606. Bianchi, Eugene C.   "Pigskin Piety." <u>Christianity and Crisis</u>.   32, No.2 (February 21, 1972), 31-34. DEHUMANIZATION, FANS, FOOTBALL FASCISM, AGGRESSION, VIOLENCE, WOMEN, RITUAL, ANALOGY BETWEEN FOOTBALL AND POPULAR RELIGION.

2607. Brailsford, Dennis. "Religion and Sport in Eighteenth-Century England: 'For the Encouragement of Piety and Virtue, And for the Preventing or Punishing of Vice, Profaneness and Immorality'." The British Journal of Sports History. 1, No.2 (September 1984), 166-183. PURITAN TRADITION, BENEFIT AND HARM, HISTORY, ENGLAND.

2608. Brody, M. Kenneth. "Institutionalized Sport as Quasi-Religion: Preliminary Considerations." Journal of Sport and Social Issues. 3, No.2 (Fall/Winter 1979), 17-27. INSTITUTIONALIZATION OF SPORTS, SOCIOLOGY OF RELIGION, ANALOGY OF SPORT AND RELIGION, SYMBOLIZATION, RITUAL, BELIEFS, FUTURE.

2609. Buhrmann, Hans G. and Maxwell K. Zaugg. "Religion and Superstition in the Sport of Basketball." Journal of Sport Behavior. 6, No.3 (October 1983), 146-157. RITUAL, PRAYER, CHURCH ATTENDENCE, RELATIONSHIP BETWEEN RELIGION AND SUPERSTITION.

2610. Carter, John Marshall. "Muscular Christianity and Its Makers: Sporting Monks and Churchmen in Anglo-Norman Society, 1000-1300." The British Journal of Sports History. 1, No.2 (September 1984), 109-124. MUSCULAR CHRISTIANITY, MONASTICISM, CHRISTIANIZATION OF SPORTS.

2611. Crawford, Scott A. G. M. "Sport and Religion: Some Selected Readings." The Journal of Physical Education. 75, No.4 (March/April 1978), 82-83. RELATIONSHIP BETWEEN SPORTS AND RELIGION, LITERATURE ON SPORT AND RELIGION, TEACHING PHYSICAL EDUCATION, USE OF RELIGION IN TEACHING SPORTS.

2612. Deford, Frank. "Reaching for the Stars: Locker Room Sermons." Sports Illustrated. 44, No.18 (May 3, 1976), 42-60. REV. BILLY ZEOLI, EVANGELISM, SUNDAY SPORTS, FELLOWSHIP OF CHRISTIAN ATHLETES.

2613. Deford, Frank. "Religion in Sport." Sports Illustrated. 44, No.16 (April 19, 1976), 88-102. ATHLETES IN ACTION, EVANGELISM, SUNDAY SPORTS, FELLOWSHIP OF CHRISTIAN ATHLETES.

2614. Deford, Frank. "The Word According to Tom (Show Biz Approach to Christianity)." Sports Illustrated. 44, No.17 (April 26, 1976), 63-69. TOM LANDRY, DALLAS COWBOYS, FELLOWSHIP OF CHRISTIAN ATHLETES.

2615. Geldbach, Erich. "Protestantism--Capitalism--Sports." Journal of Sport History. 4, No.3 (Fall 1977), 285-294. MATERIALISM, CHURCH RECRUITMENT THROUGH SPORTS, HISTORY, RELATIONSHIP OF SPORTS AND RELIGION.

2616. Genasci, James E. and Vasillis Klissouras. "The Delphic Spirit in Sports." Journal of Health, Physical Education and Recreation. 37, No.2 (February 1966), 43-45. STRUGGLE FOR PERFECTION, SELF DISCOVERY, INTEGRATION.

2617. Gerber, Ellen W. "Identity, Relation, and Sport." Quest. 8 (May 1967), 90-97. BENEFIT AND HARM, CULTURE, MARTIN BUBER.

2618. Gonzalez, Arturo F. Jr. "Detroit's Father Vaughan Quinn and His Globetrotters of Hockey Save Both Goals and Souls." People Weekly. 15, No.13 (April 6, 1981), 145-146. SACRED HEART REHABILITATION CENTER FOR ALCOHOLICS, FLYING FATHERS, PLAYING FOR CHARITY.

2619. Higgs, Robert J. "Muscular Christianity, Holy Play, and Spiritual Exercises: Confusion about Christ in Sports and Religion." Arete: The Journal of Sport Literture. 1, No.1 (Fall 1983), 59-85. SPORT AS IDOLATRY, SPORT IN COMPETITION WITH RELIGION, CHRIST, GOD, FUNCTION OF RELIGION, FUNCTION OF SPORT.

2620. Hoffman, Shirl J. "Evangelicalism and the Revitalization of Religious Ritual in Sport." Arete: The Journal of Sport Literature. 2, No.2 (Spring 1985), 63-87. SPORT AS A SECULAR RELIGION, SPORT AS A FORM OF RELIGIOUS EXPRESSION, EVANGELISM, CHRISTIANITY.

2621. Hoffman, Shirl J. "The Sanctification of Sport: Can the Mind of Christ Coexist with the Killer Instinct." Christianity Today. 30, No.6 (April 4, 1986), 17-21. RELATIONSHIP OF SPORTS AND RELIGION, FELLOWSHIP OF CHRISTIAN ATHLETES, PRO ATHLETE OUTREACH, COMPETITION, RITUAL.

2622. Jable, J. Thomas. "Pennsylvania's Early Blue Laws: A Quaker Experiment in the Suppression of Sport and Amusements, 1682-1740." Journal of Sport History. 1, No.2 (Fall 1974), 107-121. MORAL BEHAVIOR, IDEOLOGY, WORLDLINESS.

2623. Jable, J. Thomas. "The English Puritans--Suppressors of Sport and Amusement?" Canadian Journal of History of Sport and Physical Education. 7, No.1 (May 1976), 33-40. OBSERVANCE OF SABBATH, ECONOMICS, GAMBLING.

2624. Kreiter, Ted. "Gospel on the Gridiron." The Saturday Evening Post. 250, No.8 (November 1978), 48-50. EVANGEL COLLEGE, EVANGELISM.

2625. Kretchmar, Robert Scott. "Meeting the Opposition: Buber's 'Will' and 'Grace' in Sport." Quest. 24 (Summer 1975), 19-27. MARTIN BUBER, NATURE OF WILL AND GRACE, OPERATION OF WILL AND GRACE IN SOCIETY, THE DIALOGICAL ATHLETE.

2626. Lawton, Philip. "Sports and the American Spirit: Michael Novak's Theology of Culture." Philosophy Today. 20, No.3/4 (Fall 1976), 196-208. THE JOY OF SPORTS, SPORTS AS A FORM OF RELIGION.

2627. Lewis, Guy. "The Muscular Christianity Movement." Journal of Health, Physical Education and Recreation. 37, No.5 (May 1966), 27-28+. MUSCULAR CHRISTIANITY, HISTORY, SOCIAL REFORM.

2628. Lumpkin, Angela. "Athletes of the Bible and Muscular Christianity." North American Society for Sport History Proceedings and Newsletter. (1979), 34. TEACHING MORALS THROUGH SPORTS, TEACHING ETHICS, MUSCULAR CHRISTIANITY.

2629. Mangan, James Anthony. "Christ and the Imperial Games Fields: Evangelical Athletes of the Empire." The British Journal of Sports History. 1, No.2 (September 1984), 184-201. SPORT AS AN INSTRUMENT OF MORAL TRAINING, MISSIONARIES, CODE OF BEHAVIOR.

2630. Marty, Martin E. "God's Gridiron Gladiators." The Christian Century. 90, No.45 (December 12, 1973), 1239. PRAYER, PIETY IN FOOTBALL.

2631. Meilaender, Gilbert. "Hank Gathers and Cultural Christianity." First Things: A Monthly Journal of Religion and Public Life. No.5 (August/September 1990), 9-10. LOYOLA MARYMOUNT COLLEGE BASKETBALL, HANK GATHERS' DEATH, SPORTS MEDICINE, NCAA BASKETBALL, LENT, CHRISTIANITY.

2632. Meyer, Heinz. "Puritanism and Physical Training: Ideological and Political Accents in the Christian Interpretation of Sport." International Review of Sport Sociology. 8, No.1 (1973), 37-52. SPORTSMANSHIP, RELATIONSHIP BETWEEN CHRISTIANITY AND SPORT.

2633. Murray, Bill (Reviewed by Wray Vamplew). "Celtic V Rangers: Ideology or a Business In Bigotry." Journal of Sport History. 12, No.3 (Winter 1985), 295. GLASGOW, BIGOTRY, CATHOLICS VS. PROTESTANTS.

2634. Nixon, Howard L. "Idealized Functions of Sport: Religious and Political Socialization Through Sport." Journal of Sport and Social Issues. 6, No.1 (Spring/Summer 1982), 1-11. BENEFIT AND HARM OF SPORT, IDEAL AND MEANING, CONSERVATIVISM, VALUES.

2635. Overman, Steven J. "Sport as Puritanism: An Etiology of American Athletics." The Physical Educator. 43, No.1 (Late Winter 1986), 7-10. CALVINISM, WINNING AT ALL COSTS.

2636. Plowman, Edward E. "Dugout Disciples." Christianity Today. 19, No.3 (November 8, 1974), 39-40. BASEBALL CHAPEL INC., EVANGELISM.

2637. Plowman, Edward E. "Outreach at the Olympics." Christianity Today. 20, No.23 (August 27, 1976), 30-32. MONTREAL OLYMPICS, CHAPLAINCY PROGRAM FOR ATHLETES, AIDE OLYMPIQUE, AMBASSADORS IN MISSION, EVANGELISM.

2638. Poliakoff, Michael. "Jacob, Job, and Other Wrestlers: Reception of Greek Athletics by Jews and Christians in Antiquity." Journal of Sport History. 11, No.2 (Summer 1984), 48-65. WILL TO EXCEL AND WIN, SPORTS METAPHORS, SPIRITUAL SIGNIFICANCE OF GREEK ATHLETICS.

2639. Prebish, Charles S. "'Heavenly Father, Divine Goalie': Sport and Religion." The Antioch Review. 42, No.3 (Summer 1984), 306-318. IMITATION OF SPORTS BY RELIGION, CLERGY AND ATHLETES, ATHLETES IN ACTION, FELLOWSHIP OF CHRISTIAN ATHLETES, WINNING IN THE NAME OF THE LORD, PRAYER, RITUAL.

2640. Quinn, Hal and Ashley Collie. "The Christians in the Arenas." Maclean's. 91, No.27 (November 13, 1978), 50. HOCKEY PLAYERS, MATERIALISM, CHRISTIANS, HARE KRISHNAS, JEHOVAH'S WITNESSES.

2641. Redmond, Gerald. "The First Tom Brown's Schooldays: Origins and Evolution of 'Muscular Christianity' In Children's Literature, 1762-1857." Quest. 30 (Summer 1978), 4-18. TOM BROWN'S SCHOOLDAYS, YOUTH, LITERATURE, HISTORICAL.

2642. Redmond, Gerald (Reviewed by Richard William Cox). "Moral Tales for Manly Boys: Christian Sport in Children's Literature 1783 to 1857." The British Journal of Sports History. 3, No.1 (May 1986), 110. TOM BROWN'S SCHOOL DAYS, CHARACTER BUILDING.

2643. Resick, M. C. "The Sports Metaphors of the Apostle Paul." The Physical Educator. 26, No.1 (October 1969), 112-113. GREEK ATHLETIC GAMES, TOOL TO REACH GENTILES, BOXING, PRIZES, RUNNING, TRAINING.

2644. Rhoden, Bill. "Athletes Search For Inner Peace Through Religions and Mind Sciences." Ebony. 30, No.9 (July 1975), 94-96+. CHRISTIANITY, TRANSCENDENTAL MEDITATION, SILVA MIND CONTROL, BUDDHISM, MUSLIMS.

2645. Roberts, Robert C. "The Sanctification of Sport: Competition and Compassion." Christianity Today. 30, No.6 (April 4, 1986), 22-23. VARIETIES OF COMPETITION, HUMOR, DEHUMANIZATION, CHILDREN.

2646. Rogers, Cornish. "Sports, Religion and Politics: The Renewal of An Alliance." The Christian Century. 89, No.14 (April 5, 1972), 392-394. HISTORY, SPORTS MYSTIQUE AND POLITICS, RELIGION AND ATHLETICS, FELLOWSHIP OF CHRISTIAN ATHLETES.

2647. Rueckert, Norbert. "The Practical Application of Christian Values in Sports." Journal of Physical Education. 70, No.2 (November 1972), 11-14. OLYMPICS, YMCA, CHARACTER BUILDING, CHARACTER VALUES, SELF REALIZATION.

2648. Ruhl, J. K. (Reviewed by Richard William Cox). "Puritanism and Sport--The Classical and Scriptural Heritage of Several Principles in the Modern Conception of Sport." The British Journal of Sports History. 3, No.1 (May 1986), 110-111. PURITAN HERITAGE, CLASSICAL SCHOLARS.

2649. Scott, Jack. "Sport and the Radical Ethic." Quest. 19, (January 1973), 71-77. VALUES, EXCELLENCE IN SPORTS.

2650. Segal, Jonathan. "Sports: Prayer Sessions Before Football Games." Esquire. 79, No.5 (May 1973), 60-64. DICK MOTTA, PRAYER, PROMOTION OF RELIGION THROUGH SPORTS, FAN REACTION.

2651. Shinobu, Abe. "Zen and Sport." Journal of the Philosophy of Sport. 13 (1986), 45-48. SPORT AND "THE WAY OF THE WARROR (BUSHIDO)," FIGHTING BOLDLY AND FAIRLY, TRANSCENDENCE, EGO DETACHMENT, JAPANESE MARTIAL ARTS, ZEN BUDDHISM.

2652. Shuster, William. "The Exercise of Religion at the Winter Olympics." Christianity Today. 24, No.3 (February 8, 1980), 67-69. LAKE PLACID OLYMPICS, COMMITTEE ON RELIGIOUS ACTIVITIES.

2653. Spoelstra, Watson. "A Training Huddle for Purposeful Pros." Christianity Today. 23, No.11 (March 2, 1979), 66-67. PRO ATHLETES OUTREACH, ATHLETES IN ACTION, PRO FOOTBALL.

2654. Spoelstra, Watson. "Sunday Brunch at Jerry's Place." Christianity Today. 20, No.12 (March 12, 1976), 48-49. GERALD FORD, EVANGELISM.

2655. Spoelstra, Watson. "Training for Pros." Christianity Today. 21, No.12 (March 18, 1977), 53. PRO ATHLETES OUTREACH, PRO FOOTBALL, NORM EVANS.

2656. Stoll, Sharon Kay. "The Sacred and the Profane in Sport." North American Society for Sport History Proceedings and Newsletter. (1982), 18. CHARACTER, CONDUCT IN SPORTS, EXISTENTIALISM.

2657. Stone, Roselyn E. "Of Zen and the Experience of Moving." Quest. 33, No.1 (1981), 96-107. JAPANESE AESTHETICS, SPORT, DANCE AND EXCERCISE AS CONTEMPLATIVE FORMS.

2658. Struna, Nancy L. "Puritans and Sport: The Irretrievable Tide of Change." Journal of Sport History. 4, No.1 (Spring 1977), 1-21. HISTORY, MASSACHUSETTS BAY, RELIGION, SPORT AS A MIRROR OF SOCIETY, ROLE OF SPORTS IN SOCIETY, VALUES, WORK AND PLAY, BENEFIT AND HARM.

2659. Swanson, Richard A. "The Acceptance and Influence of Play in American Protestantism." Quest. 11 (December 1968), 58-70. INFLUENCE OF PLAY ON THE CHURCH, CHRISTIAN EDUCATION, FINANCIAL BENEFITS, RECRUITMENT, INFLUENCE OF THE CHURCH ON PLAY.

2660. Vance, N. Scott. "Sport is a Religion in America, Controversial Professor Argues." The Chronicle of Higher Education. 28, No.12 (May 16, 1984), 25-27. CHARLES S. PREBISH, PENNSYLVANIA STATE UNIVERSITY, SPORT AS A RELIGION, IDENTITY OF SPORT AND RELIGION.

2661. VanLeeuwen, Mary Stewart. "Ben Johnson, Role Model?" Christianity Today. 32, No.18 (December 9, 1988), 15. DRUGS, OLYMPICS, FAIR PLAY.

2662. von Kortzfleisch, Siegfried. "Religious Olympism." Social Research. 37, No.2 (Summer 1970), 231-236. RELIGIOUS PHENOMENON, SPORTS IDEOLOGY, MEANING OF SPORTS, OLYMPICS, COMPETITION.

2663. Willis, Joe D. and Richard G. Wettan. "Religion and Sport in America: The Case for the Sports Bay in the Cathedral Church of Saint John the Divine." Journal of Sport History. 4, No.2 (Summer 1977), 189-207. EPISCOPAL CHURCH, HISTORY.

2664. "Winners." Christianity Today. 22, No.3 (November 4, 1977), 50-51. NEW YORK YANKEES, LOS ANGELES DODGERS, PRE-GAME CHAPEL SERVICES, "BASEBALL CHAPEL," EVANGELISM.

2665. Zimmer, Judith. "Courting the Gods of Sport." Psychology Today. 18, No.7 (July 1984), 36-39. RITUAL, COPING STRATEGY, TABOOS, WOMEN, RISK.

WOMEN AND SPORT

Books

2666. Averbuch, Gloria. The Woman Runner: Free To Be the Complete Athlete.
New York: Cornerstone Library, 1984. HISTORY, PSYCHOLOGICAL BARRIERS,
FUTURE, COMPETITION, SPORTS MEDICINE.

2667. Boutilier, Mary A. and Lucinda SanGiovanni.   The Sporting Woman.
Champaign, IL: Human Kinetics Publishers, 1983. HISTORY, PSYCHOLOGY,
SOCIOLOGY, MEDIA, POLICY, EDUCATION, FAMILY, POLITICS AND LOCAL SPORTS,
TELEVISION, DISCRIMINATION.

2668. Dyer, Kenneth Frank. Challenging the Men: The Social Biology of Female
Sporting Achievement. St. Lucia, Australia: University of Queensland Press,
1982. SOCIOLOGICAL ANALYSIS OF SPORTS, COED COMPETITION, GENDER
DIFFERENCES, CULTURAL ACCEPTABILITY OF SPORTSWOMEN.

2669. Engelmann, Larry. The Goddess and the American Girl: The Story of Suzanne
Lenglen and Helen Wills. New York: Oxford University Press, Inc., 1988.
RELIGION, ROLE OF SPORT IN SOCIETY, PRO TENNIS.

2670. English, Jane (ed.). Sex Equality. Englewood Cliffs, NJ: Prentice Hall, 1977.
COED TEAMS, SEGREGATED SPORT, EQUALITY, DISCRIMINATION.

2671. Evans, Virginia Lou. The Status of the American Woman in Sport 1912-1932.
PhD Thesis, University of Massachusetts, 1982. HISTORY, POWER, SPORT AS A
REFLECTION OF SOCIETY.

2672. Geadelmann, Patricia L. (ed.). Equality in Sport For Women. Washington,
D.C: American Alliance for Health, Physical Education and Recreation, 1977.
EQUALITY, COMPLIANCE AGENCIES, PRECEDENTS, STEREOTYPES, CHANGE,
AFFIRMATIVE ACTION.

2673. Gerber, Ellen W., Jan Felshin, Pearl Berlin, and Waneen Wyrick (eds.). The
American Woman in Sport. Reading, MA: Addison-Wesley Publishing
Company, Inc., 1974. HISTORY, ROLE OF SPORTS IN SOCIETY, PSYCHOLOGY.

2674. Gibson, Althea with Richard Curtis. So Much to Live For. New York: G. P.
Putnam's Sons, 1968. PRO TENNIS, PRO GOLF, PREJUDICE, BLACK ATHLETES.

2675. Green, Tina Sloan, Carole A. Oglesby, Alpha Alexander, and Nikki Franke.
Black Women in Sport. Reston, VA: American Alliance for Health, Physical
Education, Recreation and Dance, 1981. MINORITIES, MYTHS, PREJUDICE,
RACISM, NIGERIA, FUTURE.

2676. Greendorfer, Susan Louise. The Nature of Female Socialization Into Sport: A Study of Selected College Women's Sport Participation. Unpublished Ph.D. Dissertation, University of Wisconsin, 1974. SOCIALIZATION, CHILDREN, REWARDS FOR PARTICIPATION.

2677. Harris, Dorothy (ed.). Women and Sport: A National Research Conference. University Park, PA: Pennsylvania State University Press, 1972. PSYCHOLOGY, SOCIOLOGY, PHYSIOLOGICAL, BIOMECHANICAL CONSIDERATIONS, FANS, COACHES, BUSINESS VALUES, SOCIALIZATION, HYPNOSIS, MOTIVATION, AGGRESSION.

2678. Hoepner, Barbara J. (ed.). Women's Athletics: Coping with Controversy. Washington, D.C: American Association for Health, Physical Education and Recreation, 1974. WOMEN'S RIGHTS, INTERCOLLEGIATE ATHLETICS, AIAW, FUTURE, OLYMPICS, SPORTSMANIA, SOCIOLOGY.

2679. Howell, Reet A. (ed.). Her Story in Sport: A Historical Anthology of Women in Sports. West Point, NY: Leisure Press, 1982. EQUALITY, INTERCOLLEGIATE ATHLETICS, CASE STUDIES.

2680. Huey, Lynda. A Running Start: An Athlete, A Woman. New York: Quadrangle/New York Times Book Company, 1976. TRACK, EQUALITY, MINORITIES, OLYMPIC BOYCOTT.

2681. Johnson, William Oscar and Nancy P. Williamson. 'Whatta-Gal': The Babe Didrikson Story. Boston: Little, Brown and Company, 1977. GOLF, TRACK AND FIELD, BASKETBALL, BLACK ATHLETES.

2682. Jones, Barbara Ann Sewell. Impact of Title IX on Women's Athletic Programs of Selected State Universities in Texas: A Critical Assessment. Ed.D. Thesis, Texas Southern University, 1979. SEX DISCRIMINATION, COMPLIANCE, COLLEGE SPORTS.

2683. Jones, Betty Millsaps. Nancy Lieberman: Basketball's Magic Lady. New York: Harvey House Publishers, 1980. COLLEGE BASKETBALL, OLD DOMINION UNIVERSITY.

2684. Kaplan, Janice. Women and Sports. New York: The Viking Press, 1979. SEX AND SPORTS, COMPETITION, ROLE CONFLICT.

2685. Klafs, Carl E. and M. Joan Lyon. The Female Athlete: Conditioning, Competition and Culture. St. Louis: C. V. Mosby Company, 1978. ROLE OF SPORT IN SOCIETY, CULTURAL, COMPETITION.

2686. Lenskyj, Helen. Out of Bounds: Women, Sport and Sexuality. Toronto: The Women's Press, 1986. SPORTS MEDICINE, COMPETITION, EQUAL OPPORTUNITY, FEMINITY, ROLE CONFLICT.

2687. Lichtenstein, Grace. A Long Way, Baby: Behind the Scenes in Women's Pro Tennis. New York: William Morrow and Company, Inc., 1974. BILLIE JEAN KING, AGGRESSIVENESS, COMPETITION.

2688. Livingston, Laurie Anne. Toward An Understanding of Women Who Avoid Sports: A Cognitive-Behavorial Assessment of the Female Athletic Nonparticipant. Ed.D Thesis, Boston University, 1983. ATHLETIC PARTICIPATION, ROLE MODELS, BENEFIT AND HARM.

2689. Lumpkin, Angela. Women's Tennis: A Historical Documentary of the Players and Their Game. Troy, NY: The Whitston Publishing Company, Inc., 1981. AMATEURISM, EQUALITY, BILLIE JEAN KING, BOBBY RIGGS.

2690. Mangan, James Anthony and Roberta J. Park (eds.). From 'Fair Sex' to Feminism: Sport and the Socialization of Women in the Industrial and Post-Industrial Eras. London: Frank Cass and Company Ltd., 1987. GENDER, ROLE CONFLICTS, HISTORY.

2691. Oglesby, Carole A. (ed.). Women and Sport: From Myth to Reality. Philadelphia: Lea and Febiger, 1978. STEREOTYPES, ROLE CONFLICT, SOCIALIZATION, MYTHS, SOCIAL CHANGE, CIVIL RIGHTS.

2692. Parkhouse, Bonnie L. and Jackie Lapin. The Woman in Athletic Administration. Santa Monica, CA: Goodyear Publishing Company, Inc., 1980. MANAGEMENT, ATHLETIC DIRECTORS, COACHES, RULES, COLLEGE SPORTS, SCHOLARSHIPS, COED SPORTS, MONEY.

2693. Parkhouse, Bonnie L. and Jackie Lapin. Women Who Win: Exercising Your Rights in Sport. Englewood Cliffs, NJ: Prentice-Hall, Inc., 1980. EQUALITY, TITLE IX, LAW, SCHOLARSHIPS.

2694. Postow, Betsy C. (ed.). Women, Philosophy and Sport: A Collection of New Essays. Metuchen, NJ: The Scarecrow Press, Inc., 1983. FAIRNESS, MEDIA, COMPETITION, EQUALITY, OVEREMPHASIS ON WINNING, SEX DISCRIMINATION.

2695. Remley, Mary L. (ed.). Women in Sport: A Guide to Information Sources. Detroit: Gale Research Company, 1980. HISTORY, REFERENCE, BIBLIOGRAPHY.

2696. Simri, Uriel. A Concise World History of Women's Sports. Wingate, Israel: Wingate Institute for Physical Education and Sport, 1983. DISCRIMINATION, OLYMPICS, TITLE IX.

2697. Simri, Uriel. A Historical Analysis of the Role of Women in the Modern Olympic Games. Netanya, Israel: The Wingate Institute for Physical Education and Sport, 1977. PIERRE DE COUBERTIN, SWIMMING, TRACK AND FIELD, GERMANY, USSR.

2698. Sparhawk, Ruth M. (comp.). American Women in Sport, 1887-1987: A 100-Year Chronology. Metuchen, NJ: The Scarecrow Press, 1989. TITLE IX, BIBLIOGRAPHY, HISTORY, REFERENCE.

2699. Twin, Stephanie L. (ed.). Out of the Bleachers: Writings on Women and Sport. Old Westbury, NY: The Feminist Press, 1979. TITLE IX, QUEST FOR EXCELLENCE, HISTORY, OLYMPICS, SEX DISCRIMINATION.

2700. Zaharias, Babe Didrikson and Harry Paxton. This Life I've Led: My Autobiography. New York: A. C. Barnes and Company, 1955. WINNING, GOLF, DISCRIMINATION, BASKETBALL, TRACK AND FIELD, CANCER.

Articles

2701. Acosta, R. Vivian and Linda Jean Carpenter. "Status of Women in Athletics--Changes and Causes." Journal of Physical Education, Recreation and Dance. 56, No.6 (August 1985), 35-37. INTERCOLLEGIATE ATHLETICS, WOMEN ADMINISTRATORS AND COACHES.

2702. Acosta, R. Vivian and Linda Jean Carpenter. "Women in Athletics--A Status Report." Journal of Physical Education, Recreation and Dance. 56, No.6 (August 1985), 30-34. DECLINE OF FEMALE COACHES AND ADMINISTRATORS, HIGH SCHOOL ATHLETICS, INTERCOLLEGIATE ATHLETICS, CHANGE AND REFORM.

2703. Adedeji, John A. "Social Change and Women in African Sport." International Social Science Journal. 34, No.2 (1982), 209-218. HISTORY, SOCIAL STATUS, NEW ROLES, SOCIALIZATION, SOCIAL EMANCIPATION, SOCIO-ECONOMIC CHANGE, EDUCATIONAL AND CULTURAL CHANGE.

2704. Appenzeller, Herb and C. Thomas Ross. "Title IX Update." Sports and the Courts. 4, No.1 (Winter 1983), 12-14. SEX DISCRIMINATION SUITS, ATTITUDE OF COURTS, WOMEN'S SPORTS REVOLUTION IN REMISSION.

2705. Armitage, Shelley. "The Lady as Jock: A Popular Culture Perspective on the Woman Athlete." Journal of Popular Culture. 10, No.1 (Summer 1976), 122-132. ADVERTISING, FEMINITY/SPORT CONFLICT, ROLE CONFLICT, TITLE IX.

2706. Beezley, William H. and Joseph P. Hobbs. "'Nice Girls Don't Sweat': Women in American Sport." Journal of Popular Culture. 16, No.4 (Spring 1983), 42-53. HISTORY, INTERCOLLEGIATE ATHLETICS, AIAW, TITLE IX, DISCRIMINATION, SPORT AS A MIRROR OF SOCIETY.

2707. Belliotti, Raymond A. "Women, Sex and Sports." Journal of the Philosophy of Sport. 6 (Fall 1979), 67-72. SEXUAL EQUALITY, BASIC VS. SCARCE BENEFITS, SELF RESPECT.

2708. Bentsen, Cheryl. "When Men Coach Women--Do They Have to Score?" Ms. 5, No.2 (August 1976), 24-31. UNIVERSITY OF CALIFORNIA AT LOS ANGELES, CHUCK BEBUS, COACHES, TRACK AND FIELD, BOYCOTTS.

2709. Biles, Fay R. "Women and the 1984 Olympics." Journal of Physical Education, Recreation and Dance. 55, No.5 (May/June 1984), 64-65+. OPPORTUNITIES FOR WOMEN, INCLUSION, RELIGION, CAREERS.

2710. Birrell, Susan. "Separatism as an Issue in Women's Sport." Arena Review. 8, No.2 (July 1984), 21-29. FEMINIST ANALYSIS, SEGREGATION, INTEGRATION.

2711. Birrell, Susan. "The Woman Athlete's College Experience: Knowns and Unknowns." Journal of Sport and Social Issues. 11, Nos.1&2 (December 1987), 82-96. INTERCOLLEGIATE ATHLETICS, REFORM, DRUG USE, RETIREMENT.

2712. Blinde, Elaine M. "Contrasting Orientations Toward Sport: Pre- and Post-Title IX Athletes." Journal of Sport and Social Issues. 10, No.1 (Winter/Spring 1986), 6-14. CHANGE, ATTITUDES, ACADEMICS.

2713. Boxill, J. M. "Beauty, Sport and Gender." Journal of the Philosophy of Sport. 11 (1984), 36-47. SPORT AS ART, AESTHETICS, EFFICIENCY, VICTORY, SELF EXPRESSION.

2714. Bray, Cathy. "Sport, Capitalism, and Patriarchy." Canadian Woman Studies. 4, No.3 (Spring/May 1983), 11-13. IDEOLOGY, COMMERCIALIZATION OF SPORTS, SPORT/FEMINITY CONFLICT, INEQUALITY.

2715. Bronson, Gail. "Hitting Stride: Women, Long Ignored as College Athletes, Move Into 'Big-Time'." Wall Street Journal. 185, No.108 (June 4, 1975), 1+. MALE DOMINATION OF SPORTS, GAINS IN WOMEN'S SPORTS, MILITANT ATTITUDE OF FEMALES.

2716. Bryson, Lois. "Sport and the Oppression of Women." The Australian and New Zealand Journal of Sociology. 19, No.3 (November 1983), 413-426. SEXISM, COMPLEXITY OF THE RELATIONSHIP BETWEEN SPORT AND GENDER INEQUALITY, SPORT AS A CONTRIBUTOR TO MALE DOMINANCE, ISOLATION OF WOMEN FROM SOCIAL POWER, PATRIARCHAL IDEOLOGY, SPORT AS RITUAL.

2717. Campbell, Patricia B. "Women in Sports in Children's Books: Wealthy, White and Winning." Interracial Books for Children Bulletin. 10, No.4 (1979), 3-10. OLYMPICS, HISTORY, TITLE IX, BILLIE JEAN KING/BOBBY RIGGS MATCH, MINORITY WOMEN, ANTI-SEXIST BOOKS.

2718. Coffey, Margaret A. "The Sportswoman--Then and Now." Journal of Health, Physical Education and Recreation.   36, No.2 (February 1965), 38-41+. HISTORY, SOCIALIZATION.

2719. "Comes the Revolution." Time. 111, No.26 (June 26, 1978), 54-59. GROWTH OF WOMEN'S SPORTS, TITLE IX, REGULATIONS, FUTURE, CHANGE.

2720. Davenport, Joanna.   "The Women's Movement into the Olympic Games." Journal of Physical Education and Recreation. 49, No.3 (March 1978), 58-60. DISCRIMINATION, HISTORY, ACCEPTANCE.

2721. Davison, Fred C. "Intercollegiate Athletics and Title IX: Equal Opportunity or Federal Incursion." USA Today.   108, No.2410 (July 1979), 34-37. LEGISLATIVE HISTORY, REGULATIONS, POLICY INTERPRETATION.

2722. Diem, Liselott. "Women in Sport Today: Aspects and Problems." International Journal of Physical Education. 18, No.3 (Fall 1981), 23-26. OVERCOMING RESTRICTIONS, ROLE MODELS, COOPERATION, MALE EMANCIPATION.

2723. Duncan, Margaret Carlisle. "Women and Leisure in Feminist Fiction." Quest. 35, No.2 (1983), 120-130. DEFINITION OF LEISURE, LEISURE PATTERNS IN FEMINIST FICTION.

2724. Dunn, Kathleen. "Women Getting Olympic Runaround." The Physician and Sportsmedicine. 8, No.1 (January 1980), 20-21. LONG DISTANCE EVENTS, OLYMPICS, ATTITUDES.

2725. Dworkin, Susan. "Sexism Strikes Out: New Jersey Girls Get to First Base in Little League." Ms. 2, No.11 (May 1974), 20. SEXISM, COURT CASE.

2726. Edwards, Harry. "Desegregating Sexist Sport." Intellectual Digest. 3, No.3 (November 1972), 82-83. SEXISM, DESEGREGATION, RELIGION AND SPORT.

2727. English, Jane. "Sex Equality in Sports." Philosophy and Public Affairs. 7, No.3 (Spring 1978), 269-277. EQUAL OPPORTUNITY, GENDER DIFFERENCES, SPATIAL PERCEPTION, VERBAL ABILITY, JUSTICE, BENEFIT AND HARM, BENEFIT OF SPORTS TO WOMEN, LEARNING TO WIN AND LOSE, CHARACTER, COOPERATION.

2728. Engstrand, Gary. "Don't Expect Fair Play from the NCAA for Women." The Chronicle of Higher Education. 21, No.17 (December 15, 1980), 19. WOMEN'S VOICE IN ATHLETICS, NCAA, EQUAL OPPORTUNITY, JUSTICE, AIAW.

2729. Farrell, Charles S. "Many Women Link Anti-Sex Bias Law to Outstanding Olympic Performances." The Chronicle of Higher Education. 29, No.1 (August 29, 1984), 31-32. TITLE IX, NCAA, RETRENCHMENT, GROVE CITY COLLEGE CASE.

2730. Felshin, Jan. "The Triple Option...For Women in Sport." Quest. 21 (January 1974), 36-40. FEMINITY, DEFINITION OF SPORT, FUTURE.

2731. Felshin, Jan and Carole A. Oglesby. "Transcending Tradition: Females and Males in Open Competition." Journal of Physical Education, Recreation and Dance. 57, No.3 (March 1986), 44-47+. EXCELLENCE, DISCRIMINATION, EQUALITY, SEPARATION.

2732. Fields, Cheryl M. "Must Women Copy Men to Gain Equality in Athletics?" The Chronicle of Higher Education. 13, No.18 (January 17, 1977), 8. BAN ON PAYING COACHES TO RECRUIT, LIMIT ON SCHOLARSHIPS, GRADE POINT AVERAGES, LAW, EQUAL OPPORTUNITY, AIAW.

2733. Fields, Cheryl M. "U. S. Anti-Sex-Bias Law Covers College Sports, Federal Judge Rules." The Chronicle of Higher Education. 23, No.9 (October 28, 1981), 18. TEMPLE UNIVERSITY, TITLE IX, EQUAL OPPORTUNITY.

2734. Flygare, Thomas J. "Federal Court in Michigan Holds That Title IX Does Not Cover Athletics." Phi Delta Kappan. 62, No.10 (June 1981), 741-742. SEX DISCRIMINATION, LAWSUITS.

2735. Flygare, Thomas J. "HEW's New Guidelines On Sex Discrimination in Collegiate Athletics." Phi Delta Kappan. 60, No.7 (March 1979), 529-530. TITLE IX, LAW, EQUALITY.

2736. Footlick, Jerrold K. "Of Sports, Sex and Money." Newsweek. 97 (March 16, 1981), 98+. TITLE IX, EQUAL BUDGETS, GUIDELINES.

2737. Gaines, Lynn. "Missing Persons: How No Pass, No Play Affects Women." Women's Sports and Fitness. 8, No.11 (November 1986), 20. PROPOSITION 48, SAT SCORES, GRADE POINT AVERAGES, MINORITIES.

2738. Geadelmann, Patricia L. "Equality in Athletics: Can Separate Be Equal?" Journal of Physical Education and Recreation. 49, No.9 (November/December 1978), 32-33+. TITLE IX, SEGREGATION, DISCRIMINATION.

2739. Gerber, Ellen W. "The Controlled Development of Collegiate Sport for Women 1923-1936." Journal of Sport History. 2, No.1 (Spring 1975), 1-28. COMPETITION, CHANGES, HISTORY AND DEVELOPMENT OF WOMEN'S COLLEGIATE SPORT, ACADEMICS, SPORTS MEDICINE.

2740. Gilbert, Bil and Nancy P. Williamson. "Are You Being Two-Faced?" Sports Illustrated. 38, No.2 (June 4, 1973), 44-54. MASCULINIZATION OF WOMEN IN SPORTS, STEREOTYPES OF FEMALES IN SPORTS, INJUSTICE, MYTHS.

2741. Gilbert, Bil and Nancy P. Williamson. "Programmed to Be Losers." Sports Illustrated. 38, No.23 (June 11, 1973), 60-73. LIMITED ACCESS OF GIRLS TO ATHLETICS, AGGRESSIVENESS, WINNING, DISCRIMINATION IN SPORTS, MALE DOMINATION, JUSTICE.

2742. Gilbert, Bil and Nancy P. Williamson. "Sport is Unfair to Women." Sports Illustrated. 38, No.21 (May 28, 1973), 88-98. PREJUDICE, INEQUALITY, MONEY, DOUBLE STANDARD, PSYCHOLOGICAL DISCRIMINATION.

2743. Gilbert, Bil and Nancy P. Williamson. "Women in Sport: A Progress Report." Sports Illustrated. 41, No.5 (July 29, 1974), 26-31. DISCRIMINATION, EFFECT OF WOMEN'S MOVEMENT.

2744. Giuliani, Carla. "Sport and Women: Which Will Liberate the Other." Olympic Message. 12 (December 1985), 35-50. WOMEN GAINING GROUND, DIFFERENCES IN STATUS BETWEEN WOMEN IN THE FIRST AND THIRD WORLDS, MISCONCEPTIONS ABOUT FEMALE ATHLETES.

2745. "Giving Girls a Sporting Chance?" Senior Scholastic. 107, No.2 (September 23, 1975), 18+. DISCRIMINATION, EQUALITY, MONEY, SEPARATISM, COED SPORTS.

2746. Goodman, Cary. "Degoaling Sports." Sport Sociology Bulletin. 5, No.2 (Fall 1976), 11-13. GOAL ATTAINMENT, COMPETITION, PLAY, HIERARCHY.

2747. Grant, Christine H. B. "The Gender Gap in Sport: From Olympic to Intercollegiate Level." Arena Review. 8, No.2 (July 1984), 31-47. HOCKEY, NCAA, AIAW, VALUES, GENDER.

236 Sport and Society

2748. Griffin, Patricia S. "R. R. Knudson's Sport Fiction: A Feminist Critique." Arete: The Journal of Sport Literature. 3, No.1 (Fall 1985), 3-10. FEMINIST CRITIQUE OF SPORT FICTION FOR CHILDREN, IMAGES OF WOMEN, RELATIONSHIP BETWEEN MALES AND FEMALES, STANDARDS OF SUCCESS, SEX DISCRIMINATION.

2749. Hall, M. Ann, Dallas Cullen and Trevor Slack. "Organizational Elites Recreating Themselves: The Gender Structure of National Sport Organizations." Quest. 41, No.1 (April 1989), 28-45. GENDER, ORGANIZATIONAL BEHAVIOR.

2750. Hannon, Kent. "Too Far, Too Fast." Sports Illustrated. 48, No.13 (March 20, 1978), 34-45. WOMEN'S INTERCOLLEGIATE BASKETBALL, TITLE IX, UNRESTRAINED GROWTH, RULE-FLOUTING COACHES, RECRUITING SCANDALS, NCAA REGULATIONS, AIAW REGULATIONS.

2751. Harris, Dorothy V. "Fallacies About Women in Sports." Stratagies: A Journal for Physical and Sport Educators. 1, No.6 (June 1988), 13-17. TITLE IX, MALE DOMAIN, LAW, SEX DISCRIMINATION, BENEFIT AND HARM, ROLE MODELS, INJURIES, COMPETITION, GENDER DIFFERENCES.

2752. Hart, Marie. "Sport: Women Sit in the Back of the Bus." Psychology Today. 5, No.5 (October 1971), 64-66. ROLE CONFLICT, MALE PERFORMANCE STANDARDS, FEMININITY, MYTHS.

2753. Holland, Judith R. and Carole Oglesby. "Women in Sport: The Synthesis Begins." The Annals of the American Academy of Political and Social Science. 445 (September 1979), 80-90. CHANGES, BENEFIT AND HARM, SOCIALIZATION, AIAW.

2754. Hook, Janet. "Bell Unveils 'Flexible' Approach to Settling Complaints of Sex Bias in College Athletics." The Chronicle of Higher Education. 22, No.10 (April 27, 1981), 1+. TERREL BELL, EDUCATION SECRETARY, SEX DISCRIMINATION, UNIVERSITY OF AKRON, TITLE IX.

2755. Hoppes, Steven. "Playing Together--Values and Arrangements of Coed Sports." Journal of Physical Education, Recreation and Dance. 58, No.8 (October 1987), 65-67. BENEFIT AND HARM, PLAY, VALUES.

2756. "How Has Athletics Changed? From Title IX: The Half Full, Half Empty Glass." Graduate Woman. 76, No.1 (January/February 1982), 19-22. HIGH SCHOOLS, INTERCOLLEGIATE ATHLETICS, ATHLETIC BUDGETS, SCHOLARSHIPS, TITLE IX.

2757. Howard, Lisa. "Ms. Right and Mr. Wrong." Women's Sports and Fitness. 9, No.10 (October 1987), 45. MORAL DEVELOPMENT, COMPETITIVE WINNING AT ALL COSTS.

2758. Howe, Harold II. "Sex, Sports and Discrimination." The Chronicle of Higher Education. 18, No.15 (June 18, 1979), 72. TITLE IX, GOVERNMENT ENFORCEMENT, SEX DISCRIMINATION, BIG TIME COLLEGE SPORTS, EQUAL OPPORTUNITY.

2759. Howell, Maxwell L. and Reet A. Howell. "Women in Sport in the United States, 1900-1914." Abstracts of Research Papers. (1979), 8. CHANGING ROLE OF WOMEN, CAUSES OF INCREASED PARTICIPATION, INDUSTRIALIZATION, URBANIZATION, INVENTION, EDUCATION, HISTORICAL.

2760. Huckle, Patricia. "Back to the Starting Line: Title IX and Women's Intercollegiate Athletics." American Behavioral Scientist. 21, No.3 (January/February 1978), 379-392. INTERCOLLEGIATE ATHLETICS, MONEY, POWER, DEMAND BY WOMEN FOR GREATER RESOURCES, POLITICAL CONFLICT.

2761. Hult, Joan S. "The Philosophical Conflicts in Men's and Women's Collegiate Athletics." Quest. 32, No.1 (1980), 77-94. FUNCTION OF INTERCOLLEGIATE ATHLETICS IN HIGHER EDUCATION, NCAA, AIAW, TITLE IX, INFLUENCE OF SOCIAL AND CULTURAL FACTORS ON ATHLETICS.

2762. Jackson, Susan A. and Herbert W. Marsh. "Athletic or Antisocial? The Female Sport Experience." Journal of Sport Psychology. 8, No.3 (September 1986), 198-211. ROLE CONFLICT, SEX-ROLE IDENTIFICATION, SELF CONCEPT.

2763. Jordan, Pat. "From the Land of Cotton." Sports Illustrated. 43, No.23 (December 8, 1975), 86-98. WILLYE B. WHITE, TRACK AND FIELD, UNESCO, FAIR PLAY AWARD, RACE RELATIONS.

2764. "Just One of The Boys." Newsweek. 80, No.1 (July 3, 1972), 43. SHEILA MORAN, FEMALE SPORTS WRITERS, SEXISM.

2765. Karlsberg, Elizabeth. "Battle of the Sexes: Do Girls Have a Sporting Chance?" Teen. 32, No.3 (March 1988), 80-81. GENDER DIFFERENCES, LAWSUITS, BENEFIT AND HARM, WINNING AT ALL COSTS.

2766. Kirkpatrick, Curry. "Getting Into the Picture." Sports Illustrated. 42, No.16 (April 21, 1975), 84-96. FEMALE SPORTSCASTERS, JEANNIE MORRIS, LIZ BISHOP, ANITA MARTINI, JANE CHASTAIN, TELEVISION.

2767. Klein, Frederick C. "Girls Wooed Today Are Often Wooed for Athletic Ability." Wall Street Journal. 193, No.88 (May 4, 1979), 1+. RECRUITING, AIAW, ABUSES.

2768. Krotee, March L. "The Battle of the Sexes: A Brawl in the Locker Rooms." Journal of Sport and Social Issues. 5, No.2 (Fall/Winter 1981), 15-23. CONFLICT BETWEEN THE AIAW AND THE NCAA, TITLE IX.

2769. La Noue, George R. "Athletics and Equality: How to Comply with Title IX Without Tearing Down the Stadium." Change: The Magazine of Higher Learning. 8, No.10 (November 1976), 27-30+. MEANING OF EQUALITY, INTERCOLLEGIATE ATHLETICS, SEXUAL INEQUALITY, SEPARATE BUT EQUAL TEAMS, COED TEAMS, REFORM.

2770. Ladd, Tony. "The Girl Who Broke and Set the Gender Barrier in Baseball." North American Society for Sport History Proceedings and Newsletter. (1978), 31. CONSERVATIVE SOCIAL FORCES, SOCIAL CHANGE.

2771. Leaman, Oliver. "Sport and the Feminist Novel." Physical Education Review. 5, No.2 (Autumn 1982), 100-106. EXCLUSION OF SPORT IN FEMINIST NOVELS, FEMALE ALIENATION FROM SPORTS.

2772. Leepson, Marc. "Women in Sports." Editorial Research Reports. 1, No.17 (May 6, 1977), 331-348. STEREOTYPING, STATUS OF FEMALES IN PRO SPORTS, TITLE IX, NCAA, UNEQUAL TREATMENT, REFORM, FUTURE.

2773. Lemley, Ann T. "Women's Sports at Cornell: Moving Toward Parity." Human Ecology Forum. 11, No.1 (Summer 1980), 19-21. TITLE IX, HISTORY, RECRUITMENT, FACILITIES.

2774. Lenskyj, Helen. "We Want to Play...We'll Play: Women and Sport in the Twenties and Thirties." Canadian Woman Studies. 4, No.3 (Spring/May 1983) 15-18. COMPETITION, SPORT/FEMINITY CONFLICT, DORIS BUTWELL CRAIG, GLADYS GIGG ROSS, HILDA THOMAS SMITH.

2775. Ley, Katherine. "Women in Sports: Where Do We Go From Here, Boys?" Phi Delta Kappan. 56, No.2 (October 1974), 129-131. TITLE IX, EQUALITY, VALUES, BENEFIT AND HARM.

2776. Lichtenstein, Grace. "A Fight to Remember." World Tennis. 36, No.4 (September 1988) 26+. BILLIE JEAN KING, BOBBY RIGGS, HISTORY.

2777. Lichtenstein, Grace. "The Wooing of Women Athletes." The New York Times Magazine. (February 8, 1981), 26-27+. BIG BUSINESS, CORRUPTION, AGENTS.

2778. Lichtenstein, Grace. "Women in Sports." Horizon. 21, No.7 (July 1978), 50-57. EXPLOSION OF INTEREST IN WOMEN'S SPORTS, TELEVISION COVERAGE, MONEY, CONTACT SPORTS.

2779. Lieberman, Nancy. "Sexism in 'Men-only' Sports: Why I'm Not a Victim." Glamour. 85, No.8 (August 1987), 64. BASKETBALL, INTIMIDATION, COED SPORTS.

2780. Lopiano, Donna A. "A Political Analysis of the Possibility of Impact Alternatives For the Accomplishment of Feminist Objectives Within American Intercollegiate Sport." Arena Review. 8, No.2 (July 1984), 49-61. NCAA, FUTURE, MALE SUPREMACY.

2781. Lopiano, Donna A. "Fair Play for All (Even Women)." The New York Times. 139 (April 15, 1990), S10. UNIVERSITY OF OKLAHOMA, DISCONTINUATION OF WOMEN'S BASKETBALL, FORMULA FOR SUCCESS OF WOMEN'S SPORTS TEAMS.

2782. Malmisur, Michael C. "Title IX Dilemma: Meritocratic and Egalitarian Tension." Journal of Sport Behavior. 1, No.3 (August 1978), 130-138. IDEOLOGIES, STATUS OF TITLE IX, POLITICAL ACTION.

2783. Messner, Michael A. "Sports and Male Domination: The Female Athlete as Contested Ideological Terrain." Sociology of Sport Journal. 5, No.3 (September 1988), 197-211. ORGANIZED SPORTS, POLITICS OF GENDER RELATIONS, MALE SUPERIORITY, EQUALITY, SELF DEFINITION.

2784. Middleton, Lorenzo. "Equal Spending for Men's, Women's Sports Endorsed by U.S. Civil Rights Commission." The Chronicle of Higher Education. 19, No.3 (September 17, 1979), 15-16. FEDERAL REGULATIONS, EQUAL SPENDING, TITLE IX, SUBSTANTIALLY EQUAL CONCEPT.

2785. Middleton, Lorenzo and Cheryl M. Fields. "NCAA Votes to Widen Role in Women's Sports; Action is Bitterly Debated, 'Power Play' Charged." The Chronicle of Higher Education. 21, No.19 (January 19, 1981), 6. NCAA, AIAW, POLICIES, LACK OF AUTONOMY.

2786. Mitchell, Sheila. "Women's Participation in the Olympic Games, 1900-1926." Journal of Sport History. 4, No.2 (Summer 1977), 208-228. PIERRE DE COUBERTIN, INTERNATIONAL OLYMPIC COMMITTEE.

2787. Nabil, Philip A. "Women in Society and Sport: Democracy or Hypocrisy?" The Physical Educator. 32, No.4 (December 1975), 180-181. SPORTS AS A REFLECTION OF SOCIETY, CHANGE.

2788. Novak, Michael. "Can Girls Play Football, Daddy?" Commonweal. 97, No.16 (January 26, 1973), 366+. WOMEN'S LIBERATION, SPECIALIZATION, HEROISM.

2789. Oberlander, Susan. "Soft-Spoken Woman May Be In Line to Strike a Blow for Equality of the Sexes in Sports Administration." The Chronicle of Higher Education. 34, No.18 (January 13, 1988), A37-38. CHARLOTTE WEST, SOUTHERN ILLINOIS UNIVERSITY, ACTING ATHLETIC DIRECTOR.

2790. Oberlander, Susan. "Trial Begins in Sex-Bias Lawsuit Against Temple University; Charge is Added Under New U. S. Civil-Rights Act." The Chronicle of Higher Education. 34, No.31 (April 13, 1988), A43-44. TEMPLE UNIVERSITY, SEX DISCRIMINATION TRIAL, VIOLATION OF CIVIL RIGHTS RESTORATION ACT, TITLE IX.

2791. Oliphant, Judith Lee. "Title IX's Promise of Equality of Opportunity in Athletics: Does It Cover the Bases?" Kentucky Law Journal. 64, (1975/1976), 432-464. EQUAL PROTECTION STANDARD, ATHLETIC DISCRIMINATION SUITS, EQUALITY OF OPPORTUNITY IN EDUCATION, LEGISLATIVE HISTORY OF TITLE IX, DEVELOPMENT OF REGULATIONS FOR TITLE IX, JUSTICE.

2792. Oriard, Michael V. "Jennifer Levin's Water Dancer and the Feminist Sports Novel." North American Society for Sport History Proceedings and Newsletter. (1986), 9-10. FEMINISM, TITLE IX, MYTHS.

2793. Orleans, Jeffrey H. "Title IX and Athletics: Time Out?" Educational Record. 63, No.1 (Winter 1982), 40-44. EXEMPTION FOR REVENUE-PRODUCING MEN'S SPORTS, INTERCOLLEGIATE ATHLETICS, ANTITRUST.

2794. Park, Roberta J. "'Embodied Selves': The Rise and Development of Concern for Physical Education, Active Games and Recreation for American Women, 1776-1865." Journal of Sport History. 5, No.2 (Summer 1978), 5-41. TITLE IX, SPORTS MEDICINE.

2795. Phillips, Terry Don. "HEW's Interpretation of Title IX Leaves Questions Unanswered." Athletic Purchasing and Facilities. 3, No.9 (October 1979), 16+. ATHLETIC ADMINISTRATORS, DISCRIMINATION, HEW.

2796. Pogge-Strubing, Marianne. "The Sexist Underground in Sports." Update on Law-Related Education. 7, No.2 (Spring 1983), 16-19+. TITLE IX, GUIDELINES, CONTACT SPORTS, ENFORCEMENT.

2797. Postow, Betsy C. "Masculine Sports Revisited." Journal of the Philosophy of Sport. 8 (Fall 1981), 60-63. SEXISM, ANDROGYNISM, MALE SOLIDARITY, IMAGE OF FEMALE INFERIORITY, PHYSIOLOGICAL DIFFERENCES.

2798. Postow, Betsy C. "Sport, Art, and Gender." Journal of the Philosophy of Sport. 11 (1984), 52-55. SPORT AS AN ART FORM, SEXISM, RULES, REFORM.

2799. Postow, Betsy C. "Women and Masculine Sports." Journal of the Philosophy of Sport. 7 (Fall 1980), 51-58. GENDER IDENTITY, ANTIANDROGYNISM, SEX SEGREGATION.

2800. Potera, Carol. "Women in Sports: The Price of Participation." The Physician and Sportsmedicine. 14, No.6 (June 1986), 149-150+. TRAINING, INJURIES, HEREDITY.

2801. Pottker, Janice and Andrew Fishel. "Separate and Unequal: Sex Discrimination in Interscholastic Sports." Integrated Education: A Report on Race and Schools. 14, No.2 (March-April 1976), 3-7. TITLE IX, PARTICIPATION RATES, FUNDING LEVELS, CHANGE, SOURCE OF FUNDING.

2802. Riley, Marie. "Title X: A Proposal for a Law to Guarantee Equal Opportunity for Nonathletes." Journal of Physical Education and Recreation. 46, No.6 (June 1975), 31. EQUALITY, DISCRIMINATION, NON-ATHLETES.

2803. Rohrbaugh, Joanna Bunker. "Feminity on the Line." Psychology Today. 13, No.3 (August 1979), 30-42. GENDER IDENTITY, ROLE CONFLICT, MASCULINIZATION, ATHLETIC PERSONALITY, COMPETITION, EQUALITY.

2804. Rohrbaugh, Joanna Bunker. "Superwomen to Match Supermen." Psychology Today. 13, No.3 (August 1979), 38. TITLE IX, REACTION BY MALE AND FEMALE ATHLETIC DIRECTORS, ATHLETIC SCHOLARSHIPS FOR FEMALES, WINNING IS EVERYTHING ATTITUDE.

2805. Rothlein, Lewis. "A Taboo Whose Time Has Gone." Women's Sports and Fitness. 10, No.7 (October/November 1988), 56. WILSON REPORT, ACCEPTANCE OF GIRLS IN SPORTS, BIAS.

2806. Sabock, Ralph J. and Carol J. Kadingo. "Sports and Ethics: Survey Indicates Female Athletes Have Proper Behavioral Attitudes." Interscholastic Athletic Administration. 13, No.3 (Spring 1987), 14-15. GENDER DIFFERENCES, HIGH SCHOOL SPORTS, FAIR PLAY, EMPIRICAL STUDY.

2807. Sage, George H. and Sheryl Loudermilk. "The Female Athlete and Role Conflict." Research Quarterly. 50, No.1 (March 1979), 88-96. GENDER, PERCEPTIONS VS. ACTUALITY.

2808. Sandler, Bernice. "Title IX: Antisexism's Big Legal Stick." American Education. 13, No.4 (May 1977), 6-9. INSTITUTIONS COVERED BY TITLE IX, DISCRIMINATION, SINGLE SEX SPORTS.

2809. Satterthwaite, Frank. "Men Competing With Women." Esquire. 99, No.5 (May 1983), 101-104. ATTITUDES, EXCELLENCE, QUOTAS, FUTURE, COED SPORTS.

2810. Seligman, Daniel. "New Rules About Sex." Fortune. 101, No.1 (January 14, 1980), 33-34+. TITLE IX, HEW REGULATIONS, EQUAL EXPENDITURES.

2811. Sewall, Gil. "The New Sex Rules." Newsweek. 94 (December 3, 1979), 84. SEX DISCRIMINATION, TITLE IX, ENFORCEMENT, HEW GUIDELINES.

2812. "Sex Discrimination and Intercollegiate Athletics: Putting Some Muscle in Title IX." The Yale Law Journal. 88, No.6 (May 1979), 1254-1279. REGULATIONS, MIXED AND SEPARATE TEAMS, EQUAL OPPORTUNITY AND ATHLETIC SCHOLARSHIPS, EQUAL EXPENDITURES.

2813. "Sex Discrimination in Athletics: Conflicting Legislative and Judicial Approaches." Alabama Law Review. 29, No.2 (Winter 1978), 390-425. EQUAL PROTECTION, CLASS ACTIONS, SEPARATE BUT EQUAL DOCTRINE, EQUAL RIGHTS, TITLE IX, ENFORCEMENT, LAWSUITS, FUNDING.

2814. "Sex Discrimination in High School Athletics." Minnesota Law Review. 57 (1972-1973), 339-371. EQUAL PROTECTION DOCTRINE, SEX DISCRIMINATION IN ATHLETICS, SEPARATION OF SEXES, CLASSIFICATION, FUTURE.

2815. Sharp, Kathy. "Lady Referees Face the Barrier of Male Domination in the Professional Soccer Ranks." Soccer World. 6, No.4 (July/August 1979), 34-37. KNOWLEDGE OF THE GAME, PROVING ONESELF, NASL, FEMININITY.

2816. Sisley, Becky. "A New Breed: The Woman Athletic Director." Journal of Physical Education and Recreation. 46, No.6 (June 1975), 47-48. ATHLETIC DIRECTORS, COMPETENT LEADERSHIP, EQUALITY.

2817. Sisley, Becky. "Challenges Facing the Woman Athletic Director." The Physical Educator. 32, No.3 (October 1975), 121-123. TITLE IX, RESPONSIBILITIES, LEADERSHIP NEEDS, SEX DISCRIMINATION, ATHLETIC DIRECTORS.

2818. Slaughter, Mary. "Should Women Athletes Be Allowed to Play on Men's Teams?" The Physical Educator. 32, No.1 (March 1975), 9-10. TITLE IX, GENDER.

242   Sport and Society

2819. "Sportswomanlike Conduct." Newsweek. 83, No.22 (June 3, 1974), 50-55. EXCELLENCE, WOMEN'S RIGHTS, SALARIES, ROLE CONFLICT.

2820. Stark, Elizabeth. "Women's Tennis: Friends vs. Foes." Psychology Today. 18, No.7 (July 1984), 17. COMPETING AGAINST FRIENDS, PAM SHRIVER, MARTINA NAVRATILOVA.

2821. "Sultanas of Sweat." Time. 108, No.2 (July 12, 1976), 50. FEMALE SPORTS REPORTERS, EQUALITY, HURDLES.

2822. Theberge, Nancy. "A Critique of Critiques: Radical and Feminist Writings on Sport." Social Forces. 60, No.2 (December 1981), 341-353. SPORTS AS AUTHORITARIAN, EXCESSIVELY COMPETITIVE AND EXCLUSIONARY, SPORTS AS MALE-DOMINATED AND MASCULINE, INEQUITY, SECULARIZATION AND NATIONALIZATION OF SPORTS, REFORM.

2823. Theberge, Nancy. "Toward a Feminist Alternative to Sport as a Male Preserve." Quest. 37, No.2 (1985), 193-202. GENDER, INEQUALITY, ROLE CONFLICT, SOCIALIZATION.

2824. Thomas, Ann Victoria and Jan Sheldon-Wildgen. "Women in Athletics: Winning the Game But Losing the Support." The Journal of College and University Law. 8, No.3 (1981/1982), 295-330. TITLE IX, CHANGES, LEGAL DEVELOPMENTS, CONFLICT BETWEEN ORGANIZATIONAL REGULATIONS, NCAA, AIAW, FUTURE.

2825. Truby, J. David. "The Team of '48: Stinnett High's Notorious Right Tackle." Ms. 7, No.10 (April 1979), 26. FRANKIE GROVES, RULES, TITLE IX, GIRLS ON FOOTBALL TEAMS.

2826. Uhlir, Ann. "The Wolf Is Our Shepherd: Shall We Not Fear?" Phi Delta Kappan. 64, No.3 (November 1982), 172-176. MALE DOMINATION OF HIERARCHY, REFORM, JUSTICE, EQUALITY.

2827. Uhlir, Ann. "Women's Sports Education Today." The Education Digest. 48, No.8 (April 1983), 32-35. AIAW, CHANGE AND REFORM, TITLE IX, INEQUALITY.

2828. Uhlir, G. Ann. "Athletics and the University: The Post-Woman's Era." Academe: Bulletin of the American Association of University Professors. 73, No.4 (July/August 1987), 25-29. TITLE IX, AIAW, LACK OF FEMALE ADMINISTRATORS, COACHES, FINANCIAL AID DISCRIMINATION.

2829. Ulrich, Celeste. "Three, to Get Ready." Coaching: Women's Athletics. 7 (March/April 1981), 46-47. PREJUDICE, INJUSTICE, GENDER DIFFERENCES, NCAA, AIAW, TITLE IX.

2830. Unsworth, Robert E. "First Baseperson? Heroines in Young Adult Sports Fiction." School Library Journal. 27, No.9 (May 1981), 26-27. TITLE IX, GIRLS IN SPORTS NOVELS, BIBLIOGRAPHY OF GIRLS' SPORTS NOVELS.

2831. VanHorn, Elizabeth and LeRoy G. Seils. "Equality in the Use of Athletic Facilities." Journal of Physical Education and Recreation. 51, No.5 (May 1980), 22-23. EQUITY, POLICY, GENDER, JUSTICE.

2832. Vecsey, George. "Will Women Ever Play in the World Series?" Seventeen. 40 (October 1981), 100. COED LITTLE LEAGUES, JACKIE MITCHELL.

2833. Vertinsky, Patricia. "Feminist Charlotte Perkins Gilman's Pursuit of Health and Physical Fitness as a Strategy for Emancipation." Journal of Sport History. 16, No.1 (Spring 1989), 5-26. TURN-OF-THE CENTURY FEMINIST, HISTORY, FEMINISM, NON-CONFORMITY, POETRY, LIFESTYLE, WRITER, BENEFIT AND HARM OF SPORTS.

2834. Vertinsky, Patricia. "Sexual Equality and the Legacy of Catherine Beecher." Journal of Sport History. 6, No.1 (Spring 1979), 38-49. GYMNASTICS FOR GIRLS AND WOMEN, NINETEENTH CENTURY, GENDER DIFFERENCE, RELIGION, METHODISM, CALISTHENICS FOR WOMEN.

2835. Voigt, David Quentin. "Sex in Baseball: Reflections on Changing Taboos." Journal of Popular Culture. 12, No.3 (Winter 1978), 389-403. HISTORY, SEXUAL FREEDOM, INDIVIDUALISM, EQUALITY, WOMEN OWNERS, GENDER DIFFERENCES.

2836. Weiland, Walter E. "The Changing Scene in Women's Intercollegiate Athletics: Point with Pride, View with Alarm, 1971-81." The Physical Educator. 45, No.2 (Spring 1988), 74-79. AIAW, DECISION MAKING, SCHOLARSHIPS, RECRUITING, INTERCOLLEGIATE ATHLETICS.

2837. Westcott, Marcia and Jay J. Coakley. "Women in Sport: Modalities of Feminist Social Change." Journal of Sport and Social Issues. 5, No.1 (Spring/Summer 1981), 32-45. SPORT AS A CONTEXT FOR CHANGE, ASSIMILATION.

2838. Wheeler, Elizabeth. "Is There a Future for Title IX?" Ms. 9, No.9 (March 1981), 17. ENFORCEMENT OF TITLE IX, GUIDELINES, OFFICE OF CIVIL RIGHTS.

2839. Whiddon, Sue. "Title IX Encourages Growth." Coach and Athlete. 43, No.5 (March 1981), 48. BENEFIT TO WOMEN, FENCING, MONEY, FACILITIES, OPPORTUNITY FOR COMPETITION.

2840. "A Whole New Ball Game for Women." Ebony. 37, No.10 (August 1982), 116-117+. SEXISM, RACISM, CHANGE, TITLE IX.

2841. Williams, Roger M. "Education Now." Saturday Review. 5 (January 21, 1978), 56-57. TITLE IX, MALE PRESERVE, MONEY, EQUAL FACILITIES, BIG TIME COLLEGE SPORTS.

2842. "Winning Her Point in a Man's Arena." Ebony. 30, No.8 (June 1975), 44-46+. DOROTHY RICKEY, FEMALE HEAD COACH, CHICAGO STATE UNIVERSITY.

2843. Wittig, Arno F. "Sport Competition Anxiety and Sex Role." <u>Sex Roles: A Journal of Research</u>. 10, Nos.5&6 (March 1984), 469-73. COMPETITION ANXIETY, GENDER, SPORT/FEMININITY CONFLICT.

2844. "Women Want a Sporting Chance." <u>The Economist</u>. 255, No.6877 (June 14, 1975), 43-44. NCAA, AIAW, TITLE IX.

2845. "Women's Sports Boom--Too Slow For Some." <u>U. S. News and World Report</u>. 85, No.1 (July 10, 1978), 79-80. SEXUAL EQUALITY, TITLE IX, LAWSUITS, BUDGETS.

2846. Young, Iris Marion. "Throwing Like a Girl: A Phenomenology of Feminine Body Comportment, Motility, and Spatiality." <u>Human Studies</u>. 3, No.2 (April 1980), 137-156. EXISTENTIAL PHENOMENOLOGY, FEMINIST THEORY.

Reference Works

Books

2847. Burns, Grant. The Sports Pages: A Critical Bibliography of Twentieth-Century American Novels and Stories Featuring Baseball, Basketball, Football and Other Athletic Pursuits. Metuchen, NJ: Scarecrow Press, Inc., 1987.

2848. DeSensi, Joy Theresa. Exploring the Potential for Relationship in Sport. Buffalo, NY: The Philosophic Society for the Study of Sport Proceedings, 1982.

2849. Givler, Mark A. Sports and Literature: A Rationale and Guide for the Use of American Sports Literature in the Teaching of a College Undergraduate General Education Course in Fiction. PhD Thesis, University of Maryland, 1980.

2850. Gratch, Bonnie, Betty Chan and Judity Lingenfelter (comps.). Sports and Physical Education: A Guide to the Reference Resources. Westport, CT: Greenwood Press, Inc., 1983.

2851. Higgs, Robert J. Sports: A Reference Guide. Westport, CT: Greenwood Press, Inc., 1982.

2852. Robinson, Rachel Sargent. Sources for the History of Greek Athletics. Chicago: Ares Publishers, Inc., 1981.

2853. Shoebridge, Michele. Women in Sport: A Select Bibliography. London: Mansell Publishing Ltd., 1987.

2854. Wise, Suzanne. Sports Fiction for Adults: An Annotated Bibliography of Novels, Plays, Short Stories and Poetry with Sporting Settings. New York: Garland Publishing, Inc., 1986.

Articles

2855. "Annotated Bibliography of Children's Sport." Sociology of Sport Journal. 3, No.3 (September 1986), 279-287.

2856. "Bibliography of Sports Medicine--1983." The American Journal of Sports Medicine. 13, No.1 (January/February 1985), 66-79.

2857. Burgener, Louis. "Sports and Politics: A Selected Bibliography." Cultures. 4, No.2 (1977), 137-181.

2858. DeSensi, Joy Theresa. "PSSS Bibliography of Sport Philosophy--Update II." Journal of the Philosophy of Sport. 13 (1986), 109-117.

2859. DeSensi, Joy Theresa. "PSSS Bibliography of Sport Philosophy--An Update." Journal of the Philosophy of Sport. 12 (1985), 101-107.

2860. DeSensi, Joy Theresa. "Update--PSSS Bibliography of the Philosophy of Sport--1988." Journal of the Philosophy of Sport. 15 (1988), 95-96.

2861. Struna, Nancy, L. "In 'Glorious Disarray': The Literature of American Sport History." Research Quarterly for Exercise and Sport. 56, No.2 (June 1985), 151-160.

2862. Vanderwerken, David L. "Sports Literature Anthologies: A Scorecard." Journal of the Philosophy of Sport. 6 (1979), 95-100.

2863. Vanderwerken, David L. "The Joy of Sports Books: A Tout Sheet." The Georgia Review. 33, No.3 (Fall 1979) 707-712.

Author Index

The numbers here refer to page numbers, not entry numbers.

Subject Index

The numbers refer to entry numbers, not page numbers.

Ciulla, Tony 787
Civil liberties 543
Civil rights 303, 359, 483, 2190, 2199,
    2210, 2283, 2314, 2692, 2790
Civil War 2406
Clements, William 1646, 1667, 1686
Clemson University 325, 485, 600, 1617,
    1907
Cleveland Browns 431, 528
Cleveland Indians 2113
Coaches 35, 57, 67, 71, 78, 106, 137, 139,
    160, 164, 183, 191, 196, 221, 227,
    234, 237, 256, 259, 264, 271-272, 320,
    334, 390, 454, 471, 494, 496, 505,
    516, 530, 536, 548, 575, 583, 587,
    594, 596, 601, 607-608, 610, 618, 637,
    639, 646, 657, 665, 682, 700, 744-745,
    807, 809-810, 824, 848-849, 894, 900,
    911, 922, 976, 978, 1017, 1022, 1039,
    1048, 1072, 1074-1075, 1080, 1084,
    1161, 1169-1172, 1177, 1184, 1199,
    1236, 1239, 1266, 1281, 1293, 1307,
    1320, 1331, 1339, 1390, 1393, 1418,
    1424, 1449, 1452, 1478, 1515, 1534,
    1556, 1615, 1639-1640, 1652, 1697,
    1705-1706, 1711, 1729, 1732,
    1738-1739, 1746-1747, 1751-1752,
    1757-1758, 1762, 1787, 1791, 1797,
    1807-1808, 1823, 1849, 1851, 1858,
    1860, 1862, 1865-1866, 1874,
    1886-1887, 1889, 1905, 1907,
    1998-1999, 2109, 2126, 2140, 2186,
    2274, 2319, 2322, 2328-2329, 2347,
    2358, 2377, 2440, 2450, 2475, 2599,
    2601, 2678, 2693, 2708, 2732, 2750,
    2828, 2842, 2854
Coaches and players 5, 173, 194, 268,
    1820
Coaching 244, 904
Coach-player relations 1820
Cobb, Ty 2500
Cocaine 279-280, 287, 292, 308-309, 318,
    340, 344, 376-377, 413, 430-431, 437,
    461, 467, 472, 500, 519, 528, 539,
    545, 560, 584, 1732, 1779, 1868, 1901,
    2476
Cochell, Earl 871
Cockfighting 1230, 1333
Code of conduct 620, 636, 864, 875, 890,
    913, 945, 1001, 1761, 1791
Code of ethics 15, 612-613, 623, 886, 2518,
    2537, 2629
Coed sports 2693
Colgate University 485, 1216
Collective bargaining 1549, 1563, 1572,
    1577, 1589, 2443, 2452, 2457
Collective behavior 922, 925, 937

College basketball 207, 212, 218, 220-221,
    234, 239, 327, 376-377, 467, 472, 526,
    598, 602, 607-608, 639, 729, 773, 834,
    991, 949, 1000, 1012, 1019, 1028,
    1037, 1039, 1041-1044, 1359, 1439,
    1613, 1617, 1628, 1640, 1642, 1669,
    1672, 1681, 1707, 1732, 1827, 1867,
    1881, 1886, 1905, 1907, 2143, 2243,
    2523, 2584, 2631, 2684, 2750, 2781
College football 139-140, 196, 199-200,
    244, 254, 269, 482, 589, 595, 710,
    731, 735, 748, 750, 766, 771, 786,
    1056, 1216, 1236, 1238, 1320, 1431,
    1445, 1464, 1469, 1557, 1571, 1613,
    1619, 1621, 1623, 1634, 1643-1644,
    1646-1647, 1652, 1659, 1667-1668,
    1670-1671, 1677, 1680, 1684, 1686,
    1691, 1697, 1708, 1716, 1729, 1731,
    1735, 1820, 1823, 1834, 1839, 1842,
    1852-1853, 1859-1860, 1863, 1865,
    1903, 2102, 2120, 2307-2308, 2477,
    2489, 2521
College hockey 1335
College presidents 35, 604, 619, 644, 666,
    673, 678-679, 684, 706, 719, 791,
    1387, 1418, 1467, 1524, 1593, 1635,
    1637, 1639, 1648, 1657, 1693, 1887,
    2298
College sports 42, 143, 232, 588, 603, 619,
    654, 657, 668, 676, 703, 792, 810,
    858, 1419, 1524, 1542, 1558,
    1610-1613, 1618, 1627, 1629, 1652,
    1683, 1685, 2088, 2096, 2166, 2168,
    2225, 2231, 2249, 2299, 2321, 2345,
    2373, 2385, 2453, 2486, 2520, 2547,
    2683, 2693, 2739
College volleyball 2174
College wrestling 200
Collins, Sonny 1056
Columbia University 1658
Commercialism 662, 1558, 1682, 1735,
    1951, 1964, 1980, 2033, 2084, 2547,
    2575
Commercialization 67, 652, 673, 721, 851,
    923, 959, 1269, 1366, 1410, 1461,
    1548, 1555, 1565, 1576, 1579, 1604,
    1612, 1685, 1716, 1887, 1970, 2004,
    2079, 2249, 2318, 2320, 2332, 2355,
    2449, 2470, 2502, 2559, 2714
Commonwealth games 2242
Communism 1936, 1950, 2411, 2546, 2560
Community 1528, 2383
Competition 7, 14, 26, 29, 31, 34, 56,
    62-64, 67, 80, 83, 85, 120, 124, 134,
    160-161, 173, 176, 186, 188, 198, 201,
    210, 220, 222, 272, 405, 514, 547,
    588, 641, 655, 672, 721, 769, 806,
    809, 811, 814, 823, 825-826, 829,
    831-832, 840, 842-843, 846, 851, 857,

Loaded bats 759, 799
Locke, Taylor O. 1617, 1907
Lombardi, Vince 89, 163, 186, 210, 215, 807, 872, 1171
Long Island University 1019
Los Angeles 1292, 1829
Los Angeles Dodgers 295, 1818, 2158, 2216, 2588, 2664
Los Angeles Lakers 151, 1319
Los Angeles Olympics 451, 558, 1217, 1932-1933, 1949, 1964, 2044, 2051, 2077, 2079, 2388, 2554
Los Angeles Raiders 206, 2475
Loschiavo, John 739
Losing 804, 810, 835, 1751, 1819, 1827, 2504
Louis, Joe 1843, 2112, 2154, 2178, 2194, 2275, 2287, 2305, 2378
Louisiana State University 139, 207, 1876, 1905
Lowe, Dick 1694
Lowery, Joseph 2190
Loyola Marymount University 2631
Lucchesi, Frank 1253
Luckett, Walter 805
Luke, Steve 1313
Lysiak, Tom 2488
Madden, John 1171
Mafia 782
Mailer, Norman 1277
Malamud, Bernard 177
Mamby, Saoul 1235
Management 264
Managers 193, 590, 873, 1169, 1818, 1845, 1873, 1892, 2179, 2295
Mancini, Ray 1392
Mandell, Arnold 315, 465, 571
Manhattan College 1019
Maple Leafs 1294
Mapscam 760
Marijuana 279, 292, 367, 462, 502
Marksmanship 1089
Martial arts 1935
Martin, Billy 193, 873
Martin, Jerry 430
Martini, Anita 2766
Marx, Karl 108, 1566
Marxism 1375, 1492, 1505, 2015, 2049, 2348, 2548, 2561, 2568, 2571
Maryland 395
Maslow, Abraham 182
Mason, Tony 1601
Mass society 1576

Mass sports 2359
Massachusetts Bay 1321, 2433, 2658
Massachusetts Institute of Technology 1445
Materialism 1011, 2082, 2615, 2640
Mayo, Carl 2500
Mays, Willie 1058, 2111
Mazza, Patrick 436, 438
McCray, Shirley 236
McEnroe, John 820, 874, 891, 901
McLain, Denny 1005, 1034, 1052
McLain, Gary 472
McLeod, Barry 805
McLuhan, Marshall 2510
McVea, Warren 2120
Media 3, 27, 35, 41, 46, 86, 106, 132, 206-207, 282, 398, 509, 520, 530, 557, 623, 658, 671, 942-943, 990, 1014, 1030, 1053, 1074, 1080, 1212, 1240, 1264, 1267, 1336, 1347, 1357, 1364, 1371, 1382, 1499, 1508-1509, 1581-1582, 1598, 1660, 1669, 1682, 1821, 1845, 2063, 2148, 2157, 2192, 2220, 2227, 2240, 2265, 2319, 2328-2329, 2335, 2342-2343, 2350, 2353-2354, 2360, 2366, 2372, 2387, 2459, 2467, 2477, 2491, 2493, 2495, 2514-2515, 2538, 2546-2547, 2668, 2695, 2705
Medieval 1115
Meggyesy, Dave 1902
Mehre, Harry 894
Memphis State University 234, 1018, 1039, 1339, 1642
Mergers 1544
Metaethics 111
Metaphors 79, 123, 1772, 1793, 2558, 2580, 2638, 2640
Metaphysics 45, 48, 60, 63, 72, 96, 127, 1062, 2438
Methodist Church 786, 1429, 2491, 2834
Methodology 112, 2412
Mexico City Olympics 424, 2108
Miami Dolphins 287, 423, 1901
Michael, Gene 155
Michaels, Al 2503
Michigan 2734
Michigan State University 1722
Mikhailov, Boris 1908
Military 1, 730, 2371
Miller, Merrill 1216
Mills, Jack 145
Milton, Fred 2299
Minnesota Vikings 1900

About the Author

DONALD G. JONES is Professor of Social Ethics at Drew University. His most recent books include *Business, Religion, and Ethics: New Ventures in Management Development* (1982) and *A Bibliography of Business Ethics* (1986).